# Peace in the Thought of Thomas Aquinas

*Philosophy, Theology, and Ethics*

# Peace in the Thought of Thomas Aquinas

## Philosophy, Theology, and Ethics

JOHN M. MEINERT

FOREWORD BY GREGORY M. REICHBERG

The Catholic University of America Press

*Washington, D.C.*

Cataloging-in-Publication Data is available
from the Library of Congress
ISBN : 978-0-8132-3792-3
eISBN : 978-0-8132-3793-0

# Contents


Abbreviations of Aquinas's work    vii

Foreword by Gregory M. Reichberg, Ph.D.    ix

Introduction    xiii

1. Aquinas's Sources and Treatments of Peace    1

2. A Thomistic Philosophy of Peace    50

3. A Thomistic Theology of Peace    113

4. Thomistic Ethics and Peace    185

5. Peace and Thomistic Sacramental Theology    267

Conclusion    281

Bibliography    289

Index    299

# Abbreviations of Aquinas's works

| | |
|---|---|
| *In Phys.* | *Commentaria in octo libros Physicorum* |
| *Comp. Theo.* | *Compendium theologiae ad fratrem Raynaldum* |
| *De Rat.* | *De rationibus Fidei* |
| *De Regno* | *De regno ad regem Cypri* |
| *In Or. Dom.* | *Expositio in orationem dominicam* |
| *In Symb.* | *Expositio in Symbolum Apostolorum* |
| *Super Is.* | *Expositio super Isaiam ad litteram* |
| *Super Iob* | *Expositio super Iob ad litteram* |
| *In Jer.* | *In Jeremiam prophetam expositio* |
| *In de Div. Nom.* | *In librum B. Dionysii De divinis nominibus expositio* |
| *In Ps.* | *In psalmos Davidis expositio* |
| *Quodl.* | *Quaestiones de Quolibet* |
| *De Malo* | *Quaestiones disputatae de malo* |
| *De Pot.* | *Quaestiones disputatae de potentia* |
| *De Ver.* | *Quaestiones disputatae de veritate* |
| *De Virt.* | *Quaestiones disputatae de virtutibus* |
| *Sent.* | *Scriptum super Sententiis* |
| *In Eth.* | *Sententia libri Ethicorum* |
| *In Meta.* | *Sententia libri Metaphysicae* |
| *ScG* | *Summa contra Gentiles* |

# Abbreviations

| | |
|---|---|
| *ST* | *Summa Theologiae* |
| *De Trin.* | *Super Boethium De Trinitate* |
| *Super Col.* | *Super Epistolam B. Pauli ad Colossenses lectura* |
| *Super Eph.* | *Super Epistolam B. Pauli ad Ephesios lectura* |
| *Super Gal.* | *Super Epistolam B. Pauli ad Galatas lectura* |
| *Super Heb.* | *Super Epistolam B. Pauli ad Hebraeos lectura* |
| *Super Phil.* | *Super Epistolam B. Pauli ad Philipenses lectura* |
| *Super Rom.* | *Super Epistolam B. Pauli ad Romanos lectura* |
| *Super Tit.* | *Super Epistolam B. Pauli ad Titum lectura* |
| *Super Io.* | *Evangelium S. Ioannis lectura* |
| *Super Matt.* | *Evangelium S. Matthaei lectura* |
| *Super I Cor.* | *Epistolam B. Pauli ad Corinthios lectura* |
| *Super I Thess.* | *Epistolam B. Pauli ad Thessalonicenses lectura* |
| *Super I Tim.* | *Epistolam B. Pauli ad Timotheum lectura* |
| *Super II Cor.* | *Epistolam B. Pauli ad Corinthios lectura* |
| *Super II Thess.* | *Super II Epistolam B. Pauli ad Thessalonicenses lectura* |
| *Super II Tim.* | *Super II Epistolam B. Pauli ad Timotheum lectura* |

# Foreword

This is a book I wish I had written. Ever since my earliest days as a student of Thomas Aquinas, I have been intrigued by his discussion of peace in *Summa theologiae* II-II, q. 29. There, in a scant three pages, the learned saint reflects on the theological, metaphysical, and moral dimensions of peace. His aphorisms have been a source of wonderment for me: *all things desire peace* (quoting St. Augustine), *whoever desires anything desires peace; there can be no true peace except where the appetite is directed to what is truly good; true peace is only in good men and about good things; the peace of the wicked is not a true peace but a semblance thereof; even those who seek war and dissension, desire nothing but peace; peace is in a sense the final end; there is no other virtue except charity whose proper act is peace; charity, according to its very nature causes peace; perfect peace consists in the perfect enjoyment of the sovereign good.*

Yet the capaciousness of these insights made me recoil before the challenge of explaining their meaning. How can it be possible that all things (without qualification!) desire peace? Why is peace solely in the good and not the wicked? And how is this consistent with saying that even those seeking war also seek peace? And, most fundamentally, what is peace and how does it differ from goodness, unity, justice, tranquility, cessation of conflict, joy—terms to which it is often joined or compared? I accordingly took the easier, more travelled path, and wrote a book on Aquinas's approach to the moral problem of war. But even there the question of peace could not be evaded. War and violence, for St. Thomas, are first and foremost sins against peace. And if some wars can be just, it is only because they are waged with the aim of restoring a peace that has been disrupted. War is first and foremost a privation of peace; the former becomes intelligible only against the background of the latter. Peace is indeed much wider than war; war cannot be conceptualized without reference to peace, but peace can be well understood in its intrinsic nature without reference to war. I accordingly appended "peace" to my book's title and by way of introduction ventured some cursory remarks on the topic.[1]

But the itch remained. Invited to give a lecture at the Iranian Institute of Philosophy in Tehran, and cognizant that for Islam "Giver of Peace" (*As Salam*) is counted among the attributes of God (Quran 59:23), I chose "The Idea of Peace in the Christian Thought of Thomas Aquinas" as the theme of my presentation. At that time, I was still writing on just war—a topic I preferred to avoid in Tehran. Setting down to pen my initial thoughts on the metaphysical aspects of peace, I sought clarity in St. Thomas's commentary on the *Divine Names* of Dionysius, but my old perplexities were renewed. Peace is there described as akin to a transcendental property, namely as something co-extensive and convertible with being. Peace emerges when desire is unimpeded and fulfilled, when it outflows in union or is reduced to unity. Is peace a function of goodness or does it flow rather from oneness? Unable to parse the difference, I again took the easier route and set it down under the heading of both. By this time, I was in Istanbul awaiting arrival of my visa for travel to Iran. Like all good tourists I made way for the Topkapi Palace where the Ottoman sultans once lived. Walking through the palace gate, to my left was an edifice that resembled the much larger Hagia Sophia. Walking over for a closer look, I learned it was a church that had been constructed in the early fourth century, several years prior to the famed cathedral

---

1. *Thomas Aquinas on War and Peace* (Cambridge: Cambridge University Press, 2017).

of Constantinople. Called *Hagia Irene* (Holy Peace), it was dedicated to divine peace of God. Now a museum, the exhibit explained how Hagia Irene was one of three shrines—together with Hagia Sophia (Wisdom) and Hagia Dynamis (Power)—that the Christian emperors had devoted to God's attributes.

This encounter with Hagia Irene stimulated my still incomplete reflections on St. Thomas's conception of peace. Did he deem peace a name of God? Indeed, in his commentary on Dionysius's treatise St. Thomas does refer to divine peace (*divina pax*) and the peace of God (*pax Dei*) as pertaining to God, but why then is peace not listed in the first part of the *Summa Theologiae* alongside the other attributes of God (unity, goodness, truth, infinitude, wisdom, love, power, and the like)? And if peace merits inclusion among names of God, on what specific rationale should it be deemed a divine attribute? Although not failing to venture some thoughts on the matter, here too I was reduced to stammering.

Regrettably my visa to Iran didn't arrive in time. A colleague read my paper in Tehran (a Lutheran pastor having no background in Aquinas, he found the content most enigmatic) and it was subsequently published in a volume devoted to conceptions of peace in the medieval age.[2]

Around this time, John Meinert shared with me his plan for a book length study on peace in the writings of Aquinas. I was impressed by the rich detail of his outline and found hopeful solace in the thought that my divagations around the meaning of peace might soon come to an end. I have not been disappointed—far from it! Gratuitously crediting me for having identified the lacuna the book aimed to fill, the book succeeds at filling that lacuna beyond all reasonable expectation. It carefully sifts through Aquinas's many comments about peace—considerably more numerous than I had been aware—and organizes them systematically around key themes. Peace is therein elucidated in all its rich connections—to our moral

---

2. "Human Nature, Peace, and War," in *A Cultural History of Peace in the Medieval Age, 800–1450*, Walter P. Simons, ed (London: Bloomsbury Publishing, 2020), 33–49.

life, the inner life of God, the political ordering of communities, the creative causality of God as manifested in the natural world, the outpouring of grace in the sacraments, our activities of peacemaking in this world, and alas by its absence, in war and our other collective human failings. What emerges from this sustained reflection is the first comprehensive treatment of peace in Aquinas's writings. *Peace in the Thought of Thomas Aquinas: Philosophy, Theology, and Ethics* is destined to remain the gold standard on this topic for many years to come.

Peace represents a more challenging topic of inquiry than war. War is more circumscribed than peace; it relates to a limited sphere of our terrestrial existence, while peace touches all aspects of our lives and even reaches below and above human existence, from the realm of nature all the way up to God. It is perhaps for this reason that Thomists have shied away from careful examination of peace and have concentrated instead on delineating the nature and scope of just war—which, from Cajetan, Vitoria, Suárez and beyond has been a staple of Thomistic commentaries. But in neglecting peace, a fertile opportunity to engage with the deep yearnings of humanity has been missed. It is thus highly propitious that John Meinert has seen the full potential in St. Thomas's thought on peace; professor Meinert has seized the opportunity, and in the process has he has charted ever so luminously the philosophical and theological contours of peace for the great benefit of contemporary readers. May this book find the wide audience it richly merits.

*Gregory M. Reichberg, Ph.D.*

# Introduction

Thomas Aquinas and the Thomistic tradition are not usually associated with the study of peace. In the scholarly literature (and in our current polarized climate), Aquinas belongs to the 'just war camp'. The study of peace, on the other hand, is usually the concern of pacifists. Aquinas either does not appear in studies on peace or is summarily dismissed. This is only partly an omission by scholars of peace. The Thomistic tradition, though it has expanded, studied, and defended Aquinas's conception of just war is largely silent on the topic of peace itself. This has led Gregory Reichberg to write that "In the secondary literature, [Aquinas's] conception [of peace] has rarely been thematized in its own right."[1] Those who devote themselves to the study of peace rarely study Aquinas, and those who study Aquinas rarely go to him for guidance on peace. Whatever one thinks about Aquinas's thought on war (which receives most attention both within and outside of Thomism), there is clearly a lacuna in the current scholarship concerning Aquinas and peace.[2]

When one begins to look at Aquinas's explicit treatments of peace a possible explanation arises for this inattention. Aquinas's treatments of peace are largely happenstance, occasional, and

---

1. Gregory Reichberg, *Thomas Aquinas on War and Peace* (Cambridge: Cambridge University Press, 2016), 2.

2. For more information concerning Aquinas's knowledge of military practices and war, see Edward Synan, "St. Thomas Aquinas and the Profession of Arms," in *Medieval Studies,* vol. 50 (1988): 404–37.

cursory. They usually only arise because the text on which Aquinas is commenting mentions peace, because he borrows a structure from another author (e.g. enumerating peace amongst the fruits of the Spirit as St. Paul does in Galatians), or because peace is mentioned in an objection concerning another topic (e.g. happiness). These situations require Aquinas to say something about peace and what he says is often deep and profound, but his primary intention is rarely to elucidate peace. Because of this, Aquinas's treatments are often brief and in seeming tension with each other; it is an exegetically and hermeneutically difficult task to explicate his thought.

Though one might hope for it, the Thomistic tradition does not fill this gap in Aquinas's own corpus. If Aquinas's attention to peace is often happenstance and brief (though potent and deep), the Thomistic tradition's is practically non-existent. This is especially true since a large part of Aquinas's thought on peace is found outside his major syntheses, in his biblical commentaries and his *Commentary on the Divine Names*, which have received much less scholarly attention. Even in places where you would expect commentators to expand on Aquinas's conception, they do not. The *Summa Theologiae* gave them pretense to treat peace (*ST* II-II q. 29) and yet none took it up with much substance (especially given the length at which they treat other topics!): Capreolus, Cajetan, John of St. Thomas, Contensen, Billuart, Bañez, Suarez, the Salamancan commentary, etc. either bypass the topic entirely or are so perfunctory that they are (mostly) unhelpful in beginning to sort out Aquinas's thought.[3] The commentators certainly have insights to offer, but one does not find among them serious attention to peace.[4]

---

3. If one finds some attention to peace in the Thomistic tradition, it is usually found in ascetical or spiritual theology. For an example, see Louis of Granada's *La Guía de Pecadores* or Garrigou-Lagrange's *Three Ages of the Interior Life*. Alternatively, peace gets treated as a political reality clearly and easily separable from interior peace or questions of metaphysics. Here one thinks of John Finnis in *Aquinas*. Put simply, peace seems to have particularly suffered from the Post-Tridentine separation of moral and spiritual theology. This certainly helps explain why one struggles to find substantial theological or metaphysical reflection on peace in the Thomistic tradition.

4. This does not mean that the commentators' thought is irrelevant. For example,

In the Neo-Thomist revival of the 20th century, Thomistic attention to peace begins to gain traction. Francis McMahon has an article focusing metaphysically on peace.[5] Santiago Ramirez, bucking
the trend amongst the commentators,[6] spends 14 pages commenting on q. 29 and has two other independent articles on peace.[7] Likewise, in 1952 the International Eucharistic Congress contains some
important contributions to a Thomistic understanding of peace.[8]
Furthermore, there has been a growing interest, relative to previous eras at least, amongst scholars in the last 30 years.[9] Finally, there

---

Bañez's interpretation of peace as the proportion/relation between powers/subjects is
important. See Domingo Bañez, *Scholastica Commentaria in Secundam Secundae Angelici
Doctoris S. Thomae*, XXIX, a. 4, 432.

5. Francis McMahon, "A Thomistic Analysis of Peace," in *The Thomist*, vol. 15, no. 4
(1952): 1–52.

6. Another exception is Pietro Casella, *La pace in San Tommaso* (*Summa Theologiae:
II-II, Q. 29*): *interiorizzazione e attualità di un concetto*, Ph.D. dissertation (Piacenza: Tipolito Moderna, 1978). Unfortunately, I have been unable to obtain a copy.

7. Santiago Ramirez, *De Caritate*, Opera Omnia Tomus XII (San Esteban: Salamanca, 1998). "*La Eucaristía y la Paz*," is an appendix in this commentary. Ramirez, "La Eucaristía y la Paz Individual en la Teología de Santo Tomas de Aquino," in *Ciencia Tomista*
79 (1952): 163–228.

8. Santiago Ramirez. "La Eucaristía y la Paz Individual en la teología de Santo Tomas de Aquino," Adolphus Hoffman. "Eucharistia ut Sacramentum Pacis secundum
S. Thomam," Godefridus Geenen."*L'adage Eucharistia est sacramentum ecclesiasticae unionis dans les oeuvres et la doctrine de S. Thomas d'Aquin*"), and Ephrem Longpré, "L'Eucharistie est le sacrement de la paix mystique," in *La Eucaristía y la Paz*, XXXV *Congreso
eucarístico internacional* 1952: *Sesiones de estudio*, vol. 1 (Barcelona: Planas, 1953), 171–83
(Ramirez), 163–67 (Hoffman), 275–81 (Geenan), and 158–62 (Longpré).

9. Heather McAdam Erb, "Interior Peace: *Inchoatio vitae aeternae*," in *Wisdom's Apprentice: Thomistic Essays in Honor of Lawrence Dewan, O.P.*, ed. Lawrence Dewan and
Peter A. Kwasniewski (Washington, DC: The Catholic University of America Press,
2007), 260–81; Matthew Tapie, "For He is our Peace: Thomas Aquinas on Christ as
Cause of Peace in the City of Saints," *The Journal of Moral Theology* 5.1 (2016): 111–28;
Gregory Reichberg, "Thomas Aquinas between Just War and Pacifism," *Journal of Religious Ethics* vol. 38, n. 2 (June 2010): 219–41; Gregory Reichberg, "Human Nature, Peace,
and War," in *A Cultural History of Peace in the Medieval Age*, ed. Walter Simons (New
York: Bloomsbury Academic, 2020); John Meinert, "*Alimentum Pacis*: The Eucharist and
Peace in St. Thomas Aquinas," in *Nova et Vetera*, English edition, Vol. 14, No. 4 (2016):
193–212; John Meinert, "Peace and the Transcendentals: The Case of Thomas Aquinas,"
in *European Journal for the Study of Thomas Aquinas*, 37 (2019): 18–34; Diego Fernando
Barrios-Andrade, "Educación para la paz: una reflexión desde Tomas de Aquino," *Educación y Educadores* vol. 24, is. 2 (2021): 181–96; Liliana Irizar, "Sabiduría y paz. Explorando sus conexiones intimas desde Tomas de Aquino," in La sabiduría en Tomas de

is Reichberg's own book *Thomas Aquinas on War and Peace,* which not only offers an invaluable interpretation of *ST* II-II q. 29, but also identifies the very lacuna this book aims to fill. "In the secondary literature, [Aquinas's] conception [of peace] has rarely been thematized in its own right."[10]

This book aims to begin filling this lacuna by giving a broad exposition, summary, and interpretation of Aquinas's thought on peace. Chapter One aims to introduce the reader to Aquinas's thought on peace in its sources and development. Aquinas's thought on peace is deeply influenced by his authorities. These are principally Scripture, Augustine, Dionysius, and Aristotle. I begin by briefly outlining each of these sources' approach to peace. I follow that section with a chronological exposition of Aquinas's main treatments of peace. I not only try to show Aquinas's dependence on his sources as well as the development of his thought, but also expose the occasional nature and ambiguities of his thought on peace. The questions governing the rest of the book will arise from Aquinas's thought itself.

Chapter Two concerns a Thomistic philosophy of peace. This chapter is organized around the four causes. In this way it aims to begin a Thomistic philosophy of peace by following some of the lines in Aquinas's thought. This requires not only sorting out Aquinas's multiple descriptions, but also relating peace to the good, analyzing the source of peace, and exposing what subjects may be at peace.

--------

Aquino. Inspiración y reflexión: Perspectivas filosóficas y teológicas (Argentina: Universidad Sergio Arboleda, 2017): 107–34; Tyler Wittman, "Not a God of Confusion but of Peace: Aquinas and the Meaning of Divine Simplicity," *Modern Theology,* 32.2 (April 2016): 151–69; Ignazio Genovese, "Dalla concordia degli animi alla tranquillità dell'ordine: per una fondazione interiore della pace nella Summa Teologia di Tommaso d'Aquino," in *Rassegna di Teologia* 63 (2022): 577–96; F. Truini, *La pace in Tommaso d'Aquino,* Città Nuova, Roma 2008; Gerhard Beestermoller, *Thomas von Aquin und der Gerechte Krieg: Friedensethik im theologischen Kontext der Summa Theologiae* (Germany: J.P. Bachem Verlag Koln, 1990); Lawrence Boakye, *Peace Building: the Person, Community, and Authority, A Contemporary Thomistic Approach* (Self-Published, BookSurge, 2009); finally, there is a recent dissertation by Irenej Siklar (2022) entitled *Ce que tous cherchent: Une étude sur la paix chez Thomas d'Aquin,* but I obtained a copy too late to incorporate any of Siklar's findings.

10. Reichberg, *Thomas Aquinas on War and Peace,* 2.

By analyzing peace using the four causes, we shall see that Aquinas approaches the study of peace from a fundamentally metaphysical perspective, which is essential for understanding the rest of Aquinas's thought.

Chapter Three attempts to outline a Thomistic theology of peace. Aquinas is a theologian, and this is preeminently the case in his thought on peace. Aquinas is willing, and does, relate peace to almost every other theological topic (though it is often not recognized in secondary literature). In treating each of these topics, we can see the potency of Aquinas's thought and the importance of peace. Peace is not simply a political or ascetical category, but fundamentally a Trinitarian reality. God is the fundamental exemplar of peace, and he pours peace into the world through the Trinitarian relations and missions. Christ not only embodies peace in his person but incarnates to give a share of it to creation. In this way, other things come to share in the very peace of God. The Church is the prime locus of this outpouring and thereby becomes a community of peace, a community animated by the Spirit of peace.

The fourth chapter tries to answer questions concerning an ethics of peace, treating how Aquinas's philosophical and theological vision of peace impacts the practical order. How does peace relate to happiness, charity, wisdom, and justice? What is our responsibility to make peace with God, ourselves, others, and creation? What counsels would Aquinas have for pursuing peace? Is it possible to achieve peace? I argue that Aquinas's philosophical and theological vision has serious implications for his ethics and transforms the way we understand his thought about happiness, virtue, joy, justice, and other ethical topics. Not only this, but Aquinas also has concrete counsel for us about both the responsibility to pursue peace as well as the means and the possibility of achieving it—both individually and socially. This chapter is likely to be the most interesting for those concerned with peacebuilding, but I would caution reading it apart from the previous two. Aquinas's ethics of peace flow from his philosophical and theological vision.

The final chapter concerns the sacraments and their relation to peace. In many ways this chapter is a microcosm of the whole book. In the sacraments, we find Aquinas's thought at its most concrete and tangible. Aquinas draws a straight line from the peace of God to the Eucharist, the very means by which God communicates his peace to the world. Nevertheless, seeing this picture requires answering a couple of questions concerning worship and the sacramental order. How does peace relate to worship in general? How does the sacramental order relate to peace? Chapter Four answers these questions and thereby, hopefully, uncovers the depth and profundity of Aquinas's sacramental thought and its relation to peace. As it turns out, Aquinas's thought on the sacraments serves as a microcosm of his thought on peace. Not only is the sacramental order peaceful in itself, but it is directly ordered to the introduction and maintenance of both individual and social peace. In this it completes the mission of Christ and the Spirit to unite what was divided.

Attempting a recovery of Aquinas's thought on peace is not only worthwhile in itself, but is also helpful for supplementing our understanding of other, more well-trod topics in Aquinas (in addition to aiding us in articulating a theology and philosophy of peace relevant to today). Of course, first among these topics is war or conflict. Studying peace obviously helps us better understand in what sense war is related to peace for Aquinas. It also reveals the absurdity of trying to study Aquinas's thought on war without any reference to peace. Peace is the metaphysical basis, intelligibility, and context for war. One cannot study a privation without reference to the good. In addition, the implications of peace (as we shall see) extend well beyond the topic of war. For example, Aquinas's thought on peace relates to his metaphysics and could expand and deepen our understanding of the transcendentals. Aquinas's thought on peace relates to his trinitarian theology and could expand our understanding of the Trinitarian Relations, divine naming, divine exemplarity, and creation. Based on these, Aquinas's thought on peace has implications for his theodicy, ethics, and sacramental theology. Examples could be multiplied, but these implications are not the purpose of this book. Again, its aim is simply to expose and interpret Aquinas's thought on peace in itself. Nevertheless, these implications are never far from my mind in writing the text. Aquinas's thought is a whole and so an exposition of one aspect cannot be ignorant of others.

In closing the introduction, I would like to note how difficult the study of peace is, both in Aquinas and in general. In general, the study of peace (for Aquinas, at least) involves relating diversity and unity. It is intrinsically metaphysical and theological, but also deeply anthropological and social. It does not lend itself to easy answers. As G.M. Manser says, "Unity and multiplicity . . . is such a dark and difficult problem."[11] Likewise, the issue does not become much easier just limiting it to Aquinas (as I have). Treating peace in Aquinas requires more than a passing familiarity with almost all his texts and thought. Undoubtedly, I have missed some and distorted others in my attempt to understand Aquinas and approach peace from a Thomistic perspective. Surely, I have missed larger questions and approaches by simply focusing on Aquinas. For both these reasons, I cannot say it better than MacIntyre: "even if some large parts of my interpretation could not withstand criticism, the demonstration of this would itself strengthen the tradition which I am attempting to sustain and extend."[12]

11. G.M. Manser, "Begriff und Bedeutung der transzendentalen Beziehung," *Divus Thomas*, 19. (1941): 356: "Einheit und Vielheit des Weltalls richtig zu klaren, fast mochten wir sagen 'zu versöhnen', denn es gibt gegensätzliches in dem Verhältnis der beiden, welch ein dunkles und schwierigen Problem!"

12. Alisdair MacIntyre, *After Virtue*, 3rd ed. (Notre Dame, IN: University of Notre Dame Press, 2010), 260.

# Peace in the Thought of Thomas Aquinas

*Philosophy, Theology, and Ethics*

1

—:—

# Aquinas's Sources and Treatments of Peace

Aquinas's thought on peace, just like his larger theology and philosophy in general, is highly eclectic in its sources.[1] Therein, he combines scriptural, Augustinian, Dionysian, and Aristotelian thought. Because of this, at least an elementary grasp of these authors is necessary to understand Aquinas's thought on peace. In other words, it is necessary to begin with his authorities. After a consideration of Aquinas's sources, I pass to an overview of his explicit treatments of peace. I begin with his early *Scriptum* and end with his mature *Commentary on the Psalms.* Undoubtedly, this makes for uninteresting reading—both surveying the authors on whom Aquinas relies, as well as Aquinas's own thought. This survey does, however, ground my positive construction of a Thomistic philosophy and theology of peace. In other words, from this chapter arises both the fundamental concepts with which I am working as well as the problems I am trying to solve. Likewise, a survey of Aquinas's sources and texts gives the reader a glimpse of Aquinas's own creativity, the texts he had available as well as his positive statements and understanding of

---

1. For an extended study of Aquinas's philosophical sources, see Leo Elders, *Thomas Aquinas and his Predecessors* (Washington DC: The Catholic University of America Press, 2018).

peace. Finally, a survey gives the reader the basis from which to dialogue with my claims in order to see precisely what judgments I've made, as well as disagree with my interpretations.

AQUINAS'S SOURCES

Scripture

Aquinas was a *magister sacrae paginae,* and no work on Aquinas should forget this. He produced commentaries on most of the books of the New Testament, as well as a few of the Old Testament. Scriptural teaching is the ever-present foundation of Aquinas's thought. This is true of his thought on peace as well. Obviously, the scriptural data in its totality is well beyond the scope of this book.[2] Nevertheless, it is important to note here the very broad contours of biblical teaching on peace.

In the Old Testament, the Hebrew word for peace, *shalom,* occurs many times and in many different contexts. It can signify a greeting (cf. Jgs 6:23), a state of abundance, a lack of conflict, safety, and many other things (cf. Lv 26:6–10). Nevertheless, among these seemingly divergent meanings, one stands out and unifies the rest. It is because of this central meaning that the Hebrew word *shalom* was used in an extended sense to greet, indicate good harvests, identify prosperity, and provide safety from enemies and beasts. This central meaning is covenantal. In the covenantal sense, peace signifies the gift of living faithfully in God's covenant, a wholeness and well-being that goes beyond a mere lack of conflict and signifies right relation with God.[3] It certainly implies a lack of conflict, but only because of the goodness (righteousness as at Is 60:17) that comes from living rightly in relation to God and neighbor. In this sense peace is a

---

2. For a summary of the biblical concept see David Gushee & Glen Stassen, *Kingdom Ethics: Following Jesus in Contemporary Context* (Grand Rapids, MI: Eerdmans, 2016), Chapter 16; Selva Rathinam, SJ, "Biblical Understanding of Peace," in *Jnanadeepa,* vol. 21, n. 1 (Jan 2017): 11–24.

3. Scott Hahn, ed, *The Catholic Bible Dictionary* (New York: Double Day, 2009), 688.

totality of good relationships: spiritual well-being in all its senses. Peace goes beyond a mere lack of conflict, it requires righteousness (cf. Is 48:18). Hence, there is no peace for the wicked (cf. Is 48:22).

Because of the centrality of covenantal peace, the Old Testament's concept of peace shares in some of the other aspects of covenants. Just as a covenant is a gift, so too is peace (cf. Lv 26:6, 1 Kgs 2:33, Is 26:12). Just as covenants are communal, so too is peace. It is given to a people, as a whole (and thus often lacks the sense of interior peace with which Aquinas often associates the word). Likewise, just as Israel looked forward to a fulfillment of the covenants at the end of time, peace too is hoped for as an eschatological reality (cf. Ez 34:25–31). It is an integral part of the new creation. The Messiah, who will fulfill the covenants, will also restore peace (cf. Jer 29:11). He is the prince of peace (cf. Is 9:6).

In the New Testament, the central covenantal sense of peace continues, but is fulfilled by Jesus as the eschatological prophet. He is the expected Messiah who brings peace. He does this by reconciling humans to God through his sacrifice on the cross (as the new high priest and new paschal victim). This new sacrifice is the basis of a new communal covenant. This covenant is the inbreaking of eschatological perfection, a perfection in which God and humans can live in right relationships to each other. In this sense, the New Testament concept of peace is simply the beginning of the fulfillment of Old Testament hopes. It is an inbreaking of eschatological peace.

The New Testament certainly emphasizes the social aspect of peace but also expands it to include an interior dimension. Paul is adamant that Christians must live in peace with one another, since Christ is our peace (cf. Rom 14:19; 1 Cor 14:33; 2 Cor 13:11; 1 Thes 5:13). In addition, Christ produces an interior peace in individuals (cf. Phil 4:7, Col 3:15, Rom 8:6, Rom15:13). Likewise, it is from community, the Church, that peace will be spread to the whole world, through the proclamation of the gospel. The gospel will overcome old standards of division (especially Jew and Gentile) and will draw all into right relationships with God and each other, producing harmony and peace. The interior and social dimensions are not in competition with each other, but mutually imply each other. If one is a recipient of the covenant as part of the Church, one will be interiorly at peace amidst the variation and contingency of this world. As leaven, one can carry the peace of Christ to others and draw them into the Church.

Because Christians saw themselves as recipients of a covenant and a mission to the world, the sense of connection between peace and material prosperity drops out in the New Testament.[4] What is emphasized is spiritual blessings. Hence, peace occurs with righteousness, mercy, love, joy and life. We find the conjunction of grace and peace many times in the Pauline letters. In this sense, peace is produced in believers through Christ and is a fruit of the Spirit (cf. Gal 5:22). God is the God of peace (cf. Rom 15:33; Phil 4:9) and the gospel is the gospel of peace (cf. Eph 6:15). The Church has a mission to bring peace to the world through the covenant established in the blood of Christ.

### Augustine of Hippo

While Scriptural teaching is a prime influence on Aquinas's thought, Augustine is the controlling factor.[5] In other words, Augustine's thought on peace is the hermeneutical lens through which Aquinas interprets scriptural teachings on peace. One can see this in Aquinas's penchant for Augustine's definition of peace as *tranquillitas ordinis*. Indeed, as we shall see, a significant amount of Aquinas's thought on peace is borrowed directly from Augustine, but reinterpreted in a more medieval and Aristotelian framework.

Augustine's thought on peace is born from his Neo-Platonic metaphysics, from his reflections on the one and the many. What is

4. Dewey, J., (2011), "peace," In M. A. Powell (Ed.), *The HarperCollins Bible Dictionary*, revised and updated (Third Edition, p. 763). New York: HarperCollins.

5. In what follows, I am heavily in debt to Donald Burt, O.S.A., "Peace," in *Augustine through the Ages*, ed. Allan D. Fitzgerald (Grand Rapids, MI: Eerdmans, 1999), 629–32. See also Henri Rondet, S.J., *Pax, Tranquillitas Ordinis* (Real monasterio de San Lorenzo de El Escorial, 1954).

one, is unified, is *ipso facto* at peace. It cannot conflict with itself or have dissension with itself. Conflict is made possible by multiplicity. If many things are to be at peace with each other, it will be because they return to unity.[6] Therefore, Augustine focuses on order in his definition of peace: "the arrangement of like and unlike things whereby each of them has its proper place."[7] An order allows for many things to be made one in a certain respect. Since they are unified, they cease to conflict. "Unrest is always symptomatic of disorder."[8]

The emphasis on order in Augustine's thought recalls his teaching on creation. God creates all things with order, number, and weight. For Augustine, these are transcendental (to use Aquinas's language); they are coterminous with being. Hence, inasmuch as something is good it observes its order, number, and weight. Evil is a privation of any one of these three aspects. Because of order's centrality to creation, Augustine holds that all things can be at peace and desire their proper place in that order.

Humans are particularly marked by their place in creation. All humans desire to be happy, this is their *pondus*. By desiring to be happy, humans desire to be at peace. The possession of the good is the cause of happiness, but one cannot truly possess a good unless one possesses it securely and without fear it will be lost. In other words, one does not really possess the good unless one is at peace. This is why Augustine holds that peace is among the highest goods one can achieve.[9]

For humans, peace depends on ordered loving.[10] This is what

6. For another good summary of the metaphysical elements of Augustine's thought see Johannes Brachtendorf, "Augustine: Peace Ethics and Peace Policy," in *From Just War to Modern Peace Ethics,* eds. Heinz-Gerhard Justenhoven and William Barbieri (Berlin: Walter de Gruyter, 2012), 49–70.

7. Augustine, *De civitate dei contra paganos,* 19.13.1 (PL 41): "*Ordo est parium dispariumque rerum sua cuique loca tribuens dispositio.*"

8. George Lawless, "Interior Peace in the *Confessions* of St. Augustine," in *Revue des études augustiniennes,* vol. 26 (1980): 45–61. See page 54.

9. Cf. Augustine, *De civitate dei,* 19.11.

10. It goes without saying, then, that interior peace is a gift of God's grace. See Augustine, *De civitate dei,* 19.13.2.

results in harmony within individuals and between individuals. "Internal peace depends on good order between body and soul and health in living whole."[11] This is certainly difficult, since we live in a world of weakness and decay. The body is disintegrating; we are tempted; at the very least, we are constantly distracted. We are never free from fear and anxiety. Even one who attains internal peace in this world will constantly have to fight to maintain it.[12] For peace with others, what Augustine calls *concordia* (to be together in heart), peace requires a proper order between individuals. This is, at the very least, doing them no harm and trying to do good to them.[13] Above and beyond that being of one heart finds its ideal in friendship.[14] Friendship unites people by the things that they love.[15] On the other hand, just as interior peace is precarious in this life, so too is concord. We are constantly changing, and we do not know if the concord will survive those changes.[16] Because of this precarity, peace must be a gift of God.[17] Only God can order our loves.

Because we can only possess the good precariously in this life, Augustine holds that peace is precarious in this life as well. This is especially true of earthly peace, a kind of peace found by seeking and possessing the good things of this world. These goods diminish when consumed and when shared.[18] Thus, there is often conflict and selfishness. For the citizens of the heavenly city, this is not their only peace, though they seek the good things of this world also. True peace only comes in the *patria*, where God is beheld and cannot be lost. Yet even in this life believers are united to him in love and possess him in hope.[19] They are united in a true *concordia* by their

11. Donald Burt, O.S.A, "Peace," 629.

12. Cf. Augustine, *Sermones,* 61 n. 7 (PL 38).

13. Cf. Augustine, *De civitate dei,* 19.14.

14. Cf. Augustine, *Sermones,* 357.1.

15. Cf. Augustine, *De civitate dei,* 19.24.

16. Cf. Augustine, *De civitate dei,* 19.5.

17. Cf. Augustine, *De civitate dei,* 15.4.

18. Cf. Augustine, *Sermones,* 357.1.

19. Cf. Augustine, *Enarrationes in psalmos* (PL 36.147.20); 122.9; *sermones,* 229H.3 and 242A.1

mutual love of him; in this way they are made one. They are ordered internally and preserved to a certain extent from the vicissitudes of this world by their love of him.[20] In heaven, they will experience the fruit of their lives, a final unity with God and others resulting in the final peace of resting in God.[21] No conflict is possible here. Body and soul are in harmony, no temptation, no dissension, no quarrels, no war, no death.

### Dionysius the Areopagite

The third major influence on Aquinas is Dionysius. This is especially true of his work, *On the Divine Names*.[22] Aquinas was, no doubt, introduced to Dionysius through his teacher, Albert the Great. Albert commented on the works of Dionysius from 1248–1250, when Aquinas was his assistant. A recent scholar has shown that Albert even used marginal notes of Aquinas in writing his own commentaries.[23] It is during this time in which Aquinas was serving as Albert's assistant, that Aquinas composed his own commentaries on Isaiah, Jeremiah, and Lamentations. It was not until later that Aquinas writes his own commentary on *The Divine Names*, though it is disputed whether it comes from his time in Orvieto (1261–1265) or while in Rome (1265–1268).[24] Jean-Pierre Torrell agrees with R.-A. Gauthier in placing the composition of this work during Aquinas's time in Rome, dating this work to 1266.[25]

Dionysius treats the theme of peace most directly in Chapter 11 of his work *On the Divine Names*. As with Augustine's thought on

20. Augustine, *In Evangelium Ioannis tractatus centum viginti quatour, patrologia latina* (PL 35), 104.1.

21. Augustine, *Confessiones* (PL 32.13.36.51-37.52).

22. Dionysius, *The Complete Works,* trans. by Paul Rorem (New Jersey: Paulist Press, 1987). I often compare my translation to that of Rorem.

23. Maria Burger, "Thomas Aquinas's Glosses on the Dionysius Commentaries of Albert the Great in Codex 30 of the Cologne Cathedral Library," in *Via Alberti Texte—Quellen—Interpretationen* (Münster: Aschendorff, 2009), 561–82.

24. Jean-Pierre Torrell, *Saint Thomas Aquinas: The Person and his Work,* trans. by Robert Royal (Washington DC: The Catholic University of America Press, 2005), 346.

25. Jean-Pierre Torrell, *Initiation à saint Thomas d'Aquin: Sa personne et son œuvre* (Paris: Les Editions du Cerf, 2015), 460.

peace, Dionysius is deeply influenced by Neo-Platonism, especially the works of Plotinus.[26] Because of this, Dionysius also identifies
peace with unity. Things are at peace to the degree they are unified,
and not at peace to the degree they are disunified. The more things
pass into multiplicity and non-being, the more strife is possible. The
closer, however, they draw to God, "the perfect source and cause of
all peace,"[27] the more perfectly they will be made one with God and
others.

Though Dionysius is clearly influenced by Neo-Platonism in his
thought on peace, he is likewise influenced by Scripture. It is no mistake that the problem of peace is not simply the problem of unity
and multiplicity, but how humans are united with themselves, others, and God. The individual must be unified within himself to be at
peace. "For everything loves to be at peace with itself, to be made
one with itself, to be inseparable from and unmoved with itself."[28]
When one is unified with oneself one is "preserved from all factions
within oneself and detachment from others."[29] Peace with oneself
does not destroy individuality,[30] but rather guards it so that all things
"are fixed and stable in their power."[31] Likewise, individuals must be
unified with others and the angels to be at peace. "But we must learn
from it [the loving kindness of Christ] to stop fighting ourselves,
each other, and the angels."[32]

Because all things desire to be what they are, they implicitly desire peace.[33] Dionysius is quite explicit that all things desire peace,

---

26. Plotinus, *Enneads,* with an English translation by A. H. Armstrong (Cambridge,
MA: Harvard University Press, 1966). For a good introduction to his works see Dominic
J. O'Meara, *Plotinus: An Introduction to the Enneads* (New York: Oxford University Press,
1993).

27. For the Greek citations of Dionysius see Thomas Aquinas, *De divinis nominibus,*
ed. Marietti (Turin and Rome, 1950): XI, l. 1, n. 403 (948d). All translations are from the
Greek and cross-checked with the Latin available to Aquinas.

28. Dionysius, *De divinis,* XI, l. 1, n. 415 (952c).

29. Dionysius, *De divinis,* XI, l. 3, n. 416 (952c).

30. Dionysius, *De divinis,* XI, l. 3, n. 415 (952b).

31. Dionysius, *De divinis,* XI, l. 3, n. 416 (952c).

32. Dionysius, *De divinis,* XI, l. 3. 1, n. 420 (953a).

33. Dionysius, *De divinis,* XI, l. 1, n. 401 (948d).

even if they seem to desire its opposite.[34] To desire the opposite of peace would be tantamount to desiring non-existence. Perfect peace with oneself requires not only internal unity, but also freedom from conflict and confusion with other things. This is only possible if all things act in accord with what they are, their "own motion;"[35] to be at peace they engage in "the activity proper to themselves."[36]

The fact that everything desires peace makes more sense if one realizes that for Dionysius peace is universal. This is because unity is universal: "There is nothing which has totally fallen away from unity."[37] To do so would be to totally fall away from peace, but given even a modicum of unity, there is a degree of peace. This is because, and here the Neo-Platonism is evident, "for whatever is totally unstable, unbounded, unestablished, undefined, is neither a being nor among those things which have being."[38]

The cause and superabundant perfection of peace is God, whom Dionysius calls "the one who stands under [ὑποστάτις] peace itself [αὐτοειρήνης] both of the whole and of each instance."[39] The name of peace is given to God to indicate "how God is still unmoved and acts in tranquility [ἡσυχίαν ἄγει] and how he is in himself, within himself, and wholly united with himself. He does not enter into himself and multiply himself thereby losing the very union, but proceeds to all things within the whole while remaining in the preeminence of his union [ὑπερεχούσης ἐνώσεως] which exceeds all things."[40] Yet this must be understood within Dionysius' apophaticism. Strictly speaking, God is beyond peace for he is beyond all knowing and being.[41] He is "unspeakable and unknowable."[42] He is the cause of peace.

34. Dionysius, *De divinis,* XI, l. 3, n. 420 (953a).

35. Dionysius, *De divinis,* XI, l. 3, n. 417 (952c).

36. Dionysius, *De divinis,* XI, l. 3, n. 417 (952d). Translation taken from Rorem.

37. Dionysius, *De divinis,* XI, l. 3, n. 418 (953a): "ἐνώσεως/*unitione.*"

38. Dionysius, *De divinis,* XI, l. 3, n. 418 (953a).

39. Dionysius, *De divinis,* XI, l. 2, n. 406 (949c) and XI, l. 4, n. 422 (953c).

40. Dionysius, *De divinis,* XI, l. 2, n. 405 (949b).

41. Cf. Dionysius, *De divinis,* XI, l. 2, n. 422 (953d).

42. Dionysius, *De divinis,* XI, l. 2, n. 405 (949b): "ἄφθεγκτον και ... ἄγνωστον. *Ineffabile et ... ignotum.*"

Yet Dionysius still calls him "wholly absolute peace [ἡ τῆς παντελοῦς εἰρήνης ὁλότης] who ranges through all things according to his simplicity and purity, powerfully making everything into one by his presence."[43] All things have one source in God for their being, "through whom there is one unshakable combination of all things, being placed according to a divine harmony, fitted in a harmony, drawn together without confusion and without division."[44] The divine peace is indivisible, abiding in absolute unity,[45] but "[he] made all to be a family indivisibly with respect to unity, identity, union, gathering/communion."[46] He is perfect peace because he is the cause of unity in all other things.[47] These names signify a source and are thus applied to the "one transcendent cause and source beyond all things."[48] These perfections, peace included, "come forth plentifully as a stream overflowing from God the unpartakable."[49]

## What about Aristotle?

Typically, when scholars list the influences on Aquinas's thought on peace, Aristotle does not make the cut.[50] In some sense, this is totally understandable. When Aquinas writes about peace, he rarely cites "the philosopher." Likewise, many of the points one might trace to Aristotle could just as easily be traced to Augustine or Dionysius. On the other hand, there are points of Aristotle's thought that do influence the way Aquinas thinks about peace. These are,

---

43. Dionysius, *De divinis*, XI, l. 1, n. 411 (952a).

44. Dionysius, *De divinis*, XI, l. 1, n. 410–11 (949b–952a).

45. Cf. Dionysius, *De divinis*, XI, l. 1, n. 413 (952b).

46. Dionysius, *De divinis*, XI, l. 1, n. 412 (952a): "καὶ πάντα ὁμογνια ποιοῦσα ταῖς ἑνότησι ταῖς ταυτότησι ταῖς ἑνώσεσι ταῖς συναγωγαῖς ἀδιαιρέτως"/"*faciens unitatibus, identitatibus, unitionibus, congregationibus, indivisibiliter.*"

47. Cf. Dionysius, *De divinis*, XI, l. 1, n. 402 (949a): "By sharing in the divine peace (Τῇ μετοχῇ τῇ θείας εἰρήνης/*participatione divinae pacis*), the more fundamental of the gathering powers, are made one (ἑνοῦνται/*uniuntur*) with themselves, others, and the one principle of peace of the world (εἰρηναρχίαν/*pacis-principatum*).

48. Dionysius, *De divinis*, XI, l. 4, n. 425 (956a).

49. Dionysius, *De divinis*, XI, l. 4, n. 426 (956b).

50. For example, Heather Erb's excellent article does not include Aristotle as an influence.

especially, his metaphysics of division, unity, and wholeness as well as his thought on friendship, the *polis*, and justice.

Aristotle outlines his views on the one and the many in *Metaphysics* X. This is an extremely dense and convoluted discussion, but I will try to pull out those parts that are essential for Aquinas's thought on peace. In Book X, Aristotle is especially concerned to answer the question of what the one is. In this he answers that it's essential note is indivisibility (ἀδιαίρετος/*indivisibilis*). This is the way that the one and the many are distinct—the one is indivisible, but the many is divisible. The ways in which one is said (things continuous by nature, of wholes, of a singular thing, and of a universal) are all indivisible. It is because the one is indivisible that it can serve as a measure (what Aristotle calls its strictest sense) especially in the category of quantity (but also extending to quality). Yet Aristotle does not mean to limit "one" to those categories and says that it is (along with being) the most universal of predicates and "cannot be a genus."[51] This is because "unity is said in the same number of ways as being is."[52]

Aristotle extends his thought on unity to many other topics, including friendship. As Aristotle says, "friendship consists in association/communion."[53] Aristotle, famously, divides friendship into three types (based on the good): the useful, the pleasurable, and the virtuous—the three objects of love. What Aristotle calls perfect friendship (a friendship of virtue) is that which brings the deepest unity, but the others qualify as friendship to the extent that they also bring a type of unity, albeit to a lesser extent.[54] Aristotle even

51. Aristotle, *Metaphysics,* ed. W.D. Ross (Oxford: Clarendon Press. 1924), 1053b24. I often compared my translation to that of Hugh Tredennick. See Aristotle, *Metaphysics,* Loeb Classical Library, trans. by Hugh Tredennick (Cambridge, MA: Harvard University Press, 1933).

52. Aristotle, *Metaphysics,* 1053b24-1054a13.

53. Aristotle, *Ethica Nicomachea,* ed. by J Bywater (Oxford, Clarendon Press, 1894), 1159b. I often compared my translation to that of Rackham. See Aristotle, *Nicomachean Ethics,* Loeb Classical Library, trans. by H Rackham (Cambridge, MA: Harvard University Press, 1934).

54. David Bostock, *Aristotle's Ethics* (New York: Oxford University Press, 2000), 169–70.

categorizes political relationships as friendship and correlates the types of political friendship with the types of regimes, though these undoubtedly have far less unity than friendship taken strictly. "Each of the types of citizenship seem to be friendship, founded upon the whole and the just."[55] So although friendship extends to all types of unity, where unity is totally lacking, there is no type of friendship.[56] In this way, justice and friendship are almost identified by Aristotle. In all common things there is justice and friendship.[57] Justice and friendship deal with the same things.[58] Both are founded on sharing.[59]

Aristotle's thoughts on politics extend his thought about unity between persons to that of the *polis*.[60] "Political concord also seems to be a type of friendship."[61] Again, the *polis* (like friendship) is established in view of some good. "Every state is a community of some kind, and every community is established with a view to some good; for mankind always act in order to obtain that which they think good. But, if all communities aim at some good, the *polis* or political community, which is the highest of all and which embraces all the rest, aims at good in a greater degree than any other, and at the highest good." Nevertheless, Aristotle views political relations as a type of useful friendship and so if it attains a deeper degree of unity ceases to be political friendship at all.[62] "Is it not clear that a city may become so unified that it is no longer a city? The nature of the city is a multitude [πλῆθος]. If it becomes more unified [μία μᾶλλον] it is a household in the city or an individual in the household. For a house-

---

55. Aristotle, *Nicomachean Ethics*, 1161a10.

56. Aristotle, *Nicomachean Ethics*, 1161a32.

57. Cf. Aristotle, *Nicomachean Ethics*, 1159b.

58. Cf. Aristotle, *Nicomachean Ethics*, 1159b.

59. Cf. Aristotle, *Nicomachean Ethics*, 1159b.

60. For a modern recovery of this project see Paul Ludwig, *Rediscovering Political Friendship: Aristotle's Theory and Modern Identity, Community, and Equality* (New York: Cambridge University Press, 2020).

61. Aristotle, *Nicomachean Ethics*, 1167bb2.

62. For an extended treatment of the relation between friendships of utility and the *polis* see Ludwig, *Rediscovering Political Friendship: Aristotle's Theory and Modern Identity, Community, and Equality*, 72ff.

hold is more unified than a city and an individual than a household. So if someone could accomplish such a thing, it ought not to be done. It would be the destruction of the city."[63]

The kind of unity that marks a *polis* does not preclude conflict. Humans who accord in a *polis* enjoy harmony not absolute unity. Hence, Aristotle says that agreement about certain subjects (he gives the example of the heavenly bodies) does not pertain to the notion of political friendship. Rather, members of a *polis* must agree on what is useful and about things to be done and things that can be commonly achieved (in other words, what belongs to the unity if the *polis* in itself). In this case, Aristotle says, "everyone gets what he seeks."[64]

This position on agreement, harmony, and conflict also extends to Aristotle's virtue ethics. As Terrance Irwin says, "Aristotle identifies virtue with harmony between the rational and non-rational part."[65] In other words, it shares something the note of unity with friendship and politics. It is in this way, Irwin says, that Aristotle advances an account of virtuous action that consists in moderate rather than extreme harmony (such as the Stoics). The upshot of moderate rather than extreme harmony is the possibility of conflict even in the virtuous person's action. Again Irwin, "If [the virtuous person] did not feel [regret or anger], his emotions would not accurately represent the different aspects of value in the situation; they would only represent the value all things considered."[66] Aristotle's account of the possible conflict even in the virtuous person, in this way, mirrors his account of conflict amongst friends as well as fellow citizens.

63. Aristotle, *Aristotle's Politica*, ed. W. D. Ross (Oxford, Clarendon Press), 1957. See 1261a. I often compared my translation to that of Rackham. See Aristotle, *Politics*, Loeb Classical Library, trans. by H. Rackham (Cambridge, MA: Harvard University Press, 1932).

64. Aristotle, *Nicomachean Ethics*, 1167b2.

65. Terrance Irwin, *The Development of Ethics* (New York: Oxford University Press, 2014), 157.

66. Irwin, *The Development of Ethics*, 158.

### AQUINAS'S TREATMENTS OF PEACE

Aquinas mentions peace multiple times in different texts and these texts range from his youthful *Scriptum* on Peter Lombard's *Sentences* to his mature *Summa Theologiae* and *Commentary on John*. In only a few works, however, does Aquinas devote direct attention to the topic of peace. Most of his treatments are happenstance and occasional; peace is mentioned by an objector, treated in conjunction with another topic, or present in the *auctor* on which Aquinas is commenting. Even in his direct treatments of peace, Aquinas only treats the topic cursorily. For example, in the *Summa Theologiae* (Aquinas's most mature and direct treatment of peace), Aquinas devotes one question and four articles to the topic. His mature *Commentary on John* concerning the words "My peace I give you …" is mostly concerned with a single aspect of his thought.

The brevity of his direct treatments coupled with thousands of asides can be bewildering for any interpreter.[67] Because of this, I will limit myself to a summary and review of Aquinas's explicit and direct treatments. In this section, I will not attempt any (extended) interpretation or reconciliation, nor any incorporation of smaller and more peripheral texts. I shall do my best simply to present Aquinas's thought itself. In Chapters 2–5, I will try to build a systematic picture based on Aquinas's thought. This only comes by interpreting, uniting, and reconciling Aquinas's explicit treatments with other isolated comments and surreptitious asides. Undoubtedly, this format is difficult and cumbersome for the reader. Nevertheless, it gives the reader a sense of the brevity, occasionality, plurality, and tension of Aquinas's texts. It also gives the reader a basis from which to assess my interpretations.

---

67. For an extensive and historically embedded chronology of Aquinas's works/passages on peace see Truini, *La Pace in Tommaso d'Aquino.*

## Aquinas's Youthful Treatments
## of Peace (1251–1259)

Aquinas only directly discusses peace twice in his early corpus, those works he composed while in Paris for the first time either as a student or as a master regent.[68] Both of these texts are brief, and peace is only discussed because the text on which he is commenting mentions it or an objector uses it in an objection. The first discussion comes in his *Commentary on Isaiah* c. 2, l. 2 and Chapter 26. The second is in his commentary on the *Scriptum.* Through these two *loci,* one can get a picture of Aquinas's early thought on peace.

*Expositio super Isaiam ad litteram* (1251–1252)

Though Aquinas mentions peace in passing throughout his exposition of the Prophet Isaiah, he only treats the topic directly in two places. Nevertheless, even in these two places, he does not devote more than a paragraph to peace and it is punctuated with a myriad of quotations (as is typical in his biblical commentaries).

The first mention, c. 2, l. 2, is precipitated by an expected pericope: Is 2:4–2:9 ("and they shall beat their swords into plowshares …"). Here Aquinas says that God is promising the peace of the convert, and giving the cause, sign, and fruit of peace. The cause of peace is the judgment of the king expressed in the law and correcting sin. The sign of this peace is the beating of swords into plowshares. The fruit is the removal of enemies. Aquinas does not explain more here, but does meet a challenge. How is it possible that God promises peace and yet there are still many wars? Aquinas offers two possible interpretations, while quietly bypassing the Gloss. The first interpretation claims that even in the time of the greatest persecution the saints still have peace. The second is Christological and claims, "that it refers to the peace which was made by Christ, which will be complete in the future."[69]

---

68. Torrell, *Initiation,* 421–22.

69. *Super Is.,* c. 2, l. 2: "*Vel Melius dicendum, quod referatur ad pacem factam per Christum, quae complebitur in futuro.*"

The second place Aquinas mentions peace is in c. 26 and 33 of the same commentary. Therein, he specifies what makes for peace in the future, the peace made by Christ, who is "the *princeps* of peace."[70] It is the fullness of all goods. It is safety from all evils. It is also *immobile*, or stable.[71] He gives similar characteristics of the future peace of heaven in c. 32. Therein he says that the peace is only full *in patria*. In heaven, peace will be beautiful, because it will not be false [peace], it will be uninterrupted and full (*plena*). This peace of the fatherland is desirable because of the firmness of divine power, the purity of each conscience (there is no peace for the wicked),[72] and the removal of enemies. This peace is the fruit of justice.[73]

*Scriptum Super Sententiis* (1252–1253 & 1256)

Aquinas treats peace directly in four major places in the *Scriptum*,[74] but IV, d. 49, q. 1, a. 2 is the most extensive. The others do not amount to more than asides. Nevertheless, this article is not a question specifically about peace. The question herein is whether beatitude is something uncreated. In *quaestiuncula* 4, an objector claims that beatitude is identical to peace. This requires Aquinas to clarify peace so that he can claim that beatitude is not identical with peace. Aquinas begins his response by quoting Augustine's definition of peace as *tranquillitas ordinis*. From this, it follows that peace is produced when something is not impeded from right order.[75] Aquinas immediately specifies this order as the order of the appetite to the good. Something is at peace when it is not impeded from the good it seeks, either individually or civilly (in the will of the leader). This even applies to natural appetites and their proportionate ends.

---

70. *Super Is.,* c. 9, l. 1.

71. Cf. *Super Is.,* c. 26.

72. Cf. *Super Is.,* c. 48 and *In Jer.,* c. 14, l. 4.

73. Cf. *Super Is.,* c. 26.

74. *Cf.* III *Sent.,* d. 27, q. 1, a. 3, ad 5 and d. 2, q. 1, a. 6, d. 34, q. 1, a. 4, co.; IV *Sent.,* d. 49, q. 1, a. 2.

75. Cf. IV *Sent.,* d. 49, q. 1, a. 2, qc. 4: "*ratio pacis assumitur quod aliquid non impeditur a recto ordine.*"

Since happiness is an operation, Aquinas continues, if it is to reach the good it must be unimpeded (being impeded from the good detracts from perfection).[76] This provides Aquinas a vital link between happiness and peace. Beatitude requires peace, not as an essential part of it, but as removing the impediments to it. Because of this necessary connection the desire for happiness includes the desire for peace as the negative corollary. If you want to be happy, you necessarily, and naturally,[77] also desire to achieve and hold that good which causes happiness without impediments. In other words, Aquinas sees peace as the most proximate disposition to beatitude, something without which beatitude will not be had, but not identical with it.[78] It is the removal of obstacles.

This dispositive reading of peace is confirmed in two other sections of the *Scriptum:* d. 27, q. 1 and d. 34. In d. 27, a. 1. Therein, Aquinas says that peace is not distinguished from love (*amor*) but is something of love (*aliquid amoris*). He clarifies that peace is a medium between desire and love, between desire for the end and love of the end. It is thus dispositive and enables desire to attain the end.[79] In other words, to be at peace means that the appetitive order toward the good (or joy) is unimpeded.[80] Peace is not something positive which follows from the attainment of the end but is simply the lack of impediments to the attainment of the end. Desire proceeds to love if unimpeded, in other words. In this, it is *propinquissima*

76. Cf. IV *Sent.,* d. 49, q. 1, a. 2, qc. 4: "*quia impedimentum aliquid de ius perfectione detraheret.*"

77. Cf. IV *Sent.,* d. 49, q. 1, a. 2, qc. 4, co.

78. Cf. IV *Sent.,* d. 49, q. 1, a. 2, qc. 4, ad 3: "*Ad tertium dicendum, quod pacem omnia desiderant, non sicut finem, sed sicut id sine quo finis haberi non potest.*"

79. Cf. III *Sent.,* d. 27, q. 1, a. 3, ad 5: "*Ad quintum dicendum, quod pax non distinguitur ab amore, sed est aliquid amoris: dicit enim quasi quietationem appetitus; sed amor dicit ulterius transformationem, et quamdam conversionem ipsius in amatum; unde pax est medium inter desiderium et amorem.*" This makes more sense when you realize that for the young Aquinas the relation between desire and love is the opposite of his mature position. In his youthful position, desire comes before love. In his mature position, love gives birth to desire. See Christopher Malloy, "Thomas on the Order of Love and Desire: a Development of Doctrine," in *The Thomist* 71 (2007): 65–87.

80. Cf. III *Sent.,* d. 34, q. 1, a. 4–5, co.

*dispositio ad finem.*[81] This is so because the ultimate end is an operation, not the termination of motion. Yet peace, which is rest, is the end of motion. Though it is closer to the end than the motion itself, it is not the end. Likewise, when Aquinas speaks of peace between two people, concord, peace is dispositive. If, he says, peace is not to be totally reduced to concord, it is because concord is the union of wills itself and peace is the lack of discord. Again, peace is merely the removal of obstacles. It is not the union of wills itself.

### *De Veritate* (1256–1259)

The final youthful text where Aquinas mentions peace directly is q. 22, a. 1, ad 12 of the *De Veritate.* In this question, Aquinas is dealing with questions about the good. The 12th objection claims that all things desire peace (as Augustine and Dionysius maintain) and nature is determined to one thing. Hence, all things do not desire the good (or else they would not tend to peace). This objection puts Aquinas in a bit of a bind, for in the *Scriptum* he claimed that though all beings desire peace, peace is distinct from the end (the good); it is implied in the desire for the end. Hence, it seems like it is subject to a diverse desire for the end and all are not determined to one (the good) but to two (the good and peace). Alternatively, peace and the good are identical in some way or subject to one and the same desire.

Aquinas goes for the latter option, the unity of desire for peace and the good. In other words, Aquinas wants to retain the claim that nature is determined to one end, but also claim that all things necessarily desire peace and goodness by that one desire. He does this by claiming that when desire terminates in the good and peace, it does not terminate in diverse things (*diversa*). In explaining how this is possible, he returns to appetite. Whenever one desires something, he or she desires the removal of impediments to it. Hence, by the same appetitive tendency the will desires the good and peace. Peace remains dispositive in this text but is implied by desire for the good

---

81. IV *Sent.*, d. 49, q. 1, a. 2, qc. 4, ad 1.

such that when you desire the good you *simul* desire peace. Accordingly, peace is "the removal of disturbances and impediments to the *adeptionem boni.*"[82]

## Aquinas's Middle Treatments
## of Peace (1259–1268)

During Aquinas's time at Orvieto and Rome his attention to the topic of peace increases. This is not to say that it begins to be treated independently of other topics, but only that the texts on which he is commenting themselves mention peace more often. This is especially true for his lectures on the Pauline corpus and his commentary on Dionysius' *On the Divine Names.* In Dionysius' text, especially in Chapter 11, Aquinas treats peace extensively (which is not surprising). Whereas the problem in Aquinas's youthful corpus is a dearth of treatments, the problem in his middle corpus is a surplus of treatments—but, again, most are still occasional and very brief (and then only being precipitated by clear references in the text on which he is commenting). Nevertheless, the panoply of texts in this period of Aquinas's life complicates the relatively clear picture we saw in his youthful treatises.

### Peace in Aquinas's Pauline Commentaries (1261–1268)

If Paul mentions peace, one can, with some certainty, expect Aquinas to say something about it. For example, the Pauline salutation, grace and peace, receives a consistent interpretation in Aquinas's commentaries: whereas grace is the beginning of goodness, peace is its end. Peace is the final of all goods and the last end (*finis ultimus*) of the human person.[83] In addition to this unified explanation of the Pauline salutation, Paul mentions peace again in most of his letters. For this reason, Aquinas treats peace at least one other time in most of his Pauline commentaries. To give a sense of Aquinas's thought

---

82. *De Ver.,* q. 22, a. 1, ad 12: "*Pax autem importat remotionem perturbantium et impedientium adeptionem boni.*"

83. See, for example, *Super Col.,* c. 1, l. 1, n. 7 or *Super Tit.,* c. 1, l. 1, n. 9.

on peace as found in his Pauline commentaries, I will pull out these more extensive passages and arrange them in a somewhat systematic order beginning with God and ending with what is contrary to peace.[84] In this way we can begin to see both the sweep of Aquinas's middle thought as well as the happenstance (and sometimes contradictory) nature occasioned by Paul's thought.

In Aquinas's *Commentary on Hebrews*, Aquinas speaks most directly about the relation of God to peace. This is not a surprise. In verse 13:20, the author calls God the "God of peace."[85] Elaborating on this saying, Aquinas calls peace the "the unity of affections (*unitas afectuum*)"[86] which allows him to explain in what sense God is the God of peace. It is through God that the heart is united, that all affections are united. This unity comes through love, which is the bond of perfection. Because of this, only God can cause peace; only God unites all affections in the virtue of charity. God is not only the "God of peace," but "to make peace is God's characteristic effect [*proprius effectus*]."[87] In other words, God is the God of peace because he is the sole primary cause of interior peace in humans. Yet Aquinas goes further than apophaticism. Peace "flows from that depth [God himself], in which peace exists."[88]

In his *Commentary on Colossians*, Aquinas elaborates the relation between Jesus and peace. This is also not surprising since Paul writes: "Christ reconciles all things to himself, making peace by the blood of his cross ..."[89] To explain what Paul means by reconciliation, Aquinas writes that it is to agree in willing one thing (exterior peace–concord). It is in Christ that the wills of men, God, and the angels are reconciled—agree on willing one thing. Sin divides

84. Cf. *Super Heb.*, c. 13, l. 3; *Super I Tim.*, c. 2, l. 1; *Super II Thess.*, c. 3, l. 1; *Super Col.*, c. 1, l. 5 and c. 3, l. 3; *Super Phil.*, c. 4, l. 1; *Super Gal.*, c. 5, l. 6; *Super Eph.*, c. 2, l. 5 and c. 4, l. 1; *Super II Cor.*, c. 13, l. 3.

85. Heb 13:20: "Ὁ δὲ θεὸς τῆς εἰρήνης."

86. *Super Heb.*, c. 13, l. 3, n. 766.

87. *Super Heb.*, c. 13, l. 3, n. 766 : "*Proprius enim effectus Dei est facere pacem.*"

88. *Super Phil.*, c. 4, l. 1, n. 159: "*Ab isto profundo, in quo est pax, derivatur ...*"

89. Col 1:20: "καὶ δι' αὐτοῦ ἀποκαταλλάξαι τὰ πάντα εἰς αὐτόν, εἰρηνοποιήσας διὰ τοῦ αἵματος τοῦ σταυροῦ αὐτοῦ, δι' αὐτοῦ εἴτε τὰ ἐπὶ τῆς γῆς εἴτε τὰ ἐν τοῖς οὐρανοῖς."

and causes discord. For example, the Law divided Jew from Gentile. Christ comes to reconcile all these things in his body, i.e. cause their wills to tend to one. Christ does this through the virtue of charity (whose nature is to be a bond), which not only unites all the virtues of humans, from which peace is immediately derived (*mox oritur*), but also human wills. Likewise, love also gives rise to joy, which follows from peace, the peace Christ established between God and man.

This picture is confirmed in Aquinas's *Commentary on Ephesians*. At Eph 2:14, Paul says: "for he [Jesus] is our peace."[90] Commenting on this Aquinas, says that Paul is speaking emphatically to explain that through Christ we are drawn near to each other. Christ is the total cause of peace: "whatever peace is in us is caused by Christ."[91] He announced this peace when he rose from the dead and removed whatever divided humans. Between the Jews and Gentiles, this was the Old Law, which divided them as a law of fear. Christ brings love, which "cements singular individuals with others and with Christ."[92] Christ comes to unite and: "whatever unites must unite into one something [*aliquo uno*]... Christ makes them one in himself."[93] He does this by removing the enmity, that is sin, and drawing people to make peace with their neighbor, for that is the way to peace with God.[94] The cause and form of this peace is also the Holy Spirit through whom people are united, and through whom Christ works. "We are united by the union of the Holy Spirit."[95]

Aquinas complements this picture concerning the Spirit in c. 4, l. 1 where Paul exhorts the Ephesians to "keep the unity of the Spirit

90. Eph 2:14: "Αὐτὸς γάρ ἐστιν ἡ εἰρένη ἡμῶν."

91. *Super Eph.*, c. 2, l. 5, n. 111: "*Quia ergo quidquid pacis est in nobis causatur a Christo.*"

92. *Super Eph.*, c. 2, l. 5, n. 113: "*Quae est quasi cementum conglutinans singulos sibi invicem, et omnes simul Christo.*"

93. *Super Eph.*, c. 2, l. 5, n. 116: "*Quae autem uniuntur, oportet uniri in aliquo uno, et quia lex dividebat, non poterant in lege uniri.*"

94. Cf. *Super Eph.*, c. 2, l.5, n. 118: "*Sciendum est quod dilectio proximi est via ad pacem Dei.*"

95. *Super Eph.*, c. 2, l. 5, n. 121: "*Causam autem pacis et formam ostendit dicens quoniam per ipsum habemus accessum ambo, id est, duo populi, in uno Spiritu, id est, uniti unione Spiritus Sancti.*"

in the bond of peace."[96] This gives Aquinas space to reflect on what destroys the unity produced by the Spirit. He identifies four vices, in particular, that destroy peace: pride (through producing *dissension*), anger (through *turbationes*), impatience, and inordinate zeal (producing *turbatio*). Charity, and the other relevant virtues, remove these problems and maintain unity among the faithful. The unity of the faithful is not the *unitas carnis,* which is used for evil. The unity of the faithful is the unity of the Spirit which is good and for the doing of good. The unity of the faithful, which is charity (*caritas enim est coniunctio animorum*), is preserved by peace for objects cannot last unless they persist in a common bond. Peace is this bond since it is tranquility of mode, species, and order where each has what is his own. Thus, Aquinas follows, justice maintains peace. However, the unity of the Church is compared to the unity of the body, which is the order of one member to another so peace orders one member to another just as in a singular body. Believers are also united in one Spirit, which is another type of unity, like body and soul making a *tertium quid.* Hence, believers have one spiritual consensus through the unity of faith and charity.[97]

Commenting on Gal 5:22, Aquinas continues outlining the relation between the Spirit and peace. Paul gives occasion by listing the fruits of the Spirit and including peace, love, goodness, and joy. This requires Aquinas to disambiguate in what sense all these are fruits and relate them to each other. According to Aquinas, the fruits of the Spirit arise in the soul from grace and perfect one either inwardly or outwardly. Interiorly, humans are perfected and directed concerning the good and the evil. With respect to the good, humans are perfected first in love. Just as in natural movements there is an inclination to the good, so also the first human movement is toward the good and accordingly the first of the fruits is charity, which is the inclination

---

96. Eph 4:3: "σπουδάζοντες τηρεῖν τὴν ἑνότητα τοῦ πνεύματος ἐν τῷ συνδέσμῳ τῆς εἰρήνης."

97. Alternatively, Aquinas writes, one body is unity with neighbor and one spirit is unity with God. Believers have and mutually enjoy something equally, that is the eternal reward.

to God. The last inward end is joy which proceeds from the presence of the thing loved. For joy to be perfect it requires two things. The first is peace, which is the sufficient possession of what is loved. Likewise, the perfect enjoyment of the thing loved is also had by peace since when you enjoy something perfectly, you cannot be hindered.[98] In this way, joy is the fruition of charity, but peace is its perfection. Through both joy and peace, man is perfected in relation to the good. Interiorly, the Holy Spirit also perfects (through patience) the person by removing the obstacles that disturb peace. Against the obstacles to love, the Holy Spirit teaches longanimity to wait for the beloved object. Goodness, Aquinas continues, is what perfects man in relation to his neighbor: a right and good will. Benignity regards the good deeds regarding one's neighbor: a burning, yet kindly (*bene*), fire (*ignis*) that moves man to relieve the needs of others and to meekly undergo their evil (mildness). To God, the Spirit establishes right order through faith and in relation to our body, modesty. Continence refers to the fruit that, assailed by desires, reason does not fail whereas chastity guards from any attacks.

In his *Commentary on II Thess.,* c. 3, l. 2, Aquinas gives a clearer exposition of peace and explains why God is necessary for it. Therein, he writes that peace consists in man's concord with himself and with others. These two concords (and thus two types of peace) cannot be had without God. Personally, one is only in harmony with oneself if what one seeks to fulfill one desire suffices to fulfill them all. Aquinas does not explain why this is the case, but does claim this can only be God. Likewise, humans are united by what is common and God is the most common (and so it is implied that God brings the deepest peace between individuals). Hence, Aquinas continues, this is why Paul writes that God gives peace, not temporal peace but spiritual peace. This spiritual peace begins here among all the faithful but is completed in heaven.[99]

---

98. Cf. *Super Gal.,* c. 5, l. 6, n. 330: "*Secundo vero ut adsit perfecta fruitio rei amatae, quod similiter per pacem habetur, quia, quidquid superveniat, si perfecte aliquis fruatur re amata, puta Deo, non potest impediri ab eius fruitione.*"

99. Cf. *Super II Thess.,* c. 3, l. 2, n. 89–90.

In Second Corinthians, Paul gives Aquinas occasion to begin to relate peace to the body of the Church. Paul says: "For the rest, brethren, rejoice, be perfect, be exhorted, be of one mind, have peace. And the God of peace and of love shall be with you" (2 Cor 13:11).[100] In explaining this passage, Aquinas says that bodies cannot be preserved and ordered unless their members are ordered to one another, so also the Church members must be ordered and united with one another. This unity is both interior and exterior. The interior union is by faith and love—that they believe and love the same things. The exterior is peace. He moves on to Paul's final clause saying that Christ is the God of peace because he himself is the giver, author, and lover of peace. Christ also dwells in peace. Christ is not only the God of peace but also of love, and these are connected, because he who has true peace of heart and body has charity. Aquinas then moves on to Paul's sign of peace (kiss), which Aquinas says is fitting because one breathes when one kisses, a sign of uniting their spirits toward peace. The sign of peace gives Aquinas the opportunity to distinguish a true sign from a false sign and false peace. Here Aquinas identifies the possibility of a simulated peace—when one seems to be at peace, but evil is in one's heart. There is also an evil and shameful peace, which is when people come together to do evil. This is distinct from the holy peace which is united in holiness, a sign of which is the kiss as a sign of charity and union.[101]

In his *Commentary on 1 Timothy*, Aquinas makes a rare foray into political peace and contrasts it with the peace of the Church. Aquinas treats peace in c. 2, l. 1. Paul writes that kings are in authority in order for us to live a "quiet and tranquil life." This leads Aquinas to say that subjection is useful to obtain our good. Useful is the operative word, for what Paul (according to Aquinas) references is the peace of this world (*pax mundi* or *pax terrena*). According to Aquinas, in these two things (quiet and tranquility) consists the entirety

---

100. 2 Cor 13:11: "Λοιπόν, ἀδελφοί, χαίρετε, καταρτίζεσθε, παρακαλεῖσθε, τὸ αὐτὸ φρονεῖτε, εἰρηνεύετε, καὶ ὁ Θεὸς τῆς ἀγάπης καὶ εἰρήνης ἔσται μεθ' ὑμῶν."

101. Cf. *Super II Cor.*, c. 1, l. 1, n. 8 & c. 13, l. 3, n. 539–40.

of the peace of the world (which is shared commonly between those of the Church and those not). Yet, Aquinas claims, the Church has a peace which is proper to it and not shared with the world. The difference between these two types of peace is that earthly peace can be disturbed both from within (against quiet) and from without (against tranquility). Likewise, the impious and the pious use this peace for different ends: the impious for idolatry and lascivious actions and the saints for the worship of God and chastity. Hence, they are distinct by end.[102]

Finally in his commentary on c. 4, l. 1 of Philippians, Aquinas treats the contrary of peace and claims that *perturbatio* of order is the destruction of peace. This is so because peace is tranquility of order. Aquinas considers this peace in three ways. First, in its principle: God. He writes: "From that depth in whom it exists, peace flows first and more perfectly to the beatified, in whom there are no perturbations (neither of blame nor guilt). Then it flows into the saints. For inasmuch as one is holy, to that extent one suffers less perturbations of the mind."[103] In its source, God, peace surpasses all created understanding. As it exists in the beatified, it surpasses angelic understanding. As it exists in those on earth, it surpasses the knowledge of those who lack grace. Aquinas then goes on to specify that peace is a matter of affections and its loss is the loss of affection for the good. Jesus is the cause of our affections remaining trained on the authentic good and the fruits of this good action is God. If you do what is good, God will be with you.

*De Divinis Nominibus* (1266–1268)

Aquinas's *Commentary on the Divine Names* is extensive, and what he says there about peace resists easy summary. Indeed, Aquinas devotes the entirety of Chapter 11 to the discussion of peace. With the

---

102. Cf. *Super I Tim.*, c. 2, l. 1, n. 59.

103. *Super Phil.*, c. 4, l. 1, n. 159: "*Ab isto profundo, in quo est pax, derivatur primo et perfectius in beatos, in quibus nulla est perturbatio, et nec culpae, nec poenae, et consequenter derivatur ad sanctos viros. Et quanto est magis sanctus, tanto minus patitur perturbationem mentis.*"

proper reservations one must bring to the commentary genre,[104] this text represents the most extended treatment of peace in Aquinas's entire *ouvre*. Therein, he discusses peace under two broad categories. The first is found in Chapter 11, l. 4 and considers peace's relation to the divine nature in the abstract and answers objections. The second is found in Chapter 11, lectures 1–3, and considers how God causes peace in creatures, both in general and in particular.

In Chapter 11, lecture 4 and the beginning of lecture 2, Aquinas treats peace in relation to the divine nature. In other words, unlike Chapters 1–3, Aquinas is not considering peace in relation to God's causality, but rather as it exists in God himself. He begins by denying that we can fully comprehend God, and hence he is called "ineffable." God is *immobile* and above all (creaturely) processions, and although his similitude is poured into things, he is above all of them having *quies et immobilitas*. We are not able to say how he acts in silence and rest or how he is *supereminenter unita* in himself in which consists the divine peace. This does not, however, stop Aquinas from predicating peace of God. *Unitio* pertains to the *ratio* of peace, Aquinas says. In creatures, thus, peace comes from being united into one something, *aliquo uno*. Yet God is *unitus* in himself. Humans can be diverse in themselves by containing many; they are not *unus*. They are divisible. God has no diversity and so is *unus*. Aquinas goes on to specify in what senses *unus* is said and so clarify how it applies to God. Some things are *unus* in themselves because they do not have divisible parts but are not totally united to themselves because one part is not another. God, however, is united totally to himself because he has no parts, but is in every way simple. So is his *unitio*, which remains total. God is peace itself because he is *unitus*.

In Chapter 4 Aquinas not only discusses peace, but also the other attributes under discussion in Dionysius' text: life and virtue. Yet, his discussion of these has a bearing on the predication of peace.

---

104. Cf. Christopher Kaczor, "Thomas Aquinas's Commentary on the Ethics: Merely an Interpretation of Aristotle?" in *American Catholic Philosophical Quarterly*, Vol. 78, No. 3 (2004): 353–78.

Likewise, in interpreting these texts Aquinas softens Dionysius' apophaticism somewhat. In predicating peace of God, it seems that Dionysius wants to claim that the cause of something in others is also maximal and first in that category and yet beyond that same trait. Hence, things do not participate in God who is beyond all participation. God is said to be a trait because he is the cause of this trait, in other words. Indeed, this is how Aquinas reads Dionysius. He says that it is manifest that what is *per se vita* is prior to all the living so that we praise God as cause of the prior, he is the cause of all. God himself is beyond "through a certain excess."[105]

Yet Aquinas continues to say that what is *per se vita* is the cause and principle of all the living. This excludes the error of the Platonists for whom life would be a separate and subsisting thing. Rather than hierarchically arranging the ideas, Aquinas claims that all goods are subsumed under *esse* and that when we say that God is the cause of life, we do not mean a life other than God's own. God is the cause of all the living and is therefore *per se vita*. He exceeds all the participations by creatures in his life while remaining the principle of life and being of all things. He even interprets Dionysius' claim that God is *imparticipabilis* (ἀμέθεκτος) to mean that no one creature exhausts the supereminent perfection found in God and God is not part of the creature, not that God is simply the cause of these perfections but they do not properly apply to God.[106] As Aquinas says in another place of the commentary, God stands immobile in himself but in another sense he is the exemplar of all created peace and his similitude passes to all things.[107] In other words, the divine peace proceeds to all things through its similitude. Yet it remains in itself *supereminenter unita*. God is subsisting *unitas*. Hence, he is simply and essentially one.[108] It is this peace that God "pours into the world through Christ."[109]

105. *In de Div. Nom.*, 928.
106. *In de Div. Nom.*, 934.
107. Cf. *In de Div. Nom.*, 912
108. *In de Div. Nom.*, 912.
109. *In de Div. Nom.*, 923: "*Effundit pacem in mundum per Christum.*"

In Chapters 1–3, Aquinas explores the causality of God in relation to peace and divides it into the universal and the particular. Concerning God's universal causality of peace, Aquinas begins by defining peace: the rest (*quies*) of appetite in its proper good.[110] This happens when there is nothing impeding this rest either interiorly or exteriorly. Hence, Aquinas follows, something has peace when it has a certain union with the good by which all repugnant things are excluded. Though God causes peace in all creatures, this is most manifest in rational creatures. Humans have peace when their wills agree with others *in uno* such that one is not against the other. Humans accord in one because they share in one.

Aquinas follows that the *ratio* of peace consists in two things. The first is that humans are united and, second, that they agree toward one. This is why all things, even natural things, are at peace. They all agree in their desire for the ultimate end. This desire for unity, just as the desire for *esse et bonum*, is natural to the creature for it is by its division that things are corrupted. This is how the divine peace causes unity in all things—by uniting them as parts of the universe. Hence, the divine peace is the final cause of all things. Indeed, even if in their proximate ends things are contrary to one another, they agree in the order of the universe. In this all things participate in the divine peace, which has the *rationem finis*.

Aquinas then moves to the particular causality of God with respect to peace. He claims that all things have a triple union by their participation in divine peace. They are *unum* with themselves. They are united, *unio*, with others in an order which is truly one. They are united with the principle of all things and of peace, which is God. This is the threefold union—self, others, God. Though God unites lower creatures through the ministry of the higher, it is all reduced to God as the ultimate end and first cause. What God causes in all things is the unity of peace, which consists in a tranquil order (citing Augustine). This requires three things: distinction (*distinctio*), not exceeding of the limits of one's nature, and stability of this

---

110. *In de Div. Nom.*, 880.

distinction (*diffinitio et terminatio*). In other words, God introduces the distinction of things in order to build a harmonious whole. The last, stability, pertains to the conservation of peace. Hence, God does not allow things to tend to something infinite and without termination and end. This would oppose the triple unity in things. *Unio* would be destroyed by this.

Aquinas also treats the way God creates peace in angels, humans, and in the whole universe. In describing the ways in which God causes peace in these three groups, Aquinas says that, "the effect of divine peace in the rational animal is reduced to unity."[111] This holds also for the angels, since the three ways Aquinas identifies are three ways they are united. With respect to the entire universe, Aquinas claims that God fits all creatures together in one order which remains indissolubly and is a certain harmony: "That is, the causality of a proportionate concord."[112] This concord is produced in creatures through consensus, of wills, and connaturality, of natural appetites. That is, they belong to a certain order and have a connection to each other. In other words, God makes peace in all things through making unity in them. God does this by "reducing all things to a certain order."[113] Hence, all things have a certain "connatural friendship" by their shared ordination to enjoy God as an ultimate end.[114]

Aquinas follows this with an extended discussion of the ways in which unity is said, since the "*ratio* of connection is perfected in unity. Hence, the from the modes of unity one considers the modes of connection."[115] This helps him to specify the ways in which God causes unity in other things. The first is what is *secundum se unum*. That is, something is one through itself. The second concerns a way something is said to be one, but through relation to another. This is

---

111. *In de Div. Nom.*, 906.

112. *In de Div. Nom.*, 908: "*idest proportionata condoria causatur.*" Harmony is a nothing other than *concors consonantia*.

113. *In de Div. Nom.*, 910.

114. *In de Div. Nom.*, 910.

115. *In de Div. Nom.*, 911: "*Ratio autem connectionis in quadam unitate perficitur et ideo, secundum modum unitatis, attenditur modus connexionis.*"

through reason or name alone as two names point to the same person or other according to the thing, as Socrates and Plato are the same in species or a horse and a cow are the same generically. For one is said absolutely but the same is relative. Next, some things are not one simply but in a relative sense since they are gathered from many (as a composite). This is a union. Finally, Aquinas says, something can be called one through relation. Congregations have less the *ratio* of *unitatis* than *unita*. What is *secundum quid unum* is not simple but is able to be said to be united. God causes peace by causing unity by the mode of simple unity or the mode of identity, or the mode of union, or the mode of congregation.[116]

In Chapter 11, lecture 3, Aquinas provides an exposition of Dionysius' objections to the aforesaid presentation. The first objection is that not all things desire peace, but always desire to move. The *ratio* of peace is *unitas* and *quies* and so they would be adverse to it. Aquinas, in response, claims that even to desire such separation is to desire peace, for they will to be united to themselves and to what is proper to their nature. They want to be preserved in themselves. They want to have their natures immobile and without loss. This is to desire peace. God, likewise, preserves this by his activity. God preserves each thing in its nature and its proper boundaries by his providence. The divine peace guards things so they don't escape their natural limits as well as moving them to proper operation. Likewise, distinction and alterity are not contrary to peace, so those who desire it still desire peace. Alterity and distinction belong to the very *ratio* of peace. Since the *ratio* of peace is *unio*, none fall from this completely. Each thing desires and loves that which is in conformity with itself and rejects what is contrary. The third objection concerns the many who rejoice in alterity and separation in their rational appetite. Even these still desire peace, according to an obscure similitude, Aquinas says. They still desire to have their appetites satisfied, even if they desire what will ultimately disturb them more. They would be wiser if they turned their many desires toward the one desire of true peace.

---

116. *In de Div. Nom.*, 911.

## Aquinas's Mature Treatments
## of Peace (1268–1273)

In Aquinas's late works, those composed by his time in Paris and Naples, Aquinas continues to treat peace as occasions arise. These occasions are especially prominent in his *Commentary on John, Summa Theologiae,* and *Lectures on the Psalms.* Though we find Aquinas's most mature theology in these texts, it is still occasional: precipitated by the text in front of him mentioning peace.

### *Super Matthew* (1269–1270)

Aquinas treats peace in two major places in his *Super Matt.* (through the lecture notes taken by one of his students and so meriting a more critical eye) c. 5, l. 2 and c. 10, l. 2. In c. 5, l. 2, Aquinas is explaining the beatitudes. He begins by refuting the opinion of those who think that happiness consists in something other than the virtues of the contemplative life. When mentioning the active life, which is the closest (Aquinas remarks) to true happiness, Aquinas mentions peace for the first time. The virtues of the active life are ordered to oneself or to another. If they are ordered to another their *finis est pax.* Since they are ordered to another, they are not beatitude itself. The peacemakers are not blessed because they make peace but because they tend toward something else: being children of God. When Aquinas comes to that beatitude itself, he says that "blessed are the peacemakers" is the second beatitude which pertains to love of neighbor. He says there that beatitudes which are dispositive are toward the vision of God or to love. This beatitude is one of them since "peace disposes toward love of God by which we are called (and are) sons of God."[117] On this basis peace disposes one to love of neighbor. In this way peace is an effect of justice and mercy. After claiming that peace is dispositive to love, Aquinas goes on to explain peace itself.

---

117. *Super Matt.,* c. 5, l. 2, n. 436: "*ita pax ad dilectionem Dei disponit, qua filii Dei nominamur et sumus.*"

He begins by citing Augustine: peace is the tranquility of order. Order, he says, is "the disposition assigning to each its place, the equal or the unequal."[118] Peace is each remaining in this place: the mind subject to God, the other powers subject to the mind, and having peace with others. This order is only possible in the saints, Aquinas notes. They have "interior peace" whereas the wicked have no peace. Interiority is the peace the world cannot give. Yet interior peace is not enough, the saints ought to make peace where there is discord. Neither of these types of peace can be perfect here though, one's passions are never wholly subject to reason.

Aquinas then moves to the reward: to be a son of God. He notes that those who are sons of God do what is required of a son. Now the Son came to gather what is dispersed. Through peace and charity one arrives at the kingdom, where you are a son. Where there is peace, additionally, there is no resistance. One is not able to resist God. Aquinas finishes by mentioning that the beatitudes all point toward the same reward, but add to one another. The seventh beatitude is adapted to the gift of wisdom, for it is wisdom that makes men sons of God. Peace is placed in the seventh beatitude, just as rest on the seventh day. He finishes by noting that persecution can take away exterior peace, even possibly entirely, but not interior peace.

The next place Aquinas mentions peace in his *Super Matt.* is in explaining the dominical saying, "I have not come to bring peace, but the sword" (Mt 10:34). As Aquinas reads it, this is firstly a warning to the disciples to preach the truth despite insults and fear of death. In this way it is a warning for the disciples to not abandon their mission for some sense of false exterior peace. In other words, as Aquinas says, there is a bad peace (*pax mala*) and a good peace (*pax bona*). Evil peace is the peace of carnal affects, which is not the peace that Christ brings or was announced at his birth. When Christ said he came not to bring peace, Aquinas interprets this to mean he

---

118. *Super Matt.*, c. 5, l. 2, n. 438: "*Ordo autem est parium dispariumque sua loca cuique tribuens dispositio.*"

came not to bring carnal peace. He says that true peace signifies *concordia.*

*Commentary on John* (1270–1272)

Aquinas's *Commentary on the Gospel of John* affords him the opportunity to elaborate on peace in multiple places, but especially c. 14, l. 7, c. 16, l. 8, and c. 17, l. 5.

It is no mistake that c. 14, l. 7 is primarily about peace. It is Aquinas's commentary on Christ's saying: "Peace I leave with you, my peace I give unto you: not as the world give, do I give to you. Let not your heart be troubled, nor let it be afraid."[119] The entire lecture, though short, is an important source of Aquinas's mature thought on peace. He begins by noting that the gifts of wisdom and knowledge are appropriated to the Son, while the gift of peace is appropriated to the Holy Spirit, since he is *amor,* and *amor* is the cause of peace.[120] Yet since the Spirit proceeds from the Son, the gifts which are appropriated to the Holy Spirit can also be attributed to the Son.

Aquinas follows this clarification by offering a description of the gift of peace, calling it the tranquility of order. Inasmuch as order is undisturbed (*inturbatus*), one remains in peace. In humans there is a threefold order: to oneself, to God, and to neighbor. Thus, there is a threefold peace. The first is intrinsic, when "one is pacified with oneself and one's powers are without perturbation."[121] The other is with God when "one is totally subject to his ordination." The third is with neighbor, which Aquinas does not explain here. Aquinas then further specifies interior peace, which must include the intellect, will, and sense appetites. These are well ordered when the will is directed by the mind and the sense appetites are directed by the intellect and will. In this our mind is unencumbered by disordered affections, the will is trained on God, its object and the bond of love is had with our neighbor in the *consortium* of love of God.

119. Jn 14:27: "Εἰρήνην ἀφίημι ὑμῖν, εἰρήνην τὴν ἐμὴν δίδωμι ὑμῖν· οὐ καθὼς ὁ κόσμος δίδωσιν ἐγὼ δίδωμι ὑμῖν. μὴ ταρασσέσθω ὑμῶν ἡ καρδία μηδὲ δειλιάτω."
120. Cf. *Super Io.,* c. 14, l. 7, n. 1961.
121. *Super Io.,* c. 14, l. 7, n. 1962.

To have any of these totally is not possible now, for there are always disturbances, Aquinas warns. Yet Christ gives us his peace now so that we can conquer enemies and love one another. It will be perfect in heaven. Nevertheless, both types of peace—in this world and in heaven—are that of Christ. For the present peace Christ is alone its author (*tantum auctoris*), and of the future peace Christ is its author and its possessor. Christ himself is always without conflict, and though he leaves us his peace ours is with conflict. Alternatively, Aquinas says, one could say that both peace sayings refer to this time and then it is Christ who leaves his example by power and strength.

"Not as this world gives to you." Aquinas explains this by distinguishing the peace of the saints from the peace of this world in three ways. The purpose is different. Temporal peace is for the quiet and calm enjoyment of the things of this world. It could help people to sin. The peace of the saints is for eternal goods. So the ends are different. Christ gives peace in this world so that we can obtain eternal things. They also differ in that the peace of this world is simulated—it is only exterior peace. The peace of Christ is true because it is both interior and exterior. Finally, they differ in perfection since the peace of this world is imperfect since it only concerns externals but Christ brings tranquility both interiorly and externally.

In Chapter 16, l. 8, Aquinas says that the benefit (*utilitas*) the Lord's teaching gives is peace. All his teaching was aimed to return humans to God so that we may have peace in him. Hence, the purpose of the gospel is peace in Christ. Here Aquinas identifies peace as opposed to perturbations. Those who are evil have troubles without peace, for they do not have God. Whereas the saints have peace with troubles, yet their joy super-exceeds those evils and the evils do not remain. Even on this earth they have peace: "for our purpose (*finis*) here ought to be having peace in God."[122] We need this peace to meet all the vexations of this world.

The final major place that Aquinas treats peace in this commentary

---

122. *Super Io.*, c. 16, l. 8, n. 2174: "*Finis enim noster hic debet esse ut pacem habeamus in Deo.*"

is c. 17, l. 5. One would not know it based on word count. The word peace only occurs twice in this treatment. Yet Aquinas reads the entirety of Christ's high priestly prayer as a prayer for peace. The key is the identification between peace and unity: "For God is not a cause of dissension, but of peace."[123] Aquinas then, with copious citations of the Fathers, expounds what this unity means. Christ prays that they may be *unum* and this is to pray for goodness since people may be one in evil. God seeks unity in good. Believers are united in the Father and Son because we seek and believe one thing together. Otherwise, Aquinas reasons, believers' affections would be scattered. Charity is what unites our affections and makes us one with God. Whereas God is united in essence and love, believers are united to God in remote likeness in grace. The oneness of believers is a remote likeness to the oneness of God—both in nature and in love.[124] In this way they are one and at peace.

*Summa Theologiae II-II* (1271–1272)

Aquinas treats peace in a more extended fashion twice in the *Summa Theologiae*. Both concern the fruits of the Spirit. Aquinas treats the fruits directly in I-II q. 70. Nevertheless, Aquinas's thought in II-II q. 29 on the interior and exterior effects of charity (among which he locates peace) is also deeply influenced by Paul's listing in Galatians 5 (love, joy, peace ...). In I-II q. 70, Aquinas attempts to give an intelligible order to the fruits by dividing them between the disposition of man toward good and against evil. Love relates to the good and thereby grounds the others. In other words, it is the root

123. *Super Io.,* c. 16, l. 8, n. 2241: "*Non enim est Deus dissensionis causa, sed pacis.*"

124. Cf. *Super Io.,* c. 16, l. 8, n. 2240: "*Patre et Filio est duplex unitas, scilicet essentiae et amoris; et secundum utramque Pater est in Filio, et Filius in Patre. Quod ergo hic dicit sicut tu, Pater, in me, et ego in te, potest referri uno modo ad unitatem amoris, secundum Augustinum, ut sit sensus: sicut, te, Pater, es in me per amorem, quia caritas facit unum esse cum Deo; quasi diceret: sicut Pater diligit Filium, et e converso; ita ipsi diligant Patrem et Filium. Et sic ly sicut non dicit aequiparantiam, sed quamdam remotam similitudinem. Vel secundum Hilarium, potest referri ad unitatem naturae: non quidem quod eadem natura numero sit in nobis cum Patre et Filio, sicut est in eis; sed quod unitas nostra per hoc sit quod assimilamur illi divinae naturae, per quam Pater et Filius sunt unum. Hoc etiam modo ly sicut dicit imitationem quamdam. Et inde est quod invitamur ad imitationem dilectionis divinae.*"

of all. Joy follows from this, since every love rejoices at the joining with that which is loved. Charity, since it is affective union with God, causes God to dwell presently in the soul, and so joy follows. Aquinas puts peace third here, saying it perfects joy in two ways. The first is that it perfects joy by removing exterior disturbances. In explaining how peace removes exterior disturbances, Aquinas identifies peace and charity. He continues: there is no perfect joy when it is disturbed by external things, but it is charity itself that explains how exterior disturbances are removed. The lover accounts them as nothing. In other words, charity regards all other objects as nothing and so is not disturbed by them. In this way, peace perfects joy. Second, peace perfects joy in the sedation of fluctuating desire. In other words, it makes us count the object of our love as sufficient. In these two perfections, both seemingly provided by charity itself, Aquinas finds peace. Peace implies both that we are not disturbed and that our desires rest together in one object. Hence, peace is "placed third."[125]

In ST II-II q. 29,[126] Aquinas has four questions concerning peace and locates peace as one of the "interior effects of charity."[127] Interior effect seems to be what effect peace has on the individual. Explaining the order of interior effects, Aquinas uses the model of the passions.[128] All the effects of charity follow from charity's principal act, which is *dilectio.* As Aquinas is fond of saying—when many effects follow from one, they must come in a certain order. In that order, again, Aquinas follows Paul. Hence, after love comes joy: "for joy is caused by love either through the presence of the loved good or on account of the existing (*inest*) and conservation of the good of the loved good in the lover."[129] The second is properly spiritual joy because God is in those who love him through charity.

---

125. *ST* I-II q. 70, a. 3, co.: "*Unde post caritatem et gaudium, tertio ponitur pax.*"

126. For a close reading of this question, see Ramirez, Reichberg, and Genovese.

127. *ST* II-II q. 28, pr.

128. Nicholas Lombardo, O.P., *The Logic of Desire: Aquinas on Emotion* (Washington DC: The Catholic University of America Press, 2011), 75ff.

129. *ST* I-II q. 28, a. 1, co.: "*Gaudium enim ex amore causatur vel propter praesentiam boni amati; vel etiam propter hoc quod ipsi bono amato proprium bonum inest et conservatur.*"

After Aquinas treats joy, he comes to peace. Is peace the same as concord? Do all things desire peace? Is peace an effect of charity? Is peace a virtue? These four questions represent the most extended and direct treatment of peace in Aquinas's *oeuvre*. Two things should keep us from claiming that these questions exhaust the whole of Aquinas's thought. First, the questions Aquinas treats here are largely set by the time he gets to this mature treatment. In other words, the questions Aquinas asks about peace replicate themes he has treated elsewhere and are precipitated by the questions Augustine and Dionysius are asking about peace. Elsewhere, however, we have seen him take up other themes when the text in front of him demands it. In other words, though the *Summa* is Aquinas's most extended treatment it is neither his most personal nor is it complete. Second, we can see Aquinas's thought on peace morphing and developing as he encounters new topics related to it (both across his thought and even within q. 29). Aquinas was, as Reichberg shows, developing as he wrote this question and the inclusion of war expands his thought.[130] Though war is not the topic of this book, the spontaneous inclusion confirms the largely occasional and ad hoc nature of Aquinas's thought even in his most direct treatment. Something similar could be said concerning contention, strife, and sedition. In q. 34, he only lists two sins against peace, but then goes onto treat 5.[131] Likewise, in q. 29 he distinguishes peace from concord (as interior and exterior union), but then lists only sins against exterior peace (i.e. concord) not interior (what he called peace). These reasons should not stop us from recognizing q. 29 as Aquinas's most extensive and direct treatment of peace, but it should temper our hopes that we will find here something other than what we've found elsewhere: a largely occasional and ad hoc attention to peace.

Concerning the identity of peace and concord (q. 1), Aquinas claims that peace is the more general of the two. Peace includes

---

130. Reichberg, *Thomas Aquinas on War and Peace*, 18ff.

131. Judging from the *sed contra* of each article, he revisited Galatians 5 in the sins against peace and strove to include more of them.

concord, but also adds something. "Hence wherever there is peace there is concord, but concord does not always include peace, properly speaking."[132] Concord is between people, i.e. when their wills consent to the same good thereby making their appetites one in a certain respect. Peace is something beyond this for it indicates the union (*unio*) of the diverse appetites in man (either in one power for multiple and contradictory objects or of multiple appetites). Concord, Aquinas continues in response to the objectors who argue that peace and concord are the same thing, can only be an ordered concord, i.e. fitting to each (*convenit utrique*). If one of the two parties consents to the shared good out of fear, or if all his appetitive movements do not agree, then concord is not identical with peace. The concord will not bring an individual's appetitive movements to rest together. So peace is not the same as concord; peace does this. Indeed, one person can consent to the same thing with another without it perfectly uniting all his appetitive movements. Only the dissension of one man and another is opposed to concord, which is fully compatible with internal dissension. Concord and peace, though diverse, are integrally related. Peace is the more general here. Concord is integral to peace.

In article 2, Aquinas is arguing that all things desire peace. His argument rests on desire. All who desire something *ipso facto* desire to remove those things that can impede achievement. This could be a contrary desire or the desire of another. Both are removed by peace, since it is the union of all appetites: rational, sensitive, and vegetative. Aquinas concludes: "It follows of necessity that any individual who desires anything also desires peace inasmuch as they want to come tranquilly and without impediments to that which they desire. In this is the *ratio* of peace, which Augustine defines as tranquility of order."[133]

In response to the objectors, who claim that not everyone desires

---

132. ST II-II q. 29, a. 1, co: "*Unde ubicumque est pax, ibi est concordia, non tamen ubicumque est concordia, est pax, si nomen pacis proprie sumatur.*"

133. ST II-II q. 29, a. 2, co.: "*Et ideo necesse est quod omne appetens appetat pacem, inquantum scilicet omne appetens appetit tranquille et sine impedimento pervenire ad id quod appetit, in quo consistit ratio pacis, quam Augustinus definit tranquillitatem ordinis.*"

peace, Aquinas is forced to provide some clarifications. Even those who seek war desire peace. They seek to replace a defective peace with a fuller peace (at least as they see it). Aquinas explains this by claiming that there is no peace when you have concord with another even though you more greatly desire something else. War breaks the concord since it is a *defectum pacis* and seeks to have all the objects of one's will fulfilled, i.e. a fuller peace. In other words, the desire behind war is to obtain peace in which nothing is contrary to the will. This does not, however, mean that those who wage war are always correct in their wills. Peace consists in the rest and union of appetites. Since appetite can be mistaken about what is good in fact, thus peace may be too. True peace is the appetite directed to the true good: evil may calm the appetite in some respect but is lacking in others which will disturb desire. True peace is only about to be in the good and about good things. The peace of the wicked is merely apparent. Yet even the peace of the good is not perfect. Perfect peace is the unity of rest in one: the highest good. This is the ultimate end of the rational creature. Imperfect peace is here since our chief movement of appetite rests in God, but internal and external things disturb this.

In the third article, Aquinas asks whether peace is the characteristic/special effect (*proprius effectus*) of charity. He begins his argument by noting that the ratio of peace is a twofold union (*unio*): one's own appetites directed to one object and one's appetite concurring with others. Each of these unions is an effect of charity. Interiorly, God is the only achievement which can fulfill all one's desires. By referring all things to him, one tends to one object and thus a unity of desire. Appetitive desire with others comes through friendship, since that makes us want to fulfill our neighbor's will as our own. This is only possible with grace and so without grace, peace is only apparent. This concord with others requires not absolute unity of will but is compatible with dissension in small matters. It requires concord in the goods that conduce to life (*in bonis conferentibus ad vitam*), especially the most important. Opinions concern the intellect, but peace resides in the appetite. Charity, according to its proper *ratio*, causes peace. Love is a unitive force, and peace is union. Yet the mind precedes the will, so if two minds do not agree on the greater good, they will not have peace. Yet given agreement in the greater goods, the two (or more) can disagree about particular goods: one thinking it is a part of their shared good and the other not. Their more fundamental agreement is not negated. This kind of disagreement, however, is not compatible with perfect peace and will not be present in heaven.

In the final question, Aquinas asks if peace is a virtue (a *habitus*). He answers no. When acts follow from one another and according to the same *ratio* from the agent, they are from a single cause. Charity causes peace in its very *ratio* as love of God and neighbor, the union of affects within a person and between persons. Hence, "peace is the *proprius actus* of charity."[134] Hence, it is not a separate virtue. Aquinas explains this further with a comment in q. 30. Not only is peace an act of charity, but this is why peace adds nothing beyond the *ratio* of the good which is the object of charity (*pax nihil adiiciunt super rationem boni*). It has no special aspect like mercy.[135] Peace is thus meritorious as an act of charity, which is why it is among the beatitudes. It is a fruit because it is the final good and has spiritual sweetness.

In the *Summa*, Aquinas treats the vices contrary to peace under three headings: those contrary to the heart (discord), the mouth (contention), and acts (schism, strife, sedition, and war). Discord is a *disgregationem voluntatum*. Aquinas seems to want to make discord general and place all the others *sub discordia*.[136] Discord occurs

---

134. *ST* II-II q. 29, a. 4, co.

135. Cf. *ST* II-II q. 30, a. 3, ad 3: "*Ad tertium dicendum quod gaudium et pax nihil adiiciunt super rationem boni quod est obiectum caritatis, et ideo non requirunt alias virtutes quam caritatem. Sed misericordia respicit quandam specialem rationem, scilicet miseriam eius cuius miseretur.*"

136. Aquinas does this explicitly with sedition and schism (*ST* II-II q. 42, a. 1, ad 3), but it is clear that the others are being held to similar standards—e.g. contention is a type of discord because it involves the will turning away from the truth or turning toward its private good in acrimony of speech. Both involve elements of sinful discord in the will.

when there is voluntary privation of union/order between individuals.[137] This is culpable if it involves the heart turning directly against
the divine good or the good of one's neighbor. In other words, for
discord to be a problem it must concern directly turning against the
good and concern things necessary for salvation or be accompanied
by undue obstinacy. If one of those two factors does not obtain, one
could have discord of a type, but Aquinas calls this *per accidens* discord and not *per se*.[138] Contention is discord in speech. Contention
only occurs when one speaks in one of two ways: against the truth
(as one knows it—if one unknowingly contends against the truth
it is not the sin of contention), or defends the truth but inordinate-
ly (e.g. by acrimony of speech). Finally, Aquinas treats those things
contrary to peace in actions; these wrongly dissolve/harm union/
order. Schism is contrary to the union/order of the church, strife
contrary to the union with our neighbor by deeds (not words)—in-
flicting harm on our neighbor privately, and sedition to the unity and
peace of a multitude. War is contrary to the union/order between
diverse multitudes, *multitudinis ad multitudinem*. All these are prob-
lematic because they turn the individual against the good of one's
neighbor, but not if they turn one from a *mala concordia*.

*Lectures on the Psalms* (1272–73)

Though Aquinas also mentions peace in his mature *Commentary
on Romans* and there claims that peace is perfect in heaven when "the
will rests in the fullness of every good and has immunity from every
evil" and that the Holy Spirit is the "union and bond between the
Father and Son"[139] and so peace is his final gift (*ultimum*), Aquinas's
most extensive late treatment of peace is found in his *Commentary on*

137. Interestingly, All the sins against peace in the *Summa* are sins against concord.
There are no sins listed against interior peace.

138. *ST* II-II q. 37, a. 1.

139. *Super Rom.*, c. 1, l. 4, n. 70: "*Aliud autem, scilicet pax, est ultimum quod in beatitudine perficitur. Ps.: qui posuit fines tuos pacem. Tunc enim erit perfecta pax, quando voluntas
requiescet in plenitudine omnis boni, consequens immunitatem ab omni malo.*" And "*Persona
autem Spiritus Sancti expresse non ponitur, quia intelligitur in donis eius, quae sunt gratia et
pax; vel etiam quia intelligitur in duabus personis Patris et Filii, quarum est unio et nexus.*"

*the Psalms*. Therein, especially commenting on Psalms 33, 36, 37, and 45, Aquinas elaborates his most mature thought on peace.

In commenting on Psalm 33 (34 by Masoretic numbering) especially the verse wherein the psalmist admonishes one to "depart from evil and do good, seek peace and pursue it." Aquinas offers two possible readings of this text. The first claims that if someone is fighting with you, then it is your responsibility to pursue peace and if someone seeks peace with you, you should follow his lead. He follows this by a qualification of the type of peace we can have in this world, which is necessarily imperfect because the flesh fights against the spirit and vice versa. In the future it will be perfect. The second possible reading is Christological (a theme that appears throughout his commentary on the Psalms). He suggests that to inquire after peace is to inquire after Christ, who is our peace.

In commenting on Psalm 36 (37), Aquinas has a chance to further elaborate on peace. The psalmist writes that the meek will inherit the earth and will delight in the fullness of peace.[140] In commenting on this verse, Aquinas says that peace is intensely enjoyable (*valde delectabilis*), and it is enjoyed in its fullness because in heaven there is *multiplex pax*. Here there are wars, among humans and within humans (Galatians 5). In heaven all will be in one pacified whole. Within an individual, we lack peace when the "will is against itself by diverse desires." There our wills "will not be divided but united in the Lord." Here that is not possible because we make war on the Lord through sin, but there we will have peace with him.[141] He continues this line of thinking in his commentary on the next psalm, 37 (38). Therein he elaborates that iniquity, and our many grave sins, destroy peace. Inquietude is against peace, and its remedy is through

---

140. Aquinas's Latin here is different than the modern translation of the Hebrew, which is translated by the RSVCE 2nd edition as "will delight themselves in abundant prosperity." Aquinas's edition accurately reflects the Septuagint version on which it is based: "κατατρυφήσουσιν ἐπὶ πλήθει εἰρήνης."

141. Cf. *Super Ps.*, 36: "*Secundo ponuntur eorum deliciae, cum dicit, et delectabuntur in multitudine pacis. Haec enim pax est valde delectabilis. Dicit autem, in multitudine, quia ibi est multiplex pax; hic vero sunt bella. Quoddam est enim ad homines; sed hoc non erit ibi, quia omnes erunt in unum pacifici*"

consolation and hope in the Lord. This inquietude is twofold: one of the concupiscible and one of the irascible appetites. Inasmuch as we lack rest in our concupiscible appetites, it is because of sin and the miserable creature is one who turns from God in sin. This sin is heavy and prevents the affects of humans from "tending to the superior." Aquinas then goes on to treat the sadness caused by this and counsels a remedy: the sadness of the penitent. With hope one can move toward good acts and tend toward spiritual and interior goods By doing this one reverses the cause of sadness (tending toward exterior goods and temporal goods).

The final place Aquinas treats peace in his *Commentary on the Psalms* is psalm 45 (46): "He makes wars cease to the end of the earth."[142] Aquinas comments that to remove war is the work of peace and then divides the psalmist's intention into three: the work, the magnitude, and the utility. The utility of peace is shown that in the time of Christ's birth the whole world was at peace. Christ himself came to make peace between God and human nature. The magnitude was universal because during the time of Octavian peace extended, as if to the whole world and showed the peace of Christ is meant for all humans. This peace will also last for a long time and this is shown by the removal of the weapons of war. In other words, Christ brings perpetual peace. Continuing, Aquinas speaks of the *finis* as peace. Yet there are types of peace and so types of *fini*. Aquinas says that, according to the philosopher, the purpose of temporal peace is the contemplation of truth. Peace is useful (*utilis*) for the active life and peace is ordained to contemplation. Augustine complements this saying that God gave the *Pax Romana* so that the apostles could travel and evangelize. Hence, Aquinas follows, that God gives peace not for evil works, but for contemplation of truth.[143]

---

142. Ps 46:9 (RSV).

143. Cf. *Super Ps.*, 45: "*Vacate et videte. Hic finis est pacis. Finis pacis temporalis, secundum philosophum, est contemplatio veritatis. Unde pax est utilis finis vitae activae, et pax ordinatur ad contemplationem. Et secundum Augustinum, Christus procuravit pacem Romani imperii, ut apostoli discurrerent per totum mundum. Et ideo dicit ex quo est tanta pax, vacate et videte. Unde patet quod Deus dat pacem ut non vacent malis operibus, sed contemplationi veritatis: 1 Cor. 7: ut vacetis orationi: Eccl. 39: et in prophetis vacabit.*"

### The Trajectory and Ongoing Issues
### of Aquinas's Thought

From Aquinas's youthful *Commentary on Isaiah* to his mature *Commentary on the Psalms,* Aquinas's thought on peace has constants, developments, ambiguities, and tensions. It is from these constants, ambiguities, tensions, and asides that any Thomistic theology of peace must develop. This section's purpose is to take stock of them so that one can see where the promises and difficulties lie. I also do not want to belabor them here by representing, citing, and explaining the tensions and ambiguities. In some sense they will be with us throughout the text and will receive (hopefully) adequate explanation in each of those sections.

Aquinas's constants are the bedrock of his thought on peace and no Thomistic account of peace can diverge from these and remain Thomistic. First and foremost, Aquinas is committed to a theological vision of peace. Peace is ultimately attributed to God, the God of peace. How it is attributed to God is ambiguous, but that it is attributed is clear. Likewise, peace is ultimately a gift of God and is given to the world through Christ and the Holy Spirit. True peace is the effect of grace in humans and has a special relation to the gifts of wisdom and charity. This is what brings the individual into right order interiorly—the subordination of mind to God, will to mind, and affections to both. Without God, there is no solid or lasting peace. Interpersonally, grace brings peace between humans. This peace comes to humans because Christ brings reconciliation between God and men, preeminently in the Church. Most particularly, Aquinas links the Eucharist to peace. This sacrament is the "sacrament of unity and of peace."[144] Christ overcomes division and brings union. Aquinas also is clear that whatever peace is, it is strongly linked to the appetitive order toward the good, either interiorly or exteriorly. Peace is also linked to union, order, rest, tranquility, a lack of conflict, a lack of obstacles, and security in holding the good.

---

144. IV *Sent.,* d. 25 q. 2 a. 2 qc. 2 co.

The major development I see in Aquinas's thought comes in relation to his reading of Dionysius and Paul in his middle years (though he could have, but does not seem to have, gleaned the same points from Augustine's thought). In both of these authors, peace is identified with union or unity, to the making of one out of what is many. Contact with these authors marks a shift in Aquinas's thought, though not a fully developed one. In his early treatises, he treats peace primarily as negative and dispositive to the good (though this does not disappear in his mature treatises!). In his early treatments, peace is not love, it is not the end: it is a lack of obstacles to the end. It is not concord, but the lack of obstacles to concord. It is primarily negative and dispositive—when peace is present love can proceed to its object. After Aquinas comments on both the *Divine Names* and the Pauline corpus, he begins to identify peace much more with order/union itself (either as interior or exterior peace), not simply the lack of obstacles to order/union. Peace becomes something positive and not purely negative and dispositive. Likewise, in those texts Aquinas begins to more closely associate peace with *quies* and not simply lacking obstacles to *quies*. This development in Aquinas's thought is a major shift, but one that sits uneasily with his previous thought. Likewise, nowhere does Aquinas reconcile these descriptions and sources. They are found side by side in his mature works.

In addition to the above quasi-development, there are also many ambiguities and tensions in Aquinas's thought on peace. These ambiguities are mostly caused by Aquinas's treatments of peace being occasional, i.e. subordinated to other topics and drawn from different sources. His point is often to explain the text in front of him, not usually peace itself. Indeed, most of the tensions in Aquinas's treatments can be explained this way. Put differently, Aquinas treats peace often in terms of love, the fruits of the Spirit, in relation to war, and because the author on whom he is commenting mentions it. He does not thematize it nor does he seem particularly worried that the explanations he gives of differing authors and contexts are in tension with one another. Most of these tensions and ambiguities are implicit in the summaries above, but a short sketch will be helpful here. It is against these that I hope to develop my account of peace and they govern the structure of the rest of the book.

The first set of ambiguities surrounds peace itself; these ambiguities can be divided using the four causes: final, formal, efficient, and material. Considering final causality, the relation between peace and the good (as well as *unum*)[145] is ambiguous in Aquinas. In his early thought, he gives a definite (but somewhat unclear) dispositive reading where peace is simply the lack of appetitive obstacles to the good. Dispositive readings of peace remain throughout his thought. On the other hand, also present is a less dispositive reading of peace (the development of which roughly corresponds with a greater association of peace with *unio* in his middle thought). He says the will terminates in the good and peace. They are not diverse things. Likewise, peace is order/union and rest/tranquility (not simply the removal of obstacles to it), which are aspects of the good. He even claims that peace adds nothing beyond the *ratio* of the good in the *Summa*. Are these claims reconcilable? In other words, Aquinas's position on the metaphysics of peace requires some clarification. Second, and related to the first, Aquinas gives various descriptions of peace. Of course, Aquinas constantly uses the Augustinian description of peace. Yet Pauline and Dionysian (as well as Augustinian) elements are also given as descriptions (union/rest). He claims all of them pertain to the essence of peace. Apart from these two main descriptions, Aquinas gives myriad other descriptions which are not easily reducible to these two main descriptions. Likewise, at times he claims that peace is entirely exterior and at other times that it is entirely interior. He makes diverse claims about the relation of interior and exterior peace. At the very least, some clarification is necessary. Finally, considering efficiency, Aquinas seems to link peace very closely with the appetitive order, and yet admits that the intellect has a relation to peace too (e.g. wisdom). What is this relation?

---

145. Genovese, "Dalla concordia degli animi alla tranquillità dell'ordine: per una fondazione interiore della pace nella Summa Teologia di Tommaso d'Aquino," 595–96.

Likewise, other statements of his seem to link other virtues and human powers to peace (e.g. the intellect resting, *quies,* or justice causing peace), but what is that relation? Clearly in some sense peace is non-appetitive, but what is this sense? Related to this ambiguity is the question of what things can be at peace. What is the subject of peace? Obviously, it is closely tied to the rational appetite for Aquinas, but can only beings with rationality be at peace? Does peace require an appetite? In what sense? Not only are these ambiguous in Aquinas's thought, but the difficulties interpenetrate such that an answer to one (e.g. peace and the good) impacts the way one answers all the other questions and brings up new questions. The purpose of Chapter 2 is to attempt a philosophy of peace in answer to these questions (and more that arise along the way).

The second set of ambiguities surrounds the relation of peace to the divine nature and to the Trinity or to Aquinas's theology of peace. Aquinas seems to predicate the peace of God in his *Commentary on the Divine Names,* but does not explain what it would mean to predicate peace of God. How does this predication fit within Aquinas's more well-known theology of the divine names? How does it relate to the *ratio* of peace defended in the previous chapter? Relatedly, Aquinas also seems to predicate peace of the Trinity, and especially the Holy Spirit. Is it possible to predicate peace of both the divine nature and the Trinity? In what senses? Furthermore, Aquinas suggests that God is the exemplar of peace. Yet he does not explain more: is the exemplar of peace the divine nature? The Trinitarian persons? The divine ideas? All three? Aquinas also strongly suggests that God gives peace to creatures in creation. What does this mean? What does it mean for creatures to participate in God's peace? If creatures participate in God's peace, then why is there so much disorder? Aquinas also suggests a very close link between the incarnation, life, and mission of Christ and peace. Christ is peace and comes to bring/preaches peace. Rarely does Aquinas elaborate. The same could be said for the Spirit and the Church. Aquinas clearly thinks that there is a particular link here between these aspects and peace, but extended discussions are lacking. These are the questions that will occupy me in Chapter 3, which will attempt a Thomistic theology of peace.

The next set of ambiguities relates to Aquinas's ethics. Obviously, the cascade of questions here begins to gain momentum, and one can see how previous answers have implications. Likewise, some of the same ambiguities surface in Aquinas's ethics as we have seen above. For example, Aquinas clearly says peace is an interior act of love and yet in other places suggests that it is not merely one act of love, but is present in every act of love. He even identifies peace with union and union with charity itself. So, peace is one interior act of love but also identical with charity? Elsewhere, he suggests that peace is merely exterior and found in security or a lack of obstacles to the good, the perfection or preservation of the good. Certainly, it cannot be all of these things, or at least it will take some explaining as to how this can be. Following from this ambiguity, Aquinas is also unclear on the relation of peace and joy, suggesting both that peace comes before joy and also after. He even identifies peace with joy at times (or rather both with *quies*). So which is it? These ambiguities open more questions: What is the precise relation between grace and peace, wisdom and peace, justice and peace? Aquinas is clear that they each have a special relation, but does not explain it at length and this invites a more extended Thomistic ethics of peace.

The relation of justice to peace brings in other dimensions of Aquinas's thought that are not overtly related to peace. For example, Aquinas suggests that satisfaction, especially in the cross of Christ, has an intimate relation to peace (indeed, Christ comes to bring peace and effects it by his cross) but does not elaborate or relate it to human satisfaction. Furthermore, Aquinas is adamant in his *Commentary on the Psalms* we have a serious responsibility to make peace. From where does this responsibility come? What are the means Aquinas would suggest for making interior and exterior peace? What are the prospects? Can we have hope to enjoy peace in this world and in what sense? Is it a fruitless task? Finally, Aquinas very briefly suggests that peace with sub-rational creation is an integral part of peace. On what grounds does he suggest this and what are the means for pursuing it? Chapter 4 takes up these questions, and others, and attempts to elaborate a Thomistic ethics of peace.

Finally, the last chapter relates to the ambiguities found in Aquinas's corpus on the relation of peace to worship and the sacraments. One would expect Aquinas's thought on peace to culminate here, but in some sense, it is the least developed. Where one would expect the most extended discussion, one finds the least extended. Aquinas certainly suggests that peace is had by worshipping God and has a special relation to whole sacramental order, particularly the Eucharist. He even calls the Eucharist the sacrament of unity and peace. Yet elaborations are largely lacking and only implicit in his texts. The purpose of Chapter 5 is to draw on the previous chapters and offer some kind of coherent and defensible conception of the relation of the sacraments to peace, especially the Eucharist.

2

A Thomistic Philosophy of Peace

The prospects for a Thomistic philosophy of peace seem bleak. As seen in the last chapter, Aquinas's philosophical treatments of peace are disjointed and often in tension with one another. On the other hand, I think Aquinas's texts contain all the building blocks necessary to conceptualize a rich doctrine of peace. The key is bringing them together, interpreting them, and reconciling them. To do this, I will treat peace according to the standard Thomistic division of the causes: formal, final, material, and efficient. Though this heuristic is somewhat artificial to Aquinas's own treatments of peace, I find it consonant with his larger Aristotelian approach to philosophical topics.

WHAT IS THE *RATIO* OF PEACE?

It might seem that the *ratio* of peace is settled in Aquinas. He certainly has two central descriptions. The first description of peace is from Augustine: peace is *tranquillitas ordinis*. The second he draws from Paul and Dionysius (as well as other parts of Augustine): peace is *unio et quies*. Related to both, he uses the language of essential description—saying at different times that all four (tranquility, order, union, and rest) are of the essence of peace. This makes the relatively simple question about the *ratio* of peace more complicated. In addition, a full scan of Aquinas's corpus gives a bewildering number of descriptions: the removal of impediments to attaining the good, rest of the will in the fullness of good and immunity from all evil, putting things in right order, harmony with ourselves and others, the quiet of the mind in the end, ordered harmony, security against the loss of goods, tranquility of mind, tranquility arising from order, and the cessation of all desire.[1] How is one to sort out this kind of plurality? Does Aquinas have a unified description or conception of peace or do his occasional treatments resist unification?

I think Aquinas does have a unified vision of the *ratio* of peace, but this is a point that must be argued. I think the first step is working with the two primary descriptions Aquinas gives and reconciling them. In doing this, I argue that Aquinas means the same thing by *unio* and *ordo* as well as *tranquillitas* and *quies*. Indeed, we shall see that Aquinas seemingly reduces both *unio* and *ordo* to relation (at least in subject), to being *ad aliud*. This reduction helps us to see the unity of Aquinas's primary descriptions of peace. *Quies* and *tranquillitas*, on the other hand, Aquinas understands as negations following from union and order. They are not *aliqui* but negations of discord/disunion. They denote that the union/order is undisturbed. Then, based on this unified description, one can integrate the more occasional descriptions. I claim that all those descriptions can be reduced to a reconciled Augustinian/Pauline/Dionysian description. In other words, all the descriptions of peace Aquinas gives are

---

1. Cf. *De Ver.*, q. 22, a. 12, co. (the removal of impediments to attaining the good); *Super Rom.*, 1, l. 4, n. 70: "*Tunc enim erit perfecta pax, quando voluntas requiescet in plenitudine omnis boni, consequens immunitatem ab omni malo*"; *ST* II-II q. 45, a. 6, co. (putting things in right order); *Super II Thess.*, 3, l. 2, n. 89: "*Pax enim consistit in duobus, ut scilicet homo concordet ad seipsum, et ad alios*"; *Super Gal.*, 1, l. 1, n. 11: "*... pax, quae est quietatio mentis in fine ...*"; *Super II Tim.*, 2, l. 4, n. 80: "*Pax autem importat ordinatam concordiam*"; *Super Rom.*, 2, l. 2, n. 204: "*Non enim potest esse pax hominis perfecta quamdiu aliquis timet se amissurum bona quae habet, sed tunc aliquis habet veram pacem cordis, quando habet omnia quae concupiscit et ea perdere non timet*"; *Super Gal.*, 6, l. 5, n. 376: "*Pax, inquam, qua quietentur et perficiantur in bono. Pax enim est tranquillitas mentis*"; *Super Io.*, 14, l. 7, n. 1962: "*Sciendum est, quod pax nihil aliud est quam tranquillitas ordinis: tunc enim aliqua dicuntur pacem habere quando eorum ordo inturbatus manet*"; *Super I Thess.*, 1, l. 1, n. 6: "*Et pax quae est finis, quia tunc est pax, quando appetitus totaliter pacatur.*"

merely reiterations, synonyms, or aspects of either *tranquillitas ordinis* or *unio et quietus.*

## *Unio/Ordo*

Beginning with the first description (tranquility of order), order is naturally prior and so merits attention first. In other words, tranquility presupposes order; order is conceptually more fundamental. But what is order? This is a central question, and Aquinas treats it explicitly. We are not left guessing his thought. Likewise, Ramirez has paid explicit (and extensive) attention to order and so can serve as a guide for interpreting Aquinas.[2]

According to Aquinas, all order obtains among those things that are distinct. In other words, distinction is part of the very *ratio* of order (or as Ramirez puts it things must be *realiter plura*).[3] One cannot have order where there is absolute singularity. Yet order is not merely distinction, but a certain fittingness/connection between distinct things. It is how distinct things come to be fitting that constitutes order itself. This Aquinas claims is by sharing a common principle. Hence, he always speaks of order in relation to a principle.[4] From the divergence of causes/principles comes the divergence of orders: final, efficient, formal, or material.[5] In other words, the connection between things is intrinsically related to causality. Distinct things are fitting by their causal relation to each other or by their relation to a singular (shared) cause.

Furthermore, all created orders include the notion of prior and posterior according to their proximity to the principal of that order (degree of influence from the cause—and therefore of the equal and

2. Santiago Ramirez, *De Ordine Placita Quaedam Thomistica* (San Esteban: Salmanticae, 1963).

3. *ST* I-II q. 104, a. 4, s.c.: *"ubi est ordo, oportet quod sit distinctio."* Ramirez, *De Ordine,* 14.

4. Cf. *ST* I q. 42, a. 3, co.

5. Cf. *ST* II-II q. 26, a. 1, co.; *ST* I q. 105, a. 6, co: *"a qualibet causa derivatur aliquis ordo in suos effectus, cum quaelibet causa habeat rationem principii. Et ideo secundum multiplicationem causarum, multiplicantur et ordines, quorum unus continetur sub altero, sicut et causa continetur sub causa."*

unequal).[6] It is here that we begin to see the most concrete way Aquinas formally describes order. As Aquinas says, "Order is a disposition by which things of equal and unequal nature are each given a place."[7] Place in the order is based on their proportion/disposition to the principle of the order, which gives each its place and relation to other parts of that same order. Hence, order is "nothing other than a determinate relation of one part to another."[8] As Ramirez puts it "*ordo est relatio*."[9] Aquinas confirms this when he says, "Relation, which is in things, consists of a certain order of one to another." And "Relation itself is nothing other than the order of one thing to another."[10] In other words, this relation is formally the most concrete way Aquinas describes order; it is the very fittingness or connection between distinct things.[11]

It seems likely that when Aquinas speaks of *unio* being of the *ratio* of peace, he is referencing the same reality as *ordo*.[12] In *ST* I q. 39, a. 8, co., Aquinas is forced to specify the difference between unity (*unitas*) and union (*unio*), though elsewhere he uses the terms seemingly interchangeably because of their conceptual relation. In this question he speaks precisely. Herein, Aquinas says that "*unitas* is said absolutely and does not presuppose anything else."[13] Unity denotes oneness, simply speaking.[14] It is the predication of indivisibility in itself (either actually undivided or indivisible).[15] Union, on the other hand, "implies unity of two somethings." Unity does

---

6. Cf. Ramirez, *De Ordine*, 15.

7. *ST* I q. 96, a. 3, s.c.: "*Ordo autem est parium dispariumque sua cuique loca tribuens dispositio.*"

8. *In I Meta.* 11, l. 12, n. 2: "*Positio vero non addit supra ubi, nisi ordinem partium determinatum, qui nihil aliud est quam determinata relatio partium ad invicem.*"

9. Ramirez, *De Ordine*, 14.

10. *In I Meta.*, l. 17, n. 1904 and *De Pot.*, q. 7, a. 9, ad 7.

11. Cf. Ramirez, *De Ordine*, 15.

12. Cf. *ST* II-II q. 29, a. 3, co.; *In de Div. Nom.*, c. 11, l. 2, n. 896 & c. 11, l. 3, n. 914.

13. *ST* I q. 39, a. 8, co.

14. Cf. *ST* I q. 39, a. 3, co.: "*In creaturis autem non invenitur una forma in pluribus suppositis nisi unitate ordinis, ut forma multitudinis ordinatae.*"

15. For more on this see David Svoboda, "Thomas Aquinas on Whole and Part," in *The Thomist*, vol. 76 (2012): 273–304. See pages 296ff.

not require distinction, but union does.[16] This is why union is "the conjunction of many into one."[17] In this way, "unity surpasses union [qua oneness]."[18] Union has distinction in its very meaning, but unity does not.

Aquinas speaks of modes of union in multiple places.[19] We saw one of them above in his *Commentary on the Divine Names*.[20] One need not go through them all again to see the consonance between union and order. One need only look at the way Aquinas treats the union of the Incarnate Word. When Aquinas begins to defend the position that the union of the incarnate word takes place in the divine person, he says "the union about which we are speaking [between the divine and human nature] is a certain relation which is considered between the divine nature and human nature inasmuch as they are united in one person of the Son of God."[21] He continues in the next article to distinguish union from assumption by saying: "that the first and principal difference between union and assumption is that union conveys the relation itself (*importat ipsam relationem*), and assumption the action by which it is said someone is assuming or a passion according to which it is said someone is assumed."[22] Elsewhere he rejects that habitual grace can be the *medium unionis*, i.e. the midpoint between the divine and human natures of Christ.[23] The union is the relation itself. It is the relation itself

16. Cf. *ST* II-II q. 17, a. 3, co.: "*Unio autem est aliquorum distinctorum.*"

17. *ST* III q. 2, a. 9, co.: "*quod unio importat coniunctionem aliquorum in aliquo uno.*"

18. *ST* II-II q. 26, a. 4, co.: "*unitas potior est quam unio.*"

19. Cf. *ST* III q. 2, a. 7; *SCG* II c. 57; *ODA* I.10.

20. Cf. *In de Div. Nom.*, 911.

21. *ST* III q. 2, a. 7, co.: "*Respondeo dicendum quod unio de qua loquimur est relatio quaedam quae consideratur inter divinam naturam et humanam, secundum quod conveniunt in una persona filii Dei.*"

22. *ST* III q. 2, a. 8, co.: "*Sic igitur dicendum est quod prima et principalis differentia inter unionem et assumptionem est quod unio importat ipsam relationem, assumptio autem actionem secundum quam dicitur aliquis assumens, vel passionem secundum quam dicitur aliquid assumptum.*"

23. *Quodl.*, IX, q. 1, a. 1: "*Ad tertium dicendum, quod gratia habitualis non intelligitur ut medium unionis, quod secundum intellectum praecedit unionem: nec est medium quod causet unionem vel unibilitatem: sed medium quod facit ad congruitatem unionis, sicut decora vestis facit ad congruitatem coniunctionis matrimonialis. Et similiter scientia et omnes aliae*

which is the grace of union. Looking at the other modes of union strengthens the case that union is the relation/connection between distinct things.[24]

An additional consideration is the way Aquinas treats the union in the Trinity. This confirms that union is relation as well. The Trinitarian Persons are one in essence, but also share the one essence by relations/unions of mutual opposition. The union is the relation. More particularly, Aquinas calls the Holy Spirit the union between the Father and Son.[25] The Holy Spirit is not the principle of the union between the Father and the Son, nor is the union which is the Holy Spirit an effect of the love of Father and Son. Aquinas means that the subsistent relation which is the Holy Spirit is the union, the love.[26] Again, for this to be true, union must be relation.

Further, we see this when Aquinas discusses different types of unions: a substantial union, an effective (real) union, and an affective union. A substantial union, called elsewhere a union of likeness, does not seem to be a union properly speaking, for Aquinas uses it to reference a person's identity with himself. There are not really two

---

*perfectiones Christi possent dici medium unionis; et pro tanto gratia habitualis Christi potest dici gratia unionis. Verius tamen puto, quod gratia unionis dicatur vel ipsa gratuita Dei voluntas, quae gratis, nullis meritis praecedentibus, unionem fecit; vel potius ipsum donum gratis datum humanae naturae, quod est esse in divina persona. Si tamen anima unita corpori praeintelligitur ad assumptionem, solvendum est ut prius."*

24. Aquinas gives a few other modes of union, and even in those union reduces to relation. The first he calls *per modum confusionis*, which Aquinas says is union without order. The second is *unio per modum commensurationis*, which includes order. He rejects these as possibilities for the incarnational union because the union is merely accidental and so there is no absolute unity, only *secundum quid* unity. The two things would have many acts and not one. The third possibility he considers is *per modum complexionis* which is a combination as many elements in a mixture. He rejects this as well because it requires change on the part of all elements. The fourth possibility is a union of imperfect things which are not mixed or changed, as man is made of body and soul. This also cannot be said of the incarnation because each nature has its perfection, cannot be parts, and there would be a third thing neither human nor divine. The only suggestion here that union and order are conceptually distinct is the first mode of union, *modum confusionis*. I treat this question below in the text.

25. Cf. *I Sent.*, d. 10, q. 1, a. 3, ad 1; *ST* I q. 39, a. 8; *De Pot.*, q, 10, a. 5, ad 11.

26. Cf. Gilles Emery, *The Trinitarian Theology of St. Thomas Aquinas* (New York: Oxford University Press, 2010), 239ff.

here and so it would more properly be called a unity and only *secundum quid* (inasmuch as we can distinguish the principles of an individual, e.g. soul and body) is it a union.[27] An affective union is the aptitude/proportion/disposition for the object (and for this reason participates in it).[28] Finally, the effective union is the conjunction of one with another not in proportion, inclination, or aptitude but in fact. It is the attainment of the term and the full union with it. What should be noticed about all of these is that both affective and effective unions are relations (and union of likeness, if one introduces alterity). An affective union is the relation of the lover to the beloved, an inclination or proportion is a type of relation (a connection or *convenientia*). An effective union is the conjunction of the lover to the beloved itself. Throughout his corpus, Aquinas speaks of union as relation, "the very relation of union."[29] Backing up this interpretation, Capreolus interprets Aquinas's thought on the mode of the union of the incarnation in just this way, that the *unio* is *relatio tantum*.[30] It is the highest of created unions, created relations.[31]

Here we begin to see the consonance between union and order and the possibility of reconciling Aquinas's two main descriptions of peace. Both union and order stand in the more conceptually general position in describing peace. Peace is the tranquility of order. Peace is the rest of union. Neither order nor union can be with absolute singularity. Both presuppose two somethings (have distinction in their *ratio*) and are marked by the making one out of two, the connection of the two.[32] Finally, and most importantly, Aquinas

27. Cf. *ST* II-II q. 25, a. 4, co.: "*unicuique autem ad seipsum est unitas, quae est potior unione. Unde sicut unitas est principium unionis....*" This is why Aquinas talks about the union of matter and form. See *ST* I q. 76: "*De unione animae ad corpus.*"

28. Cf. *ST* I-II q. 25, a. 2, ad 2; *ST* I-II q. 28, a. 1, co.

29. *ST* I-II q. 25, a. 2, ad 2; q. 26, a. 2, ad 2; *ST* I-II q. 28, a. 1, co.; *ST* III q. 2, a. 7, co.

30. John Capreolus, *Defensiones theologiae divi thomae aquinatis,* v. 5, b. 3, d. 5, q. 1, a. 1, page 53. See also: *III Sent.,* d. 5. q. 1, qa 1, co.: "*unio relatio quaedam est.*"

31. Cf. Capreolus, *Defensiones,* v. 5, 3, d. 5, q. 1, a. 1, page 54.

32. Aquinas seems to correlate relation with the types of wholes they inhabit. In other words, he claims that different types of orders (relations) follow from different types of wholes. According to Aquinas, there are three types of wholes: universal, integral, and potential. These are ways in which things can be made one, *secundum quid*.

seems to claim that both union and order are reduced to relation. We saw above that order is nothing but a definite relation. He seems to say the same thing for union. In other words, both order and union seem to be referring to the same *res,* and I will use them interchangeably as Aquinas does.[33] Put differently, the fittingness/relation of distinct things is a kind of union, the weakest kind of unity.[34] The relation that is order is the most minimal of being and so is the most minimal union.[35] The two track onto each other. The positive element of the *ratio* of peace would then be the relation (*ordo*), the union, of distinct constituents of a being or diverse beings.

On the other hand, at least once, Aquinas does explicitly distinguish union and order, saying it is possible to have union without order. This comes in *ST* III q. 3, a. 7, co. when Aquinas is outlining possible modes of incarnational union (and rejecting all but one). The first mode of union Aquinas discusses is the *modum confusionis.* Aquinas says explicitly that this is union without order. This may make it seem that order and union cannot be identified, since in *ST* III q. 3, a. 7, co. Aquinas distinguishes them. The union *per modum confusionis* is union, but not order.

I think there are four possible readings of Aquinas's use of this term, *unio per modum confusionis.* All four preserve the preceding interpretation of Aquinas that union and order both describe relation. The first claims that the *modum confusionis* does, in spite of

33. According to Aquinas, diverse terms can denote the same reality or subject under different formalities. This seems to be true for union and order. Union denotes the oneness of order the sharing in one form through relation/connection/nexus between two. It denotes the relation as sharing and uniting. Order, on the other hand, denotes relation more distinctly as driving or inclining one thing to another. They are conceptually distinct and not strictly synonyms. We can see this in what Aquinas says about the *ratio* of the good. "The *ratio* of the good implies a relation, not because the name good signifies only a relation, but because it signifies something upon which a relation is consequent along with the relation itself." See *De Ver.* q. 21, a. 6. It seems likely that something similar could be said of *ordo* and *unio.* Order signifies the determinate relation directly. Union signifies both the conjunction of many into one and that from which it follows, the determinate relation.

34. A. Krempel, *La Doctrine de la Relation chez Saint Thomas: Exposé historique et systématique* (Paris: Libraire Philosophique, 1952), 615.

35. Cf. *De Pot.,* q. 7, a. 9, co.; q. 8, a. 1, ad 4; q. 9, a. 5, ad 2; q. 9, a. 5, ad 14.

what Aquinas says, have order. Aquinas only uses this term (*modum confusionis*) one other time in his corpus and makes it clear that this type of union does have order, "as rocks in a pile."[36] The second goes the other way, so to speak, and claims that there is no real union here (even though Aquinas uses the term union). If there is no relation between the parts, no real whole to speak of, then there is no union (no oneness). Things that are wholes in any sense, but are not necessarily *unum* in the strict sense, have a union of order.[37] Order and union again track onto one another. A *per accidens* order is a *per accidens* union. Third, one could say that Aquinas does not mean there is no order at all here, but rather that it is purely external order, i.e. relations of proximity/place, but it is still order of some kind, otherwise one would not be able to call it one in even a qualified sense, but Aquinas does this.[38] He says they are one by "touching," which is a type of relation between them and could be the foundation in action/passion.[39] Finally, if the above are all incorrect, then one might say that the union here is merely logical and not real. The order (and thus the union too) is merely logical. Yet order/union still track onto each other even if they are both merely logical. In other words, what Aquinas calls 'relations of reason' will also result in unions of reason. If one of the two correlative terms in the union is not real, not distinct, has a lack of grounding, then the relation, order, and union will be of reason only.[40]

## Aquinas on Relation, Order, and Union

The importance of Aquinas's thought on relation for his thought on peace should be clear by now. Aquinas calls both order and union essential to peace and then explains them using relation. Because

36. *In de Div. Nom.*, c. 5, l. 1: "*sicut adunantur lapides in acervo.*"

37. Cf. *I Meta.*, l. 1, n. 5.

38. Cf. *VII Meta.*, l. 17, n. 1672–74.

39. XI *Meta.*, l. 10, n. 2346.

40. Gilles Emery, "*Ad aliquid:* Relation in the Thought of St. Thomas Aquinas," *in Theology Needs Philosophy, Acting Against Reason is Contrary to the Nature of God*, ed. Matthew Lamb (Washington DC: The Catholic University of America Press, 2016): 175–201. See page 190.

of this, at least the basics of Aquinas's thought on relation is essential for understanding peace. This section will attempt to cover those basics and explore more the consonance between union and order (thereby getting closer to understanding Aquinas's descriptions of peace).

Following Emery's excellent article on the subject, one can find four aspects of (categorical) relations in Aquinas:

> The subject of the relation, that is the thing which is ordered and the name which formally signifies this ordered thing (the 'relative': *relativum; ea quae sunt ad aliquid*); the foundation (*fundamentum*) or cause of the relation,[41] that which brings about the relation in the subject; the correlative term, that toward which the relation tends; the order or relationship to the term (*respectus, habitudo, ordo, comparatio,* etc.), which constitutes the formal reason (*ratio*) of the relation and by virtue of which a thing is (and is called) relative.[42]

One can immediately see the identity of Aquinas's thought on relation with his thought on peace. When he is speaking about the more general *ratio* of peace, order/union, he is speaking about relation (connection/*convenientia*/etc.). Taking relation in its most technical sense, not as subject, foundation, or term, gives us the purest sense of what Aquinas means by *ordo/unio*. Order/union . . . "consists in the connection to something (*quod sit ad aliquid*)."[43] They "signify only a relationship to another (*solum respectum ad aliud*)."[44] Just as "Relation . . . consists only in the fact of being referred to something else (*relatio . . . consistit tantum in hoc quod est ad aliud se habere*)"[45] so too order/union are merely that connection, that *ad aliud* that joins one to another. Hence, the more general *ratio* of peace simply posits a reference/connection/union/order to some-

---

41. Cf. Aquinas holds that only two foundations can cause relation relations, quantity and action/passion. See Emery, "Ad aliquid," 185.

42. Emery, "Ad aliquid," 176.

43. Emery, "Ad aliquid," 179.

44. Emery, "Ad aliquid," 179.

45. Respectively: *De Pot.,* q. 2, a. 5, c.; *ST* I, q. 28, a. 1, c.; *ST* I, q. 28, a. 2, obj. 3; *ST* I, q. 40, a. 2, ad 4; *ST* I, q. 32, a. 2, c.; *III Phys.,* lect. 1, p. 6.

thing else, *ad aliud*. It "does not posit anything in the subject."[46] As Emery puts it, "it does not posit *aliquid,* but *ad aliquid.*"[47] This is why Aquinas says that relation has the weakest being.[48]

If this is right, then metaphysically Aquinas's distinctions concerning relations are relevant to his thought on peace. The first and most fundamental of these is the distinction between a real and a logical relation, or relation of reason. Real relations exist outside our mind, *secundum rem,* and are not merely beings of our mind. Logical relations only exist in our minds, only in the intellect. They're existence is dependent on the mind (like a privation or negation).[49] However, Emery warns that this distinction "does not touch the generic *ratio* of the relation … but it touches on the existence of the relation."[50] Relation, even when it exists in a subject by mode of inherence (as an accident) is not signified in the manner of a property that inheres in the subject."[51] A relation of reason is an ordering of concepts in the intellect.[52] Some of these relations/orders/unions are invented by our intellect (such as genus) and others are flow from our mode of knowing.[53] According to Emery, real (categorical) relations only obtain in the following conditions. Two terms are real, really distinct, belong to the same order/union, and results from a foundation which causes it to be in the subject.[54] The relation is the ordo, the *ad aluid* to the term. According to Emery, if any one of the conditions above does not obtain, the relation is a relation

46. *IV Sent.,* d. 26, q. 2, a. 1, co.

47. *Quodl.,* IX q. 2, a. 3, co.

48. Cf. *De Pot.,* q. 7, a. 9, co.

49. Cf. Gyula Klima, "The Changing Role of Entia Rationis in Medieval Semantics and Ontology," in *Synthese,* 96.1 (1993): 25–29.

50. Emery, "*Ad aliquid,*" 184.

51. Emery, "*Ad aliquid,*" 184.

52. Cf. *De Pot.,* q. 7, a. 11, co.

53. Cf. Emery, "*Ad aliquid,*" 189

54. Cf. Emery, "*Ad aliquid,*" 185. Belonging to the same order need not require a common principle, since creatures are really related to God as creator, but they do not have a common principle (belong to the same order). I think the criteria of belonging to the same order could be put more precisely as belonging to the same order or one being principle of the order.

of reason and not a real relation (though I qualify this somewhat below).[55]

One type of real relation is called by Thomists a transcendental relation.[56] Though there has been denial of this concept by some Thomists, one suspects because of antipathy toward Scotism,[57] most Thomists accept this as a doctrine of Aquinas. As Manser explains it: "The name 'transcendental' relation means that it . . . stands above all the categories."[58] If put this way, it is a relatively simple matter. Some things are said, *ad aliud* (and the mode of predication follows the mode of being here),[59] but the relation is not something which has a mode of being *inesse*, but rather the principle or thing itself is a relation/order/union with its correlative principle. One can see this doctrine clearly in Aquinas's thought on the relational transcendentals (though the relation between the transcendentals themselves is a relation of reason). In other words, though relation is certainly categorical, it is also a transcendental concept. These are called transcendental relations.[60] According to this doctrine, relation can also transcend the categories and apply to act/potency, essence/existence, form/matter, substance/accident, etc.[61] As De Raeymaker

55. Cf. Emery, "*Ad aliquid*," 188. Part of this requires explaining. If one of the aspects of a real relation is belonging to the same order, then how can order be reduced to relation? It seems circular at best. I think the best way to explain this is to claim that Aquinas is explaining a subsequent relation by a more fundamental one (and that order is a relation) that grounds the relation in question. For example, by their fundamental relation to God, order to God, creatures are related to each other. It is not that the order/relation come apart, so to speak, but that there are nested orders and the more fundamental the relations/order are the explanations for subsequent relations being real and not merely logical. Those more fundamental unions/relations, it seems, could be real or logical.

56. The denial of transcendental relation, or at least a lack of attention to it, leads some Thomists to deny the identity of order and relation. See Andrew Woznicki, *Being and Order: The Metaphysics of Thomas Aquinas in Historical Perspective* (New York: Peter Lang, 1991), 83ff.

57. Cf. Emery, "*Ad aliquid*," 198ff.

58. Manser, *Begriff*, 354

59. *V Meta.*, l. 9, n. 889.

60. Cf. Wippel, *The Metaphysical Thought of Thomas Aquinas* (Washington DC: The Catholic University of America Press, 2001), 320 n. 96.

61. For an example in the relation of form to matter, see Markus Schulze, *Leibhaft und Unsterblich: zur Schau der Seele in der Anthropologie und Theologie des Hl. Thomas von*

says, "[Each of these principles] is identified entirely with the relation which binds it to its co-principle, and it does not contain anything which is not referred to this other principle."[62] For example, when we use the language of potency being ordered to act we are not positing an accidental relation somehow adhering in potency, but rather claiming that potency as a principle is *ad aliud* toward act. Put differently, each of these principles is in union with the other. Likewise, their union is indivisible because they are relations to the other principle. They are distinct as principles but indivisible from each other.[63]

Following from the modes of relation, both categorical and transcendental, peace's positive *ratio* would be both categorical and transcendental. In its transcendental aspect, as I will claim later, peace belongs to the *ratio* of the good—as a transcendental concept. In its categorical aspect, it is reduced to categorical relation, with a subject, term, and foundation. This claim, that peace belongs both to the transcendental and categorical orders, should not surprise a Thomist. It follows from Aquinas's thought on relation and mirrors the moves he makes with other transcendentals. Aquinas claims *unum* is both transcendental and categorical and distinguishes between them.[64] I think we can do the same thing with relation (and thus peace). It is both a transcendental order/union as well as a categorical order/union. It admits of both real and merely logical instantiations that are the same conceptually but differ in *esse*.

### Quies et Tranquillitas

The above section merely concerns the logically prior *ratio* of peace, but what of the other elements of Aquinas's descriptions, *quies et tranquillitas*? Do they also describe the same reality? If the above

*Aquin* (Freiburg: Universitätsverlag Freiburg Schweiz, 1992), 138f: "*druckt eine Relation aus zwischen Seele und Leib . . . keine akzidentelle, sondern eine wesenhafte Relation.*"

62. For the source of this quotation see Wippel, *The Metaphysical Thought of Thomas Aquinas*, 320 n. 96.

63. Cf. Ramirez, *De Ordine*, 46.

64. Cf. *ST* I q. 11, a. 2, co.

argument concerning order/union is correct, then it would seem to follow that the other elements of Aquinas's description would also be identified in some sense. The purpose of this section is to argue just that, using the rational appetite as an example, though the solution analogously holds for anything since Aquinas is clear that anything can be at peace.[65] In this section, I argue that both *quies* and *tranquillitas* are negations (and hence beings of reason) that follow from *ordo/unio* as well as address some texts of Aquinas where he explicitly distinguishes them. If this is right, then Aquinas does have a unified description of peace despite the semantic differences.

When Aquinas analyzes the rational appetite, he uses a triad of actions to describe its motion toward an end: love, desire, and joy. Love is the initial proportion/relation/union to the good.[66] Desire follows when full union with that good is lacking; desire is the motion of a merely appetitive union toward an effective union.[67] Joy is the fruition of the will caused by the possession of the object of the rational appetite, the good. It is within this triad that we can locate Aquinas' thought on tranquility/rest and see their identity with each other and thereby the unity of Aquinas's two main descriptions of peace.

In *ST* I-II q. 70, a. 3, Aquinas relates peace to the will's ongoing order/union with the good. Therein, Aquinas claims that peace is the perfection of joy in two ways. The first is that one's joy is undisturbed by others or by other appetites. The other is the sedation of restless desire (*sedationem desiderii fluctuantis*).[68] Aquinas follows by saying that "peace implies both of these,"[69] both an exterior lack of disturbance and rest of the appetite. What is important to note, for now, is that both of these descriptions are negations. These two negations (lack of obstacles to the good and rest in it) are exactly what

---

65. Cf. *In de Div. Nom.*, c. 11, n. 885.

66. Cf. *ST* q. 25, a. 2, ad 2.

67. Cf. *ST* I-II q. 26, a. 2, ad 2.

68. *ST* I-II q. 70, a. 3, co.

69. *ST* I-II q. 70, a. 3, co.: "*Haec autem duo importat pax, scilicet ut neque ab exterioribus perturbemur; et ut desideria nostra conquiescant in uno.*"

Aquinas means by tranquility/rest. The first aspect is that one's seeking of the good is without obstacles/conflict.[70] This negation seems to be antecedent to one's achievement of the good and these obstacles could be contrary internal appetites or other persons' actions. Importantly, the lack of obstacles must be born of another, distinct, union (either with others or within oneself). In other words, what removes an obstacle to one union/order is another union/order. The second aspect is rest (*quietus*). This element is the rest of all faculties in the good.[71] Rest is a lack of motion, the termination of motion.[72] This element of tranquility seems to be subsequent to the achievement of the good, though naturally and not temporally. In other words, tranquility (also) denotes the lack of motion that comes from achieving the good which satisfies desire entirely.[73] Hence, as Aquinas says, peace is present to the degree one rests in the good.[74] I shall return to this aspect of Aquinas's thought in subsequent chapters. The important thing to recall here is that both *quies* and *tranquillitas* are negations. In other words, the *ratio* of peace is not merely order/union, but also a negation that follows from order/union.

On the other hand, this text does not seem to help us find a unified description of peace. In this text, as well as some others, Aquinas seems to distinguish between rest and tranquility.[75] By tranquility, Aquinas often means a lack of interior and exterior obstacles, the negation of obstacles/impediments to the good.[76] Either interior

---

70. Cf. *ST* II-II q. 29, a. 2, co.

71. Aquinas even goes further to claim that all faculties must rest in the same good. If they are to inhabit the same order, they must be organized by the same good, i.e. have the same principle. Only in this case can conflict be precluded.

72. Cf. *IV Sent.*, d. 49, q. 1, a. 2, qc. 4, ad 4: "*et secundum hoc quies ad quam terminatur motus*". *Super Is.*, c. 26.

73. Aquinas tends to use tranquility and rest synonymously, but on occasion distinguishes them. When distinguished, he uses tranquility to denote the lack of exterior disturbances and quiet/rest to denote a lack of interior desire/motion. E.g. *Super I Tim* c. 2, l. 1.

74. Cf. *IV Sent.*, d. 49, q. 1, a. 2, qc. 4, co. & ad 4.

75. When distinguished, he uses tranquility to denote the lack of exterior disturbances and quiet/rest to denote a lack of interior desire/motion. E.g. *Super I Tim* c. 2, l. 1.

76. Cf. *ST* II-II q. 29, a. 2, co.: "*Et ideo necesse est quod omne appetens appetat pacem, inquantum scilicet omne appetens appetit tranquille et sine impedimento pervenire ad id quod*

or exterior obstacles would serve to derail the will's achievement of the good. By rest, on the other hand, Aquinas seems to mean a lack of motion caused by the achievement of the good.[77] This makes for two interpretive problems. The first is descriptive and I will try to deal with it here. A plain reading of the text would seem to distinguish them and thus frustrate any attempts at a unified description of peace. The second follows from my solution to the first, namely that it implies that Aquinas identifies joy and peace. I will treat that issue in Chapter 4. The description problem concerns me here. How is it possible that peace has both these *rationes*? If rest and tranquility are distinct, how do they both describe peace?

In addition, the best textual evidence that rest and tranquility are diverse is based on *ST* II-II q. 29, a. 1. Therein, as we saw earlier, Aquinas argues that concord, the union of appetites of different people, is integral to peace, but is not peace, *proprie sumatur.* "Wherever there is peace there is concord, but it is not' wherever there is concord there is peace."[78] Wherever you have peace, you must have concord (though Aquinas qualifies this somewhat),[79] but the reverse doesn't hold (though this too seems suspect on Aquinas's terms as we shall see later), for peace is the union of appetites within an individual (rational, animal, and natural appetites).[80] In this way,

---

*appetit, in quo consistit ratio pacis, quam Augustinus definit tranquillitatem ordinis."* The lack of interior obstacles seems to be what Aquinas means by tranquility, i.e. one's desire for the good is tranquil and not disturbed by contrary desires. When Aquinas references impediments, he seems to mean exterior obstacles. This makes sense with the definition of peace—tranquility of order—which applies to interior peace. Exterior peace is an integral part of this.

77. Cf. *In de Div. Nom.,* c. 11, n. 880.

78. *ST* II-II q. 29, a. 1, co.

79. One can see why in cases of persecution. The rest of one's appetites will be disturbed by others, to put it lightly. You and the other do not inhabit the same order and so will inevitably experience conflicts of various sorts. Yet even if one's life is taken or one is tortured, the highest desires can continue to rest in God. Hence, one can have peace without concord, but it will only be peace in one's will and not in one's sensual appetites. Full peace, which is what Aquinas seems to mean in *ST* II-II q. 29, a. 1, cannot be had without concord. This makes perfect sense, because the full order/union of the individual cannot be obtained without recognizing the social nature of the individual.

80. Cf. *ST* II-II q. 29, a. 1, co.

tranquility stands to rest as concord stands to peace. Conceptually, tranquility is antecedent to the achievement of the good but rest is concomitant with it (ST I-II q. 4, a. 4, co.). Thus, strictly speaking, rest is the most proper *ratio* of peace, even if rest and tranquility will occur simultaneously (the desire for the good, if not impeded, will proceed to the good desired). This is why Aquinas sometimes identifies rest and a lack of impediments. They are both effects of order/union, but are distinct as interior and exterior. This seems to be the most straightforward interpretation of Aquinas and claims that rest and tranquility describe diverse negations. Tranquility is the more specific *ratio* of concord and rest is the more specific *ratio* of peace, but they are not identified with each other (even if one is essential for the other). Concerning peace, tranquility is a lack of exterior obstacles and rest is the lack of motion toward the good caused by its achievement.

On the other hand, this does not seem exactly right. If the above divergent interpretation of *quies et tranquillitas* is to be sustained, then concord must be tranquil, and peace must be at rest (diversity in the negative *rationes*). Especially when we look closer at what Aquinas means by concord, problems begin to emerge. By concord, Aquinas means the sharing in one form by two people (by their common willing), an order/union between them.[81] The more general *ratio* of peace is clearly present in the mutual order/union which is concord. This is why Aquinas calls concord peace on occasion and calls peace the concord of our powers. In other words, if one is to claim that rest and tranquility are different this difference cannot flow from their positive *rationes*. Both are *unio/ordo*. They may be distinct as negations following from differing orders/unions (one interior and one exterior) but they are not conceptually distinct.

In other words, looking more closely it seems that conceptual identity follows in the negative *ratio* of peace as well. In order to share in the same form, have a order/union to the other of some kind, the will of the two individuals must rest in a common good.

---

81. Cf. *ST* II-II q. 29, a. 1, co.: *"voluntates simul in unum consensum conveniunt."*

Yet rest in the good by a will is exactly what Aquinas means by *quies*. In other words, what Aquinas above called the more specific element of peace (rest) is also the more specific element of concord. The wills of each must be informed together, and wills are informed by resting in the good, not by a lack of obstacles to the good. One cannot rest in a lack. This is concord (but this is also peace).

Likewise, Aquinas's claim that concord and peace are distinct is predicated on the possibility of there being concord without peace, as we see in the evil concords, in coercion, or in what is only *secundum quid* voluntary, and peace without concord (as in persecution). Yet this also has difficulties based on other texts of Aquinas. The concord the evil have is not a true sharing in a form because what they seek is not truly good (and so cannot be the basis of an order/union between them). Their love cannot amount to more than a love of concupiscence, with each terminating in himself: a distorted love of self.[82] In other words, there is not union here between them for the good is false and thus their wills cannot terminate in *uno aliquo*; their love is not a union with the other. This is why Aquinas elsewhere says that the evil cannot have peace.[83] If it is true considering the diverse appetites within a human, that they cannot be brought into true order and rest by being directed to what is evil, then I do not see how it could be true of diverse appetites between humans. The two stand or fall together.[84] Love of evil cannot bring interior order/union and Aquinas often recognizes this, calling the peace merely apparent. Loving evil with more than one person does not change this. Just as there is true and false (interior) peace, there is true and false concord (exterior peace).

On the other hand, the plain reading of *ST* II-II q. 29, a. 1 is not wholly wrong. Peace and concord are distinct. This is not because they are conceptually distinct (hence both are peace) but rather that

---

82. Cf. Anthony Flood, *The Metaphysical Foundations of Love* (Washington DC: The Catholic University of America Press, 2018), 88ff.

83. Cf. *Super Is.*, c. 48; *In Jer.*, c. 16, l. 1; *Super Gal.*, c. 5, l. 6; *Super II Cor.*, c. 13, l. 3; *Super Matt.*, c. 10, l. 2; *ST* I q. 98, a. 1, co.

84. Cf. McMahon, "A Thomistic Analysis of Peace," 185.

they are diverse orders/unions (one interior, between the person's potencies, and one exterior, between persons). This is what the divergence reading gets right. Yet both peace and concord realize the essential notes of what Aquinas means by peace more generally as union/order and rest/tranquility. If this is right, then Aquinas's above discussion of the relation of concord to peace must be qualified somewhat. In that text, he means to limit the term "peace" to interior peace. So in speaking of interior peace, the rest of the will in a common good with another individual is not to be identified with the order/union of the faculties of the individual, but is integral to it. Nevertheless, if one takes a more general perspective on peace, the same *ratio* obtains in both. Both peace and concord are order/union and rest/tranquility. The issue is merely semantic, as Aquinas clearly calls concord peace elsewhere, as we saw in the last chapter. For these reasons, Ramirez says that rest and tranquility are really identical. "The same name indicates it: *tranquillitas* = *trans-quies*, that is complete and overflowing quietude."[85] And yet, Aquinas still does want to retain the sense that interior peace is peace "in the most precise sense."[86] The principal sense of peace is interior.[87] This leads him, on occasion, to speak of rest/tranquility as diverse and relate them, but I do not think we should interpret this in a stronger sense than their distinction based on interior/exterior orders/unions.

If this interpretation is correct, then one can see here also the connection of Aquinas's two main descriptions of peace and why he uses all four terms essentially. Peace is *unio/ordo*. This is the affirmative aspect of peace and denotes the order/union between diverse beings/appetites within beings. This order/union is caused by their sharing one cause. *Quies* and *tranquillitas* denote negations of both conflict/contrary desires and motion. As Aquinas says, "[peace is had] from a certain union by which everything repugnant

<hr>

85. Ramirez, "La Eucaristía y la Paz Individual en la Teologia de Santo Tomas de Aquino," 174.

86. Ramirez, "La Eucaristía," 174: *"en todo el rigor de la palabra."*

87. Cf. Ramirez, *De Caritate,* 858: *"placentera y principalmente interior."*

is excluded."[88] It is the lack of conflict and rest that union with the good provides. The relation between these two elements is also clear. The positive element (*unio* or *ordo*) precludes conflict and is marked by rest.[89] Inasmuch as the diverse powers of an individual are unified/in order, they do not conflict and are marked by rest in the good. Inasmuch as the wills of diverse individuals are truly unified/ordered, then this also precludes conflict and causes rest.

Should we call this description (an intentionally vague term) a definition of peace? Aquinas does use definitional language to refer to peace, but only once.[90] His usual language is not that of definition, but rather of what the *ratio* of peace imports/implies.[91] I think, for reasons to be explained in the next section, that we should treat Aquinas's description of peace as non-definitional. A negation, rest/tranquility, cannot serve as a true specific difference.[92] Likewise, order/union is not a genus; one cannot find anything outside of it to divide it. Peace, as rest/tranquility, is realized everywhere there is order/union. Rest/tranquility does not serve to distinguish peace from anything else but rather to show what follows necessarily and conceptually from order/union: what it negates.[93]

The relationship between the two elements is more akin to the relation between *ens* and *unum* in Aquinas's thought.[94] Negations

88. *In de Div. Nom.*, c. 11, l. 1, n. 880: *"ex quadam unione qua omnis repugnantia excluditur."*

89. Cf. *ST* II-II q. 29, a. 1, co. Notice that whenever Aquinas talks about a lack of conflict, it is caused by diverse appetites (of different individuals or within one individual) inhabiting the same order/being unified.

90. Cf. *ST* II-II q. 29, a. 1, co.

91. See, for example, *Super Eph.*, c. 4, l. 1, n. 194 (*quae est*); *Super Heb.*, c. 13, l. 3, n. 766 (*nihil aliud est, nisi unitas affectuum*); *Super II Tim.*, c. 2, l. 4, n. 80 (*importat*); *Super I Tim.*, c. 2, l. 1, n. 59 (*est*); *Super Col.*, c. 3, l. 3, n. 164 (*est*); *Super Phil.*, c. 4, l. 1, n. 158 (*est*); *Super II Cor.*, c. 1, l. 1, n. 8 (*est/accipiatur*); *De Regno* I c. 4, co. (*quae pax dicitur*); *In de Div. Nom.*, 885 (*ratio pacis consistat*), 891 (*consistit*); 896 (*ad rationem pacis pertinet*); 914 (*consistat*), 920 (*pertinent ad rationem pacis ... consistit*); *ST* I-II q. 113, a. 2, co. (*consistit*); *ST* II-II q. 29, a. 2 (*consistit*), a. 3 (*est de ratione pacis*).

92. Cf. David Svoboda, *Aquinas on One and Many* (Neuenkirchen-Seelscheid: Editiones Scholasticae, 2015), 51.

93. Cf. *In de Div. Nom.*, c. 11, l. 1, n. 880.

94. Cf. *ST* I q. 11, a. 1. co.

are beings of reason and so wherever order/union is realized—it is restful and tranquil.[95] Using *ens* and *unum* as an example, what is being lacks division inasmuch as it is being. What is ordered/unified lacks conflict and motion to the extent it is ordered/unified. In this way, just as one should not say that Aquinas defines the good as the *appetible*, but rather that he describes the good by its effect on us, so too we should not reduce peace to its effect (rest/tranquility). That is merely the way it is known to us and this seems to be why Aquinas uses similar language for picking out the essence of the good as picking out the essence of peace.

Furthermore, it seems also that the other descriptions of peace Aquinas gives can be reduced to one of these two, either to the positive or negative *ratio* of peace. The lack of impediments is clearly a reference to either concord or tranquility, the lack of conflict resulting from order/union. Immunity from evil is the same. Peace as putting things in right order is, of course, a reference to order/union. Harmony with ourselves and with others references the order/union that is the positive *ratio* of peace precluding conflict, as well as ordered harmony. Two of Aquinas's descriptions though do not seem as easily reduced to order/union or rest/tranquility. These are the security against the loss of the good and the tranquility or rest *of the mind*. To begin with the latter, it might seem difficult to see why Aquinas would affirm that peace can be the rest of the mind when he clearly thinks of peace as predominately appetitive. Nevertheless, inasmuch as one thinks of the intellect as specified by its object, truth, one can see why Aquinas could hold that peace is the rest of the mind (or the general *finis* of the mind, as Aquinas says elsewhere). The intellect's good is truth and inasmuch as it rests in it, it is at peace. Likewise, Aquinas's identification of peace with security against the loss of goods also makes sense vis-à-vis Aquinas's claim that peace is order/union removing conflict. To the extent one removes conflicts and dissension (by having order/union), one's possession of the good is secured. Likewise, one cannot fully rest unless

95. Cf. Svoboda, *One and Many,* 51.

such possible disturbances are removed. Both are an effect of order/ union, having one order/union can remove obstacles to another, and pertain to rest/tranquility.

## Analogicity of Peace

Given Aquinas's *rationes* of peace, peace must be an analogous concept.[96] This is something we should expect not only because analogy is near the heart of Aquinas's thought, but because there is an intrinsic link between analogy and order/union. Equivocation is to "signify the many as many."[97] In other words, to equivocate is to signify with no clear union or order between the usage of terms or the *res* to which they refer.[98] To use terms analogously is simply to claim that there is an order/union between the things to which these terms refer. Order/union and analogy are coterminous for Aquinas and so it should be no surprise that peace, which is order/ union, is an analogous concept itself for it enters the very meaning of analogy.

The analogicity of the concept of peace, which mimics the analogicity of the term goodness (this is no mistake, as we will see in the next section),[99] allows a Thomistic account of peace to distinguish three "types" of peace: supernatural, natural, and false (each of which can be subdivided into interior/exterior as well as perfect/ imperfect—depending on the order/union in question).[100] Exegetically, Aquinas mentions all of these in passing in different contexts, but nowhere presents them systematically. Yet, all of them are order/ union marked by rest/tranquility, so the most general descriptive

96. For Aquinas's thought on analogy see John Wippel, *The Metaphysical Thought of Thomas Aquinas*, 75–85. See also Domenic D'Ettore, "*Una ratio* versus *Diversae rationes*: Three Interpretations of *Summa Theologiae* I, Q. 13, aa. 1–6," in *Nova et Vetera*, vol. 17, n. 1 (Winter 2019): 39–55.

97. Ramirez, *De Ordine*, 4

98. Cf. Ramirez, *De Ordine*, 13: " . . . *casu aequivoca, nullus ordo aut repectus attenditur unius ad alterum, sed omnino per accidens est quod unum nomen diversis rebus attribuitur.*"

99. Cf. *Super Rom.*, 1, l. 4, n. 70: "*Aliud autem, scilicet pax, est ultimum quod in beatitudine perficitur;*" *Super II Cor.*, 1, l. 1, n. 8.

100. For alternative divisions, see Tapie, "'For He is Our Peace,'" 116–17; Reichberg, "Human Nature, Peace, and War," 38ff.

unity of peace presented above still obtains. This section should not be viewed as an exhaustive presentation of the 'types' of peace in Aquinas, but rather a description of the typical places Aquinas analyzes peace.

This makes sense given the *ratio* outlined above. Could one catalogue and describe every order/union in Aquinas's thought?[101] I would think not and yet in every order/union, one finds peace (e.g. between essence/existence or substance/accident or elements, etc.). Nevertheless, there is still value in describing Aquinas's typical examples of peace. Each of these types of order/union has interior and exterior aspects: the ordering of diverse desires within the same power and within different powers and the ordering of diverse humans to a common good.

The full meaning of peace, like that of virtue,[102] occurs only supernaturally. Aquinas claims this because only with God can one find true order/union. Two considerations make it apparent why this is the case. First, to belong to the same order, different desires must converge upon the same good. If you have desires for different goods, they belong, in themselves, to different orders (e.g. the sensitive appetite and intellectual appetite). These diverse desires can be further ordered to one good. If this happens then they belong to the same order. In other words, if we are going to bring order to diverse human desires, they must first all be ordered to one good. Second, this one good cannot just be any good. To order each desire intelligibly implies that the unifying good can fulfill each of those diverse desires. If this were not the case, one could not intelligibly order one's desires to that good. Clearly only God, who super-eminently contains the good of all created things, can fulfill both requirements. Hence, Aquinas says that peace is obtained by submitting to and obeying God.[103] Yet God cannot have this integrating function,

---

101. For a much more extensive treatment of orders in Aquinas's thought see Ramirez, *De Ordine.*

102. Cf. Brian Shanley, "Aquinas on Pagan Virtue," *The Thomist* 63 (1999): 553–77.

103. Cf. *Super Rom.,* 5, l. 1, n. 382: "Let us have peace with God, that is by submitting ourselves and obeying him."

union with the highest good ordering all appetites,[104] without habitual grace (and especially the virtue of charity caused by habitual grace).[105] As Aquinas says, "without sanctifying grace one cannot have true peace, but only apparent [peace]."[106] In other words, without the virtue of charity ordering all of our acts and habits to God, they may fulfill the first requirement and inhabit the same order by being commanded by general justice, but inevitably the *polis* cannot fulfill the second requirement.[107] This will be a topic treated more extensively in the ethics chapter.

Exteriorly, supernatural concord (order/union) between humans is caused by seeking the common good of God, i.e. inhabiting the same supernatural order. It is by inhabiting the same order/being in union that conflict between persons is precluded. When the good around which humans gather is God, and humans are supernaturally ordered to God as friends of God, then there is a supernatural concord. As Aquinas says, "Men are not united amongst themselves unless it is by something held in common, and this is maximally God."[108] The higher the good, the greater its unifying power. As is commonly known, Aquinas holds God to be the separate common good of the entire universe, that to which all other things are ordered and by which ordering they are in union to each other. Nevertheless, in order to have supernatural concord each individual must be ordered to God as a friend by sanctifying grace and the charity it causes in the soul.

Full peace (supernatural interior and exterior peace), the *pax ecclesiae*,[109] can in turn be divided into imperfect and perfect. Perfect

---

104. Cf. *In de Div. Nom.*, 11, l. 1: "*Et quia divina pax causat unitatem in rebus, ideo concludit quod omnia suo modo desiderant divinam pacem, inquantum etiam est omnium unitiva.*"

105. Cf. *Super Col.*, 3, l. 3, n. 163.

106. See also *ST* II-II q. 29, a. 3, ad 1: "*Et propter hoc sine gratia gratum faciente non potest esse vera pax, sed solum apparens.*"

107. Cf. *ST* I-II q. 2, a. 8, co.

108. *Super II Thess*, 3, l. 2, n. 89: "*Item homines non uniuntur inter se, nisi in eo quod est commune inter eos, et hoc est maxime Deus.*"

109. *Super I Cor.*, 12, l. 3, n. 750.

peace, i.e. the full proper order of things (including with God, one another, and within oneself), the complete rest of desire, and freedom from all evils can only be had in the beatific vision. Yet, an imperfect participation in this type of peace can be had in this life.[110] Supernatural peace is imperfect in activity, but not in object. Imperfect because in full concord (external peace) since even though all love God as the highest good, those in the Church have differing opinions about God in small matters, *in aliquibus parvis*.[111] The peace of the Church on earth is imperfect in interior peace since "even if the soul's principal movement rests in God, still there remain certain obstacles, both within and without, which disturb this peace."[112] These remaining obstacles are signs that though the highest order/union is intact, other orders/unions are lacking. Neither of these negate the true peace of the earthly Church, but neither will be present in heaven nor that the supernatural peace had in this world is continuous (a foretaste) of heavenly peace.[113]

The next type of peace in Aquinas is natural peace. Certainly, Aquinas does not use this term (as far as I am aware), but he does imply its existence since he suggests that there is a natural order and its goods can be sought apart from sanctifying grace. For natural peace to obtain the good sought must be authentically good, not merely apparently so. Any truly natural good sought without

110. Cf. *Super Io.*, 14, l. 7, n. 1962.

111. *ST* II-II q. 29, a. 3, ad 2: "*Ad secundum dicendum quod, sicut philosophus dicit, in IX Ethic., ad amicitiam non pertinet concordia in opinionibus, sed concordia in bonis conferentibus ad vitam, et praecipue in magnis, quia dissentire in aliquibus parvis quasi videtur non esse dissensus. Et propter hoc nihil prohibet aliquos caritatem habentes in opinionibus dissentire. Nec hoc repugnat paci, quia opiniones pertinent ad intellectum, qui praecedit appetitum, qui per pacem unitur. Similiter etiam, existente concordia in principalibus bonis, dissensio in aliquibus parvis non est contra caritatem. Procedit enim talis dissensio ex diversitate opinionum, dum unus aestimat hoc de quo est dissensio pertinere ad illud bonum in quo conveniunt, et alius aestimat non pertinere. Et secundum hoc talis dissensio de minimis et de opinionibus repugnat quidem paci perfectae, in qua plene veritas cognoscetur et omnis appetitus complebitur, non tamen repugnat paci imperfectae, qualis habetur in via.*"

112. *ST* II-II q. 29, a. 2, ad 4: "*Quia etsi principalis animae motus quiescat in Deo, sunt tamen aliqua repugnantia et intus et extra quae perturbant hanc pacem.*"

113. Cf. *ST* I-II q. 3, a. 1, co. This seems to be the necessary interpretation of *Super Io.*, 14, l. 7, n. 1964 where Aquinas claims that the peace Christ gives is perfect.

the aid of grace that brings people together, i.e., causes order/union, can cause a type of concord, a degree of external peace, and internal rest.[114] Obviously, the highest candidate for this good follows an Aristotelian account. The *polis* provides for the good life and when all the members order their acts and habits to the good of the city in general justice, then they are ordered amongst themselves and within themselves by the provisioning of the city for human needs. Natural peace and its accompanying partial ordering and quieting of the appetites can be had by all. It does not require grace, though it does require virtue (so its possibility after sin is mitigated).[115] This includes, but is not limited to, what Aquinas calls "the peace and quiet of enjoying temporal things."[116] The peace and quiet caused by temporal things inasmuch as it falls under natural peace requires a virtuous ordering to those things. Nevertheless, one can also see why this type of peace will necessarily be imperfect both in object and in activity. The *polis* is not God and cannot provide for the full rest of each of our desires, so interior conflict is inevitable. Likewise, in activity without the help of grace, sin will inevitably mar both interior peace and exterior peace.

The final sense of peace is the order/union and rest/tranquility found in a merely apparent good.[117] False peace is distinct from natural peace, in other words, because natural peace involves a real (common) good. False peace is the semblance of peace caused by unity in malice.[118] Order/union based on a merely apparent good might seem to be peace; there is a kind of concord and a kind of internal order. Aquinas wants to admit this—there is a type of order/

114. Another way of stating this is that both the natural law and the civil law produce a type of natural peace. See Erb, *Interior Peace,* 265–66.

115. This could still obtain even in the most pessimistic interpretation of Aquinas on the power of fallen humans without grace. All must at least admit the following possibilities: not only "building houses and planting vineyards" but also "friendship" and "conservation of citizenship." See *ST* I-II q. 109, a. 2; a. 5; *ST* II-II q. 23, a. 7.

116. *Super Io.,* 14, l. 7, n. 1964: "*Nam pax mundi ordinatur ad quietam et pacificam fruitionem temporalium.* . . ."

117. Cf. *ST* I-II q. 29, a. 3, ad 1: "*non potest esse vera pax, sed solum apparens.*"

118. Cf. *Super Rom.,* 12, l. 3, n. 1010.

union between a band of thieves. They cooperate toward a common end/goal so it can preclude (some) interpersonal conflict. Their desires are all ordered/in union with that end so it can seem to provide interior rest.

Yet, given Aquinas's metaphysics, he must qualify this picture as we saw earlier. The order/union found in something evil cannot be peace, for peace is a *ratio* of the good (as we shall see in a later section). Evil is parasitic on the good and thus parasitic on peace. In addition, evil can never quiet or order the appetites; it will not give rest. The peace of a band of thieves (their union/order) or of someone who orders their lives around a finite good as final end is not peace at all. The metaphysics of this will be explained more in the next section, but Aquinas clearly admits this:

> Peace consists in the rest and union of one's appetites, and just as one can desire the good simply speaking or a merely apparent good, so too peace can be either true or apparent. Indeed, peace is not able to be without the true good since every evil, though it seems good from some angle, and so quiets the appetite in part, it has so many defects that the appetite remains restless and disturbed.[119]

It is more difficult to catalogue what Aquinas calls worldly peace, *pax mundi*, or temporal peace, *pax temporalis*.[120] In one sense of this term, Aquinas simply means peace (natural or supernatural) had in this world.[121] This use of the term is not a separate type of peace but reduces to either imperfect supernatural peace or imperfect natural peace. A second sense of worldly Aquinas claims that the good and evil share,[122] it could help people to sin, and is distinguished

---

119. *ST* II-II q. 29, a. 3, co.: "*quia pax consistit in quietatione et unione appetitus; sicut autem appetitus potest esse vel boni simpliciter vel boni apparentis, ita etiam et pax potest esse et vera et apparens, vera quidem pax non potest esse nisi circa appetitum veri boni; quia omne malum, etsi secundum aliquid appareat bonum, unde ex aliqua parte appetitum quietet, habet tamen multos defectus, ex quibus appetitus remanet inquietus et perturbatus.*"

120. The differences between these two terms should not be exaggerated. Aquinas seems to use both freely to describe any peace had in this world. See *Super Io.*, 14, l. 7, nn. 1963–964.

121. Cf. *Super Io.*, 14, l. 7, n. 1963.

122. Cf. *Super I Tim.*, 2, l. 1, n. 59.

from the peace of Christ in three ways. Any account of the *pax mundi* must consider all these features.

When Aquinas treats the *pax mundi* in the most depth, he distinguishes it from the peace of Christ, supernatural peace, in three ways. First, they differ in end. The purpose of Christ's peace is to enjoy and contemplate eternal goods as well as to evangelize.[123] The purpose of the *pax mundi* is temporal things. They differ as the simulated from the true. Worldly peace is simulated because it is only peace on the outside (though I do not think Aquinas would categorically deny any interior rest to the *pax mundi*).[124] Finally, they differ in perfection inasmuch as the peace of Christ gives interior order and tranquility, but the peace of the world is only concerned with externals (again, with the above qualifications Aquinas makes in other texts). In this way, the *pax mundi* could help people to sin.[125]

Clearly, Aquinas does not think the *pax mundi* can be reduced to supernatural peace. The real question comes in whether it is reduced to natural peace or false peace. I think its reduction depends on the order/union Aquinas has in mind at the time. The key to recognizing this is that the *pax mundi* seems to primarily refer to the lack of conflict *inter patrias et intra patriam*.[126] As we know from above, a lack of

123. Cf. *Super Ps.*, 14, n. 8: "*Vacate et videte. Hic finis est pacis. Finis pacis temporalis, secundum philosophum, est contemplatio veritatis. Unde pax est utilis finis vitae activae, et pax ordinatur ad contemplationem. Et secundum Augustinum, Christus procuravit pacem Romani imperii, ut apostoli discurrerent per totum mundum. Et ideo dicit ex quo est tanta pax, vacate et videte. Unde patet quod Deus dat pacem ut non vacent malis operibus, sed contemplationi veritatis*" Aquinas seems to suggest a more independent end for temporal peace in *Super Io.*, 14, l. 7, n. 1964.

124. Cf. *Super Io.*, 14, l. 7, n. 1964.

125. Cf. *Super Io.*, 14, l. 7, n. 1964. *Super I Tim.*, 2, l. 1, n. 59.

126. Cf. Gregory Reichberg, "Aquinas's Moral Typology of Peace and War," *Review of Metaphysics* 64 (1): 467–87; see pages 472–79. It is certainly also true that *intra patriam* (and maybe also *inter patrias*) peace falls under natural peace since there is a true political common good sought by all. For more on the primacy of the common good see (among many other possibilities), Stephen Brock, "The Primacy of the Common Good and the Foundations of Natural Law in St. Thomas," in *Ressourcement Thomism: Sacred Doctrine, the Sacraments, and the Moral Life: Essays in Honor of Romanus Cessario, O.P.*, eds. Reinhard Hütter and Matthew Levering (Washington DC: The Catholic University of America Press, 2010): 234–55.

conflict is caused by some kind of order/union.[127] If that is the case, then this type of peace reduces to natural peace or false peace, depending on whether the order/union which is precluding conflict is real or apparent, the internal order likewise being real or apparent.

This diverse reduction helps to explain one of the tensions in Aquinas's texts. He often says, in his more Augustinian moments, that the *pax mundi* is a false or simulated peace when it is not ordered to a higher good. Without grace there is only apparent or false peace. If he praises natural peace, he praises it instrumentally—it allows people to contemplate and the Church to evangelize. Yet if it is used for evil, natural peace itself becomes evil. We have seen this in multiple texts. Nevertheless, elsewhere he says that this (natural) peace is not merely instrumentally good, but intrinsically good. "The peace of the republic is something intrinsically good, nor is it rendered bad by the fact that some people make poor use of it; for there are many other people who make good use of it, and much worse evils are prevented by it . . ."[128] The tension, both claiming that the peace of the city is only true when ordered toward a higher supernatural good and also claiming it is good in itself and not purely instrumental, can be explained by a distinction Aquinas draws between the internal and external common good as well as his metaphysics of peace. When the peace of the natural city is ordered toward human happiness (its external common good), then it is true, but imperfect, peace (the internal common good). It can cause an imperfect and provisional unity and rest. When it is ordered toward something unjust or false (e.g. an unjust war), it is reduced to a false peace—the peace of a band of thieves. This also explains why Aquinas mentions

---

127. The other possibility is to claim that the lack of conflict is not caused by order but by a total lack of contact. In this sense it would seem possible to have no conflict without having order/relation. This would make sense of Aquinas's claim that the good and evil share this type of peace. This hardly seems possible though, especially *inter patrias*. Could it be possible to have no order to another member of one's country? How could this be if you share in the same common good? It might seem more possible between countries, yet the same questions hold but only in reference to the common good of the universe and the separate common good of God.

128. *ST* II-II q. 125, a. 3, ad 3.

the caveat above—that others make good use of it and it prevents other evils. If all were making bad use of it, then there would be unity in seeking evil and it would be reduced to the "peace" of a band of thieves. But this is neither union—nor peace (metaphysically speaking). In other words, natural happiness, the goal of a city, is a true good. Because of this, it can be the basis of true union/order between individuals. Nevertheless, if a city, as a whole, orders itself to a false good or engages in collective action that does not conduce to happiness, then it ceases to be unified. Because of the identity of union/order and the good, the cooperation/order/union are false and simulated. It is no longer order/union because the good sought is a mere apparent good and not a true good.

These three senses of peace: supernatural, natural, and false, are all different realizations of order/union marked by rest/tranquility. Peace is found wherever there is order/union; these are the essential notes of peace. The key to recognizing why this is ubiquitous in Thomistic metaphysics becomes clear in the next section. Order/union and rest/tranquility are *rationes* of the good. Wherever there is good, there is order/union. Hence, wherever there is good, there is rest and tranquility.

### PEACE AND THE GOOD

Final causality is undoubtedly the most important cause for understanding Aquinas's thought on peace. Whenever Aquinas discusses peace directly, he normally discusses it in terms of the good (though *unum* comes in a close second—as we shall see).[129] Good, as Aquinas says, is the correspondence of being to the will in the form of final causality.[130] Peace is an aspect of every end; peace has a *rationem finis*.[131] While commenting on Paul's salutation "Grace unto you

---

129. See, for example, *IV Sent.,* d. 1, q. 2, a. 4, ad 1, and 4; *De Ver.,* q. 22, a. 1, ad 12; *ST* II-II q. 29, a. 1, co.

130. Cf. *De Ver.,* q. 1, a. 1, co.

131. *In de Div. Nom.,* c. 11, l. 1, n. 886: *"et hoc est ex participatione divinae pacis quae, inquantum ab omnibus desideratur, habet rationem finis."*

and peace . . ." Aquinas says, "the final of all gifts is peace, because peace is the general end of the mind (*generalis finis mentis*). For in any way peace is taken, it has the concept of an end. In eternal glory, governing, and behavior, the end is peace."[132] By saying that peace is the general end of the mind and activity, Aquinas is indicating that it is not just a particular end (a particular good), but the general end of the human. He even calls peace the "universal good."[133] He says explicitly elsewhere: "Peace follows from every good"[134] and one has peace when "one is quieted and perfected in the good."[135] Aquinas even says once that peace adds nothing beyond the ratio of the good. "*Pax nihil adiiciunt super rationem boni.*"[136]

In short, as one can see, that if one wants to understand Aquinas's thought on peace, his thought on the good is indispensable. Hence, in this section I begin by giving a short introduction to Aquinas's thought on the transcendentals in general and the good in particular. Following that, I argue that the positive *ratio* of peace (order/union) can be easily understood as a *ratio* of the good. In other words, peace in its positive aspect, is simply an explanation of the good. Because of this, peace attains a kind of transcendental status. More controversial is the negative *ratio*, rest/tranquility. Should this *ratio*, and thus peace in its negative sense, be reduced to the good? I will offer arguments in favor and against and tentatively conclude that Thomistic metaphysics should hold that the negative *ratio* is also a conceptual explanation of the good. On the other hand, this should not surprise anyone who has read the previous section. If I am right that order/union is reduced to relation, rest/tranquility is

132. *Super II Cor.*, c. 1, l. 1, n. 8: "*Ultimum autem omnium bonorum est pax, quia pax est generalis finis mentis. Nam qualitercumque pax accipiatur, habet rationem finis; et in gloria aeterna et in regimine et in conversatione, finis est pax;*" *Super Heb* c. 12, l. 2; *Super I Thess.* c. 1, l. 1; *Super II Thess.* c. 1, l. 1.

133. *De Malo* q. 1, a. 1, co.: "*Rex autem qui est illo superior, intendit bonum universale, scilicet totius regni pacem.*"

134. *IV Sent.*, d. 8 q. 2 a. 4 qc. 3 expos.: "*pacem quantum ad consecutionem omnis boni;*" *Super Iob* c. 22.

135. *Super Gal.* c. 6, l. 5, n. 376: "*Pax . . . qua quietentur et perficiantur in bono.*"

136. *ST* II-II q. 30, a. 3, ad 3; cf. *ST* I q. 11, a. 2, ad 3.

realized (as a negation) wherever there is order/union, and relation belongs to the transcendental order, then clearly rest/tranquility does as well.

## The Transcendentals

Aquinas's thought on the transcendentals is a solution to a wider and older philosophical problem: the division of being (*ens*). In contrast to Parmenides, Aquinas (following Aristotle) holds that being is not univocal (ontologically or conceptually); in other words, being is not a genus. This opens a problem: If being cannot be divided in the mode of a genus, then how is it divided?

Aquinas answers this question in *De Veritate* q. 21, a. 1. Therein, he begins by distinguishing three ways in which something can be divided: by addition from outside the essence (substance/accident division), by limitation and determination (species/genus division), and by concept (privation or conceptual division). Aquinas only accepts the second and third ways as possible divisions of being. The first would assume that there is something outside of being; clearly this is false. The second yields the ten categories as particular modes of being. Being is determined to one of ten modes. The third way is how the transcendentals add to being. Being and the transcendentals are identical *in subiecto, suppositum,* or *res* but different in *ratio* and hence in *nomen.* They "add to being because the mode they express is one that is common, and consequent upon every being."[137] The categories express a certain special manner of being, being in itself (substance) or being in another (accident), but the transcendentals transcend the ten categories and apply to all of them.

*Ens* must be first because being is understood in the *rationes* of the other transcendentals but not vice-versa; all the others are included in it indistinctly. The transcendentals, in turn, unfold conceptually from *ens* in two ways. The first follows from every being absolutely considered and the second from a being considered in relation. Thus, absolutely considered we have 'thing' (*res*) to express

---

137. *De Ver.,* q. 1, a. 1, co.

that all beings have an essence by which they are and 'one' (*unum*) to express that consequent upon every being is its undividedness. In Thomistic metaphysics, "diverse" signifies what is not *unum*, what includes the negation of the other.[138] The second way, considered in relation, gives us first 'something' (*aliquid*) which expresses the dividedness of one being from another (distinctness), 'truth' (*veritas*) which expresses the correspondence of being to the intellect, and 'good' (*bonum*) which expresses the correspondence of being to the will. In other words, every being is a thing, one, something, intelligible, and appetible. These *rationes* are, likewise, the first conceptions of the human intellect.[139]

Two things are important to note from this picture and push us to admit that, for Aquinas, order/union must be transcendental concepts. First, order/union enters into the very unfolding of the transcendentals. There is a conceptual order between them; they are united in flowing conceptually from being itself as their principle. This is just what Aquinas means by transcendental order. Second, some transcendentals are relative transcendentals, especially *aliquid, veritas, et bonum. Aliquid* is not good unless ordered/unified with others. Distinction needs *bonum* to achieve order/union. These observations give us an initial footing in exploring the relation of peace to the transcendentals. Nevertheless, following Aquinas, one should explore peace and the transcendentals through the relation of peace to goodness specifically, the last of the transcendentals.

## Peace and the Good

The connection between peace and the good comes through the *rationes* of peace: *ordo/unio* and *quies/tranquillitas.* The claim of this

---

138. See Michael Rubin, "The Place of 'Thing' and 'Something' in Aquinas's Order of the Transcendentals," in *The Thomist,* vol. 81, n. 3 (July 2017): 395–436. See pages 417–18; *In X Meta.,* l. 4, n. 35: "*Omne enim quod est ens et unum in se, comparatum alteri, aut est unum ei, et sic est idem; aut non unum, aptum natum esse unum, et sic est diversum;*" *De Trin.,* q. 4 a. 1 co.: "[U]nde et ab hoc ente non diuiditur hoc ens <nisi> per hoc quod in hoc ente includitur negatio illius entis."

139. Cf. *De Trin.,* 6.4; *Quodl.,* VIII, q. 2, a. 2, co.

section is that both the positive aspect of peace (order/union) and the negative (tranquility/rest) are implicit in the *ratio* of the good. In other words, peace is a conceptual explanation of the good. This is why Aquinas says that peace adds nothing beyond the *ratio boni*. Just as the transcendentals are implicit in *ens*, peace is implicit in *bonum*.[140] In order to make this argument, first we must know something about the *ratio* of the good and then I can make some kind of claim, following Aquinas, that peace reduces to an unfolding of that *ratio*.

As seen above, good is one of the relational transcendentals. This means that there is "a double *conventia*—literally: 'coming together' or convergence—between the soul and other things, namely a cognitive and an appetitive one: 'good' expresses the correspondence of being to the appetitive faculty."[141] In other words, to be good is to be desirable or appetible (*appetibile*). Being is appetible because it is perfect (and perfective). Being is perfect inasmuch as it is in act. Act, in turn, is the very ratio of *esse*. Hence, goodness is a transcendental and coterminous with being. This is Aquinas's basic argument for the transcendental status of the good. As one can see, it trades on the concept of perfective and appetible. In other words, *appetibile* and perfective are part of the conceptual outflowing of being, yet made known by relation to a distinct being (*aliquid*) with appetite. This is why Aquinas calls *bonum* a relational transcendental. Put simply, being is not good because we desire it, but we desire it because it is good. Appetite discovers the goodness of being. This also helps explain why Aquinas thinks that goodness has the *ratio* of an end, of final causality, since what is desirable must operate as a final cause. As

---

140. One might object that the transcendentals add conceptually to being, something conceptually *supra ens*. Since Aquinas explicitly denies that of peace, it is more properly said to be a synonym of the good and not a transcendental of the good. On the one hand, this would only make the case stronger for the transcendental status of peace. On the other hand, this seems wrong for peace signifies order/union being at rest. These are certainly implicit in the *ratio* of the good, but do not seem to be conceptually identical with *appetibile*.

141. Rik Van Nieuwenhove, *Thomas Aquinas and Contemplation* (New York: Oxford University Press, 2021), 55.

he says elsewhere, the ratio of the good is "that which is perfective in the manner of an end."[142]

The Good and Order/union

The identity of peace and the good is clearest with the positive aspect of peace, *ordo/unio*.[143] Aquinas claims on multiple occasions and in multiple texts that order/union is a *ratio* of the good. For example, in *ScG* III c. 20, n. 5, he says: "Good consists in order. For something is not only good because it is an end, or because it achieves an end. Even if it does not arrive at the end, provided that it is ordered to it, it can be called good."[144] His point in making this argument concerns prime matter: not even prime matter falls outside of order to an end and can thus be called good.[145] If this applies to what is first and supreme in the genus of material causality, it would seem to apply to all aspects of potentiality.[146] Likewise, Aquinas affirms that relation is part of the *ratio* of the good. "The good ... signifies something upon which a relation is consequent along with the relation itself."[147] It is a relational transcendental after all. The good's

142. *De Ver.*, q. 21, a. 2, co.

143. While it is true that order stems from any of the four causes: final, efficient, formal, or material and this may make it seem that order does not have an exclusive relation to the good, this is not the case. The ubiquity of order is the ubiquity of final causality. In other words, though order stems from any of the four causes, it always belongs to them qua final causality or the good. *ST* I q. 105, q. 6, co: "*Respondeo dicendum quod a qualibet causa derivatur aliquis ordo in suos effectus, cum quaelibet causa habeat rationem principii. Et ideo secundum multiplicationem causarum, multiplicantur et ordines, quorum unus continetur sub altero, sicut et causa continetur sub causa.*" Causes are ordered to their effects as to a final cause.

144. *ScG* III c. 20, n. 5: "*Et licet unumquodque sit bonum inquantum est ens, non tamen oportet quod materia, quae est ens solum in potentia, sit bona solum in potentia. Ens enim absolute dicitur, bonum autem etiam in ordine consistit: non enim solum aliquid bonum dicitur quia est finis, vel quia est obtinens finem; sed, etiam si nondum ad finem pervenerit, dummodo sit ordinatum in finem, ex hoc ipso dicitur bonum.*"

145. Cf. *In de Div. Nom.*, c. 11, l. 3, n. 921.

146. Cf. Ramirez, *De Ordine*, 31: "*materia ergo prima est primum atque supremum principium analogans in hoc genere causae, cetera vero, quaplus minusve participant de ratione passivitatis potentialis receptivae eius atque imperfectionis ...*"

147. *De Ver.*, q. 21, a. 6, co.: "The *ratio* of the good implies a relation, not because the name good signifies only a relation, but because it signifies something upon which a relation is consequent along with the relation itself."

ratio is *appetibile,* as Aquinas says in *De Ver.,* q. 1, a. 1. To have appetite toward a good is to be ordered toward it, in union with it. In other words, implicit in the *ratio* of the good is order and union. In other words, all things have an inchoate order/union toward the good inasmuch as they are. On account of this relation, all things, even prime matter, can be called good. Since the positive aspect of peace is order/union, all things can be said to be at peace as well.

Here we see the relevance of Aquinas's doctrine of transcendental relation. It is easy to see why Aquinas ascribes transcendental relation/order/union to the transcendental good. This is what the good means, in part, when it is predicated of being. Whatever is ordered to another is ordered to it as to a final cause. Thus, while *bonum* comes at the end of the normative list of transcendentals, that does not mean that it does not offer further conceptual explanation of what went before. Good adds, in the most fundamental sense, that beings are appetible to the extent they are perfect. In this sense it belongs to the order of form, of essence.[148] To be appetible is to be a final cause, the implication of desirability.[149] Likewise, given that the good is a final cause, the transcendental good also implies order/relation—even of the transcendentals themselves. Only with the *bonum* do the concepts of *res, unum,* and *aliquid* achieve order/union.[150] The good is a positive addition of conceptual content to the previous two transcendentals. Being is not only appetible but also ordered/unified inasmuch as the transcendentals flow from *ens* as a principle.

This tracks very well with what Aquinas says about peace. As Aquinas says, "The unity of a multitude is peace"[151] and "when the

148. Cf. *De Ver.,* q. 29, a. 8, obj. 8 and ad 8: "*Forma habet tres actus, quia dat esse, distinguit et ordinat in finem. Hi autem actus ad invicem ordinati sunt sicut ens et unum et bonum ; nam ens a primo actu relinquitur, unum a secundum, bonum a tertio.*" And "*quod patet ex hoc quod in eodem instanti forma dat esse, ordinat et distinguit.*"

149. Cf. *ST* I q. 5, a. 3, co.

150. Cf. *In de Div. Nom.,* c. 11, l. 2, n. 896: "*Inveniuntur autem aliqua, quae in sepisis diversa sunt, sed uniuntur in aliquot uno, sicut multi homines uniuntur in una domo, sed Deus in seipso unitus est.*"

151. *De Regno,* lib. 1, c. 16, co.: "*multitudinis autem unitas, quae pax dicitur ( . . .).*"

Lord prays that the disciples be perfect in goodness, he prays that they would be one."[152] To be made one is to be ordered/unified with one another and to a common principle. In the transcendental order, the concepts are ordered/unified by their outflowing from *ens,* and this is part of what it means to be *bonum.* The positive element of the essence of peace is order/union, a determinate relation. If we are to avoid positing accidents adhering in the transcendentals (which are certainly ordered/in union), it seems that peace (as order/union) must be another name for transcendental relation inasmuch as it is an explanation of *bonum.*

Put differently, peace (as *ordo/unio*) adds conceptual content to *ens* by its being a *ratio* of the good. This seems to be confirmed not only by the analysis above, but also in a few other ways. The first way is based on creation. If one recalls Aquinas' thought about order, it is relation to a principle. Does all being have one final cause? Aquinas certainly thinks so: all creation inhabits a single order.[153] He even claims that this one order is caused by the universal desire for divine peace.[154] Divine peace is the final cause of all things.[155] This would seem to imply that *ens* is ordered. One could also make the same case based on efficient and extrinsic formal causality as well. All being is ordered/unified by its one transcendental efficient and extrinsic formal cause, God.

The second way of approaching this question focuses on transcendental composition. As said above, order/union adds conceptually to the good (inasmuch as transcendental relation is in question) that the correlative principles of being (act/potency, form/matter, substance/accident) are in union with each other, are ordered to each other.[156] This is why earlier I claimed that transcendental

---

152. *Super Io.* c. 17, l. 5, n. 2238: "*Nam, ut Platonici dicunt ab hoc quaelibet res habet unitatem a quo habet bonitatem. Bonum enim est quod est rei conservativum; nulla autem res conservatur nisi per hoc quod est una. Et ideo Dominus petens discipulorum perfectionem in bonitate, petit quod sint unum.*"

153. Cf. *ST* I q. 11, a. 3, co.

154. Cf. *In de Div. Nom.,* c. 11, l. 1, n. 886.

155. Cf. *In de Div. Nom.,* c. 11, l. 1, n. 885.

156. In this way, Aquinas admits that all compositions involve union see *De Pot.,* q. 7, a. 11, co.

relation is part of the *ratio* of the good. Hence, if the good is a transcendental and includes transcendental relation, then *ens* is ordered/unified. This too, however, pulls peace into the transcendental order. As Aquinas says, "it is impossible that some being (*aliquod ens*) would totally escape union."[157]

Finally, one might reflect on Aquinas' commitment that all things exhibit an order to the good, even prime matter. One can easily see why. To speak of order based on final causality simply is to speak of a tendency toward the good.[158] An appetite/proportion/inclination for the good is a determinate relation, an inchoate union.[159] This determinate relation to the good, a fundamental union with it, is universal according to Aquinas. All things have a tendency toward an end.[160] Even further, Aquinas argues that all things have the tendency to one (ultimate) end, God.[161] Prime matter, which according to Aquinas is being in potency, is good (and not simply in potency).[162] This is because prime matter is ordered to an end. Potency is ordered to act. If even prime matter is ordered, this would seem to be true of all other things. Peace, in its positive aspect, names this conceptual addition. *Ens* is unified/ordered.

On the other hand, one must make a distinction concerning the identity of being and peace. It is the same caveat that Aquinas makes concerning the identity of goodness and being.[163] According to Aquinas, we must distinguish between the good *simpliciter* and *secundum quid*. The good *simpliciter* requires that a being have all perfections proper to it whereas the good *secundum quid* requires only existence. Being is the reverse. The existence of substance is being

157. *In de Div. Nom.*, c. 11, 3, n. 921: "*impossibile enim est esse aliquod ens quod totaliter unitionem refugiat* ( …)."

158. Cf. *De Ver.*, q. 1, a. 1, co.; *ST* I-II q. 25, a. 2, ad 2; Jan Aertsen, *Medieval Philosophy and the Transcendentals: The Case of Thomas Aquinas* (Leiden: E.J. Brill, 1996), 299.

159. Cf. *ST* I-II q. 25, a. 2, ad 2. This is the very reason good is a relational transcendental.

160. Cf. *De Ver.*, q. 22, a. 1; *In Eth.* l. 1. See Aertsen, *Medieval Philosophy and the Transcendentals*, 301.

161. Cf. *De Pot.*, q. 3, a. 6, co.

162. Cf. *De Malo* q. 1, a. 2, co.

163. Cf. *ST* I q. 5, a. 1, ad 1.

*simpliciter* and accidents are only being *secundum quid.* Because peace is a transcendental of the good, one must make the same kind of distinction with peace. So, what is simply in being is only at peace *secundum quid.* What is at peace *simpliciter* has being *secundum quid.* As Jan Aertsen says though, "Since actuality is always the actualization of being, the absolute goodness of a thing [and hence its peace too] can also be seen as its completed and perfected being."[164]

*The Good and Rest/Tranquility*

Though the positive *ratio* of peace has a strong case for identity with the good, the negative *ratio* of peace is more difficult to reduce to the good. Because of this, there are many more plausible objections. I will treat the objections in the next section. In this section, I want to make the positive case that that rest/tranquility are also *rationes* of the good.

Based on the relation between order/union and rest/tranquility, one can make a case for this conclusion. The positive conceptual addition of peace to the good is followed immediately by a negation. What is united/ordered is not in conflict and rests to the degree of that order/union. For example, none of the transcendentals conceptually conflict with each other on account of their union in *ens* and their orderly flowing from it. The transcendental good is distinguished by being's relation to appetite. Being is appetible because it is perfect. Aquinas clearly holds that whoever desires the good desires to obtain it, hold it, and rest in it without conflict and disturbance.[165] Yet this is simply to desire peace (at least its negative *ratio*). Therefore, Aquinas is adamant that all desire peace.[166] Likewise, the degree to which the good is achieved is the degree to which appetite is brought to rest. Neither a lack of conflict nor rest adds positively to order/union. They immediately follow from the good, the way *unum* follows from *ens.* Whatever is *ens* is undivided; whatever is

---

164. Aertsen, *Medieval Philosophy and the Transcendentals,* 318–20.
165. Cf. *In de Div. Nom.,* c. 11, l. 3, n. 917.
166. Cf. *In de Div. Nom.,* c. 11, l. 3, n. 919.

good is ordered and at rest. Rest and tranquility are aspects of order/ union. In other words, when Aquinas discusses peace the type of order/union Aquinas is describing (usually) is based on final causality, on the order belonging to the good.[167]

The conceptual addition of rest/tranquility to being follows from this. Something is at rest to the extent it is in act/perfect. When arguing that good is a transcendental, Aquinas links the good with the perfect and the perfect with what is in act.[168] One can easily replicate this argument but substitute the negative *ratio* of peace (rest). The argument would go as follows. Being and peace are identical but differ only in *ratio*. The essence of peace is rest. Now a thing is at rest insofar as it is perfect, and everything is perfect insofar as it is actual. It is clear, then, that something is at rest inasmuch as it exists, since it is existence that makes all things actual. Peace adds the *ratio* of rest to being.[169]

Part of this argument requires explanation. Is something at rest inasmuch as it is perfect? That is the key question. In recalling Aquinas' thought about rest as a lack of motion, one can see why perfection implies a lack of motion/potency. Motion is a mark of imperfection, a becoming toward a new perfection.[170] Put differently, motion implies potency. Both becoming and potency imply a lack. If rest is a lack of motion/potency, it implies the achievement (effective union/full order) of some perfection, of some act. In other words, if one is not at rest it is because one lacks a perfection toward which one is moving. Yet when one achieves that perfection, one ceases to seek it and rests. Hence, it seems right to say that the negative

167. Cf. M. Labourdette, *La Charite* (Paris, *Parole et Silence*, 2016), 219: "*La paix appartient à l'ordre du bien*."

168. Cf. *ST* I q. 5, a. 1, co.

169. In Aquinas' youthful work he contrasts activity with rest. See *IV Sent.*, d. 49, q. 1, a. 2, qc. 4, ad 4. Yet this cannot be right since God, who is pure act, is also maximally at rest, As Aquinas himself says. God rests in his own goodness. Now, if rest is in contrast to activity, it is hard to see how this would not impugn God's pure actuality. See *II Sent.*, d. 15 q. 3 a. 2 ad 8 for an example of that language.

170. Cf. *IV Sent.*, d. 49, q. 1, a. 2, qc. 4, ad 4. See Joseph Pilsner, *The Specification of Human Actions in St. Thomas Aquinas* (New York: Oxford University Press, 2006), 30ff.

aspect of peace adds a *ratio* to being. Inasmuch as something is actual, it is at rest. In this way more act and less potency is realized as more peace.

Peace and the Properties of the Good

Because of peace's identity with the good in subject, peace shares in the properties of the good. It is universal in extension, it is only reduced by privation/negation, and admits of true and false instantiations. This makes perfect sense if the above section is correct. If peace is reduced to *a ratio* of the good, it will share in the same properties as the good.

Because peace is identical in subject with the good, it extends to all things. All things, inasmuch as they are, are ordered and in union. This not only follows from the previous section, but is also confirmed in Aquinas's doctrine of creation. For Aquinas, all created things are part of God's wise order.[171] It is God's peace which overflows and causes the order/union of things to each other and to God.[172] Likewise, all things are ordered to the separate common good of God and desire God's peace, "*omnia suo modo desiderant divinam pacem* ( . . .)."[173] Certainly, the proper concept of peace is more manifest in rational creatures, but it does not only appear there.[174] Everything is ordered/united in some sense.[175] Likewise, all things are part of a single order of creation inasmuch as they come from and return to a single principle. While it is certainly the case that individuals can be disordered in themselves and disordered in relation to others, they can never fall outside God's order.[176]

The second property of the good identified here (reduced only

---

171. Cf. *ST* I q. 21, a. 2, co.

172. Cf. *In de Div. Nom.,* c. 11, n. 2, n. 905.

173. *In de Div. Nom.,* c. 11, l. 1, n. 886.

174. Cf. *In de Div. Nom.,* c. 11, l. 1, n. 886: "*nomen pacis magis frequentatur in rationalibus creaturis, in quibus manifestius ratio pacis invenitur, ex eis considerandum est quid proprie sit pax et in quo ratio pacis consistat.*"

175. Cf. *In de Div. Nom.,* c. 11, l. 1.

176. According to Aquinas, if one sins (disorder in act), then one falls outside one order of God's providence and into another.

by privation/negation), should also be true of peace. If peace is a *ratio* of the good, then it's opposite must be a privation/negation and not a true contrary. Nevertheless, in order to make this argument particularly, one must clearly identify what is opposed to peace for Aquinas. This is textually difficult, to say the least. Aquinas uses a bewildering number of terms for what is contrary to peace: discord, disturbance, violence, noise, impediments, motion, shouting, annoyances, inconveniences, sadness, afflictions, bitterness in speech, evil thoughts, perturbations, dissension, separation, iniquity, sin, and evil.[177]

Though Aquinas offers many varied and diverse descriptions, there is more intelligibility (union/order!) here than first appears. Most of these can be reduced to a privation of either, or more likely both, the elements of peace: order/union and rest/tranquility. For example, evil (as a privation) here is a lack of order/union (a lack of goodness) and thus of rest/tranquility. Sin, likewise, destroys the order and union of the individual toward the good against which he sins. Motion is opposed to rest/tranquility, as are impediments. Discord is opposed to order/union, and annoyances to rest/tranquility. As one can see, it is much easier to see why Aquinas has so much variety. Anything that can be opposed to order/union or rest/tranquility can be labeled its opposite. There is no need to go through each of them individually. As one will recall, Aquinas divides order/union (in the context of peace) into external order between individuals and internal order amongst the powers of the soul. Every one of the terms above disturbs the order/union between humans or within a human (or both). Thus, they undercut the rest/tranquility that is proper to peace. This is the most general form the contrary of peace can take. In other words, in general, a lack of peace is not an *aliquid*.[178] This not only fits with the general picture presented

---

177. By way of example, see *Super Iob* c. 8; *ScG* IV c. 17, n. 20; *Super Heb.*, c. 12, l. 2; *Super II Tim.*, c. 2, l. 4; *Super I Thess.*, c. 4, l. 2; *Super Col.*, c. 1, l. 5; *Super Phil.*, c. 1, l. 1 & c. 4, l. 1; *Super Gal.*, c. 5, l. 6; *Super Eph.*, c. 4, l. 1; *De Regno* I q. 6, co.; *In de Div. Nom.*, c. 11, l. 1–4, nn. 885, 886, 891, 895, 904, 918; *De Malo* q. 9, a. 1, ad 2; *Super Io.*, c. 16, l. 8; *ST* I-II q. 98, a. 1, co.; *ST* II-II q 29, a. 1, ad 1 & q. 34, pr. & 37 pr.

178. *De Malo*, q. 1, a. 1.

above concerning the relation of order/union to the good, but also Aquinas's many statements that disorder/disunion is a privation or negation.[179]

Likewise, the arguments Aquinas makes to argue that evil is a privation of the good can all be applied to peace and disorder/disunion. When Aquinas treats the question of whether *malum* is an *aliquid* in the *De Malo,* he gives three arguments. All three are structurally and rhetorically complex. What must be noted about them is that all of them base their argument on desire, the *ratio* of the good. From there they argue and conclude that evil cannot be an *aliquid,* based on universal causality of the good, desire for the good, and desire to exist. As we saw in the last section though, order/union are part of the *ratio* of the appetible and perfect. So it would make sense that Aquinas's conclusions would apply to peace as well. For example, in the first argument Aquinas claims that since the universal good is cause of all things, it must cause particular goods. We saw in the first chapter that Aquinas makes the same claims about God's peace causing only order/union. So disorder/disunion cannot be an entity. Likewise, following from the second argument, disorder and disunion cannot be desired in itself but only indirectly (i.e. based on union/order with another perceived or real good). Order/union are part of the *ratio* of the good such that their contrary is not an entity and cannot be desired in itself. Finally, just as evil is contrary to *ens,* it must also be contrary to order/union. Things desire to preserve their order/union (peace) just as they desire to preserve their existence.[180] Making disorder/disunion an *aliquid* would not only remove peace from the transcendental order, but the good as well.

In other words, in general, disorder/disunion cannot be contrary to peace the way white is contrary to black or slow to fast or here to there. These kinds of contraries are both entities and belong to the categories such that they can be grouped under a genus.[181] Disorder

---

179. This is true of the totality of Aquinas's thought, but it is especially central to his thought on sin and disease: *ST* I-II q. 71, a. 1, co., and *De Malo,* q. 7, a. 1, co.

180. Cf. *De Malo,* q. 1, a. 1, ad 17.

181. Cf. *De Malo,* q. 1, a, 1, ad 3.

and disunion, however, are dependent on peace and not some deeper genus which is shared with peace.[182] When Aquinas is forced to speak precisely about this, he will not say that evil is the contrary of the good,[183] but the privation of it.[184] Other times, however, he will clearly say that evil is contrary to the good, but this is not because they are opposed as two species of a common genus. Disorder/disunion (and disquiet/discord following from it) work the same way; they are the privation of form or privation of order/union to the end (two things Aquinas also says about evil as contrary to the good).[185] Aquinas even says specifically that evil is directly contrary to order/union, which makes perfect sense if peace is a *ratio* of the good.[186]

Aquinas does identify human actions as functioning differently, for there good and evil serve as specific difference.[187] In whatever way Aquinas means this, it is certain he does not mean to turn evil into an *aliquid*, but rather means that the very privation of the goodness of the object is the essential difference in specifying the human action (this is why sin takes reason to specify and is contrary to reason). Something similar is true of peace. Disorder/disunion are not, technically speaking, contraries of peace. That will not stop Aquinas from saying that they are contraries elsewhere, but not in such a way that they share a genus. What would that genus be? *Ens* is the only possibility, but *ens* is not a genus. Likewise, the will of disorder/disunion seems to follow evil in the specification of sin.[188] Disorder/disunion do sometimes specify human acts, but that does not turn them into *aliqui*. The very lack specifies.[189]

On the other hand, concerning categorical orders/unions, I think

182. Cf. *ST* I-II q. 48, a. 3, co.

183. Olivia Blanchette, *The Perfection of the Universe According to Aquinas: A Teleological Cosmology* (University Park: The Pennsylvania State University Press, 1992), 113.

184. Cf. *De Malo*, q. 1, a. 1, ad 2.

185. Cf. *ST* I q. 49, a. 1, co.: "*Causam autem formalem malum non habet, sed est magis privatio formae. Et similiter nec causam finalem, sed magis est privatio ordinis ad finem debitum.*"

186. Cf. *De Malo*, q. 1, a. 1, ad 6.

187. Cf. *De Malo*, q. 1, a. 1, ad 12.

188. See Aquinas's thought on discord, for an example. *ST* II-II q. 37.

189. Cf. *ST* I q. 48, a. 1, ad 2; *ST* I-II q. 18, a. 5, co.

one must speak more precisely (just as Aquinas does of particular goods). Just as not every lack of a good is a privation, so too not all lacks of peace are privations. We lack all kinds of particular orders/unions and this is not a lack which is necessary for perfection (privation), a due perfection as Aquinas would say. For example, order/union of a marital type necessarily precludes the same type of union with another, but the lack of the second order/union is not a privation. Another union is contrary to the first and lacking it preserves the first union. Likewise, just as particular goods can conflict and become contrary, one must say that particular orders/unions can be contrary to others in the proper sense and are not negations/privations. Peace is sometimes a categorical relation, which would make sense how diverse relationships to the same end/object can all be good and exclude one another or how diverse orderings to diverse ends can come into conflict but be good in themselves.

In addition, just as relation belongs to both the transcendental and categorical orders, peace does as well. In the categorical order, one can distinguish between the subject of peace, the term of peace, and the foundation of the relation (which is an act), and the union/order itself, the *ad aliud* of relation.[190] Put differently, just as having a particular category dedicated to relation does not prevent it from also belonging to the transcendental order, so too with peace. Throughout the text, this must be kept in mind. If we are speaking of order/union which is consequent upon a subject and founded in an act, then we are speaking about categorical peace. If we are speaking about order/union that is identical to the relation, where the relation is the subject and is identical to the act, then we are speaking about transcendental order/union. The contrary of peace appears differently in these two orders—one as a privation or a negation and the other as a proper contrary. In other words, order/union could simply *per accidens* exclude another order/union in the categorical sense.[191] This is especially clear, as we shall see in the next chapter,

190. Svoboda, "Aquinas on Real Relation," in *Theologica,* vol. 6, is. 1 (2016): 147–72; see page 150.

191. Cf. *ST* I q. 49, a. 1, co.

that adherence to a deeper order/union (good) may require the loss of a lesser order/union (good) and might even require the loss of a proximate order/union with the good (e.g. sadness). Following from this, it is true that a particular order/union can introduce disorder/disunion in the sense of negation or privation.[192]

Nevertheless, even in these cases where particular orders/unions conflict, the opposite of peace (the very disorder/disunion) is still a privation or negation. Orders/unions can be particularly opposed, but when any order/union is lacking it is a privation or negation of order/union—it takes the mind to recognize non-being in other words. One does not have to make disorder/disunion an *aliquid* to recognize this. Put simply, just like evil (which Aquinas does identify as the opposite of peace at least once), disorder/disunion in the relevant sense is a privation.[193] It is true that not all things are at peace, but they are not at peace to the degree to which they lack order/union with the good, both internally and externally. In this, again, peace tracks onto the good. If the relative contrariety of one particular good to another is not an objection against the good's transcendental status, then it cannot be an objection against peace either. Something is not said to be more or less disturbed, more or less in conflict, more or less disquieted, etc. because it is a participation in disunion or disorder itself, but rather because it is more or less removes that on which it depends, *ordo/unio* (ultimately the good).[194]

Finally, peace, just like the good, admits of true and false instantiations. How it is possible to have false peace tracks onto Aquinas's explanations of how it is possible to have a false good. Metaphysically, this does not seem to be possible since something is good inasmuch as it is. Nevertheless, freedom introduces the possibility of pursuing something which is merely apparently good. The same is true for peace. By pursuing disorder/disunion or disquiet/discord

<hr>

192. Cf. *ST* I q. 49, a. 1, co.

193. Only what is evil is contrary to peace, see *ST* II-II q. 40, a. 1, ad 3; *II Sent.,* d. 37, l. 3, a. 1, ad 1.

194. Cf. *De Malo,* q. 1, a. 1, ad 13.

under the guise of order/union and rest/concord will result not only in a lack of order/union but also a lack of rest/tranquility.[195]

Aquinas is very committed to this point. It follows from his metaphysics of the good, but also some clear statements of Scripture. Authentic peace is only found in the true good.[196] The wicked cannot enjoy peace, qua wicked.[197] As Aquinas says, "[the peace of the world and of Christ] differ inasmuch as one is simulated, and one is true."[198] Though I introduced some Thomistic qualifiers to this statement earlier, one can see why Aquinas says it. When the peace of the world is based on a false good (a privation), it is a false peace and brings no true union/order. This simply follows from his metaphysics. Aquinas claims that since evil is parasitic on the good, one can never have evil itself, desire it for itself, or enjoy it by itself. Peace is the same. It would make no metaphysical sense to say that disorder/disunion exists on its own, one desires it for its own sake (without some good attending/attached), or one enjoys it. It must always be parasitic on order/union. If this is true, then we should understand Aquinas's claims that there is a false peace, a simulated peace, etc. as claiming that this is not peace at all. Though we might say that a band of thieves has some kind of union/order—some kind of grouping—the order/union (inasmuch as it turned toward evil) should not be thought of as real, but merely an *ens rationis*. It would be similar to the demonic "order" in Aquinas. The union of the demonic city in Aquinas includes no shared good and no common

---

195. David Oderberg, *The Metaphysics of Good and Evil* (Abdingdon, Oxfordshire: Routledge, 2019), chapter 1.

196. Cf. *ST* II-II q. 29, a. 2, ad 4: "*Ad quartum dicendum quod, cum vera pax non sit nisi de bono, sicut dupliciter habetur verum bonum, scilicet perfecte et imperfecte, ita est duplex pax vera. Una quidem perfecta, quae consistit in perfecta fruitione summi boni, per quam omnes appetitus uniuntur quietati in uno. Et hic est ultimus finis creaturae rationalis, secundum illud Psalm., qui posuit fines tuos pacem. Alia vero est pax imperfecta, quae habetur in hoc mundo. Quia etsi principalis animae motus quiescat in Deo, sunt tamen aliqua repugnantia et intus et extra quae perturbant hanc pacem.*"

197. Cf. *Super Is.*, c. 48; *Super Jer.*, c. 14, l. 4 & c. 16, l. 1; *Super Iob* c. 9; *Super II Cor.*, c. 13, l. 3, n. 542.

198. *Super Io.*, c. 14, l. 7: "*Secundo vero quantum ad simulationem et veritatem: quia pax mundi est simulata, quia tantum exterius.*"

will. Their wills do not terminate in the good and so have no true sharing; truly, each one's will terminates in itself and has no union/order to the others inasmuch as their cooperation is ordered toward evil. Of course, they are still a part of the union of the whole of creation/God's order, but this does not imply that they have peace in themselves.[199]

Something similar can be said of rest/tranquility. One can find some element of order/union with a good in a sinful way that will quiet the appetites partially and for a time. But this is only true because what is attained is authentically good in some other way, not because disorder/disunion quiets the appetite. In other words, it retains something of proper order/union to the good even if the disorder/disunion specifies it. The same should be said for peace. If union and order are *rationes* of the good, then what is good cannot lack order/union and concomitant rest. Only the good is identical to *esse* in subject and therefore brings with it order/union. Without the good there will be no order/union. On the other hand, in general this would (as said above) not rule out the conflict of particular unions/orders with each other, or the possibility that what is ordered/united is *per accidens* the introduction of disorder/disunion into another.

In summary, it seems that peace has a transcendental aspect that adds to the good conceptually.[200] It adds nothing beyond the *ratio* of the good but is itself a conceptual outflow of that same *ratio*. What is good is desirable; what is desirable is a final cause; what is a final cause is order. What is ordered/unified is not in conflict and is at rest. Just like what is *ens* is *unum* (lacking division), what is good is at peace (ordered/unified, at rest, and lacking conflict).

---

199. Serge-Thomas Bonino, *Angels and Demons: A Catholic Introduction* (Washington DC: The Catholic University of America Press, 2016), 280ff.

200. In addition to the argument, the historical connection of the transcendentals to divine naming strengthens the case since Aquinas calls God peace itself. See J. Aertsen, "Good as Transcendental and the Transcendence of the Good," in: S. Macdonald (ed.), *Being and Goodness: The Concept of the Good in Metaphysics and Philosophical Theology,* (Ithaca, NY: Cornell University Press, 1991), 56–73.

## Objections (and Possible Responses) to the Claim
## that Peace is a Transcendental of the Good

Inevitably the claim that peace is a quasi-transcendental will be controversial. I want to use this section to address some objections.[201] The first objection is that Aquinas uses definitional language to speak about peace. Yet, a transcendental cannot be defined. The second objection claims that if peace is a transcendental, then the other aspects of appetite—joy and desire must be transcendentals too. Yet this is absurd. According to this objection, peace is a proper accident, like joy or pleasure, which follows from the attainment of the end.[202] Finally, Aquinas says multiple times that peace is consequent (or antecedent, depending on the text) to the good but a transcendental cannot be consequent to the good. It must be identical, *in subiecto,* to the good. As we shall see, these objections seem to miss two essential features of peace. First, peace can be both transcendental and categorical. Second, peace comes in a positive *ratio* that is identical with *esse* and a negative *ratio* that is a negation (not an addition to being). Once both are grasped, it seems to be easier to articulate answers to the objections.

The first objection, that Aquinas says you can define peace but transcendentals cannot be defined is a good objection. This is because a definition requires a genus and a specific difference. What is defined must be circumscribed to one category and not another. A transcendental, on the other hand, must transcend the categories and be identical, *in subiecto,* with being. Since being cannot be defined (as there is no category broader than it and nothing outside of it), neither can the transcendentals. This is why Aquinas describes the relational transcendentals by effect, but does not define them in the strict sense.[203] In other words, if Aquinas defines peace, then it

---

201. These objections are inspired by Michael Sherwin's objections, e-mail message to the author, September 11, 2019.

202. Cf. Odon Lottin, *Morale Fondamentale* (Tournai: Desclée & Co, 1954), 160.

203. Cf. *De Ver.,* q. 1, a. 1, co.; *De Ver.,* q. 21, a. 1, co. Aertsen, *Medieval Philosophy and the Transcendentals,* 91ff.

would certainly not be a transcendental. Further, Aquinas does say that peace can be defined in *ST* II-II q. 29, a. 1, co. So, peace cannot be a (quasi) transcendental in any Thomistic sense.

What this objection misses is a wider exposure to Aquinas's writings. Aquinas only uses definitional language once and this to relay what Augustine says, not what he himself says.[204] When Aquinas is speaking in his own voice, he always uses one of two verbs to describe peace: *consistere* or *importere*. *Consistere* is the verb Aquinas uses regularly when he asks about the *ratio* of the good.[205] Aquinas also uses *importere* to describe the *ratio* of *bonum*. Likewise, Aquinas is not always precise with his terms and so it would be hasty to conclude that Aquinas thinks you can define peace because he uses the term *definire*. For example, Aquinas uses the term *definire* in relation to the good, but that does not stop him from thinking it is a transcendental.[206] He does the same with *verum*. That does not imply it is categorical.[207] Something similar should be said about peace.

I would also say that even if Aquinas uses definitional language, that does not rule out peace being a transcendental for another reason. It is the type of definition which is in question. The relational transcendentals are "defined" by effect, not by genus and species; they transcend the categories and genera. The positive *ratio* of peace, *ordo/unio,* is identical *in subiecto* with the good.[208] It is part of the essence of the good. Aquinas is quite explicit about this.[209] The negative *ratio* of peace is the effect of the positive *ratio* and is thus the most specific description of peace, but not in the sense of being a species of order/union. It is the effect order/union have on the individual—bringing rest/tranquility. Put differently, since

---

204. Cf. *ST* II-II q. 29 a. 2, co.: "*quam Augustinus definit tranquillitatem ordinis.*" Aquinas may seem to use the language in *In de Div. Nom.*, 11.1.891, but his sense of *diffinitio* there is talking about a limit to a created thing, not a definition of peace.

205. Cf. *ST* I q. 5, pr.

206. Cf. *De Malo*, q. 1, a. 1: "*secundum philosophum in I Ethic., optime definierunt bonum dicentes, quod bonum est quod omnia appetunt.*"

207. Cf. *De Ver.*, q. 1, a. 1, co.

208. Cf. *De Ver.*, q. 21, a. 1, co.

209. Cf. *ST* II-II q. 5, a. 5, co.

rest and tranquility are negations, rest/tranquility are denials that order/union can, in itself, be chaotic. Plus, rest/tranquility are negations and negations cannot be specifications of *ens reale*.[210] Furthermore, it is not precisely the case that union/order have an effect on us that is rest/tranquility. Rest/tranquility are simply claims about what union/order are. All of this is exactly what one would expect to find in the case of a transcendental. For these reasons, and those given above (where peace as order/union clearly applies to the transcendental order), it seems best to claim peace is a quasi-transcendental.

The second objection is a kind of *reductio ad absurdum*. If peace is a transcendental, then the other appetitive aspects which are part of our order to the good, desire and joy, must be also. Aquinas also says that joy adds nothing beyond the *ratio* of the good. To conclude that joy is a transcendental is absurd. Who would claim that joy is a transcendental? It is clearly a quality and an act. So too with peace, it is a quality which follows from the attainment of the end. In *ST* II-II q. 29, a. 4, Aquinas is clearly using his thought about accidents flowing from subjects in an orderly way and claiming that peace is an accident in this way.[211] It may be a proper accident, but it is not identical in subject with the good. Desire, love, and joy are clearly appetitive and ordered, but are particular ways of participating in order or being ordered; they are not order itself. They are not general enough to be transcendental.

This objection has much more force against the negative *ratio* of peace. Considering *ordo/unio* itself, the positive *ratio*, Aquinas seems to think it is essential to the good. For one must remember that the good is a relational transcendental. *Ordo/unio* is a transcendental because it is the most general form a relation can take and is part of the *ratio* of the good. Likewise, using the proper accidents of love, one

---

210. *De Pot.,* q. 7, a. 2, ad 1; *ST* I q. 16, a. 3, ad 2; *ST* I-II q. 36, a. 1, co. As Aquinas says, negations and privations do have being in the mind and can thus take on contrariety.

211. Cf. *ST* II-II q. 29, a. 4, co.: "*dicendum quod, sicut supra dictum est, cum omnes actus se invicem consequuntur, secundum eandem rationem ab agente procedentes, omnes huiusmodi actus ab una virtute procedunt, nec habent singuli singulas virtutes a quibus procedant.*"

must admit that they themselves flow in an orderly way and are in union with each other. So, peace cannot simply be one among them if it conceptually makes sense of their relation to each other and to their subject. This is true of the 10 categories also—they are related to each other (ordered/in union) by their relation to substance.[212] One of the categories cannot apply to them all. Order/union is so general, it must be thought to be a transcendental concept—it transcends the categories of substance and accident. Peace, as a particular order/union, may flow from charity, but that does not exhaust it.

Furthermore, if one admits *ordo/unio* is a transcendental of the good, then it would seem difficult to deny that rest/tranquility is too. *Quies/tranquillitas* follow immediately as what *ordo/unio* precludes. To admit one seems to be to admit the other unless order/union could be disorder/disunion, which is absurd. It is the negational/privational aspect of the *ratio* of peace that pushes us to this conclusion. Peace (as rest/tranquility) is a negation whereas love/desire/joy are positive additions to order/union, specifications in the proper sense. Peace, in its negative aspect, is not a something. Love/desire/joy are somethings, qualities of the soul and actions. The claim that rest/tranquility is a negation allows it to be of the transcendental order. If the negative *ratio* of peace were positive, then it might be different. It would be something in addition to order/union. As a negation, it cannot be a specifying difference and so can also be a quasi-transcendental. Put differently, peace is not simply an effect of the good on us, but an aspect of the good itself as well as an effect on us.

The final objection claims that peace cannot be a transcendental because it is antecedent or consequent to the good; it is based on the achievement of the good and so cannot be identical with the good. This is just an additional reason piggybacking on the second objection. Nevertheless, this objection has strong textual bases in

---

212. Cf. Ramirez, *De Ordine*, 31: "*ita accidentia substantiae corporeae dicuntur entia analogice, per ordinem, respectum vel attributionem secundum prius et posterius ad substantiam ut ad subiectum primum inhaesionis.*"

Aquinas. Aquinas explicitly distinguishes between what is essential, antecedent, and what is consequent (to the good).[213] Peace would seem to be consequent to the good, since it is caused by the achievement of it. This would seem to imply that peace cannot be of the essence of the good. Indeed, in response to an objection arguing that peace is happiness, Aquinas says specifically that peace is both antecedent to happiness as well as consequent to it, clearly implying that peace is not essential.[214]

As a response to this objection, two counter points can be made. First, in a sense, this objection proves too much. Aquinas calls *ordo* consequent and yet still says it is essential to the good. In other words, the distinction between what is essential, antecedent, and consequent is not strict. Second, it seems we should distinguish between what is consequent logically and what is consequent naturally (as an effect from a cause). Aquinas says that *ordo* is essential and consequent to the good.[215] What he seems to mean is consequent logically. In other words, consequent need not mean something is not of the *ratio* if you are speaking of logical consequence and not natural consequence. Something can be consequent conceptually and still be a transcendental. *Bonum* is consequent to *ens* and *unum*, but it is still a transcendental, identical *in subiecto* to *ens*. Something similar should be said about peace's relation to the good.

Though I do not think the case for peace's transcendental status has been made with certainty, the above arguments and responses make it probable that Aquinas *implied* that peace was a transcendental of the good. Peace is not an independent transcendental, adding conceptual content apart from the good. Peace is itself a conceptual explanation of the good. What is good is ordered/in union (as a rela-

---

213. Cf. *ST* I-II q. 3, a. 3, co.

214. Cf. *ST* I-II q. 3, a. 4, ad 1: "*Ad primum ergo dicendum quod pax pertinet ad ultimum hominis finem, non quasi essentialiter sit ipsa beatitudo; sed quia antecedenter et consequenter se habet ad ipsam. Antecedenter quidem, inquantum iam sunt remota omnia perturbantia, et impedientia ab ultimo fine. Consequenter vero, inquantum iam homo, adepto ultimo fine, remanet pacatus, suo desiderio quietato.*"

215. Cf. *ST* I q. 5, a. a. 5, co.

tional transcendental). What is good is at rest/tranquil. As Aquinas says, "God produces peace effectively *in rebus*."[216]

## PEACE: WHAT IS THE SOURCE?

Whereas understanding peace in terms of final and formal causality is relatively complicated, understanding peace relative to efficient causality is (mostly) straightforward. Relative to the efficient order, there are two important (and related) topics that need to be treated in general. First, I need to further explain the relation between peace and its principle/source (efficient cause). This will allow us to see another concrete illustration of Aquinas's commitment that order follows the causes. Second, I need to disambiguate some texts of Aquinas that seem to suggest that both the intellect and the will are the source of peace for humans.

To ask about the relation of peace to efficient causality is to ask what the agent of peace is. In other words, what is the agent or source of order/union? When asking about the agent cause of peace, I am principally asking about the positive *ratio* of peace: order/union. Peace, in its negative *ratio* is a negation. A negation cannot be the object of *per se* causality according to Aquinas.[217] So one must ask the question about peace's positive *ratio*. Nevertheless, this ropes in the negative *ratio* necessarily. Order/union preclude motion/conflict.

To begin, Aquinas claims that order/union needs a singular cause. In commenting on Jn 1:1, Aquinas writes: "... it is necessary that we find a principle in all things in which there is order."[218] In one sense this is clear. All things require a principle, so order too must require a principle/source. What is less clear is why this is the case. Why does order/union require a cause in particular? Aquinas does not explain in this passage, and so we must hunt through his works

216. *In de Div. Nom.*, c. 11, l. 1, n. 885.
217. Cf. *De Pot.*, q. 3, a. 6, ad 1.
218. *Super Io.*, c. 1, l. 1, n. 34: "*Cum enim principium importet ordinem quemdam ad alia, necesse est invenire principium in omnibus, in quibus est ordo.*"

for an explanation. Yet once one is found, it proves central for understanding his thought on the relation of order/union to its source.

In his disputed questions on the power of God, q. 3, a. 6, Aquinas argues that there must be only one principle of creation. His reasoning here proves definitive for understanding the need for a singular source of order/union (inasmuch as the order/union is one order/union). In this question, Aquinas is arguing against a dualism which would hold two principles of creation in opposition. He offers two arguments against dualism. The first goes as follows: "Whenever different things have one thing in common, they must be referred to one cause in respect of that common thing. This is true since either one is the cause of the other or they both proceed from a common cause seeing that it is impossible for that which they have in common to be derived from the properties in which they differ."[219] This is true for order/union too. If things belong to one order (i.e. have a common union to a source and to each other), they must come from a singular cause. The one order is common to them and so requires it come from a common source. The second argument complements the first. Aquinas writes: "If diverse beings would be wholly from contrary principles and not reduced to one principle, they would not be able to concur in one order except by accident."[220]

Recall the way Aquinas defines order: the determinate relation (union) of one thing to another. How do two things come to be related/in union? According to Aquinas, it is by one being the cause of the other, thereby giving rise to the order between them (or from the effect to the cause only), or by having them share a common cause. Without one of these two conditions, the two things will not have a determinate relation and so will have no real order to each other. They will not be in union in any way. Aquinas's claim that order/union must have a singular cause is thus explained. Order in intrinsically marked by its *secundum quid* oneness. If that is not there, there

---

219. *De Pot.*, q. 3, a. 6, co.

220. *De Pot.*, q. 3, a. 6, co.: "*si diversa entia essent omnino a contrariis principiis in unum principium non reductis, non possent in unum ordinem concurrere nisi per accidens.*"

is no order. That union comes from the sharing in a singular source. The unity of the agent cause is one explanation of the order/union that follows (others belonging to the other categories of causality).

Here we see again, as argued above concerning the positive *ratio* of peace, the deep consonance between union and order. Order *qua* order is marked by union. Without this it is not order at all. Yet it is not unity in the strict sense (substantial identity), but rather *secundum quid* unity, i.e. union, that marks order. Put simply, to be order there must be union between the differing elements of that order to each other and to their cause. The union as a definite relation of each to each other and to the cause is the same as the definite relation, at least *ad rem,* that constitutes the order itself. This is so because effects have something in common with their cause and so in common with others caused by that thing. The union to the cause is the metaphysical reason there is order/union/relation to others like it.

Here also we see why Aquinas defines chance relative to a certain order/union. If the source of an order/union is not one (i.e., there is no order/union), then two things can only be related *per accidens.* In other words, they do not inhabit the same order if their causes are (ultimately and totally) diverse. Chance is the production of an effect which is not intended (in the broad sense) by any of the agents.[221] Chance itself is not a *per se* being or cause.[222] It works in the reverse as well. Aquinas argues, if we find order within things and between things—they have a range of effects which come about regularly and for the most part, interacting in predictable and stable ways—order cannot be explained by chance. Further, since the presence of order/union does not indicate chance, order/union must have a single principle. That is, if order is a determinate relation, either of elements to each other or to their cause, then diverse causes will give rise to diverse relations and thus to diverse orders and only *per accidens* relations, which occur irregularly.[223] In other words, the

---

221. Cf. *ST* I q. 47, a. 1, co.
222. Wippel, *The Metaphysical Thought of Thomas Aquinas,* 483.
223. Wippel, *The Metaphysical Thought of Thomas Aquinas,* 482.

efficient cause is the source of the relation between the parts and their relation to the whole. It is the source of order/union. Chance occurs when two orders, which do not share proximate causes, meet and an unexpected outcome occurs.

The final issue for this section is that Aquinas seems to suggest that both intellect and will are the source of peace. On the one hand he says: "peace ... is the work of charity directly because charity causes [*causat*] peace according to its proper *rationem*."[224] Yet only a few questions on, he says "it belongs to charity to have peace, but to wisdom to make [*facere*] peace."[225] These do not seem to be easily reconcilable, since to make *facere* denotes a cause. In other words, Aquinas seems to say both that the wisdom (seated in the intellect) and the will (seated in the will) are the proximate sources of order/union in humans. Likewise, he regularly suggests that the will is the subject of peace. Nevertheless, he also suggests that the intellect has an order/union to its object and can be at rest (peace).[226] He also says at least once that peace is the *finis* of the mind.

Initially, two readings of these texts can be ruled out. The first would try to make a distinction between *facere* and *causere,* with the intellect doing one and the will the other. This is unlikely as a real solution since Aquinas seems to use them synonymously elsewhere and does not always use language precisely. The second, though seemingly better, also proves fruitless. It might seem that if one reads the quotations closely, that Aquinas is talking about different *rationes* of peace in each of them. Wisdom (as informing the intellect) causes peace in its positive *ratio,* order/union. Charity causes peace in its negative *ratio,* rest/tranquility. Yet this cannot be right either. Though Aquinas does say charity causes peace in its proper *ratio* (which would seem to be rest/tranquility), he explains in the same response that love is the union of appetites (*unio/ordo*). In other words, he is talking about order/union in the appetites when

---

224. *ST* II-II q. 29, a. 3, ad 3.
225. *ST* II-II q. 45, a. 6, ad 1.
226. Cf. *ST* I q. 16, a. 1, co. "*dicendum quod, sicut bonum nominat id in quod tendit appetitus, ita verum nominat id in quod tendit intellectus.*" *ST* I q. 79, a. 8.

he says that charity causes peace, not rest/tranquility. So, it does not seem possible that wisdom causes the positive *ratio* of peace and charity the negative *ratio.*

I think the most likely solution makes a distinction in the types of causality (not necessarily based on the terms Aquinas uses though) and sees intellect and will working in concert to produce peace. According to this solution, the intellect causes order/union in a formal way because it is seated in the intellect. The intellect, as we know in Aquinas's mature corpus, specifies a human action as a formal cause.[227] So when Aquinas says that wisdom *facet* peace, he means as a formal cause. The will, on the other hand, causes order/ union in an efficient way (but is order/union in another way). The will, as we know in Aquinas's mature corpus, causes as an efficient cause. It makes sense why Aquinas would use the language of causality for both the will and the intellect then. They both cause order/ union but in different ways.

There is no contradiction between these two texts because Aquinas has in mind different types of causality for the intellect and will bringing order/union to human life. The intellect recognizes and produces the right order of the universe and how actions are ordered accordingly. Informed by wisdom, it knows the highest causes and specifies them so that the will may command actions and virtues (and thoughts) accordingly. In other words, the will is the efficient cause of order/union by exercising this order and obtaining the good. Furthermore, this solution accords with what I found in the last chapter concerning the relation of peace to final causality via appetite. This solution, likewise (as we shall see in the next section), helps make sense of why Aquinas claims that the intellect can be the subject of peace as well.

227. Cf. Michael Sherwin, *By Knowledge and By Love* (Washington DC: The Catholic University of America Press, 2005), 169ff.

### WHAT CAN BE AT PEACE? PEACE
### AND *MATERIAL* CAUSALITY

As we have seen, appetite is central to Aquinas's philosophy of
peace. This leads some Thomists to severely limit what subjects can
be at peace, properly speaking. For example, Ramirez claims that
only beings with a rational appetite can be at peace.[228] Put differently, for Ramirez, only beings with rational appetites can have peace
as a subject (be the material cause). In this section, I want to claim
something radically different. Not only is Aquinas willing to predicate peace of beings with non-rational appetites (e.g.,the sensitive
appetites), but is even willing to predicate peace of a non-appetitive
power. To develop this argument, I will first make the claim that the
intellect can be the subject of peace. If this is correct, then it would
seem to allow a greater participation in peace by subjects which are
not appetitive properly speaking (as well as confirming that those
with appetite in any sense can also be at peace). Peace has a special
link to the order of appetite, certainly, but should not be limited in
subject (material causality) to that order.

The distinctions forged in the last section concerning the source
of peace: intellect (specification and formal), will (exercise and efficient), and the subject in which peace adheres (material) help to
ground my argument. The intellect, inasmuch as it is specified by
relation to the truth, is certainly not an appetite, but the *rationes* of
peace can clearly be predicated of it as a subject. The intellect, according to Aquinas, is ordered by its very nature to the truth.[229] It is
specified by this relation, in fact. In some sense, the equivalent of
affective union is present in the intellect in relation to its object: a

228. Cf. Ramirez, *De Caritate*, 887: "*Decimos en primer término que para la ver dadera
paz se requiere el orden de todos los pensamientos y deseos o afectos de cada individuo consigo
mismo, o de unos individuos con otros, según se trate de la paz individual o de la paz social.
Porque la materia propia de la paz no es el ser con sus aptitudes o apetitos innatos—a no ser
que tomemos la palabra paz en un sentido figurado y metafórico—sino el obrar racional y
libre en cuanto que se traduce y manifiesta especialmente en sus aspiraciones, en sus deseos y en
sus afectos, pues la paz tiene razón de bien, que es el objeto propio de las facultades apetitivas.*"
229. Cf. *ST* I q. 16, a. 1, co.

primordial union by which the intellect itself is specified.[230] It may take the will to exercise this order (reach the good of the intellect) and so the will is the source of this order in exercise, but the will is not the source of this order absolutely speaking. For that the will would have to cause the intellect to exist. Put differently, the will is the source in the order of exercise for all our powers, but not of their inclinations or specification. The will causes effective union with the good of a power (and then only for human acts, not acts of a human), but not primordial order/union. As one can see, the positive *ratio* of peace can be predicated of the intellect.

Likewise, Aquinas often says that the intellect rests in the truth. In other words, it can be the subject of *quies*.[231] If the will moves the intellect to obtain the truth, it is the intellect that rests therein qua truth (not the will). This is the *ratio* of peace—order/union and rest/tranquility. Likewise, it does not seem right to say that this is metaphorical language.[232] The order/union of the intellect to the truth is not simply predicated because it is like the order/union of the will to the good.[233] Clearly, the intellect can be the subject of peace for it is the intellect which is in union with the truth and rests in it. I think there is one main confusion driving the claim that only the appetitive order can be the subject of peace. First, the main confusion comes when there is a lack of distinction between the source of order/union and the subject of it. These are not the same thing, just as the efficient cause and the material cause are not the same thing. Any power of the soul or created thing can be the subject of peace, though in exercise it is always appetite/inclination/disposition which is the secondary efficient cause (and sometimes the subject also). Second, Aquinas does not limit appetite to the intellectual,

230. Cf. *ST* I q. 78, a. 1 & q. 79, a. 2.

231. Cf. *ScG* III c. 50, n. 5; *De Ver.*, q. 10 a. 12 ad s.c. 6.

232. Ramirez would probably counter that this is predication by analogy of proportionality. See Ramirez, "La Eucaristía," 174.

233. Alternatively, one might claim that this is an analogy of attribution since the appetitive and efficient order causes rest in the intellect. In some sense, it is cause and effect.

or even the sensitive, appetites. He is willing to predicate appetite (in some sense) of any existing thing. If that is the case (even if one wants to use a different term—such as inclination or disposition), it would seem to follow that there is order/union to the good there and subsequent rest/tranquility.

If the above is correct concerning the intellect, then it would seem to follow that non-rational creatures (even those without intellectual or sensitive appetites) can be the subject of peace. In other words, materially (as the subject in which peace adheres), any created being can be at peace. One can easily see why this must be the case for things are ordered toward their proper good. According to Aquinas, individuals are ordered toward the goods through disposition/inclination/appetite.[234] This is true of things both with and without intelligence, or even without appetite (if one wishes to limit the term to the intellectual or sensitive appetite). As Aquinas argues, things which exhibit regularity and achieve the best result for the most part, are clearly acting for an end. In other words, they have order/union to an end.

Nevertheless, Aquinas makes a distinction here. In those things with intelligence, their appetite is sufficiently explained by their self-direction toward the end.[235] This is because only rational beings can know the concept of an end and the relation between an act and the realization of that end.[236] In other words, only intellectual beings can produce (some) appetites in themselves (though of course this presupposes a more fundamental order to and union with the good and *synderesis*).[237] For non-intellectual beings, it is necessary to posit an external intelligence that explains why they act for ends without knowledge of an end or the relation of acts to ends.

Another way of approaching the claim that, materially speaking, anything can be the subject of peace is based on Aquinas's thought concerning form. Aquinas holds that all things have a form and from

---

234. Part of the confusion here is certainly the use of these terms.
235. Cf. *ST* I q. 2, a. 3, co.
236. Cf. *ST* I q. 6, a. 1, co.
237. Cf. *ST* I-II q. 79, a. 13, ad 3.

form necessarily follows an inclination to a range of effects/goods. "It is necessary that some inclination follow every form."[238] This is key to the claim that anything can be at peace. The relation between form, inclination, and good in all beings implies that union to the good and order to the good are a universal aspect of being, as was seen earlier in the chapter. Though it sounds odd to modern ears, Aquinas claims that all beings have inclinations, i.e. an ordering to a certain range of effects.[239] I suspect that most of the misunderstanding of Aquinas's position on this is because an individual takes 'inclination' as univocal and applies it only to conscious and self-directed desires in humans. How could a rock have an inclination or appetite? Yet for Aquinas appetite/inclination is an analogous term meaning an ordering toward certain ends/goods. For this reason, all things can be at peace. There is a primal ordering to the good/union with it as well as rest/tranquility to the extent it is achieved. Nor is rest/tranquility the predication of some kind of act on the part of a rock. Rest/tranquility is a negation. It does not involve any claim that a rock reposes in its end (if this is even the right example, since a rock more resembles a conglomerate without internal order/union than a substance).

Finally, and I think this is the best argument in favor of the claim that any being can be the subject of peace, Aquinas often predicates peace of non-rational creatures. If you look at a broader selection of Aquinas's writings, he predicates peace of non-rational appetites. Aquinas links peace to any kind of appetite: intellectual (the will), animal (sensitive), or natural.[240] He even predicates peace of internal bodily relations (health).[241] Health, obviously does not require the intellect to order/unify the body. In addition, Aquinas is willing to predicate appetite/inclination/tendency to any created being. As Reichberg says, "every single entity that exists—whether mineral,

---

238. *ST* I q. 80, a. 1, co.

239. For a modern defense see Oderberg, *The Metaphysics of Good and Evil*, 13ff.

240. Cf. *ST* II-II q. 29, a. 2, ad 1.

241. In this he is following Augustine. See Henri Rondet, S.J., *Pax, Tranquillitas Ordinis*, 345.

vegetal, animal, or rational—has an innate tendency (a 'natural inclination' or 'natural appetite') to its completion."[242] This is not metaphorical predication for Aquinas. It seems, rather, to trade on an analogous reading of the term appetite, which extends to all beings. In *de Div. Nom.*, 920 and 921, Aquinas argues that "nothing is totally able to exclude union, which is the *ratio* of peace."[243] He then argues this by linking union to existence. "In no way is something able to be existing per se or something in existence, as an accident or part, which would in every way lack union."[244] Aquinas follows this with four cases and exemplifies the principle. He concludes: "therefore nothing is totally able to exclude the union of peace for everything desires and loves that which conforms to itself and flees from that which is contrary. Thus, it is impossible for something to be *ens* which totally flees from union and desires alterity and distinction . . ."[245] Clearly then any created being, *ens,* is both at peace inasmuch as it is *ens* and can be the further subject of (categorical) peace. Treating peace according to material causality draws all of creation as subjects because order/union extend universally since they are *rationes* of the good.

242. Reichberg, "Human Nature, Peace, and War," 35.
243. *In de Div. Nom.*, 920.
244. *In de Div. Nom.*, 921.
245. *In de Div. Nom.*, 921.

3

## A Thomistic Theology of Peace

Though the previous chapter may give the picture that Aquinas's thought on peace is primarily philosophical, this is not the case. Certainly in order to discover the extent that Aquinas's thought is marked by peace, one must have some kind of conception of it. In this sense, the chapter on philosophy was necessary. Nevertheless, Aquinas is preeminently a theologian. His thought on peace is no exception to this. As we shall see, peace relates intimately to most theological topics in Aquinas. Though it takes interpretation and argument, I do not think it is an exaggeration to claim that Aquinas's thought on peace is compelling and encompasses everything from the Trinity through the Church. Peace marks the depths of God and is poured into the world through creation, which is a participation in the very peace of God. When sin and inevitable conflict disturb the peace of the world, God begins the return of all things to union with God, self, others, and creation. The goal is to create a redeemed community of peace, one animated by God's own love.

### PEACE AND THE DIVINE NATURE

It was relatively common in the Middle Ages for Islamic and Jewish philosophers to predicate peace of God, though it was a lot less common in Christian circles.[1] Historically, I will make no claim as to why this is the case, but the purpose of this section is to argue that Aquinas, at least, clearly thinks peace can be predicated of God. We saw this in chapter one. In his *Commentary on the Divine Names,* he even uses the language of *subsistens,* mimicking his typical phrase for predicating *esse* of God (*esse ipsum subsistens*).[2] The real question is how to make sense of this predication, especially in light of the *ratio* we discovered in the last chapter: *unio/ordo.*

As we saw in chapter one, Aquinas clearly predicates peace of God. This is not in dispute. When explaining how this is possible in his *Commentary on the Divine Names,* however, he uses the transcendental *unum.* Peace, he says, arises from unity. What is one in an absolute sense cannot but lack conflict. God is one in himself, admitting of no diversity.[3] In other words, God is not composed of divisible parts, is not numerical, and is in every way simple. Aquinas' language for God's simplicity and unity is forceful in this commentary. He distinguishes four ways in which unity can be said and claims God is the highest, *simpliciter and secundum se unum.*[4] He is the excess of unity, which is "above every unity."[5] Hence, God is peace itself. As is clear, Aquinas is here identifying the *ratio* of peace with the perfection of something absolutely indivisible, with the transcendental *unum.*[6]

This can be further explained using some traditional Thomistic categories. In those categories, names can be said of God affirmatively or negatively. If affirmatively it can be said absolutely or relatively (i.e. as a cause of that trait in creatures). If absolutely, it can be

---

1. Gregory Reichberg, "Human Nature, Peace, and War," 33.

2. *In de Div. Nom.,* c. 11, l. 2, n. 900: "*non est enim aliqua pax creata per se subsistens.*"

3. Cf. *In de Div. Nom.,* c. 11, l. 2, n. 896: "*Sed Deus intra seipsum est unus, quia nulla diversitas invenitur in ipso.*"

4. Cf. *In de Div. Nom.,* c. 11, l. 2, n. 911.

5. Cf. *In de Div. Nom.,* c. 11, l. 2, 896: "*sed propter excessum unitionis eius, quae superat omnem unitatem (...)*"

6. See Aertsen, *Medieval Philosophy and the Transcendentals,* 239–40 for the argument that the transcendental *unum* is a positive perfection and not simply a negation of division.

affirmed metaphorically or properly.[7] Where does Aquinas's predication of peace fall in this division? Because Aquinas likens peace to absolute unity and the transcendental *unum* is a positive perfection and not simply a denial of division, that would imply that peace too is affirmatively predicated.[8] Likewise, Aquinas uses the Dionysian language of supereminence when predicating peace of God. God's peace is the source and cause of peace in creatures surely. Peace, however, is not predicated of God simply because he is the source of it in creatures. Furthermore, it is clear Aquinas does not mean to predicate peace of God metaphorically. He wants to predicate peace of God in the strongest sense and even implies peace's identity with the divine *esse*. As he says elsewhere, "Only the divine *esse* is the principle and cause of all existing things."[9] If peace is a principle (as he also claims), then it must be reducible (in some sense) to the divine *esse*. Otherwise, Aquinas would not say that the divine peace is a cause.[10]

On the other hand, this is also puzzling. Aquinas seems to change the positive *ratio* of peace from union/order to unity. We saw in the last chapter that union and unity are not the same in concept. The positive *ratio* of peace is order/union. It has multitude or distinction in its *ratio*. Writing elsewhere Aquinas specifically distinguishes between union and unity. We saw this in the previous chapter and Aquinas makes the same distinction when discussing friendship: "each one, however, is united with himself, which is greater than union."[11] He affirms similar things elsewhere.[12] When Aquinas explains his predication of peace of God in this commentary, he

---

7. Gregory Rocca, *Speaking the Incomprehensible God* (Washington DC: The Catholic University of America Press, 2004), 318ff.

8. Aertsen, *Medieval Philosophy and the Transcendentals,* 239ff.

9. *In de Div. Nom.,* c. 11, l. 4, n. 930.

10. Cf. *In de Div. Nom.,* c. 11, l. 2, n. 898.

11. *ST* II-II q. 25, a. 4, co.

12. Cf. *In de Div. Nom.,* c. 11, l. 2, n. 911: "*Congregata enim minus habent de ratione unitatis quam unita: nam unitum absolute potest dici unum, licet non simpliciter, sed congregate absolute quidem sunt multa, sed secundum quid, unum.*" *ST* I q. 39, a. 8, co.: "*Connexio autem importat unitatem aliquorum duorum,*" *ST* III q. 2, a. 9; *ST* I q. 39, a. 8, co.

makes it clear that he means unity in the strict sense, what is *simpliciter and secundum se unum,* not what is *secundum quid unum.*[13] Peace presupposes distinction, oneness does not; *unum* is the perfection removing division.[14] Conceptually, at least, the two are distinct and this creates a problem. In what sense does Aquinas mean to predicate peace, taken strictly, of God? Is Aquinas inconsistent in claiming that unity is a *ratio* of peace?

Concerning the positive *ratio* of peace, it seems best to interpret Aquinas as claiming that unity can be predicated of God affirmatively, absolutely, and properly.[15] Because *unum* and *unitas* exceed *unio,* the perfection which is union approximates, i.e. the undividedness of being, exists preeminently in God.[16] It is important to note here in what sense *unitas* exceeds *unio.* Order/union approximates unity only inasmuch as it removes division in a certain sense by making multiple things into one in a certain respect. In other words, inasmuch as the *unio* is, it is *unum.* Once it is divided, it ceases to be *unio* because it is not *unum* in any sense. Division is overcome secondarily in *unio.* In this way, union is unity because it makes a multitude *unum* in a certain respect. Nevertheless, this is not to take order/union in its most proper sense because without the perfection of *unum* taken strictly there is still the possibility of divisibility and distinction is proper to the concept of *unio,* but not to *unum.* In this way, we can see the way in which *unio* approximates *unum* (concerning divisibility). Nevertheless, without revelation of the Trinity, one could not say there is distinction or alterity in God, both of which are required to properly predicate the positive *ratio* of peace in the strictest sense.[17] It seems that in Chapter 11 of Aquinas' *Commentary*

13. *In de Div. Nom.,* c. 11, l. 2, n. 910.

14. Cf. *ScG* IV c. 76, n. 4.

15. For an alternative reading of Aquinas, see Reichberg, "Human Nature, Peace, and War," 37.

16. In one sense, this reveals that a lack of motion/conflict is always caused by something being one. What is *unum* is not divided from itself and so cannot conflict with itself. Inasmuch as this is a perfection, it will be at rest to that extent. What is ordered/union also overcomes motion/conflict but in a more perfect way.

17. Cf. *In de Div. Nom.,* 920: *"alteritate et discretione." ST* II-II q. 29, a. 3, co.: *"duplex*

*on the Divine Names,* Aquinas is speaking philosophically. What is *secundum quid unum* is surpassed by what is *unum simpliciter* and hence one can say God is peace in a positive sense since he surpasses but also contains the perfection of what Aquinas means by peace in the strict sense—as *unio/ordo.*

Following from this one can philosophically predicate the negative *ratio* of peace of the divine nature, or rather deny motion/potency/obstacles of God. Because God is *unum simpliciter,* he is maximally at rest and without conflict. In other words, it seems that concerning the negative *ratio* of peace, *unum* can also *secundum quid* preclude motion, potency, obstacles, etc. What is absolutely indivisible in itself and related to no others (God), cannot have conflict internally or externally. From this, one could affirm that *unum* secondarily precludes conflict and the negative *ratio* of peace can be predicated following from unity. In this way, the predication of rest/tranquility is akin to the attribute *infinitum,* which implies only that God is not bound by anything. As we would expect, in this sense, Aquinas often affirms rest of God: God rests in the goodness of his own essence.[18] This is an uninterrupted and full rest. Likewise, if I am correct about *quies* being a negation, a denial of disunion/disorder, and about peace belonging to the transcendental order, then that God is at rest/tranquil is implied by his being *esse ipsum subsistens.* What is pure act must be at rest, for it lacks nothing of the good. A lack of peace implies a lack of the good. He who is unity itself must then be peace itself.

### PEACE AND THE TRINITY

It might seem that if the positive *ratio* of peace cannot be properly predicated of the divine nature, then certainly it cannot be predicated of the Trinity. If God exceeds union in his unity, then this

---

*unio est de ratione pacis*"; *ST* II-II q. 17, a. 3, co.: "*Unio autem est aliquorum distinctorum* (…)".

18. Cf. *ST* I q. 19, a. 1, co.

must be theologically true as well. However, according to Aquinas, these two predications do not conflict, even if "inasmuch as peace is considered in its very source, it exceeds all created understanding."[19] One can both predicate unity and union of God and there is no contradiction, only a *redoublement*.[20] The fact that we cannot predicate order/union of God philosophically simply comes from nescience. Nor does the claim that union only approximates the oneness of unity detract from the unity of the divine essence. Put simply, what Aquinas writes about the philosophical predication of peace does not exclude the proper predication of peace's positive *ratio*, order/union. The key to reconciling comes in Aquinas's strict definition of unity, his silence as to what constitutes the perfection of unity, and his claim that peace only requires distinction and not division.

Before attempting an explanation, I should first argue that Aquinas does think you can predicate order/union of the Trinity. Without this, no explanation is necessary. The key to predicating order/union is Aquinas's affirmation that there are real relations of opposition in God. "Certain relations are in God really."[21] What allows Aquinas to predicate relation of God is his distinction between that which is related (a substance in created things) and the *ad aliud* which is the relation. In this way, relation is unique amongst the categories, since "according to its proper *ratio* it only signifies reference to another."[22] Revelation teaches us that there are processions/persons in God and Aquinas uses this understanding of relation to make sense of revelation. According to Aquinas, person signifies what is incommunicable. In God person signifies subsistent relations of mutual opposition.[23] Hence, relation is singular among other accidents

---

19. *Super Phil.,* l. 4, c. 1, n. 159.

20. Gilles Emery, OP, "Essentialism or Personalism in the Treatise on God in St. Thomas Aquinas?," in *Trinity in Aquinas*, trans. Teresa Bede et al., 2nd ed. (Ann Arbor, MI: Sapientia Press, 2006), 165–208.

21. *ST* I q. 28, a. 1, co.

22. *ST* I q. 28, a. 1, co.

23. Cf. *ST* I q. 29, a. 4, co. & q. 36, a. 2, co.

"in being *properly* attributed to God according to its generic reason."[24] These distinctions of person arise simply from relations of origin, from the divine processions.[25] Because of the distinctions of origin between persons, one can say that there is plurality in God.[26] Aquinas is specific that this plurality is not difference or diversity, but there is distinction between the persons (subsistent relations) in God.[27] The divine essence is communicable and common, but the subsistent relations are not.

Recalling what was argued above, that order/union is reduced to relation, it seems easy to claim that there is order/union in the Trinity properly speaking. If there is (subsistent) relation in God, there must be order and union. Both union and order signify the *ad aliud* aspect of relation. What is *ad aliud* is ordered to the other and made one (in union) with the other. Relations of mutual opposition, and thus distinction, simply are both order and union. Confirming this, Aquinas spontaneously connects relation with order in his treatment of the Trinity. "When, however, something proceeds from a principle of the same nature, it is necessary that they both belong to the same order. And so it is necessary that they have relation to the other."[28] Elsewhere he uses stronger language: "If from the one person of the Father proceeds two persons, that is the Son and the Holy Spirit, it is necessary that there be a certain order between them."[29] According to Aquinas if a plurality proceeds from one, the only way they can do that without order (to each other) is with matter. That is clearly not an option, and so there must be order in God. In order to avoid positing some fourth thing which is the order, order must be reduced to the subsistent relations of the Persons. Order/union names the *ad aliud* aspect of relation; in the Trinity it names person.

24. Emery, "*Ad aliquid*," 183.
25. Cf. *ST* q. 27, a. 1.
26. Cf. *ST* I q. 30, a. 1.
27. Cf. *ST* I q. 31, a. 2, co.
28. *ST* I 28, a. 1, co.
29. *ST* I q. 36, a. 2, co.: "*Si ergo ab una persona patris procedunt duae personae, scilicet filius et spiritus sanctus, oportet esse aliquem ordinem eorum ad invicem.*"

Aquinas's thought on the Holy Spirit is a great example of this. Aquinas calls the Holy Spirit the union between the Father and the Son multiple times and in multiple places.[30] For example, in his *Commentary on Romans*, explaining why Paul does not mention the Holy Spirit at the end of his salutation. He offers two explanations. The Holy Spirit is understood in his "gifts and grace" or "is understood in the two persons of the Father and the Son, of whom he is their *unio et nexus*."[31] The Holy Spirit "proceeds from them as the unitive love of the two."[32] Love is a union because it implies the mutual indwelling of the lover and the beloved, the impression of the beloved on the lover. Because of this, St. Thomas writes: "The Holy Spirit is the bond of the Father and Son inasmuch as he is love because the Father loves himself and the Son by one and the same love. Conversely, there is expressed in the Holy Spirit, understood as love, the relation of the Father to the Son and the converse as a lover to his beloved. But from this fact, that the Father and Son mutually love each other, it is necessary that this mutual love, who is the Holy Spirit proceed from both."[33] This is so important for Aquinas that he even says that "without the Holy Spirit one could not understand the unity of connection between Father and Son."[34] This makes perfect sense if union and order are reduced to relation. The Holy Spirit is the proceeding relation of the Father and the Son, the fruit of their indwelling. He is love proceeding.[35]

---

30. Cf. *ST* I q. 37; *Super Io.*, c. 14, l. 7, n. 1961. *Super Rom.*, c. 1, l. 4: "*Persona autem Spiritus Sancti expresse non ponitur, quia intelligitur in donis eius, quae sunt gratia et pax; vel etiam quia intelligitur in duabus personis Patris et Filii, quarum est unio et nexus.*"

31. *Super Rom.*, l. 1, c. 4, n. 73.

32. *ST* I q. 36, a. 4, ad 1.

33. *ST* I q. 37, a. 2, ad 3.

34. *ST* I q. 39, a. 8.

35. Yet this gives rise to another problem. It seems clear that order is reduced to relation and Aquinas's Trinitarian theology confirms this. On the other hand, this does not seem to be possible for union. The Holy Spirit is not the relation between the Father and the Son—he is not the relation of mutual opposition between them. That would reduce the Holy Spirit to the persons of the Father and the Son or would make the Holy Spirit a medium between the Father and the Son. Neither is an option. Aquinas, however, is aware of this problem and addresses it. This tells us that he does mean to reduce union to relation or else he wouldn't see the problem. As far as making sense of how Aquinas

In short, Aquinas does claim that order/union are the Trinity. Because of this, the positive *ratio* of peace can be predicated of the Trinity. The Trinitarian Persons are subsisting order/union to each other. They are subsisting peace. This positive predication gives rise to the negative *ratio* of peace, which is predicated of God as a negation/remotion. The more particular *ratio* of peace does not require imperfection in the sense that one can be impeded or that one is not yet fully perfect. Recall, that those two things are signs that peace (as order/union) is imperfect. Rather, the negation of *rest/tranquility*, only requires that the order/union be full and undisturbed, negating motion and disturbance. God, on account of being subsisting goodness lacks nothing and has no potency. In perfect Trinitarian order/union, nothing is lacking. Hence, he is perfectly at rest and tranquil. When these terms are understood as negations, denials of imperfection, then their predication of God is seen more clearly. Furthermore, the negative *ratio* follows from the positive. If one can properly predicate order/union of the Trinity, then his rest and tranquility follow. If they did not, his order/union would be imperfect. This is not an option.

And yet a lingering question about unity and union remains. How is it possible that Aquinas affirms that both unity and order/union can be predicated of the Trinity and is yet still able to distinguish them? It turns out that Aquinas's solution to this problem is intimately linked with his thought on the transcendentals, his thought on *unum* and *multitudo*. Aquinas claims that unity (*unum*) is the denial of division.[36] Yet *unum* is not solely a negation. As Aertsen shows, *unum* signifies some kind of perfection of the being—its undividedness. "As Thomas himself remarks, a negation or privation as such is not susceptible of more or less. The reason he nevertheless

---

holds both that union is relation, the Holy Spirit is the relation of Father to Son, and that the Holy Spirit is not the principle or origin of that relation; see Emery, *The Trinitarian Theology of St. Thomas Aquinas,* 234ff. It is easy to see why this solution works, i.e. that the Holy Spirit proceeds from the union of the Father and Son (their relation of mutual opposition) and that the Holy Spirit is the blossom by which the two love each other, because union presupposes distinction (i.e. mutual opposition between Father and Son).

36. Cf. *ST* I q. 11, a. 4.

speaks of degrees of unity is that that which is denied by the one admits of gradation."[37] Multitude, likewise, for Aquinas is a perfection of being and is born of it. Aquinas distinguishes between multitude born of the numerical and multitude in the transcendental sense. In its transcendental sense, it "expresses that one thing is not another thing . . ."[38] Yet like *unum, multitudo* is not simply a negation but represents a positive perfection of being.[39]

This transcendental analysis implies that one can predicate both unity and order/union of the Trinity. Aquinas deals with this explicitly in his questions about unity and plurality in the Trinity. Therein he says, the persons of the Trinity are subsistent relations of opposition and thus distinct.[40] They are not, however, divisions of the divine nature. They are the divine nature subsisting with respect to another. Peace, in its positive *ratio*, only requires distinction. Distinction and plurality are not division.[41] What is *unum* is undivided. Peace, properly speaking, does not require division, but only distinction.[42] An ordered/unified multitude does not reintroduce division *per se*, but only requires distinction between subjects who are themselves undivided. As such relation (*ordo/unio*) is singular among the accidents. It consists solely in order/union with the other, *connexio*. It introduces no positive determination in the subject.[43] Theologically, this allows one to both make sense of the data of revelation and predicate transcendental multitude of God without implying he is not *simpliciter and secundum se unum*.[44] The trinitarian persons are

37. Aertsen, *Medieval Philosophy and the Transcendentals*, 240.

38. Aertsen, *Medieval Philosophy and the Transcendentals*, 224.

39. Cf. Aertsen, *Medieval Philosophy and the Transcendentals*, 225.

40. Cf. *ST* I q. 28, a. 3, co. Nevertheless, in predicating union and order of the Trinitarian persons, one must deny priority and posteriority. Priority and posteriority denote degree of influence from the principle. The Father is the principle of the Son and the Spirit, but both fully share the divine essence. Hence, there is no priority or posteriority.

41. Cf. *ST* I q. 31, a. 2, co.

42. Cf. *ST* I q. 30, a. 3, co.; *De Pot.*, q. 9, a. 7, co.; *ST* I q. 32, a. 2, co.: "*Unde sicubi in aliqua Scriptura authentica diversitas vel differentia personarum invenitur, sumitur diversitas vel differentia pro distinctione.*"

43. Cf. Emery, *The Trinitarian Theology of St. Thomas Aquinas*, 183.

44. Cf. Aertsen, *Medieval Philosophy and the Transcendentals*, 223ff.; Emery, *The Trinitarian Theology of St. Thomas Aquinas*, chapter 7.

not divisions of the divine nature but are distinct from one another in their very order/union to each other.[45] God is both unity and order/union, the fullness of *esse* and, therefore, of peace.

In addition, the relation of peace to Aquinas's trinitarian thought goes beyond the predication of peace outlined above. The very character of the trinitarian processions are also intimately related to peace. We see this especially in the processions of the Son and the Spirit. Aquinas's psychological analogy certainly implies this by using wisdom and love as modes of procession. So while each of the processions is order/union to the others (and are thereby tranquil/at rest), there is a particular way in which the Son and the Spirit are related to peace. We have seen this earlier when Aquinas appropriates *unio* to the Spirit. What remains to be briefly explored is Aquinas's claim that wisdom is predicated of the Son.

From about the middle of Aquinas's life, the name Word is central for his trinitarian theology.[46] It is Aquinas's preferred personal name for picking out the relation of being generated. Aquinas links the name Wisdom to the name Word. "It follows then that the same Word of God, as wisely conceived by the divine mind is properly said to be conceived Wisdom or begotten Wisdom."[47] In this way, Aquinas claims that Wisdom proceeds from the Father and fully manifests him. Yet it is in this full manifestation and sharing in nature that Wisdom also expresses God's knowledge of all creation. "The Word includes the operative plan of God's works."[48] By knowing himself, God knows all the different possible ways creatures could participate in his essence (as the divine exemplar of all things) and these are expressed in the Word, who is the exemplar of all things by appropriation.[49] As Aquinas says, "Through his

---

45. Cf. *ST* I q. 32, a. 2, co., ad 1: "*Sed diversitas requirit distinctionem substantiae quae est essentia. Et ideo non possumus dicere quod filius sit diversus a patre, licet sit alius.*"

46. In this section I am following Emery, *The Trinitarian Theology of St. Thomas Aquinas*, 192ff.

47. *ScG* IV c. 12, n. 3482.

48. *ST* I q. 34, a. 3, co.

49. Cf. *ScG* IV c. 13, n. 3490.

knowledge the Father knows himself, and in knowing himself, he knows all things. The consequence is that his Word also expresses primarily the Father himself, and following from that all other realities which the Father knows by knowing himself. Thus, because of the fact that he is the Word who perfectly expresses the Father, the Son expresses all creatures."[50] In this way, creatures have a special relation to the Word through whom they were made. This is the meaning Aquinas gives to Jn 1:3: "through whom all things were made."[51] In this way, all the possible participations in the divine nature and all the possible orders of creation have a kind of affinity with the Son.[52]

How does this relate to peace? The positive *ratio* of peace, union/order, helps us to answer this question. While the intra-trinitarian order cannot be said to be proper to the Son or appropriated to the Son, Wisdom can. Wisdom is here synonymous with the knowing of all orders/unions that creatures could have, the infinite possibilities of plurality in union that God could create.[53] In other words, all the possibilities of peace find their exemplar in the subsistent relation which is the Son. Put differently, the order/union of all creation can be said to have a relation of dependence according to formal causality on the subsistent relation which is Wisdom. There is a kind of cosmic affinity between all creatures to each other found in the Word. As Aquinas says,

> The Word has a kinship not only with rational natures, but also universally with every creature. For the Word contains the patterns of everything which God creates analogously to how the human artist has an intellectual conception which contains the models for his works of art. Thus, then, the totality of creatures are nothing but a kind of real expression and representation of that contained in the conception of the divine Word. This is why all things are said to be made by the Word.[54]

---

50. *De Ver.,* q. 4, a. 4, co.

51. *Super Io.,* c. 1, l. 3, n. 77.

52. Cf. *ScG* IV c. 42, n. 3803.

53. Jamie Spiering, "'The Divine Goodness Could Be Manifest through Other Creatures and Another Order': The Source of Aquinas's Convictions about Divine Freedom," in *The Thomist,* vo. 83, n. 1 (Jan 2019): 1–29.

54. *ScG* IV c. 42, n. 3803.

In conclusion, philosophically speaking it seems one could not predicate peace of the divine nature properly speaking. Without revelation, we have no knowledge God is a Tri-Unity. We saw in the last section that Aquinas does predicate peace, but thinks of its *ratio* only inasmuch as it denies division. This is not really the proper *ratio* of peace. The proper and positive *ratio* of peace is order/ union. This does preclude division in a certain sense (i.e. it makes things one *secundum quid*), but that is not its *per se* meaning. It's *per se* meaning does not require division, but only distinction (even if it reduces division *per accidens*). Once the Trinity has been revealed, the positive *ratio* of peace can be predicated in a straightforward way. There is distinction in the Trinity, but no division of the divine nature. The trinitarian persons are subsisting order to each other, and this requires the denial of motion/potency. In other words, peace can properly be predicated of each person and of the divine nature in different ways. In the divine nature there is unity precluding motion. God, the Trinity, in perfect subsisting act, is eternally at rest as order/union to each other. This is why creating peace is God's *proprius effectus*. God himself is peace.

### GOD'S CREATIVE ACTIVITY AND PEACE

As we saw in the first chapter, Aquinas's language is forceful concerning creature's participation in God's peace. All "participate in the divine peace."[55] We have seen how Aquinas calls peace God's "proper effect."[56] Making sense of these claims of exemplarity, participation, and causality is the purpose of this section.[57] This will require, first, a quick exposition of Aquinas's general thought on creation and then, second, an application to peace.

---

55. *In de Div. Nom.*, c. 11, l. 1, n. 892: *"dixit fieri in rebus per participationem divinae pacis."*

56. *Super Heb.* c. 13, l. 3: *"Proprius enim effectus Dei est facere pacem."*

57. Cf. McMahon, "A Thomistic Analysis of Peace," 179ff.

## God as the First Efficient, Exemplar,
## and Final Cause of the Universe

In ST I q. 44 Aquinas gives a good summary of how he conceives of God's creative activity. He divides these questions using different types of causality: efficient, formal, and final. In treating each of these types of causality, Aquinas makes it clear that God is the ultimate efficient, formal, and final cause of the universe.

God is the ultimate efficient cause of all existing things. Aquinas argues that all beings must be created by God. This is not an *ad hoc* argument for Aquinas but follows directly from how he conceives of the relation of efficient cause and effect. According to Aquinas, the cause gives a share of its perfection to the effect, which Aquinas often speaks of as form. Thus, whatever perfection is found in an effect must be in its cause (and there in a more eminent way—at least with equivocal causes). Because of this, the effect is a dependent relation on a source/cause (inasmuch as that perfection is considered). If one applies this picture to being, this implies that all beings which are not being itself must receive their being. They have perfection, *esse,* and since they are not that perfection, they must receive it from another. As Aquinas says: "Anything which is found in something through participation, it is necessary that it be caused by the very thing in which it is essentially found."[58] God is subsisting being and so all things which are beings by participation must have received their being from God.

In the creature, creation is a *"relationem tantum."* In other words, "In creatures creation is only a certain relation to the creator as the principle of its being."[59] Put another way, creation is a relation of dependence on God for existence.[60] It is not in the category of passion, but the genus of relation.[61] This implies that creatures are, in

---

58. *ST* I q. 44, a. 1.

59. *ST* I q. 45, a. 3, co.

60. I will leave open the debate of whether this dependence is the *esse* of the creature. For Aquinas's text, see *DPD* q. 7, a. 9.

61. Cf. Emery, *"Ad aliquid,"* 197

the order of efficient causality, dependent on God and thus in order/ union to him. Nevertheless, this is a mixed relation—where the relation is real on the part of creatures, but only logical on God's side. God is not ordered toward creatures; God is not in union with creatures properly speaking.[62] Rather, creatures are ordered toward/in union with God.

Exemplar causality is the next type of causality Aquinas treats. Exemplar causality is, according to Aquinas, a type of external formal causality.[63] It is necessary in the causal relationship that the effect receive a determinate form, i.e. this form/perfection instead of some other one. According to Aquinas, the determination of the perfection given can come in three ways which correspond to three types of exemplar causality: natural exemplar, external exemplar, and intellectual exemplar.[64] A natural exemplar is the agent's form inasmuch as it causes the effect to receive a determinate form.[65] Aquinas's typical example for this type of exemplarity is the univocal generation of animals[66] (though it also holds for equivocal causality).[67] Nevertheless, this is exemplarity only in a wide sense, since the agent does not determine its intended end and the form is intended by nature, not art.[68] The second sense of exemplar is an external exemplar, as the artist looks at a landscape as an external exemplar. Nevertheless, this sense of exemplar is also said improperly because the external exemplar only exercises its causality on the patient through

62. Cf. Emery, "*Ad aliquid,*" 196.

63. Cf. Gregory Doolan, *Aquinas on the Divine Ideas as Exemplar Causes* (Washington DC: The Catholic University of America Press, 2014), 42.

64. Cf. *De Ver.,* q. 3, a. 1, co.: "In one way, it is that from which a thing is formed, just as the informing of an effect proceeds from the form of the agent."

65. Doolan, *Aquinas on the Divine Ideas,* 21, n. 45: "Thomas does not himself employ the term 'natural exemplar,' although he does describe such a form as exercising a type of exemplarism. Moreover, he also notes that this sort of (natural) exemplarism can occur when the effect shares an analogous likeness to the agent's nature."

66. Cf. *ST* I, q. 44, a. 3, ad 1.

67. Cf. *De Ver.,* q. 3, a. 1, co.; *ST* I, q. 44, a. 3, ad 1.

68. Cf. Doolan, *Aquinas on the Divine Ideas,* 22. *De Ver.,* q. 3, a. 1, co. In this sense, natural exemplarity should not be thought of as accidental, but rather the end is set by a more primary agent. It is still the work of intelligence.

the intellectual exemplar.[69] The final instance of exemplarity, the intellectual exemplar, is the proper sense of exemplar. The intellectual exemplar is the form in the mind of the agent which causes a definite form in the patient by way of assimilation or imitation.[70] It measures both the end of the agent (termination of action) and the end of the patient (i.e. purpose or flourishing).[71]

As we saw above in Aquinas's trinitarian theology, Aquinas links exemplar causality very closely with order (and here we can see why). What was left out there was Aquinas's thought on the divine ideas. The divine ideas are part of divine wisdom, which devises the order of the universe in which the distinction and multitude of things are integral parts. In other words, God knows himself and by knowing his essence knows the infinite ways it can be imitated (the divine ideas).[72] This is intellectual exemplarity. These ideas are distinguished from each other by the definite mode of imitation and from God by the fact that they are all particular modes of being or deficient participations in his being.[73] As Doolan puts it, relative non-being enters into the mind of God and distinguishes the ideas from each other and from God.[74]

God's wisdom conceives of the order of this universe, the *forma totius,* and then gives it *esse.*[75] This *esse* is limited by the relative non-being of the divine idea (essence as recipient). The product thus perfectly imitates its divine idea and only participates in the divine essence, through both essence (through the divine ideas) and *esse.*[76] This most closely resembles natural exemplarity; though the

69. Cf. *ST* I, q. 44, a. 3.

70. Cf. *ST* I, q. 44, a. 3, co.; *De ver.,* q. 3, a. 1, co.; XII *Meta.,* l. 7, n. 2535.

71. Cf. XII *Meta.,* l. 7, n. 2535; *De ver.,* q. 3, a. 1, co.

72. Cf. *ST* I, q. 15, a. 2, co.: "For he understands his own essence perfectly. Whence, he understands it in all the ways by which it can be understood. God's essence is able, however, to be understood not only as it is in itself, but as it is able to be participated in according to a certain mode of similarity by the creature."

73. Cf. *ScG* I, c. 30, n. 6; *ScG* I, c. 54, nn. 4–5.

74. Doolan, *Aquinas on the Divine Ideas,* 235ff.

75. Note that though many orders are possible (*ScG* I, c. 81, n. 7), that does not preclude necessity within the order chosen. See also *ScG* II, c. 30 & 46.

76. Doolan, *Aquinas on the Divine Ideas,* 228.

causality is equivocal, there is still a certain analogical (not generic or specific) likeness and analogous predication.[77] Properly speaking, God does not have exemplar ideas of *esse* and the other transcendentals, but notions.[78] Since the transcendentals are only conceptually distinct from being, whatever God creates must have these *rationes*. In God's wisdom we are dealing with the intellectual exemplarity of all created effects. In God's creative activity, he gives *esse* and exemplifies by natural exemplarity, making other things like him in being (and those *rationes* following from it) was as they were conceived in his divine wisdom.

Furthermore, Aquinas not only claims that the divine ideas and the order of the universe are exemplified by the divine nature, but also by the divine persons. Aquinas's commitment that outside actions of the divine nature are common to the three persons is well known and an important part of his trinitarian theology. Nevertheless, this does not preclude him from claiming that the trinitarian persons are exemplars and causes of creation. Emery explains it thus:

> The Trinitarian distinctions and relations throw light on creation. The first distinction, that of the divine persons, is the cause of that other distinction which is the creation; for creation is the

---

77. Cf. *ST* I, q. 44, a. 3, co; *De Pot.*, q. 7, a. 1, ad 8: "The form of the effect is found in the agent through nature when the agent assimilates the effect to its own nature, since every agent makes something similar to itself. Now this happens in two ways. First, when the effect is perfectly assimilated to the agent, inasmuch as it is equal to the agent's power, then the form of the effect is in the agent according to the same *ratio*, as is the case for univocal agents (e.g. fire generates fire). When the effect is not truly assimilated to the agent, as it is not equal to the agent's power, then the form of the effect is not in the agent according to the same *ratio*, but in a higher way, as in an equivocal agent (e.g. when the sun generates fire). In agents who act through art, however, the effect's form preexists according to the same *ratio*, but not in the same mode of being, for in the effect the form has material being and in the mind of the artificer it has intelligible being. . . . But the divine art does not use an exterior nature for acting, but by the power of its own proper nature makes its effect. Therefore, the forms of things are in the divine nature as in an operative power, but not according to the same *ratio* since no effect is equal to that power."

78. For the distinction between notions and ideas see *ST* I, q. 15, a. 3, ad 4 & *In de Div. Nom.*, V, l. 3, n. 665. Granted, the transcendentals are, by necessity, always in God's created effects. However, no one would want to say that God produces these unknowingly or unintentionally, as if by accident. However, this does not amount to intellectual exemplarity, but only notional knowledge of being and its attributes.

production of the world really distinct from God, so creation creates a distinction. In the same way, the plurality of persons, the principle of which is relation, is the cause of the 'multiplication' of creation: the plurality of genus and species amongst creatures, and the multiplicity of individuals within species, the multiplicity of events produced within history, have the Trinitarian relations as their source. It is difficult to emphasize strongly enough what a positive value the multiplicity within the created world has. Plurality is not a falling away from unity, but rather a participation in the fullness of Trinitarian life.[79]

In other words, that goodness in its highest sense requires distinction and union is no mistake. The distinction in order/union is exemplified by God's own inner life. The very structure of the world is Trinitarian.

Not only is the distinction in order/union exemplified by the Trinity, but the specific trinitarian relations are exemplars of the peace of creation. Above we saw the linking of creation's order/union to the Son as Wisdom, that creatures receive a determinate form, are in order/union to each other and to God as part of an order of the universe is something that the particular subsistent relation of the Son contributes exemplarily as Wisdom. The Spirit, who proceeds by way of love (union), enters into creation as being the motive force for creation. As Aquinas says, "The Holy Spirit proceeds by way of the Love by which God loves himself. Therefore the Holy Spirit is the principle of all created things. . . . [for] the goodness of God is the reason for his willing other things to be, and by his will he produces things in being."[80] In this way the Son and Spirit exemplarily cause the coming forth of creatures according to their proper subsistent relations/mutual relations of opposition.

The final cause is the last of the causes Aquinas treats in *ST* I q. 44. All agents act for an end and that goal is the ultimate explanation why one effect follows instead of another. The agent aims for the goal (and then forms the effect according to some type of

79. Emery, *The Trinitarian Theology of St. Thomas Aquinas*, 357.
80. *ScG* IV c. 20, n. 2.

exemplarity). The ultimate end at which God aims in creation is the communication of his perfection, his goodness. God does not act in creation as a finite agent, as one who is both agent and patient in acting. This kind of agent acquires something by acting for an end/good and so is also a patient. God has no need and does not develop or acquire additional goods; he acts out of pure liberality.

Aquinas claims that the good of the universe is twofold, internal and external. The good of the universe "consists in a twofold order, that is the order of the parts of the universe and the order of the whole universe to the end who is God himself."[81] This order is a result of Aquinas's claim about God's being the first efficient, exemplar, and final cause of all creation. In other words, the two-fold order of the universe, all to God and thus to each other—is an effect of how Aquinas conceives causality. Efficiently considering creation, Aquinas claims created being is a relation of dependence on God.[82] All created being depends on God at every moment for its existence and thus relationally points back to him. Likewise, creatures are ordered to God as their final good. God contains the perfections of all creatures in a perfect and undivided way. Hence, when God orders creatures to their perfection, he orders them back to himself. This relation of dependence on a singular cause in the orders of efficient, formal, and final causality in turn unifies/orders all created things. This subsequent ordering amongst creation is the immanent common good. The immanent common good is for Aquinas the first and highest good of the universe.[83] Thus, it is what God primarily intends when creating the universe and that, in turn, for his glory (the external common good).

In *ST* I q. 15, a. 2, Aquinas defends the claim that God has multiple divine ideas. In the process of doing this, he makes a claim about the internal order of the universe. The final end is intended by the first agent. This is the principal end in creation: the order of creation.

---

81. *I Sent.*, d. 44, 2c: "*duplex est bonum universi. . . .*"
82. Cf. *De Pot.*, q. 7, a. 9, co.
83. Cf. *ScG* II c. 42, n. 4.

As Aquinas says, "That which is highest in existing things is the good of the order of the universe. . . . the order, therefore, of the universe is properly intended by God . . ."[84] The idea of the whole order of the universe is called by Aquinas a *"ratio alicuius totius"* and *"ultima forma."*[85] Aquinas is claiming here that the ultimate perfection of the universe, its highest good, is the order of the parts of the universe to each other and that God has one idea of this order.[86] It is from this one idea of the order of the universe comes the diversity of particular types of creatures, which are all in union through this order. In other words, distinction pertains essentially to the perfection of the universe and from the one and purely simple cause come diverse beings in union with each other and God. Aquinas goes so far as to say that this distinction is essential to the perfection of the universe and one can see why. The diversity of creatures more adequately reflects the ultimate purpose of the universe: to manifest God's glory and goodness.

Aquinas, however, does not claim that God must produce any one particular internal order. Divine freedom and the infinite goodness of the divine nature, require that we affirm the possibility of different internal orders.[87] Nevertheless, that creation is ordered to manifesting God's glory as well as it having some internal order are necessary features of creation. To claim that God creates in a haphazard way without internal order is incompatible with the divine goodness and the way Aquinas conceives of causality.

## Divine Causality and Peace

The above is relatively clear and goes a long way to explaining what Aquinas means when he says all things participate in divine peace. Recalling Aquinas's definitions of peace as order/union and quiet/tranquility, the question becomes how do order and union fit into creation. Once the question is formulated this way, one can see that

---

84. *ST* I q. 15, a. 2, co.
85. *ScG* II c. 42, n. 6.
86. For more on this point see Blanchette, *The Perfection of the Universe,* 108ff.
87. Cf. Spiering, "The Divine Goodness," 3.

peace runs throughout Aquinas's account of creation. When Aquinas speaks about this in his prologue to the *Commentary on the Sentences* he says the order of creation has three elements: the distinction between God and the world, the primacy of God in all perfections, and the threefold causality of God vis-à-vis the world (efficient, formal, and final). Obviously these are not totally distinct from one another, but help to make the point that order/union is ubiquitous in creation. As was argued in the previous chapter, order/union are *rationes* of the good. The good is a transcendental. In its aspect of order/union, the good runs through each type of causality. In other words, according to each order of causality, all things participate in God's peace.

As seen above, Aquinas conceives of God as the ultimate source of *esse* in creatures, for he is *esse ipsum subsistens*. This establishes order/union from creatures to God. Aquinas conceives of creation, in its passive sense, as nothing other than a relation of dependence on God for being (and for the relative non-being which is essence, formally speaking). This relation is, as argued above, an ordering to God and a fundamental union with God. In other words, considering efficient causality, creatures are at peace with God as their creator. The fundamental order/union of dependence on him produces an attenuated rest.[88] Since God will continue to sustain all creatures in existence, no disquiet or motion is possible on this most fundamental and substantial level.[89] At our most fundamental level, as creatures, we are at peace. Certainly, this does not preclude all those secondary perfections (including the gift of grace as a participation in the divine nature) on the basis of which we are called good (or at peace) *simpliciter*. Nor would it preclude a kind of disquiet based on

88. The extent of this rest is obviously bound up with the nature/grace debate. I do not want to enter into that debate here. Both sides would admit a kind of disquiet of the creature, but how it is explained would be diverse.

89. In *ST* I q. 104, a. 3, co. Aquinas claims that God could annihilate a creature by ceasing his creative activity. Yet in a. 4, ad 1, Aquinas claims that to annihilate creatures would fundamentally contradict the external common good of creation and so it will not happen. This allows the creature peace with God at this most fundamental level, though annihilation would not amount to a conflict (for the creature would cease to exist).

the inability of finite goods to fulfill us or desiring to know God's essence. The same would be true concerning natural secondary perfections, i.e. the acquired virtues.

The giving of *esse* efficiently, as seen above, is the last in the order of production. Naturally prior to this is the whole order of exemplar causality which determines formally the giving of *esse*. Aquinas draws a strong link between divine wisdom and the order/union of the universe. This is to make a strong claim about the peace of the entire universe, which is constituted by its order conceived by Divine Wisdom. The form of the whole determines the order of the whole universe and gives it a fundamental peace, which is identical to the internal good of the universe. This follows from the way in which Aquinas claims that *esse* and the other transcendentals are shot through all moments of exemplarity. No matter which order God conceives, it will necessarily be ordered/unified (just as it will necessarily be good and true). To create a disordered universe would be to create a universe which does not come from one principle (efficiently, formally, finally). God is the one source of creation (and so the order of creation is necessarily one); God cannot create evil.[90] This universal peace is lived concretely by the creature through the exemplarity of the divine idea of this universe and the divine ideas of each particular creature which determine their order and activity. This is because, as we saw in the previous chapter, a creatures' fundamental inclinations and ordering toward certain goods and actions flow from its form. It is the progressive activation of these powers and the attainment of the perfection that will bring creatures to a fuller peace. This fuller peace is a greater activation, the attainment of perfection.

The order of the whole universe and the particular order of creatures to each other and their respective perfections are in turn exemplified by the processions (order/union) of the divine persons ad intra. The Trinitarian persons are natural exemplars of creation. It is to himself that God looks for the exemplar of order (as for goodness,

---

90. Cf. Doolan, *Aquinas on the Divine Ideas*, 137ff.

truth, and oneness). As Aquinas says, "The eternal processions are the cause and the *ratio* of the making of creatures."[91] This is especially in "the procession of the divine persons is in a certain way what originates the procession of creatures, since what is first in any genus is the cause of what comes after it."[92] As Aquinas emphasizes—considering efficient causality in creation the action of the Trinity is common. Yet the exemplar of that coming forth is the Trinitarian relations. As Emery says, "The Word is the model of the way that God communicates himself to creation. In the same way, the Holy Spirit is the rationale of all that God communicates in the generosity of his love."[93]

This is especially why Aquinas holds that the order of the universe as a whole is the greatest natural manifestation of God's goodness. Final causality explains exemplar causality (the internal common good of order/union in this universe). The ordered/unified plurality of the universe comes the closest, inasmuch as that is possible, to the exemplar of the Trinitarian order.[94] The order of each creature to its proper activity, to other creatures, and to God are fashioned to be part of a whole that reflects God. Here, multiplicity and plurality are in union. Given what we found in the last section, this is no mistake. When God conceives of the infinite number of possible orders, each of them are ordered because the ultimate exemplar is the order/union of the Trinity. This is why, technically speaking, God does not have exemplars of order/union (or any of the other transcendentals), only notions of what they are, because these are substantially himself.[95]

All of this makes clearer Aquinas's statements concerning peace

91. I *Sent.,* d. 14, q. 1, a. 1.

92. I *Sent.,* d. 3, q. 1, a. 3

93. Emery, *The Trinitarian Theology of St. Thomas Aquinas,* 346.

94. Though this seems consonant with Aquinas's thought, I have gone beyond what he says (though hopefully not contradicted it). When Aquinas talks about creation imaging God, he does not speak about the distinction and union/order mirroring God. He speaks about the specific character of the human as in the image of God: cf. *ST* I q. 45, a. 7.

95. Cf. *ST* I, q. 15, a. 3, ad 4 & *In de Div. Nom.,* V, l. 3, n. 665.

in his *Commentary on the Divine Names.* When Aquinas explains how God produces peace in all things, he explains it using the notions of order/union. God efficiently produces peace by uniting things to each other and to God. One can see efficient, exemplar, and final causality. The divine idea of this universe is the ultimate exemplar cause of the peace of the universe. This idea is in turn exemplified by the divine nature and the divine persons. In other words, all creation is an effect of God's divine peace and a participation in it.[96] "Divine peace passes to all things, uniting them, through which he reduces all things to a certain order."[97] In other words, God himself, in his unity and plurality, is the exemplar of peace.[98] The reason God's wisdom conceives this order is, in turn, for the ultimate final cause of manifesting his goodness *ad extra.* It is for this purpose that God causes peace in all things by imparting a certain union based on fittingness to each one.[99] This union does not destroy distinction but presupposes it. God makes peace in all things through union.[100] Thus, there is no inordinateness in creation. This is not only because of the order of the whole, but each enjoys the divine peace in its own mode.[101] In other words, God creates all things in imitation of his peace.[102] This causes a kind of cosmic friendship around their desire for God,[103] more particularly around desire for the divine peace itself.[104]

Using the categories seen in the last section, all this makes more sense. In describing the peace of the universe and God's peace, Aquinas reduces them to the positive *ratio* of peace, order/union. God efficiently creates and sustains all creatures at every moment. In this fundamental way creatures are at peace with God as being ordered

---

96. Cf, *In de Div. Nom.,* c. 11, l. 2, n. 905.

97. *In de Div. Nom.,* c. 11, l. 2, n. 910: "*Haec quidem pax divina ad omnia transit, omnia uniendo, per hoc quod reducit omnia in quemdam ordinem.*"

98. Cf. *In de Div. Nom.,* c. 11, l. 2, n. 911.

99. Cf. *In de Div. Nom.,* c. 11, l. 2, n. 898.

100. Cf. *In de Div. Nom.,* c. 11, l. 2, n. 901.

101. Cf. *In de Div. Nom.,* c. 11, l. 2, n. 910.

102. Cf. *In de Div. Nom.,* c. 11, l. 2, n. 905.

103. Cf. *In de Div. Nom.,* c. 11, l. 2, n. 910; c. 4, l. 17.

104. Cf. *In de Div. Nom.,* c. 11, l. 1 nn. 885 and 886.

to him as a dependent relation, effect upon cause. This dependence on God in the efficient order complements and is generationally prior to God's causality in the orders of final causality and exemplar causality (though it posterior to them logically and naturally). In these ways, Aquinas conceives of the whole universe, the multiplicity and formal distinction of creatures, as ordered to the revelation of God's glory and the sharing in his goodness. This is the ultimate external common good of the universe. Creatures have this end in common but reach it to differing degrees depending on their goodness. When God knows himself and thus knows all the infinite ways he could be imitated (the divine ideas), he crafts an internal order to the universe, its internal common good in such a way to reach the external common good and reflects his own supereminent plurality and unity. In other words, the universe reflects the peace of God.

## Law and Peace

Aquinas' thought on the order of creation is closely tied up with this thought on law. As is well known, Aquinas divides law into the eternal law, divine law, natural law, and human law. Each of these types of law is essential for understanding peace. This is because Aquinas says that the very purpose of law is the creation and maintenance of peace. For example, in his *Quodlibetal Disputations* XII, Aquinas is faced with the question of whether a person who acquires property by prescription in bad faith must make restitution. In answering Aquinas notes that civil and canon law differ on this matter, remarking that this is because they have different *fines*. The purpose of civil law is the promotion and preservation of peace whereas the purpose of canon law is the "*quies* of the Church."[105] In other words, both types of law seem to have some aspect of peace as their very purpose.

It turns out that when one looks at Aquinas's thought more globally, the connection between peace and law is more than just happenstance. In *ST* I-II q. 90, a. 1, Aquinas gives his famous definition of

---

105. *Quodl.,* XV q. 2, co.

law, which includes four parts. The most important part of that definition for my purposes is that law is ordered to the common good. The *bonum commune* is the very *finis* of law. This common good spoken of here is the external common good of the community. By ordering members to the external common good, law produces, by mutual relation to the external common good, order/union among the members (the internal common good). Aquinas says clearly that the [internal] common good of a multitude is the order[106] and "the good . . . of a multitude is . . . called peace."[107] "The unity of the city is through peace."[108] This good is something not reducible to the individual good of each, but is a shared good of relations between each member and the external common good. For law to even count as law, it must order members to the external common good.[109]

Since order/union is the more general *ratio* of peace, the very purpose of law is to produce peace: order/union to the external common good and the order/union between each member. In many places, Aquinas takes the above formulations (the common good being the very purpose of law) and replaces the common good with peace (or unity). This is why elsewhere Aquinas says clearly that the purpose of law is peace or peace is the good of a multitude.[110] Law plays an integral part in producing and expressing order/union. It expresses the intention of the lawgiver to move a multitude toward a certain end.[111] This is why law itself must be ordained to the common good to count as law. As soon as it lacks this order to its very purpose, it ceases to partake in the good (whose essence is order/union), and so ceases to be law. Order/union do not separate from

---

106. Cf. *ST* I, q. 31 a. 1 ad 2; *ST* I, q. 92 a. 1 ad 2; *ST* I q. 103, a. 2, ad 3; *ST* I-II, q. 111 a. 5 ad 1.

107. *De Regno* I, c. 2.

108. *Super Heb.*, c. 11, l. 3; *De Regno*, c. 2; *ST* I, q. 103, a. 3, co.: "*Et ideo id ad quod tendit intentio multitudinem gubernantis, est unitas sive pax.*"

109. Cf. *ST* I-II q. 91, a. 1, ad 3. This is not true of the eternal law since God's nature is not ordered to anything.

110. See, for example: *ScG* IV c. 76, n. 4; *De Regno* I c. 2; *Super Io.*, c. 16, l. 8; *Super Is.*, c. 3, l. 1.

111. Cf. *ScG* III c. 115, n. 1.

the good, so if law is not trained on the good, it will not produce order/union and thereby cease to be law. This is how Aquinas conceptualizes the Augustinian axiom *iniusta lex non est lex*.[112] Without order/union with the common good (peace), an unjust law "is not a law but a corruption."[113]

Each of Aquinas's types of law participates in a deeper order/union and specifies that same order/union. The whole of Aquinas's treatise on law is obviously beyond the purview of this book, but it is important that we notice that Aquinas's relation between law and peace holds for each type of law. The eternal law is "the *ratio* of divine wisdom, directing all acts and motions."[114] It is this form of the whole universe that is expressed in the Son and specifies the order/union of all creatures to each other and to the external common good. It includes all created things and orders them to this end. "The eternal law is expressed by the Word himself."[115] It is the movement toward the external common good of the universe (God's glory) that is attributed to the Holy Spirit, who "proceeds as love ... which is a driving and moving force."[116]

All those types of law that participate in the eternal law are also ordered to peace. The divine law, which is divided into the old and the new, is "a certain *ratio* of divine providence for leading humans."[117] It is specified by the leading of rational creatures toward the "love of God."[118] In other words, though it is derived from the eternal law,[119] it is specified by a different purpose. It is not ordered toward God's glory directly and to all of creation passively, but that humans may supernaturally "cling to God through love."[120] It is this

112. For the relevant citations of Aquinas see Andrew Campos, "Aquinas's 'lex iniusta non est lex': a Test of Legal Validity," in *Archives for Philosophy of Law and Social Philosophy*, Vol. 100, No. 3 (2014): 368–69.
113. *ST* I-II q. 92, a. 1, ad 4.
114. *ST* I-II q. 93, a. 1, co.
115. *ST* I-II q. 93, a. 1, ad 2.
116. *ScG* IV c. 20, n. 3.
117. *ScG* III c. 128.6.
118. *ScG* III cc. 115ff.
119. Cf. *ST* I-II q. 93, a. 3, co.
120. *ScG* III c. 116, n. 1.

law that orders/unites humans to God as friend. In other words, it specifies the peace of the church. Natural law is the "participation in the eternal law by the rational creature."[121] It includes both a passive participation (firstly in the divine idea of each nature, but ultimately in God's own *esse*) that sets up "inclinations to proper acts and ends"[122] as well as our rationality "through which [the rational creature] has its inclination to a due act and end."[123] This end is most generally the glory of God, but it is also a love of God as "the common good of the whole universe."[124] Aquinas also describes this end as human happiness or flourishing.[125] Human law complements the natural law by further determining and specifying human ordering to happiness. In other words, it orders humans to "peace and virtue" just like the natural law does.[126] The people (or their designated representatives) order themselves to the external common good of the community (happiness).[127]

Aquinas also maintains this connection between the peace and the law in his thought on punishment. Aquinas maintains that punishment's purpose is also peace, interior and exterior.[128] Evil doers are those who act contrary to the internal and external common good(s) of a community. This is why Aquinas does not claim that law is essential coercive. It is only coercive in relation to those who turn their wills from the common good of that community.[129] Punishment thus aims to return them to the good of order/union within themselves and with the community. "Punishment is inflicted as a medicine that is corrective of the sin and also to restore right order violated by sin ..."[130] It primarily aims to cooperate with the

---

121. *ST* I-II q. 91, a. 3, co.

122. *ST* I-II q. 91, a. 2, co.

123. *ST* I-II q. 91, a. 2, co.

124. *ST* I-II q. 109, a. 3, co.

125. Cf. *ST* I-II q. 109, a. 3, co.: "*bonum commune totius universi, quod est Deus.*"

126. Cf. *ST* I-II q. 95, a. 1, co.

127. Cf. *ST* I-II q. 90, a. 3, co.

128. See Peter Koritansky, *Thomas Aquinas and the Philosophy of Punishment* (Washington DC: The Catholic University of America Press, 2011), 133ff.

129. Cf. *ST* I-II q. 95, a. 1, co.

130. *Comp. Theo.*, I, c. 121.

individual in restoring the good. This is even true when the individual resists the restoration. In other words, punishment is not totally coercive even with one who does not cooperate, since punishment cooperates with the will of the sinner in another way. "Punishment itself is good simply speaking, but evil to this person; and this evil God is said to create, but is said to make peace. This is because the appetite of the sinner does not cooperate with the punishment, but God does cooperate with the appetite for peace in the sinner."[131] In other words, punishment's purpose is the restoration of peace (order/union—the good) and all individuals desire peace, even those that oppose it.

Aquinas also recognizes, though, that punishment is ultimately insufficient to produce peace (since punishment, by definition, is involuntary—though as we saw above this cannot be said absolutely speaking) in any of the above orders. Peace, interior and exterior, are ultimately about order/union within and between individuals and those can only be fully present when voluntary. If the punished cooperates with the punishment, i.e. the punishment is undertaken (somewhat) voluntarily, punishment loses some of the concept of punishment not only because it is less contrary to the will, but also because the will has already evinced a return to order/union with the good. In this way punishment becomes satisfactory for Aquinas. Barring the occurrence of cooperation on the part of the evil-doer, Aquinas recognizes that on occasion one must simply punish for the sake of protecting an order/union in which the evil-doer no longer voluntarily participates. Sometimes the polity must aim at a lower good (the mere intellectual negation of conflict not following from right order/union) and protect the order/union of others to the good which would suffer without suppression of evil doers.[132] This claim does not commit Aquinas to punishment on any one particular issue; Just as he is flexible concerning what evil

---

131. *De Malo* q. 1, a. 1, ad 1.
132. Cf. *ST* I-II q. 96, a. 1, co.

actions should be made illegal,[133] he is profoundly flexible and con-
textual concerning punishments.[134]

Although Aquinas's thought on law, peace, and punishment is
relatively clear on a more general level, and the connection between
peace, law, and the good is maintained, the connection between the
civil law and peace is highly debated in Aquinas. Gerhard Beestermoller gives a good summary of this debate. He gives three possible
positions one can take on the relation of civil law to peace. The first
is that the civil law aims at peace alone, but not at virtue and not at
religion. This position claims Aquinas as a proto-liberal who claims
that the government's competence terminates at the promotion of
peace, but cannot go beyond that to promote virtue. Another possible reading of Aquinas, the second position, claims that the peace-
keeping mission of the government requires the promotion of virtue
and of belief, but not directly. It must "guarantee the existence of belief [and virtuousness]."[135] It is required for the *Staatliche Ordnung*.
Finally, the concluding position is that Aquinas in no way anticipates
the (religiously) neutral state. Aquinas envisions the state enforce-
ment of both religion and virtue explicitly and directly. The final position is the one Beestermoller thinks is the correct interpretation of
Aquinas and he makes this argument based on peace: "Peace stands
in the *Summa* as a spiritual-political unit of the faithful."[136] And it is
the "work of a supernatural God and charity."[137] Peace can only be,
for Thomas, a work of God and charity; if law aims at peace it must
aim at supernatural peace. You can only expect peace from those
who are your theological friends, which is the work of grace.[138]

133. It depends on the capability of people (*ST* I-II q. 96, aa. 1–2) and a kind of prudence that judges which course of action is better or worse for the polity as a whole
(e.g. political prudence). Nevertheless, he seems to suggest that there is a minimum (*sed
solum graviora*).

134. Cf. *ST* I-II q. 95, a. 2, co.

135. Beestermoller, *Thomas von Aquin und der Gerechte Krieg*, 62–63: "*Staatliche Ordnung ... zur äußeren Garantie gläubiger Existenz.*" "*Voraussetzung eines tugendhaften und
gläubigen Lebens sei.*"

136. Beestermoller, *Thomas von Aquin*, 63.

137. Beestermoller, *Thomas von Aquin*, 63: "*die Wirkung der übernatürlichen Gottes
und Nächstenliebe.*"

138. Cf. Beestermoller, *Thomas von Aquin*, 64–65.

My purpose here is not to enter this very contentious debate which touches on Aquinas's relations to political forms and economies, but only to make notes on these positions inasmuch as they relate to his thought on peace. I think Aquinas's more general thought on peace challenges the two extreme positions. The first position seems to suffer from two misunderstandings of Aquinas's thought on peace. First, genuine temporal peace (as order/union) could never be conceived purely instrumentally for Aquinas (this also seems to be a mistake of the final position as well).[139] It is good in itself and not simply good because it conduces to other goods. Granted, Aquinas does seem to suggest that civil peace is evil when directed to evil ends, and good when directed to good ends (which suggests instrumentality), but this does not suggest that it is purely instrumental. Civil peace, even the peace of enjoying external goods (moderately), is genuinely good (as he says elsewhere). Second, as will be clear later, peace requires virtue for Aquinas. If individuals are to be ordered toward the common good, this requires justice, and justice is not a procedural reality for Aquinas.[140] It is a virtue. So one could not say, on Aquinas's terms, that one aims at peace but not virtue in the civil sphere, if by peace one means union/order. The real question is which order/union is the aim of civil law and what virtues are necessary for that peace.

On the other hand, the final position fares no better. According to this position, "Political peace is for the *Summa* based on love of God and neighbor and includes the whole Church."[141] In this conception, peace can only be theological, and so Aquinas requires that one have the civil sphere explicitly and directly ordered to the supernatural. It is true that peace is about due order,[142] but peace is

---

139. Cf. *ST* II-II q. 123, a. 5, ad 2: "*dicendum quod pax reipublicae est secundum se bona, nec redditur mala ex hoc quod aliqui male ea utuntur. Nam et multi alii sunt qui bene ea utuntur, et multo peiora mala per eam prohibentur, scilicet homicidia, sacrilegia, quam ex ea occasionentur, quae praecipue pertinent ad vitia carnis.*"

140. Cf. Jean Porter, *Justice as a Virtue: a Thomistic Perspective* (Grand Rapids, MI: Eerdmans, 2016).

141. Beestermoller, *Thomas von Aquin,* 66.

142. Cf. *ST* II-II q. 45, a. 6, co.: "*pax constituitur ad debitum ordinem rediguntur.*"

not solely theological for Aquinas. This would amount to the claim that order/union is solely theological. This is clearly not true. One should not claim that "the first place of peace is the Church"[143] unless by first you mean principal or maximal. One must distinguish the types of peace that require grace from those that do not, supernatural good from natural good. Aquinas seems to envision a natural peace, which partially constitutes what he means by civil peace (just like natural happiness). Likewise, the relation of orders (in this case the natural and supernatural) in Aquinas is not always direct, but could be indirect and non-repugnant.[144] Believers and non-believers can share proximate ends/goods, even if those proximate ends are diversely ordered to higher goods.[145] Likewise, Aquinas is explicit that virtue and peace cannot be produced directly through fear of punishment or a mere union of feeling.[146] This evinces totalitarianism.[147] Both interior and exterior peace require the individual to be willing (at least *secundum quid* for exterior) if it is to be true peace and true concord. This is the goal of law for Aquinas.

Obviously this debate is more complex than the above picture, but any solution that follows from Aquinas's thought on peace will have to take these points into account: order is not solely theological, orders are dependent on deeper orders (but have multiple types of possible relations between them), peace requires virtue, peace is

143. Beester, *Thomas von Aquin*, 65.

144. Cf. *ST* II-II q. 23, a. 7, co.: "*Si vero illud bonum particulare sit verum bonum, puta conservatio civitatis vel aliquid huiusmodi, erit quidem vera virtus, sed imperfecta, nisi referatur ad finale et perfectum bonum.*" This is why Aquinas often says that the good and evil share some types of peace. Aquinas seems to suggest that this peace becomes false when it is not ordered to God. It becomes a true peace when so ordered. See, for example, *Super Ps.*, 45, n. 8. In this way the non-repugnance of the civil sphere, though it allows for sin, allows for a strong set (to use Jensen's language) in believers because of its inherent non-repugnance: cf. Steven Jensen, *Sin: A Thomistic Psychology* (Washington DC: The Catholic University of America Press, 2018), 75ff.

145. Cf. Jennifer Herdt, "Aquinas and the Democratic Virtues: An Introduction," in *Journal of Religious Ethics* vol 44, n. 2 (2016): 233–45.

146. Cf. *ST* I-II q. 29, a. 1, ad 1. The lack of conflict caused by punishment would not be called peace in the proper sense, since the will of the offender is turned against order/union. It would be a mere being of reason.

147. Cf. McMahon, "A Thomistic Analysis of Peace," 177

not solely an instrumental good (but identical with the good, instrumental or otherwise), and peace must be voluntary (in some sense). Likewise, a fuller solution would have to relate to other contentious issues in Aquinas, such as pagan virtue, authority, common action, and the specification of virtues.[148] I will make no pretense at solving these debates, but only note that a correct conception of peace is essential for their resolution and mistakes are made when a fuller understanding and debate concerning peace is sidelined.

## Conclusion

In the orders of efficient, final, and formal causality, the created universe is peaceful. It is ordered and in union (with God most fundamentally and on that basis with each other). This peace is, in turn, a participation in the unchanging peace of God, whether it is conceived philosophically according to oneness or theologically as order/union. The ultimate external common good of the universe is the revelation of God's peace and God shares this peace with creation. Aquinas's thought on law finds its *Sitz im Leben* in this context. Law has the purpose of producing diverse orders/unions and specifying them on a more particular level, all the way down to the civil. For these reasons, Aquinas says that "*Proprius effectus Dei est facere pacem.*"[149]

### GOD'S GOVERNANCE, EVIL, AND PEACE

If the above is true, then how does Aquinas explain the deep and ongoing presence of disorder/disunion and disquiet/discord present in creation? The presence of disquiet and discord are seemingly ubiquitous and, at the very least, cast doubt on Aquinas's claims that the very purpose of all of God's creative activity is to communicate a share of his peace to creatures. Because of this it might seem that peace must be something other than the internal common

---

148. Cf. Herdt, "Aquinas and the Democratic Virtues," 241ff.
149. *Super Heb.*, c. 13, l. 3, n. 766.

good and form of the universe; it must be something other than the dependent relation of creation on God; it must be something other than the order of all things to each other and to God. If it were, then one would not expect it to seemingly fail so often. How does Aquinas explain this?

Aquinas's philosophy of peace is important for recognizing how he would analyze the ongoing presence of disorder resulting in disquiet/discord in creation. Order/union and rest/tranquility are *rationes* of the good. Because of this, the difficulty presented above appears as another manifestation of the problem of evil. If God and creation are good, then one would not expect to find privations throughout creation. Yet we find those privations, both natural and moral.[150] If the existence of natural and moral evil is not an objection to the transcendental status of the good, the goodness of creation, or the goodness of God[151] and if I am right about the reduction of peace to the *ratio* of the good, then something similar can be said about peace. Wherever there is goodness to the same extent order/union and rest/tranquility are also realized. If the objection can be met considering the goodness of creation, it can be met concerning peace as well. Following Aquinas's explanation of the ongoing presence of evil in creation helps us to understand the ongoing presence of disorder/disunion and disquiet/discord, since Aquinas explains disorder/disunion as a privation of order/union.

### Aquinas and the Goodness of Creation

Aquinas distinguishes between God's providence and God's governance. "In [God's] governance two things are to be considered: the very *ratio* of governance which is providence itself and its execution."[152] When Aquinas defines providence he says "strictly speaking, the *ratio* of things toward their end is providence."[153] This includes the distinction of things as well as "the *ratio ordinis* of

---

150. Cf. *ST* I q. 48, a. 1, co.
151. Cf. *ST* I q. 49, a. 2, co.
152. *ST* I q. 103, a. 6, co.
153. *ST* I q. 22, a. 1, co.

things to the end or the *ratio ordinis partium* in the whole."[154] The resonance with the divine ideas and formal causality treated in the last section is unmistakable. Remember, the divine ideas determine (formally) the distinction, essence, and order of the individual to others and to the whole. This ordering of things to each other and to the whole is what Aquinas calls the internal common good of the universe and the reason why he claims there is a kind of form of the whole universe. In this sense, providence has been treated in the last section. It concerns the ordering of things to their respective ends and to the glory of God. As can be guessed, because God's providence has to do with the creative ordering of all things, it extends as far as God's causality extends: "not only to the principles of the species, but even the individual principles."[155] Nothing falls outside of God's universal ordering. Governance, on the other hand, is when God executes this order "through secondary causes."[156] Secondary agents, as is well known figure heavily in Aquinas's explanation of how God's efficacious will brings about some things through necessary causes and some through contingent.[157] This will also feature heavily in Aquinas's explanation of ongoing disorder in creation.

Aquinas's answer to the problem of evil depends on his previous claims about the goodness of God's creation as well as his providence and governance, but it also depends on his privation theory of evil. As is well known, Aquinas treats evil as a "privation of a particular good . . . and opposed to it [and therefore] opposed to the appetible."[158] It is a lack of "measure, form, and order."[159] This is distinct from negation, which is simple not being. Humans cannot fly, but this is not evil. Evil is a lack of a good which ought to be there based on the essence of the creature. Evil as a privation is again divided by Aquinas into evil suffered and evil done.[160] This division applies primarily to

---

154. *ST* q. 22, a. 1, co.
155. *ST* I q. 22, a. 2, co.
156. *ST* I q. 106, a. 3, co.
157. Cf. *ST* I q. 19, a. 9, co.
158. *De Malo* q. 1, a. 1.
159. *De Malo* q. 1, a. 4, ad 6.
160. Cf. *De Malo* q. 1, a. 4, co.

evil considered in rational subjects, but also, inasmuch as it is simply an application of the division between act and potency, also to evil in non-rational subjects.[161] When there is a loss of a particular good, this is evil suffered. Aquinas calls this the *malum poenae* when humans are being considered.[162] Actively speaking, when one takes a particular good away from something this is evil done. Evil done is again divided into *peccatum* and *culpa*. A *peccatum* is simply an action failing to reach its due end, most especially the final end.[163] Any creature, free or not, can be the subject of *peccatum*, especially in its extended sense to proximate ends. When freely chosen *peccatum* results in *culpa*. As Aquinas defines *culpa*, it is "*debitum poenae*."[164] Sin, which is "either the absence of a due act in reference to God or an act contrary to what is due to God, disturbs the universal order of divine governance."[165] Aquinas does not think that those guilty of sin desire the evil in itself, since evil is opposed to the appetible. Humans always desire to do something inasmuch as it appears good to us (appetible). Aquinas thinks of sin as a voluntary turning from the good in a certain respect. If Aquinas's defense of the goodness of creation and my claim that peace reduces to goodness are correct, then one would expect the explanation of these to apply to peace as well.

Based on this taxonomy of evil, Aquinas mounts the following defense of the goodness of creation and it is based on his claim that distinction is part of the *ratio* of the good. As will be recalled from the last chapter, the external common good of the universe is the glory of God. All creatures are ordered to this end individually, but

161. Cf. *De Malo* q. 1, a. 4, co.: "And as other things may have these two kinds of evil, so also may an intellectual nature, which acts voluntary." Though "since this division belongs to evil only as found in a rational nature." Aquinas, in the second quotation, is simply saying that punishment and fault only apply to a rational creature, but not denying the more general evil suffered and evil done to the non-rational creature. See ad 10 for a confirmation of this. When Aquinas denies the division can be said of non-rational creatures, he specifically denies fault and punishment.

162. Cf. *ST* I q. 19, a. 9.

163. Cf. *De Malo* q. 3, a. 1.

164. *ST* I-II q. 87, a. 6, co.

165. Reinhard Hütter, *Bound for Beatitude: A Study in Eschatology and Ethics* (Washington DC: The Catholic University of America Press, 2019), 180.

more especially they are ordered to reflect God's goodness as an ordered whole (the internal common good). This is God's primary intention in creating. Based on this goal, the reflection of God's glory and goodness, distinction becomes essential to the goodness of creation. As Aquinas says, "We must say that the distinction and multitude of things is from the intention of the first agent, which is God. For he produces things in being by communicating to them his goodness and representing [himself] through them. And because one creature is not able to represent him sufficiently, he produces many and diverse creatures . . ."[166] In other words, distinction and diversity are a structural part of creation. Aquinas is especially concerned here with formal diversity (different types of species) and less concerned with material diversity (different members in the species). These formal distinctions are not other than the good, but intrinsic to it (distinction is essential to order/union). Yet this diversity, if it is to remain part of the good is not created without order/union to other creatures, but as an ordered whole representing God's glory.

Nevertheless, Aquinas claims that this picture results in evil. God's glory is reflected in both the lion and the antelope, and in diverse ways. Yet, the way in which the lion reflects God's glory includes being a carnivore. The lion eats the antelope and this is good, for the lion; it is evil for the antelope. Aquinas fully admits that this is not good for the antelope to be eaten, but that it is an effect of the two-fold order of the universe (to the primary end of reflecting God's glory in living one's species' perfection and the order to each other). Aquinas does not evacuate the goodness of particular creatures or deny that there is animal suffering. Conflict is inevitable given the external common good of the universe and the subsequent diverse ordering of each type of creature to its flourishing. Likewise, even though Aquinas admits that being eaten is not good for the antelope, he also claims these conflicts are good as part of the whole. In other words, these evils are not directly willed by God inasmuch as

---

166. *ST* I q. 47, a. 1, co. 4.

they are evil but only inasmuch as they are good in light of the whole reflecting God's glory by its distinction in order/union.

Aquinas changes this picture somewhat when considering humans. Certainly, the inclusion of rational animals in creation is justified in a similar way to other creatures (to help to reflect the infinite goodness of God more adequately). However, given their rationality, he seems to take their suffering as a special case requiring more explanation than conflicting lines of causality where one species' flourishing requires the demise of another (though this does explain a lot for him). Nevertheless, when he explains human suffering, it still follows from what he claims about the order of creation. Aquinas argues that God wills justice (order/union of creation) and so permits human suffering to occur in the world. God wills justice and inasmuch as humans are not in accord with that order (they sin), he must act in punishment (i.e. allow people to suffer). It would be unjust not to punish and so a failure to punish on God's part would be a voluntary turning from what he is in his essence.[167] Because of this, God wills justice (order) directly, but that entails punishment (the deprivation of a good). The key to understanding this is that Aquinas views the human race as formally unified (not in union, but a unity). The loss is suffered by any member belonging to this species. The allowing of suffering of the species in general maintains the order of the universe. God does not inflict this suffering, but it is the natural result of any bad action: a disturbed conscience, vice, and the inability to be a friend to oneself (have one's powers unified/ordered).[168] This God permits.

This conception allows Aquinas to avoid any sense of Thomistic karma with God being an active agent in punishment. According to Aquinas, God allows suffering as punishment in general but is not coordinating suffering with individual sin (beyond the sense in which it naturally results).[169] Aquinas does maintain that individual

---

167. For a defense of the reasonableness of justice questions concerning God see John Meinert, "Divine Exemplarity, Virtue, and Theodicy in Aquinas," in *The Thomist* vol 82, n. 2 (April 2018): 235–62.

168. Scott Roniger, "Is there a Punishment for Violating the Natural Law?" in *American Catholic Philosophical Quarterly*, vol. 94, no. 2 (2020): 273–304.

169. For spiritual goods, Aquinas claims that punishment is coordinated with

sin does result in suffering,[170] but he does not want to claim that individual sin is always the explanation for that individual's suffering. That would require him to deny innocent suffering. This is not an option for any Christian (let alone being a radically insufficient explanation for why those without freedom suffer). How could one make sense of the suffering of Jesus or Mary if suffering is coordinated with individual sin? One could not.[171] God does not will justice in the sense that he coordinates each person's suffering with their sins in some kind of 1:1 divine proportionalism. People suffer who do not deserve it, and people suffer in ways not fitting with justice (which requires the loss of the good desired and sinned against). Aquinas only wants to maintain that suffering is connected, if not to the contrariety of perfection in creatures (sickness is bad for us, but not for viruses), to the loss of proper order as a species caused by sin (but not necessarily the sin of the one suffering). Obviously, this requires some strong claims about singular origins of the human race which is subject to ongoing debate in Thomism.[172]

On the other hand, Aquinas does want to maintain that even with innocent human suffering, there is a possibility for reordering this suffering. "And so it follows that we call every privation of a good that human beings can employ for good activity a punishment."[173] Aquinas claims that God (and the individual) can draw good out of this (innocent or otherwise) suffering—whether it be for the

---

individual sin, but I do not think this should be pushed more particularly than the 'loss of habitual grace'. Such an account would require that any spiritual suffering be coordinated with individual sin, which certainly does not seem to be the case.

170. See Rik Van Nieuwenhove, "Bearing the Marks of Christ's Passion," in *The Theology of Thomas Aquinas,* eds. Rik Van Nieuwenhove and Joseph Wawrykow (Notre Dame, IN: University of Notre Dame Press, 2005), 282ff.

171. Nor does the distinction between suffering, in the full sense which is involuntary, and satisfactory suffering negate this. Put differently, one cannot say that all innocent suffering is voluntary and therefore not true suffering. This would not only negate the true suffering of the cross, which is involuntary in itself, but also fail to make sense of how Aquinas allows for the innocent suffering of children who do not have the exercise of their freedom.

172. Cf. Nicanor Pier Giorgio Austriaco, O.P., "Catholic Teaching on Creation and on Human Origins," in *Thomistic Evolution,* 2nd ed. (Providence, RI: Cluny Media, 2019), 159–88.

173. *De Malo* q. 1, a. 4, co.

individual in virtue or for the good of the community in merit.[174] In this way, the orders of justice and love are maintained not only in the formal unity of humans, but also by the reordering of a manifest injustice toward justice and love. This is why Aquinas claims that nothing escapes God's providence, God's ordering of things to the good. Sin and suffering cannot thwart God's providence.[175]

What about the other type of evil Aquinas discusses, the evil of human fault (which occurs only in humans—Aquinas does not view the lion eating the antelope as a moral evil)? According to Aquinas, God does not even indirectly will the evil of fault (i.e. to maintain the order/union of the universe), not for the sake of justice or the good of the whole or for any reason.[176] As such, it requires a different kind of explanation than the suffering of evil. Sin disorders the individual most deeply, and Aquinas compares it to a sickness (loss of bodily order).[177] In the active sense, sin is in no way a part of God's order of creation. It comes about because of human freedom. According to Aquinas, God created a world in which humans were free and apparently this includes the possibility of sin, even though this sin is unintelligible to us.[178] Moral evil is a foreseen but completely involuntary (on God's part) possibility of the existence of free creatures.

So why does God not intervene and prevent sins (or at least the effect of suffering, at least on the innocent)? As Aquinas says, "God leaves nature to itself."[179] Yet doesn't God's permission of this amount to consent? Isn't this an omission on God's part since he could prevent it? The answer of McCabe is apropos here. God does

---

174. Cf. Aaron Weldon, "*Ad Totius Mundi Pacem atque Salutem* Merit for Others and the Divine Plan in Thomistic Thought," in *Nova et Vetera*, English Edition, vol. 13, n. 4 (2015): 1125–148.

175. Cf. *ST* I q. 21, a. 4 & q. 22, a. 2.

176. Cf. *ST* I q. 48, a. 6, co.; *ST* I q. 49, a. 2, ad 1.

177. Cf. *ST* I-II q. 88, a. 1, co.

178. Cf. Lawrence Dewan, *Wisdom, Law, and Virtue* (New York: Fordham University Press, 2008), 192ff.

179. *ST* I-II q. 87, a. 7, co.: "*Principaliter quidem poena originalis peccati est quod natura humana sibi relinquitur, destituta auxilio originalis iustitiae, sed ad hoc consequuntur omnes poenalitates quae ex defectu naturae in hominibus contingunt.*"

not 'permit' meaning 'consent,' but rather permits by not stopping it.[180] He is not evil for not stopping sin or suffering, for to be responsible for an omission one must be able and responsible for preventing it.[181] God is certainly able to prevent sin and the evil it visits on others. The crucial question is whether God is responsible for doing this. One must likewise be careful with what sense "responsible" carries here. In one sense, God is clearly responsible for making us good, as in he is the primary cause of our goodness by creation and by grace. Yet this is not the sense of responsible that is at play when speaking of omissions. When Aquinas claims you are blamable for an omission if you are able and responsible, his sense of responsibility is something that you ought to do based on your nature, position, status, etc.[182] In other words, the self-inflicted wound of sin (or its effects on others) cannot be an omission on God's part unless you think God owes it to all of us to make all of us impeccable and to intervene every time (miraculously) each time we fail. We may want this to happen, but I do not think we can say that God owes this to us. This would make grace due to the creature. So to blame God for not intervening is equivalent to saying the grace of impeccability is due to each creature so God can be blamed for not giving it. There is certainly a deep mystery here, but it does not seem that human sin is voluntary on God's part simply because God could prevent it and does not.

## Aquinas and the Peace of Creation

Something similar can be said about the loss of peace in creation because order/union are *rationes* of the good. Peace is "tranquility of mode, species, and order."[183] Recall that the claim that creation is peaceful is a claim about the dependence of each creature on God

---

180. Cf. Herbert McCabe, *Faith within Reason* (New York: Continuum, 2007), 91–93.

181. Cf. *ST* I-II q. 6, a. 3, co.

182. Cf. Kevin Flannery, *Cooperation with Evil: Thomistic Tools of Analysis* (Washington DC: The Catholic University of America Press, 2019), 140ff.

183. *Super Eph.*, c. 4, l. 1, n. 194.

(efficient) for its being as well as the order of each creature to other creatures and to the whole of creation (formal and final). In fact, just as with goodness, the loss of peace is an inevitable part of creation. With respect to disorder/disunion suffered, it can be explained the same way Aquinas explains the loss of goodness. The peace of one requires the destruction of peace in another. The attaining of its proper good requires the lion to eat the antelope. In one sense this does negate the peace of creation (specifically the order/union and rest of the antelope), but in another sense, creation remains properly ordered/in union as a whole.[184]

Just as Aquinas locates the goodness of creation primarily in the ordered/unified whole and preserves it this way in the face of evil, so to the peace of the whole is preserved. If the conflict between the lion and the antelope, or humans and viruses, does not negate the goodness of creation, it does not negate its orderliness or its peace as a whole. The loss of peace for the antelope is not an *aliquid*, but as the loss of life, it is the loss of the orderliness/union of the antelope's proper good. Something similar can be said about the loss of order/union in a person's life. It is certainly possible to suffer this innocently and it is permitted by God as a way of preserving the order of the universe, namely the order of justice. Does this imply that nobody would suffer disorder/disunion unless someone sinned? It seems so. As Aquinas has it, the order of our bodies (e.g., health), the union of our appetites, and the union of humans to each other and to God is a grace, a preternatural gift. The loss of grace for the

---

184. One might think that Aquinas implies that to be eaten by the lion is in fact good for the antelope. As Aquinas says, creatures are ordered to each other and to the whole. What does this 'to each other' mean except to be used by each other? If God has ordered creatures for their use by one another, it seems that one must say that inasmuch as it concerns this order, then to be eaten is good (and thus peaceful) for the victim. This is not right, however. God does not order creatures toward privations. The antelope is not ordered to death, but to life and to flourishing as an antelope. When Aquinas says that creatures are ordered to human use, what he means is that humans are ordered to use creatures in reaching their good, not that creatures are somehow ordered toward death as a good for them. This preserves Aquinas's commitment that conflict and privation in evil suffered is an inevitable consequence of the overall intention of creation: to create lots of different kinds of creatures to reflect God's glory.

human species brings about the loss of peace in general. In other words, many people innocently lose their peace on account of the sins of others. Many also lose their peace on account of their own sins (though, again, Aquinas does not want to use this as a global explanation of each particular case of losing peace). Put simply, just as the presence of suffering does not negate the goodness of creation, so too the loss of peace does not negate the peace of creation.

Aquinas's thought about free actions that cause the loss of peace follows his thought about sin. God does not even indirectly will disorder/disunion done, not for the sake of justice or the good of the whole or for any reason. This essentially brings the question back to why God created a universe in which voluntarily bringing disorder is a possibility or does not intervene to prevent people disfiguring interior or exterior peace. Again, the answer is the same: the possibility of disorder/disunion done is a foreseen but unintended possibility of free creatures. So why does God not intervene and prevent the loss of peace (especially to protect the innocent)? Again, the answer is the same for peace as for goodness. In one sense to preserve the peace of each creature would require a quasi-infinite number of miracles. Lions need meat to survive. In another sense, God is not responsible for giving us peace. Full peace, just like goodness, is ultimately a gift for the individual. Yet in some sense God does preserve the peace of the universe in the face of all our sins which damage peace. As Aquinas says, "It is impossible that the divine will not follow to its effect. Whence it seems that whatever falls away from the divine will according to one order will return to it in another."[185]

Certainly disorder/disunion can result in creation, but this is a *per accidens* feature. It is a foreseen result of chance, the intersecting of two lines of causality. Alternatively, it is identified with moral evil or its effects. These are the basics of Aquinas's explanation of ongoing disorder/disunion in creation. This defense of the peace of creation requires that disunion/disorder be reduced to evil as the privation of order/union with the attendant disquiet and discord

---

185. *ST* 19, a. 6, co.; *In de Div. Nom.*, c. 4, l. 23, n. 595.

following. It mirrors Aquinas's defense of the goodness of creation against evil and stands or falls along with that account.

### Sorrow and Peace

There is at least one (if not more than one) serious objection to this explanation of ongoing disorder/disunion in creation. According to this objection, sadness is not opposed to order/union (as well as some of the other things Aquinas identifies as contrary to peace, e.g. shouting). Sadness is obviously properly ordered at times, though it does destroy the rest/tranquility of the individual. This seems to prove that the explanation of the goodness of creation cannot map onto peace. Goodness and order could cause us to lose peace. In other words, the contrary of peace seems to admit of special considerations which are not true more generally of evil (i.e. you can lose peace without disorder). If this is true, then disorder/disunion and disquiet/discord are not just a *per accidens* features of creation or an effect of moral evil. They are much more structural and the defense of the goodness of creation fails in relation to peace. One can be good and not at peace. Likewise, this objection poses an even deeper problem for my account of Aquinas's thought. It seems to separate order/union from rest/tranquility. One can lose rest/tranquility and still retain order/union. In fact, one might lose peace precisely because of order/union. The explanation of how evil and goodness occur in creation thus cannot explain peace. Creation cannot be at peace, especially explained by relation to the good, if the good and peace can come apart so to speak.

At first glance, this objection seems conclusive against using Aquinas's explanation of evil to explain disorder/disunion. Nevertheless, it is not successful. The key in understanding its failure is that it falsely claims the example of sadness shows peace, in its negative *ratio,* to be separable from the good. This is impossible on Aquinas's conception. The key to understanding this is the positive *ratio* of peace: order/union. Order/union in one way may cause the loss of order/union in another way. The preservation of the good in one sense may entail the loss of the good in another sense. Sadness is the perfect example. If a loved one dies (or there is another loss of the good by an individual or a friend), it is properly ordered to grieve. This sadness retains the affective union with the deceased and the union, which is love, to his or her life. Nevertheless, by retaining this union, one's appetite will be disturbed in another way. Yet this disturbance is because it is in order/united in a deeper way. Put simply, virtuous sadness is an example of inter-appetitive non-moral fault disunion and so can be analyzed the same way Aquinas explains discord without sin or conflict between species. This is precisely what Aquinas says when he asks if the desire for unity is a cause of sorrow.[186] As he says there, "In the same way as concupiscence and cupidity for the good is a cause of sorrow, so also the appetite for unity, or love, is a cause of sorrow."[187]

None of this casts doubt on the peace of creation though. Recalling what I argued earlier, creation is at peace in the efficient, formal, and final orders. Sadness, though it disturbs one's peace in one sense, leaves it intact in a deeper sense. In fact, it is the deeper union/order to the good that is marked (to the extent it is union/order to the good) by rest/tranquility and gives rise to sadness due to the lack of some aspect of the loved good. Inasmuch as this concerns the disorder/disunion in creation, this makes the explanation from evil an even stronger candidate for explaining the loss of peace. The objection from sadness requires the absence of goodness and Aquinas says explicitly that the disturbance of peace comes from evils.[188] One would not be sad without the loss of the good. So the real crux of the matter in the sadness objection is the presence of evil in creation. This again links Aquinas's explanation of evil with the loss of peace.

Even if my defense against the objection from sadness is successful (and more contentiously my whole explanation of the presence of disunion/disorder in creation), I am under no illusions that the above defense of the peace of creation is wholly satisfactory. No

---

186. Cf. *ST* I-II q. 36, a. 3.

187. *ST* I-II q. 36, a. 3, co.

188. Cf. *Super Io.*, c. 16, l. 8.

such defense omitting Christ will be.[189] The presence of disorder and the loss of peace in creation is a mystery only fully revealed in Christ. In other words, a full answer to the presence of disorder/disunion in creation requires a theological analysis for Aquinas. In fact, I think one could truthfully say that for Aquinas, Christ's coming is to restore the proper peace of creation, to give the Spirit in a new and fuller way to rational creatures so that all of creation can be re-ordered/re-united to God.

### THE INCARNATION AND PEACE

Any Thomistic account of peace would be woefully and misleadingly incomplete if it remained at a defense of the peace of creation. It can give God the appearance of indifference (even if blameless) to our loss of peace. A full exploration of the peace of creation, just like a full exploration of goodness, requires theology. Peace is inherently Trinitarian, and therefore theological. God is the God of peace.[190] God gives the world a share in his own peace, and this is not just through creation. As Aquinas says "every good comes to us from the Trinity through the incarnation."[191] This includes peace, which "God pours into the world through Christ."[192] This is because the peace of creation is not only incomplete and inevitably suffers loss, but sin destroys peace as well (both our own and others', to a certain extent). Though Aquinas does not explicitly relate peace to Christ or the Church in his systematic treatments of peace, his biblical commentaries contain all the building blocks of a fuller picture.

The connection between Christ and peace goes very deep for Aquinas. This is not something one would expect. Aquinas says that we have no evidence Christ would have become incarnate were

---

189. Cf. Brian Shanley, *The Thomist Tradition* (Amsterdam: Kluwer Academic Publisher, 2002), 127.

190. Cf. *Super Io.*, c. 17, l. 5.

191. *Super II Cor.*, c. 1, l. 1, n. 9.

192. *In de Div. Nom.*, c. 11, l. 3.

we to have avoided sin.[193] Thus, sin is the "reason for the incarnation."[194] As seen above, the loss of peace is not totally reducible to sin, i.e. there could be a particular lack of order/union or rest/tranquility even if there were not sin. Because of this one would not expect Aquinas to give the restoration of peace as the purpose of the incarnation; it is not totally reducible to sin and the very reason for the incarnation is sin. Nevertheless, Aquinas says precisely that: Christ "came to restore all things to a state of peace and tranquility."[195] "Christ came to make [peace] between God and human nature."[196] And because of this purpose, "at his birth peace was immediately proclaimed to all humans."[197] Though Aquinas clearly affirms sin as the reason for the incarnation, Aquinas also affirms the restoration of peace as the reason for the incarnation. Is there inconsistency here?

I do not think so. We should not overread Aquinas's claim that sin is the very reason for the incarnation. Aquinas' question in *ST* III q. 1, a. 3 is epistemological; he is profoundly agnostic about the reality of incarnation apart from sin. I think this does commit him to seeing the restoration of the sinner as the occasion of the incarnation. This, however, does not inform us of the good being sought by the incarnation. Sin is a privation, but its remedy is not. Sin may be the occasion, but its remedy is the good sought by the incarnation. If this is true, then there would be no inconsistency in saying that we do not know if Christ would have become incarnate without sin and that sin is thus the occasion of the incarnation, and yet this not telling us what good is being sought. Likewise, the restoration of the peace of creation is intimately connected to the remedy of sin because sin destroys the order/union of creation in a much deeper way than *per accidens* conflict. So although Aquinas thinks it is possible to lose peace without

193. Cf. *ST* III q. 1, a. 3, co.: "*peccato non existente, incarnatio non fuisset.*"
194. *ST* III q. 1, a. 3, co.
195. *ST* III q. 44, a. 4, ad 3: "*qui omnia in statum pacis et tranquillitatis revocare venerat.*"
196. *Super Ps.,* 45, n. 7
197. *Super Eph.,* c. 2, l. 4, n. 114: "*Nam in eius nativitate statim pax hominibus annuntiata est. Lc. II, v. 14.*"

sin, sin is still the primary cause of the loss of peace. In other words, though Christ came to remedy the primary cause of disorder/disunion, sin, the good of peace is something beyond the remedy of sin. He recapitulates all of creation, a restoration that results in something beyond a mere return to the order of creation. He comes to return all to union, a union damaged by sin, but even more so he comes to introduce a new peace which is order/union in its fullest.[198]

On the other hand, one can see why Aquinas so closely links the purpose of the incarnation, sin, and the loss of peace. Sin is fundamentally a disordered action. "Sin is by definition a withdrawal from the order of things which has God as its purpose."[199] And "Sin is not a pure privation, but an action deprived of its due order."[200] This is what makes sickness such an apt comparison. Sickness is a disorder/disunion in the body; sin is disorder/disunion in action. This is why Aquinas calls sin a "sickness of the soul."[201] This is not only true because the loss of grace follows from (grave) sin, but also because the sin itself introduces disorder into the powers of the soul. Sin is disorder/disunion with respect to the good. Certainly mortal sin, which is an action destroying our order to God, is the most serious type of sin. This is because it disorders/disunites the human in the most fundamental order/union, that is to God. Yet every sin disorders the soul, since it is a turning away from the order/union to what is good. Since the incarnation comes to remedy sin, it comes to remedy a main cause of disorder (a main cause of a loss of peace).

## The Hypostatic Union and Peace

In exploring Christ's mission for reordering/reuniting creation, Aquinas's *Commentary on Ephesians* 2:14 is a good place to start. St. Paul is writing of Christ's reconciliation of Jew and Gentile by the cross and comments "for he himself is our peace."[202] Aquinas

198. Cf. *Super Io.*, c. 17, l. 5.
199. *ST* I-II q. 79, a. 1, co.
200. *ST* I-II q. 72, a. 1, ad 2: *"dicendum quod peccatum non est pura privatio, sed est actus debito ordine privatus."*
201. *ST* I-II q. 88, a. 1, co.
202. Eph 2:14: "Αὐτὸς γάρ ἐστιν ἡ εἰρήνη ἡμῶν."

remarks particularly on this manner of speaking. "This way of speaking, however, is customarily done when the totality of an effect depends on the cause just as we say of God that he is our salvation because whatever salvation is in us is caused by God. Therefore, whatever peace is in us is caused by Christ. . . ."[203] This passage is replete with metaphysical commitments and implicitly contains all of Aquinas's thoughts on the relation of the incarnate Christ to peace. To be the cause of peace, Christ himself must have an intimate relation to peace in his person. A cause must possess a form in a more perfect way than its effect. So, it must be with Christ and peace.

On the other hand, other texts of Aquinas would seem to challenge this picture. For example, when commenting on Jn 14:27: "Peace I leave with you, my peace I give to you,"[204] Aquinas distinguishes a two-fold relation of Christ to our peace. The first is as *auctor*. This Aquinas correlates with the imperfect peace we have in this world where "we are not able to have undisturbed peace either with God or our neighbor."[205] For the imperfect peace of ours, Christ is merely *tantum auctoris*. In contrast, Christ is *possessor* of our future peace. This is the perfect peace which Christ always possesses since he is without disorder/disunion. Aquinas seems to be saying here that Christ is merely the source of human peace because it is marked by ongoing imperfections, but his perfect peace is not. Aquinas almost seems to be suggesting that one cannot predicate peace of Christ positively and affirmatively, but only by remotion or mere cause without possession.[206]

Nevertheless, this cannot be the case. The term *auctor,* even with the adjective *tantum,* does not necessarily imply complete apophaticism. Aquinas uses the term throughout his theology.[207] It does not

203. *Super Eph.,* c. 2, l. 5, n. 111: "*Hic autem modus loquendi fieri consuevit, quando totum quod est in effectu dependet ex causa, sicut cum dicimus de Deo quod ipse est salus nostra, quia quidquid salutis est in nobis causatur a Deo. Quia ergo quidquid pacis est in nobis causatur a Christo, et per consequens quidquid appropinquationis, quia homo quando pacificatus est cum alio, secure potest ambulare seu appropinquare ad ipsum, ideo dicit quod est pax nostra.*"
204. Jn 14:27: "Εἰρήνην ἀφίημι ὑμῖν, εἰρήνην τὴν ἐμὴν δίδωμι ὑμῖν."
205. *Super Io.,* c. 14, l. 7, n. 1962.
206. Cf. *ST* I q. 13, a. 2, co.
207. For a small selection of Aquinas's usage, see: *ST* I q. 22, a. 2, ad 3; *ST* I q. 32, a. 3,

imply that the source does not also have the fullness of the particular effect, as Aquinas's metaphysics require. Likewise, the addition of the *tantum* does not seem to change that. What it does seem to imply is that the way we possess peace is not the same (in perfection) as Christ's fullness. He is the mere author not because our peace is not a participation in his peace but because he does not possess peace in the same way (with imperfection) as fallen humanity.[208] It is as if Aquinas is saying that Christ is the mere author of peace with disturbance because Christ possesses peace in its fullness without disturbance. This seems to be the force of the *tantum* in relation to our peace, i.e. to deny Christ's peace has any disorder/disunion (at least post resurrection). This seems to be right because Aquinas, as we saw above, claims elsewhere our imperfect peace is a share in Christ's perfect peace. For example, "Christ is called the God of peace because he is the giver of peace.... He is also the author of peace.... He also dwells in peace."[209] Clearly the relation of Christ to peace is more than one of mere source. As Aquinas says, "We do not know the way of peace if we do not know Christ."[210]

In searching for a more precise statement of the relation of the incarnate Christ to peace, one clear place to begin looking is what I found in the last chapter concerning the Trinity and peace. To recall what was written there, the Son as Wisdom is the exemplar cause of the order/union of the world. It is this character of the Son that (partly) explains why God "pours peace into the world through Christ."[211] It is this way that the eternal Son's procession is the exemplar of all of creation's order, and therefore of its peace. Nevertheless, this does not tell us in what way Christ's human nature is related to

---

ad 4; *ST* I q. 33, a. 1, ad 2 & a. 4, ad 1; *ST* I q. 42, a. 4, ad 1; *ST* I q. 43, a. 4, ad 1; *ST* I q. 43, a. 7, ad 4; *ST* q. 46, a. 1, ad 9.

208. Cf. Matthew Tapie, "For He is our Peace: Thomas Aquinas on Christ as Cause of Peace in the City of Saints." In *The Journal of Moral Theology* volume 5, issue 1 (2016): 111–28; 119.

209. *Super II Cor.*, c. 13, l. 3, n. 540: "... *sed ideo Christus dicitur Deus pacis, quia est dator pacis et amator.... Ipse etiam est auctor pacis ... Ipse in pace habitat.*"

210. *Super Ps.* 13, n. 5.

211. *In de Div. Nom.*, 11, l. 3.

our peace. For that we must look more particularly at Aquinas's reasons for the Son's incarnation, the particular fittingness that he become incarnate.

As is well known, Aquinas holds that any person of the Trinity could have become incarnate, but it is supremely fitting that it is the Son. The reasons he gives are especially tied to the reintroduction of peace (order/union) in creation. In other words, the restoration of peace forms the key premise for Aquinas's arguments from fittingness for the incarnation of the Son. In *ST* III q. 3, a. 8, Aquinas gives three reasons for the fittingness of the incarnation of the Son: fittingness of like being in union with like, the sharing of his eternal procession as Son, and Wisdom overturning the sinful seeking of knowledge of Adam and Eve.[212] All three of these presuppose what was seen above concerning the exemplar causality of the Word/Wisdom. In God's Wisdom, the Father speaks all that he is and all that can be. Hence, the *rationes* of all creatures are spoken in the Son. Likewise, all creation happens through the Son. "God makes nothing except through the *ratio* of his intellect, who is wisdom conceived from all eternity, namely, the Word of God and Son of God."[213] And "The whole world is nothing other than a certain representation of the divine Wisdom conceived in the mind of the Father."[214] This creates a fundamental participation of creatures in the exemplar causality of the Son and therefore the supreme fittingness that he would become incarnate. Given the aforesaid order/union of all creatures to the Son's exemplar causality, it makes perfect sense that the restoration of the order/union of creation would take place through the Son.[215] The loss of order/union (peace) in creation is restored by the original Wisdom through whom it was made.[216] Although it is particularly premised on the disorder introduced by sin, the restoration

---

212. Cf. *ST* III q. 3, a. 8, co.

213. *Super Io.*, c. 1, l. 2, n. 77.

214. *Super Io.*, c. 1, l. 5, n 136.

215. Cf. Dominic Legge, *The Trinitarian Christology* (New York: Oxford University Press, 2018), 67ff.

216. Cf. *Super Rom.*, c. 1, l. 5, nn. 197–198.

of the order/union of creation goes well beyond that and restores all things to perfection.[217] This likewise shows an additional reason why it was fitting that Christ became incarnate. Wisdom is the very cause of peace by introducing order/union into a multitude. As we saw in the previous chapter, Aquinas names the procession of the Son from the Father as wisdom. Christ, as the eternal wisdom of God, is thus perfectly fitted to reintroduce order/union back to creation. He does this by assuming it, uniting it to himself, and ordering it in his very person.

To further explore how the Eternal Son's incarnation restores the peace of creation, one should look at Aquinas's thought on the ontological constitution of the incarnation, "the union of the Word to creatures not in a participated way but a personal way."[218] Not only is it supremely fitting that the second person of the Trinity reintroduce peace to creation as Wisdom, but also as Son. Aquinas's conception of the hypostatic union holds the key to the more precise way in which Christ possesses peace and the way God reintroduces peace to creation through him. This should not surprise us. Recalling what we found in the previous chapter, *unio/ordo* is the positive *ratio* of peace. When Aquinas outlines the mode of the hypostatic union, he is giving us a fuller picture of Christ's relation to peace personally and the restoration of peace to creation in his person.

Aquinas calls the unique relation between the assumed human nature (body and soul) and the second person of the Trinity, the "grace of union."[219] By this he means that by the common activity of the whole Trinity, the human nature of Christ is assumed as a *terminus* into the subsistent relation of the Son. As Aquinas says, this union is "a certain relation which is considered between the divine nature and human nature according to which they come together in one person, the Son of God."[220] Aquinas does not claim that

217. Cf. Legge, *The Trinitarian Christology*, 73.
218. *ST* III q. 3, a. 8, co.
219. *ST* III q. 6, a. 6, co.
220. *ST* III q. 2, a. 7, co: "*dicendum quod unio de qua loquimur est relatio quaedam quae consideratur inter divinam naturam et humanam, secundum quod conveniunt in una persona filii Dei.*"

a human person was assumed, for that would create two persons, but that human nature was assumed, one "univocal with other humans."[221] Because the human nature of Christ is related to the divine person such that they are one person, the human nature of Christ shares in the personal *esse* of the subsistent Trinitarian relation who is the Son. Now the subsistent relation of the Son subsists "*in duabus naturis*."[222] This is the invisible mission of the Son made visible. As Dominic Legge puts it:

> Aquinas is signifying the divine being itself, but *according to the unique personal mode* in which the Son subsists, a mode that is purely relational: the Son *is* the infinite and perfect divine *esse as received* from the Father, because the Son proceeds from the Father as his word, by way of intellect. The Son 'has being from the father . . . from whom he also has his nature, because he is God from God.' Only the Son subsists according to his unique mode, but because it is relational, this mode cannot even be conceived apart from the other divine persons, nor could it ever be separated from them.[223]

This very short summary of Aquinas's thoughts on the grace of union reveals a deep and abiding relation of the incarnate Christ to peace and bears out the metaphysical insight earlier articulated concerning cause and effect. If the incarnate Christ is the principle of our peace, then he must have it in a supreme and maximal way.[224] Aquinas clearly affirms that Christ is the cause of our peace, so he must also be that peace in the fullest sense.[225] The peace of creation is a share in the peace of Christ because he is order/union to the Father. The one subsistent person of the Son, who is order to the Father and Spirit, takes a human nature into his person such that he (through his human nature) relates to the Father and Spirit in a new

---

221. *ST* III q. 2, a. 5, co.

222. *ST* III q. 2, a. 6, co.

223. Legge, *The Trinitarian Christology*, 111.

224. Cf. Ramirez, *De Caritate*, 890: "Ese primero y ese supremo es precisamente el principio, la causa, la razón ultima de toda la ordenación de los demás de la serie."

225. Cf. *Super Heb.*, c. 13, l. 3; *Super I Tim.*, c. 1, l. 1; *Super col.*, 1.5; *Super Eph.*, 2.5; *Super Io.*, c. 14, l. 7; *Super Rom.*, c. 3, l. 2; *Super Ps.* 34, n. 18.

mode.[226] The Incarnate Son is "the created effect in which the Word is sent into the world."[227] The Son, who is peace with the Father and Spirit, takes a human nature such that it shares his filial *esse,* is his peace with the Father and Spirit lived through a human nature.

In other words, the grace of union turns out to be the ontological foundation of Christ's peace. From the grace of union thus follows the negative *rationes* of peace: *quies et tranquillitas.* Christ is fundamentally without disunion/discord in his order/union to the Father and Spirit, this is the grace of union. As such his peace will always be greater, in kind, than the peace of any human person for the grace of union takes place in a Divine Person.[228] From the grace of union flow all Christ's graces, which are formally distinct from it: capital grace, habitual grace, and the rest of the virtues and gifts.[229] They flow from the grace of union since by it the whole Trinity dwells in the human nature of Jesus Christ.[230] It is through these graces (most proximately) that creatures come to share in the peace God intends to reintroduce through Christ. It is by a share in these graces that a share in the filial mode of the hypostatic union will be given to humans and, for that very reason, a share in his peace.

Nevertheless, since Aquinas is clear that the grace of union does not preclude imperfections in Christ's body and soul,[231] it cannot preclude imperfections in his possession of peace. Aquinas is clear that Christ "assumed all those defects which follow from the sin common to all nature but not repugnant to the perfection of

---

226. Technically speaking, the Son does not begin to relate to the Father and Spirit in a new mode, but the human nature taken into his person relates in a new way, though it is attributed to the person.

227. Legge, *The Trinitarian Christology,* 118.

228. Cf. *ST* III q. 2, a. 10, co.: "*Maius autem est ipsa res quam similitudo eius participata.*" On the other hand, this does not imply that his peace cannot be disturbed. Undoubtedly, if pressed, Aquinas would claim that the perfect peace Christ enjoys as *comprehensor* does not preclude the disturbance of peace in his lower appetites.

229. Cf. *ST* III q. 7, a. 30, co.

230. For an excellent treatment of the relation between the grace of union and Christ's personal graces, see Legge, *The Trinitarian Christology,* 135–57.

231. Cf. Thomas Joseph White, O.P., *The Incarnate Lord* (Washington DC: The Catholic University of American Press, 2017), 455.

knowledge and grace."[232] These include, for Aquinas, defects of both the body and soul, which would render Christ's peace imperfect; he is *viator*. This would not preclude the hypostatic union and the graces flowing from it from being the fullness of peace inasmuch as it can be possessed by human nature and thus from Christ's ability to communicate this peace to those who love him. Nevertheless, it does mean that perfect and uninterrupted order/union is lacking in Christ (prior to the resurrection)—either because of the legitimate conflict of appetites (without sin) or because of external causes.[233]

These deeper metaphysical reflections reveal why Aquinas says that God pours peace into the world through the Son and the Son is "peace itself."[234] Therefore, "we are pacified by his coming."[235] In his person, he is the peace between human and divine natures.[236] Because of that, he can give a share of this order/union to creatures. Just as the "Father is the *auctor* from whom the Son proceeds eternally in his divine nature, and from whom he has every good that he possesses in his human nature,"[237] so also Christ as incarnate is the very *auctor* of the peace of creation. He gives humans a share in his order/union with the Father, a share in his filial mode of existence. Just as believers' graces are a share in the grace of Christ, so too, it is from this profound source that all believers receive peace.[238]

Because of the very purpose of the incarnation is peace and it is expressed ontologically in the very person of Christ, it would make sense that his whole ministry and teaching would reflect that and work for the restoration and perfection of the peace of creation. Aquinas says this explicitly. Christ "preaches what is useful to peace."[239] He preaches the "gospel of peace,"[240] and "the advantage [his] teaching

232. *ST* III q. 14, a. 4, co.: "*Illos igitur defectus Christus assumere debuit qui consequuntur ex peccato communi totius naturae, nec tamen repugnant perfectioni scientiae et gratiae.*"
233. Cf. *ST* III q. 15, aa. 5–6.
234. *Super Matt.*, c. 1, l. 3: "*Utrumque autem significat Christum, quia ipse est pax.*"
235. *Super Ps.*, 12, n. 1.
236. Cf. *ST* III q. 2, aa. 7–8.
237. *ST* III q. 21, a. 3.
238. Cf. *ST* III q. 8, a. 5, co.
239. *Super Rom.*, c. 10, l. 2.
240. *Super Rom.*, c. 10, l. 2.

gives is peace."[241] He announces the peace which is his very person: the peace to be had with all men, and peace with himself.[242] He instructs his apostles to do the same, to preach peace.[243] Christ came to "gather those who are dispersed."[244] Indeed, according to Aquinas, the very *finis* of Christ's teaching is peace, that is "everything in the whole gospel is aimed at returning you to me [Christ] . . . the purpose of the gospel is peace in Christ."[245] This recalls the metaphysics of union seen above. The proper order and perfect union Christ is in his person is not an end in itself. He aims to share it with the rest of creation. He is calling people to a share in his filial mode of existence and thereby attain supernatural order/union to God.

Aquinas gives a more concrete picture of what he means by sharing in this filial mode of existence in multiple places. In every place, he says it consists in the return of proper order/union to the individual and between individuals. In some places he identifies this as the proper order of one's powers; elsewhere he says it is proper order between God, self, and neighbor. In other words, Christ comes to return order/union both interiorly and exteriorly and this is the gospel he preaches.

> For peace consists in two things, such that a man be in harmony with himself and with others. Neither can be had sufficiently without God. For without God a man does not have harmony within himself, much less with others, because a man's affections are in harmony with themselves when what is desired for one suffices for all. Nothing but God can do this. . . . For anything else other than God is not sufficient [to quiet] for all [desires], but God is sufficient.[246]

---

241. *Super Io.,* c. 16, l. 8, n. 2174: *"utilitas doctrinae est pax. . . ."*

242. Cf. *Super Rom.,* c. 10, l. 2.

243. Cf. *Super I Tim.,* l. 3, c. 1.

244. *Super Matt.,* c. 5, l. 2, n. 439: *"ut congregaret dispersos."*

245. *Super Io.,* 16, l. 8, n. 2174: *"et propter hoc scilicet omnia quae dixi vobis in sermone, vel omnia quae in toto Evangelio locutus sum vobis, ut, ad me redeuntes, in me pacem habeatis. Finis enim Evangelii est pax in Christo."*

246. *Super II Thess.,* 3, l. 2, n. 89: *"Pax enim consistit in duobus, ut scilicet homo concordet ad seipsum, et ad alios. Et neutrum potest habieri sufficienter nisi in Deo: quia sibi non concordat sufficienter nisi in Deo et minus aliis quia tunc affectus hominis concordat in seipso*

In fact, at the very point where you would expect Aquinas to qualify the claim that peace is the very purpose of the gospel, Aquinas doubles down. This place, of course, is Mt 10:34 where Christ says: "I have not come to bring peace, but the sword." In Aquinas's lecture on this passage, he comments: "For this reason, peace is two-fold, that is good and evil . . . I have not come to make this peace (of carnal affection), but there is a good peace about which it is said in Eph 2:14: he is our very peace who has made many into one . . ."[247] In other words, Aquinas claims that Christ has not come to bring the peace of carnal affection, but has come to bring true peace. Aquinas makes a distinction so that he can maintain that the very purpose of the gospel is peace. This distinction mirrors Aquinas's distinction throughout his corpus between the peace of evildoers, which is not true peace, and the peace brought by goodness, true peace. He merely invokes this distinction here to maintain that Christ, in fact, does come to bring peace.

In summary, Aquinas's thought on the grace of union allows us to say that Christ himself is the peace between the divine and human nature, a nature estranged from the divine love and brought back by its assumption into a divine person. The grace of union bears this out and explains the deeper metaphysics of Christ's causality of peace. Christ is not simply the cause of peace but is, in his person, the order/union between humanity and divinity. "Heavenly inheritance is not given except to sons . . ."[248]

---

quando quod appetitur secundum unum, sufficit quantum ad omnes, quod nihil potest esse praeter Deum. . . . Quaecumque enim alia, praeter Deum, non sufficiunt ad omnes, sed Deus sufficit."

247. *Super Matt.*, c. 10, l. 2, n. 844: "*Ideo dicendum quod duplex est pax, videlicet bona, et mala. Nomine pacis concordia significatur. Est pax mala, de qua habetur Sap. XIV, 22: sed in magno viventes inscientiae bello, tot et tam magna mala pacem appellant. Ista pax est carnalium affectuum. Istam non veni ponere. Unde Apoc. VI, 14: datum est ei ut sumeret pacem de terra. Est et pax bona, de qua Eph. II, 14: ipse est pax nostra qui fecit utraque unum; et ideo angeli cecinerunt, Lc. II, 14: et in terra pax hominibus bonae voluntatis.*"

248. *ST* III q. 3, a. 8, co.

### The Cross, the Resurrection, and Peace

As was seen earlier, though the causes of disorder/disunion and disquiet/discord are not totally reducible to sin, sin is their primary cause for humanity in general. Because of this, Aquinas's comments that Christ came to bring peace and he is incarnated because of sin are not in tension. Sin is fundamentally a disordered action (and results in more disorder) and the incarnation and cross are particularly intent on remedying sin. The cross and resurrection are thus the restoration of order/union (or at least the beginning and cause of a reunification and restoration of order). Put differently, the cross, for Aquinas, is the main way God strikes at the very root of disorder/disunion. Because of this, Aquinas says "the passion itself was the maker of peace."[249] And "To cure [the disturbances of peace] Jesus offers them the peace of reconciliation with God ... which he accomplished by his suffering."[250] Though much could be said on this topic, three claims of Aquinas are particularly important for understanding the relation of the sacrifice of the cross to peace. The first is that according to Aquinas, one can satisfy for another only if one is united to that other in love. In other words, fundamental peace (order/union) is a prerequisite for satisfaction on behalf of another. Second, Christ's satisfaction for our sins derives from his love and obedience. In other words, it is derived from his fundamental order/union to God and with us. Third, Aquinas describes the restoration of this order in multiple ways, but they center around two primary descriptions: union of appetites and union with God, self, and others.

Aquinas's deepest metaphysical commitments about the incarnation ground his understanding of Christ's salvific action. Aquinas writes, "And because it happens that those who differ in the debt of punishment are one according to will in the union of love, one car-

---

249. *Super Matt.,* c. 16, l. 3, n. 1398: *"Voluit igitur ibi pati ad ostendendum, quod mors eorum fuit signum passionis Christi. Item Ierusalem dicitur visio pacis; sed ipsa passio pacifica fuit."*

250. *Super Io.,* 20, l. 4, n. 2532.

ries the penalty voluntarily for another."[251] Aquinas's metaphysics of satisfaction and justice require this because union with the deserving sinner makes the undeserving take on willingly the punishment of the other. In other words, out of love (union) with another one thereby takes on the sufferings of another. Christ undertakes this union fundamentally in his being.[252] He is thereby united to all rational creatures, and by extension to all of creation.[253] Justice is satisfied because the one deserving is united to another who aids. Yet Christ's stepping in is not based on justice, it being merely fitting, but on the love (union) with the sinner. Put simply, the metaphysics of the incarnation allow for Christ's satisfaction, and it is Jesus' fundamental peace with the Father and with humans (grace of union) that allows both the fitting suffering of Christ for the sins of the human race and also the return of his peace to the human race.

Understanding the hypostatic union this way avoids any substitution theory.[254] Substitution theory requires that there be no order/union between the one punished and the one substituted. Yet, Christ is united with us both in the hypostatic union and in volitional love (another union). Therefore, the cross is fitting in justice. This is why redemption extends to the whole human race, to all Christ's members.[255] Christ is head of the whole human race and thus whatever he merits affects all his members.[256] Likewise, a full substitutional theory requires nothing on the part of the one deserving punishment. Aquinas's conception includes participation. Christ doesn't replace our participation in his redemptive act, but enables it.[257] Union in

---

251. *ST* I-II q. 87, a. 7, co.: "*Et quia contingit eos qui differunt in reatu poenae, esse unum secundum voluntatem unione amoris, inde est quod interdum aliquis qui non peccavit, poenam voluntarius pro alio portat.*" See also *ScG* III c. 158, n. 7.

252. Aquinas does not want to push this point as far as Anselm does. The one in union with the other fittingly suffers on the other's behalf on account of their oneness. Justice is still preserved, but he suffers out of love and not justice.

253. Cf. *Super Io.*, c. 1, l. 8, n. 189.

254. In this section I am following, Rik Van Nieuwenhove, "Bearing the Marks of Christ's Passion."

255. Cf. *ST* III q. 48, a. 2, ad 1.

256. Cf. *ST* III q. 19, a. 4, co. q. 48, a. 2, ad 1; q. 49, a. 1, co.

257. Cf. *Super Rom.*, c. 8, l. 3, n. 651.

one direction (from Christ to us) does not replace union in the other (from us to Christ); relation in one direction does not replace relation in the other. It is perfectly possible to have a relation from one term to another, but not the reverse; this is exactly what happens if someone does not take up the cross of Christ him or herself.

Christ's fundamental union with us enables us to enter union with him. His cross enables ours.[258] This is why you must be united to Christ in order to receive the effects of his redemption, and it is by that union that one has already received the effects.[259] Put differently, the effects of redemption are not automatically applied to the whole human race. The fundamental union of the incarnation is enough to give the foundation for satisfaction, since by it Christ is united to all humans in nature and love, but the receipt of those affects require that the order/union/relation go both ways. If one does not love Christ, the effects of the redemption are inhibited.[260]

More particularly, Aquinas states that Christ offered satisfaction through love and obedience.[261] Aquinas conceives of the essence of sacrifice simply as a self-offering done *propter reverentiam diviniam* where something is done to that which is offered to God.[262] It can be internal, which is indeed the principal and primary sense of sacrifice, and external (which is ordered to and a sign of the internal). When Aquinas is pressed to explain what he means by doing something out of reverence for God, he reverts back to the desire to retain order/union to God. Hence, he explains that something has the *rationem sacrificii* if it is "an act done so that we may dwell with God in holy fellowship."[263] This explains why he sees every act of Christ

258. Cf. *ST* III q. 48, a. 6, ad 3.

259. Cf. *ScG* c. 55, n. 29.

260. Aquinas's metaphysics of union make fertile ground for rethinking his very pessimistic assessment of the salvation of those after the coming of Christ in light of Vatican II's *Nostra Aetate's* more positive assessment of the possible salvation of those outside of the Church on the basis of order/union.

261. Cf. *ScG* IV c. 55, nn. 25–26.

262. *ST* II-II q. 85, a. 2, co. & 85, a. 3, ad 3.

263. *ST* II-II q. 85, a. 3, ad 1: "*Et ideo cuiuscumque virtutis actus rationem sacrificii accipit ex hoc quod agitur ut sancta societate Deo inhaereamus.*"

as a sacrifice, but culminating in the cross. Each act of Christ was done so that he may dwell with God in fellowship, for indeed he is that fellowship in his person. Since the real cause of our salvation is his self-offering to God, which occurred in every act, we can see that the hypostatic union is the real metaphysical ground of redemption.

Jesus' divine personhood lived through a human nature makes for the perfect order/union between human nature and God. This in turn is what enables his acts of virtue on account of reverence for God, the very locus of redemption which is the oblation of his whole life in the filial mode. Yet these are made perfect, in the biblical sense, on the cross, in the perfect sacrifice. It is there that Christ offers himself in the fullest way by giving all his soul's goods, bodily goods, and external goods.[264] This love and obedience calls forth our love and obedience. "Love calls forth love."[265] Thus, Aquinas says that each of our actions should be a self-offering to God.[266] This is the heart of his sacrifice: to save us he offered himself to God. In this way, we see again the depth of Aquinas's vision. It is by participation in the one who is at peace with God that we become at peace. It is by participation in his acts of self-offering that we come to self-offer. It is by participating in his filial mode of order/union that all of us become reordered/united to God.[267] It is by participating in the fundamental peace which Christ has that we come to be at peace.

This is born out if one looks closer at how the effects of redemption are received by humanity. Aquinas describes the effects of Christ's redemption as the restoration of order/union in terms of our fundamental relationships. He reconciles all things in himself and hence, "he is our peace."[268] This makes perfect sense since, as I argued in the previous chapter, that order/union express different aspects of relations: order expressing the *ad aluid* aspect and union

264. Cf. *ST* II-II q. 85, a. 3, ad 2.
265. Ramirez, "La Eucaristía y la Paz Individual," 173: *"El amor llama al amor."*
266. Cf. *ST* III q. 48, a. 3, ad 2.
267. Cf. *Super Rom.*, c. 12, l. 1, n. 957–967.
268. *Super Col.*, c. 1, l. 5.

expressing the fact that the same relation renders the two parties one *secundum quid*. Hence, to restore order/union is to restore relationships with God, self, and others. Yet, as said above, this does not happen without our participation. We must love Christ to receive the fruits of his redemption. It is the love of Christ (objective genitive in this case) that orders our loves, which is the very fruit of redemption. Christ's cross gives the gift of right order/union with God and others. Put differently, our participation in the cross of Christ by union (love) is that which also restores our appetites and fundamental relationships. Love for Christ not only unites us to the source of redemption, but *ipso facto* reorders human life. I'll have more to say about this in the next chapter when I explore Aquinas's thought on grace and the virtue of charity, but for now the more general point suffices: Aquinas envisions the redemption as the restoration of order/union, the restoration of peace. In every way that sin disorders our relationships, Christ's sacrifice restores them. This is not only internal, i.e. our affections, but also our relationships to one another and to the world. Aquinas is fond of describing the redemption as restoring relationships to God, self, and others. He also recognizes that this re-ordering extends to sub-rational material creation.[269]

The resurrection completes the trajectory of Christ's mission of reintroducing peace to creation. According to Aquinas, the cross and the resurrection form one total efficient cause of our redemption. "Two things occur in the justification of souls: the remission of guilt and newness of life through grace. Inasmuch as one considers efficient causality, which is through the divine power, both the passion of Christ and his resurrection are the cause of justification."[270] Because of this unity of causality between the cross and resurrection, in every way the cross causes peace, the resurrection does as well. Possibly according to efficient causality one could distinguish

269. Cf. *Super Rom.*, c. 8, l. 4, 660.

270. *ST* III q. 56, a. 2, ad 4: "*dicendum quod in iustificatione animarum duo concurrunt, scilicet remissio culpae, et novitas vitae per gratiam. Quantum ergo ad efficaciam, quae est per virtutem divinam, tam passio Christi quam resurrectio est causa iustificationis quoad utrumque.*"

the cross as the beginning and the resurrection as the completion, but they remain fundamentally one efficient cause. Hence, in every way above that we explored the relation of the cross to sin likewise applies to the resurrection as well. In other words, the resurrection is the completion of Christ's satisfaction for sin. Presupposing the hypostatic union, Christ enters into deeper relation with us in the resurrection and his love for us is brought to completion. The resurrection of Christ is the fundamental beginning of the reintroduction of peace back into creation.

Although the cross and resurrection form a coherent causal whole of our salvation, occasionally Aquinas divides the causality of the cross from that of the resurrection. He is clear that efficiently speaking the cross and resurrection are united in being the sole cause of redemption and that it is through the whole mystery of Christ that peace is brought to creation.[271] Nevertheless, if one speaks of formal causality, one can divide their causality. The cross deals with the remission of faults and merits justification and resurrection causes justification.[272] Put differently, the cross removes evil and the resurrection unites to the good. That Aquinas would divide the paschal mystery's exemplar causality this way makes perfect sense both because the passion is particularly tied to sin in the Bible and because this schema mirrors well Aquinas's thought on how grace moves the subject from sin to the good, the remotion of evil coming generationally prior to the unity with the good.[273] This division reveals that the resurrection, more than the cross, is particularly tied to the reintroduction of peace. Peace is a *ratio* of the good and so the exemplar cause of the good will be particularly tied to its reintroduction.

When Christ is the focus, one can see the special connection of the resurrection to peace. The movement toward perfect peace occurs firstly in Christ. In Christ, the resurrection perfects his peace

---

271. Cf. *Super Heb.*, c. 13, l. 3.
272. Cf. *ST* III 56, a. 2, ad 4.
273. Cf. *ST* I-II q. 110, etc.

by removing his subjection to imperfections. Aquinas certainly does not think Christ was sinful, but that does not mean he is not subject to some of the imperfections and sufferings which naturally accompany the human state.[274] These imperfections can be understood as ways that Christ is not fully in union with the good, not perfectly ordered internally and externally (in this case what is lacking is other's relation to him, not his to them). Certainly, this disorder cannot be traced back to any sin on his part, but it can be (some of it anyway) traced to the loss of original justice and Christ's voluntary assumption of our fallen state.[275] The resurrection, on the other hand, removes even these and puts Christ perfectly in union with the good. He is beyond sadness or anger (both of which, though virtuous, presuppose the existence of evil). He is beyond suffering of any kind. Nothing can remove this internal or external order, Christ's perfect peace. As Thomas Joseph White says, "He is raised from the dead, then, no longer to live simply as one who is like us in all things but sin, but as one who is the perfect exemplar of our human nature transfigured by grace."[276] In other words, the resurrection completes Christ's relation to God qua human, so that he has order/union even in the body—rest from any disorder/disunion, security from all evil, and a perfect relationship to all humans.

If we want to study a perfect Thomistic vision of human peace, it must begin with Christ's peace post resurrection. It is only after the resurrection that the human nature of Christ enjoys perfect order/union with God, others, and creation. No longer will it be possible for one appetite to conflict (sinlessly, of course) with another. Christ's perfect unity to God in soul and body mean that the infinite goodness of God is the fulfilling good for each of his appetites. There can be no disorder/disunion between them because one good fulfills them all. This has effects for the way Christ's internal union of appetites operates and overflows into his body. Likewise, no external cause

---

274. Cf. *ST* III q. 14.
275. Cf. *ST* I-II q. 85, a. 3, co.
276. White, *The Incarnate Lord,* 455.

can disturb this union with God. It is eternal and imperturbable. He is the picture of perfect interior peace as it can be had by humans.

Furthermore, Christ's relation to each human as head is perfected in the resurrection. He is perfectly ordered/in union with everyone who has human nature. So, while humans can certainly have a lack of union/order toward Christ, he cannot have a lack of union with them. His order/union with them is secure. In other words, he is perfectly united/ordered to all humans now and even if this is not reciprocal, it cannot disturb his peace with them. Finally, by the perfection of his order/union with God, Christ has a perfect relation to the rest of material creation, and the rest of material creation finds in him the beginning of its restoration to the full communication of God's glory.[277] It is in the restoration of these orders, the restoration of union with God/others/creation, that we see a true picture of lasting peace.

Because of Christ's perfection, and the metaphysical commitment that whatever is perfect in an order is the source of that perfection for all others in that order, Aquinas is clear that Christ's resurrection is the cause and exemplar of our own.[278] In other words, Christ's resurrection functions as a sacrament of our life with God.[279] Jesus becomes "the universal progenitor of the human race in the order of grace."[280] In a very real sense, the incarnate Christ is the *ratio* according to which God redeems us. He is God's idea of perfect peace. This implies, since the resurrection is the exemplar cause of proper human order/union in the order of grace, that Christ is the universal progenitor of supernatural peace. This ultimately fulfills the fundamental purpose of the incarnation: the restoration of the peace of creation. In the resurrected Christ we see a perfect picture of true peace. The restoration of proper order is the restoration of union with God, others, and creation. This begins exemplarily with Christ's

---

277. Recall that for Aquinas the fall of the rest of creation is caused through the fall of man; its restoration, likewise, comes through man. I would not go as far as Christopher Thompson does in *The Joyful Mystery* in saying that the rest of creation is unfallen though. When humans fall, creation falls. See *De Rationibus Fidei*, c. 5.

278. Cf. *ST* III q. 56, aa. 1–2.

279. Cf. *Super Rom.*, c. 6, l. 2, n. 491.

280. White, *The Incarnate Lord*, 460.

resurrection and it is from his person and mystery that we are given a share. What this looks like more particularly is treated in the next chapter, but for now it is important to note that whatever it is, it is a deeper participation in the very peace of Christ who reveals to us what a human redeemed by grace becomes. As Ramirez says, "He himself is the bond of union between us and God."[281]

### THE HOLY SPIRIT, THE CHURCH, AND PEACE

Yves Congar, the great retriever of Thomistic ecclesiology, claims that Aquinas's primary designation for the Church is *congregatio fidelium*.[282] George Sabra disagrees somewhat and claims that *Corpus Christi Mysticum* also holds pride of place in Aquinas's thought.[283] It is not my purpose to decide who is correct. It is the place where these two designations converge that matters here. In both *congregatio* and *corpus* the theme of order/union is heavily stressed.[284] The Church is the gathering of many into the one of Christ's headship. Both these images are explanations of the *multitudo* and *unio* of the Church.[285] The Church is the new Jerusalem, the city of peace.[286] It is in this theme of multiplicity and union that we find the relation of the Holy Spirit to peace, who is Aquinas's ultimate explanation of the union of the Church. The Spirit is the great gatherer, the great unifier and finisher of Christ's work. In other words, though the above section gives a picture of the incarnate Christ's relation to peace, this picture would in no way be complete, or even accurate, without understanding the Holy Spirit's relation to peace as well.[287]

---

281. Ramirez, "La Eucaristía y la Paz," 915: " . . . *El mismo el lazo de union entre Dios y nosotros por su propria condicion de Dios y Hombre verdadero.*"

282. Cf. Yves Congar, "'Ecclesia' et 'populus (fidelis)' dans l'ecclésiologie de S. Thomas," in *St. Thomas Aquinas 1274–1974: Commemorative Studies*, vol. 1, ed. Armand A. Maurer et al. (Toronto: Pontifical Institute of Mediaeval Studies, 1974), 162.

283. Cf. George Sabra, *Thomas Aquinas' Vision of the Church: Fundamentals of an Ecumenical Ecclesiology* (Mainz: Matthias-Grunewald-Verlag, 1987), 71.

284. Cf. Sabra, *Thomas Aquinas' Vision of the Church*, 64 & 71.

285. Cf. Sabra, *Thomas Aquinas' Vision of the Church*, 65.

286. Cf. *Super Gal.*, c. 4, l. 8; *Super Io.*, c. 2, l. 2.

287. For a more extended treatment of the relation between Christ, the Spirit, and

As Dominic Legge says: "It is impossible, according to Aquinas, to separate the divine missions of the Son and the Holy Spirit from their eternal processions, since a divine mission includes and discloses the eternal procession upon which it is founded ... The Son does not act in the world without the Spirit, and so the whole of the mystery of Christ aims at and is accomplished in the outpouring of the Holy Spirit on the world."[288] This gives us a general reason to suppose that if Christ is intimately related to peace, so is the Spirit.

The Spirit is the ever-present accompaniment to the historical actions of Christ. Not only does the Spirit dwell preeminently in Christ (which is not the topic of the current discussion),[289] but to effect redemption simply is to give the Spirit.[290] The reordering and reunification of creation to its creator, within itself, and between subjects is planned and effected by the Son and the very means by which it is effected is the communication of the Holy Spirit. This is why, though peace is intimately related to the ontological constitution of Christ and the sharing in his filial life given by the incarnation, Aquinas more intimately relates peace to the Spirit, for the Spirit is the very gift of that life.[291] The Spirit, who is the *nexus* or *unio* between the Father and the Son, becomes the very gift by which peace is restored to creation. We are likened to him by exemplary causality in the *unio* that is love.[292] It is this love that ultimately is the peace any human enjoys between himself or herself, God, others, and creation.

According to Aquinas, the visible and invisible missions of the Son and Spirit follow their eternal processional pattern. As Legge puts it: "That Christ sends the Spirit to the world as the divine Son, therefore manifests in the world the order of the eternal processions within the Triune God."[293] Christ gives the Holy Spirit in his

---

the Church see Martin Grabmann, *Die Lehre des heiligen Thomas von Aquin von der Kirche als Gotteswork* (Regensburg: G. J. Manz, 1903), 160ff.

288. Legge, *Trinitarian Christology*, 212.

289. Cf. Legge, *Trinitarian Christology*, Chapters 5–7 for an excellent treatment.

290. Cf. Legge, *Trinitarian Christology*, 217.

291. Cf. II *Sent.*, d. 26, q. 1, a. 1; *ScG* III cc. 151–153;

292. Cf. *ScG* IV c. 21, n. 1–2 .

293. Legge, *Trinitarian Christology*, 211.

very humanity as an instrumental cause of his divinity. "He received the gifts of the Spirit without measure, he has the power of pouring them out without measure."[294] Given the intra-Trinitarian character of the Spirit, his eternal place within the order of the Trinity as 'gift' and 'love' exemplifies his temporal mission. The Spirit is present throughout the work of Christ, the ever-accompanying effect of this redemption. Since Aquinas identifies the reintroduction of order/union into creation as the very purpose of Christ's incarnation, life, preaching, death, and resurrection, the Spirit is the very gift of that reordering/reunification. Again, the eternal procession of *unio* between the Father and Son is the very person who is given to reorder/reunite creation. The Holy Spirit is the bond and unity between the Father and the Son, so he is the gift given to humans. He bonds and unifies them in the mode of love, love of Christ. To give grace and to give the Spirit are interchangeable terms for Aquinas. It is the presence of the Spirit which returns the peace of creation. Put differently, redemption is accomplished by Christ's death and resurrection efficiently and exemplarity, but the very effect of it is the presence of the Holy Spirit's indwelling. This reordering of the individual is peace. This is why Aquinas calls the "form of peace" union in the Holy Spirit.[295] It is this peace that Aquinas says imitates God's peace.[296]

The Spirit is the ever-present bond reordering/reuniting what was divided. Considering individuals, Aquinas pulls on his metaphysics of order/union to explain how this takes place. The indwelling of the Holy Spirit orders/unifies the appetites of the individual by causing in them the theological virtues. These virtues reorder the faculties of the individual to God. Preeminently it is charity which is a love of God above and beyond all things. This reordering of appetites to one (the Triune God) *ipso facto* unites them to each other. It brings them into a single order, gives them a common cause. This is only possible, without destroying each individual appetite, because God contains

---

294. *Comp. Theo.*, c. 215
295. *Super Eph.*, c. 2, l. 5.
296. Cf. *ST* I-II q. 69, a. 4, co.

eminently the goods of all human appetites. Each potency finds its fulfillment in him. God is "that through which all appetites are united by rest in one."[297] Each can find there what is "fitting to each."[298] This ordering of many to one makes each appetite part of one order to God and thus precludes, inasmuch as the order remains undisturbed, disunion. Relating this back to the Son, this is what Aquinas means when he says the Son gives a share of his filial existence through the gift of the indwelling of the Holy Spirit. This share is an imitation and participation in the life of Christ, who in his person, is the peace that God wishes to reintroduce to creation. All our appetites, and indeed our whole life, begin to be oriented toward the Trinity through the indwelling of the Holy Spirit. Obviously, there is a difference in kind between Jesus' grace and the individual believer's. Only Christ is the hypostatic union. Nevertheless, individual believers come to share in that relation.[299] For all these reasons, Aquinas says that peace is gained from "the presence of the Holy Spirit."[300]

The Church mirrors this reintroduction of order/union on a social level. What causes the union of appetites in each individual simultaneously unites/orders that individual to others. This is how Aquinas describes the Church: a union of many. They are "gathered into one something."[301] This is why Aquinas describes the form of peace as union in the Holy Spirit.[302] There is a wholeness to the Church that Aquinas compares, based on St. Paul, to the human body. The Church is the community of those who are in union with God and with each other.[303] This comes about explicitly through the Holy Spirit and Aquinas uses the metaphor of the body and soul to explain this. "As we see that there is in one man one soul and one body, yet diverse members; so the Catholic Church is one body and has diverse members. The soul which vivifies this body is the Holy

297. *ST* II-II q. 29, a. 2, ad 4: "*per quam omnes appetitus uniuntur quietati in uno.*"
298. *ST* II-II q. 29, a. 1, ad 1: "*utrique convenit.*"
299. Cf. *Super Io.,* c. 17, l. 5, n. 2247 & 2240: "*quamdam remotam similitudinem.*"
300. *Super Io.,* c. 14, l. 7, n. 1961.
301. *Super Eph.,* c. 2, l. 5, n. 116.
302. Cf. *Super Eph.,* c. 2, l. 5.
303. Cf. *Super I Tim.,* c. 3, l. 3, n. 127.

Spirit."[304] The Holy Spirit is the form, the active principle, uniting and ordering each particular element within the body to each other and to the good of the whole.[305]

This union of the Church is brought about by the same means that the individual's faculties are reordered and brought into union, by the indwelling of the Holy Spirit. It is through the gift of the Spirit, his indwelling, and the effects it has on us (including the theological virtues) that we are united by faith, hope, and love to Christ.[306] Likewise, there is no opposition between the unity of the Church being through the theological virtues and through the indwelling of the Spirit. They are related as ultimate and proximate causes of order/union.[307] Ultimately it is the same Spirit who dwells in the whole body and in each member who is numerically one and the same.[308] Yet this indwelling affects us and recreates us by causing habitual grace and the theological virtues. The same Spirit's indwelling causes the unity ultimately and secondarily it is caused by the Church being a community of those who know and love God.[309] "Because there is a sharing of God with people according to the communication of God's own happiness to us, a kind of friendship can be grounded in that sharing."[310] Aquinas explicitly connects his metaphysical thought about order/union to the order/union of the Church. The Church is *unum* and that is good.[311] Likewise, the sins against the union of the Church are sins against the oneness and goodness of the Church. "Someone moves away from the unity of the Spirit by seeking to transform the Church's good into their own. Just as in the terrestrial state peace is removed by the fact that individual citizens seek their own benefit."[312]

---

304. *In symb.*, a. 9, n. 971.

305. Cf. III *Sent.*, d. 13, q.2, a. 2.

306. Cf. *Super Io.*, c. 7, l. 7, n. 972–973.

307. Cf. Sabra, *Thomas Aquinas' Vision of the Church*, 102. For more on the debate between Mura and Journet see E Vauthier, *Le saint-Esprit principe d'unite* (1949).

308. Cf. III *Sent.*, d. 13, q. 2, a. 2.

309. Cf. *Super Eph.*, c. 4, l. 1.

310. *ST* II-II q. 23, a. 1, co.

311. Cf. *Super Rom.*, c. 17, l. 5.

312. *ST* II-II q. 183, q. 2, a. 3.

This is also what right leadership means in the Church. Leadership in the Church is one who directs an 'ordered multitude'[313] for the purpose of union with God and neighbor (peace).

In other words, the Spirit is gifted to individuals as part of a congregation, as part of those "called together."[314] "Each human being has a body and a soul and through them diverse members. So it is with the Catholic Church: one body and yet different members; the soul vivifying this body is the Holy Spirit."[315] In considering the Church, Aquinas's thought about it flows from his metaphysics of peace and mirrors the redemption of the individual. The Spirit is the bond of the Church because he "makes many into one."[316] This in turn overcomes division (but not distinction).[317] Indeed, Aquinas understands the unity of the Church as a union of friendship with God and with others.[318]

Aquinas often calls this union between individuals *concordia*. Here we see the absolute heart of Aquinas's ecclesiology. The drawing of an individual into the Church is through the reception of the Holy Spirit given by Christ. This reception transforms the hearts of individuals and bonds them together. To share one life, the life of the Spirit, is the very essence of the Church. It is a community of those who love God and love their neighbors. It is a *unio* of *multitudo,* to use the language of the transcendentals.[319] This union between individuals too comes about through the Holy Spirit since humans are united by a shared good, the most common good, God, will bring the most unity. "Men are not united amongst themselves unless it is by something held in common, and this is especially God."[320] Each of the offices and services point at a similar goal, this is the reason

313. *ST* I q. 108, a. 2.
314. *Super Eph.,* c. 4, l. 1, n. 196.
315. *Sermon on the Apostles Creed,* n. 125
316. *Super Ps.,* 36, n. 8.
317. Cf. *Super Eph.,* c. 2, l. 5.
318. Cf. *SCG* IV c. 21.
319. Cf. *Super Ps.* 36, n. 8.
320. *Super II Thess,* 3, l. 2, n. 89: *"Item homines non uniuntur inter se, nisi in eo quod est commune inter eos, et hoc est maxime Deus."*

for diversity in the Church. It assists life and order—it is beauty.[321] The Church is a "multitude of people ordered to a goal according to distinct acts and offices."[322]

As one can see, Aquinas's thought on the Spirit is intimately related to peace. Both the peace of the individual and of the Church are brought about by his indwelling. The Spirit, who is *unio*, love, and gift, indwells in the body of the Church and within all of the individuals bringing about a reordering of their faculties, their relations, and their lives. Aquinas explicitly connects the Holy Spirit to the peace of the Church since the Holy Spirit is the source of the union and order of the Church. "In the body of the Church the peace among diverse members is sustained by the power of the Holy Spirit who vivifies the body of the Church."[323] The Spirit preserves the peace of the Church.[324] It is a double order of both interior order/union within an individual and exterior order between individuals.[325] In this, the Church follows the Spirit who leads it to peace.[326] This is what the Church is for Aquinas, a congregation of those who love Christ, who have returned his love, effected by the hypostatic union and redemption on the cross, toward them in love. They are now ordered toward him by the Holy Spirit and are thus in right order/union with others and the rest of creation. This is what the Church is in its very essence, a gathering of many into one body—a gathering that is peace.

---

321. Cf. *ST* II-II q. 183, a. 2, co.
322. *ST* III q. 8, a. 4, co.
323. *ST* II-II q. 183,.2. ad 3
324. Cf. *ST* II-II q. 183, a. 2, ad 3.
325. Cf. *Super II Cor.*, c. 13, l. 3.
326. Cf. *Super Rom.*, c. 8, l. 1.

# 4

## Thomistic Ethics and Peace

As mentioned in the introduction, contemporary attention to Aquinas's thought on peace is almost always related to his writings on politics or war. This is undoubtedly worthwhile and born from Aquinas's own thought. As we have seen peace has an irreducible social dimension. Politics and war, however, do not exhaust Aquinas's thought on peace and its relation to ethics; in some sense Aquinas's thought on war is dependent on all his previous thought and only a footnote to his larger theory of peace. In other words, Aquinas's thoughts on politics and war (as well as the entirety of his ethics, as we shall see) are applications of a fundamentally metaphysical and theological vision. Peace is *ordo/unio*—and this marks all things inasmuch as they exist. To have peace is to participate in the very life of God. We inevitably lose this peace through conflict or sin, but God restores it through giving the Spirit, "who makes us live [Christ's] life, which was ordered in the highest sense."[1] Put simply, without all the philosophical and theological background, Aquinas's ethics of peace would be contextless, at best.

Aquinas gives a basic vision of his ethics at the beginning of the *Secunda Secundae*. After treating of God and those things that come forth from God in the first part, Aquinas says: "It remains now to

---

1. Ramirez, "La Eucaristia y la Paz," 918: *"ella nos transforma en Cristo y nos hace vivir su vida que era ordenadisima."*

consider his image, that is man, according to which he is himself the principle of his works, having free will and rules over his actions."[2] Aquinas's ethics are inescapably teleological and theological. This is why he begins the *Secunda Secundae* with *de ultimo fine humanae vitae*.[3] Theological ethics deals with the implications of a theological vision of the world. How should we act, given that the world comes forth from God and returns to him, that all of creation is born of peace and desires to return to it? So that is the guiding question for this chapter: How should people act given the metaphysical and theological vision of peace outlined above?

### PEACE, JOY, DELIGHT, AND HAPPINESS

In Chapter 2, I tried to clarify how peace relates to the good. I think, in general, this metaphysical picture holds up in Aquinas's ethics. On the other hand, Aquinas's thought on the relation between peace, joy, and happiness is not as clear as one would like.[4] His texts are often contradictory and do not show a clear trajectory of development. Though Aquinas's early thought shows a marked preference for a dispositive reading of peace, this is qualified by claims in his middle and mature thought, especially after he produces his *Commentary on the Divine Names*. After that, I have claimed, one can defend a reading of Aquinas's works where the positive *ratio* of peace is essential to the good as a relational transcendental and the negative *ratio* of peace is consequent to the good logically by denying that order/union is chaotic (disquiet or discord). The dispositive reading, however, does not disappear in Aquinas's mature

---

2. *ST* I-II, prol: *"restat ut consideremus de eius imagine, idest de homine, secundum quod et ipse est suorum operum principium, quasi liberum arbitrium habens et suorum operum potestatem."*

3. *ST* I-II q. 1, a. 1, pr.

4. In what follows I will use 'joy' to refer to both *gaudium* and *fruitio*. The debate concerning their distinction is not directly relevant. For the position that *gaudium* belongs to the passions and *fruitio* to the will, see Daniel DeHaan, *"Delectatio, gaudium, fruitio.* Three Kinds of Pleasure for Three Kinds of Knowledge in Thomas Aquinas," *Quaestio* 15 (2015): 543–52.

works concerning the relation of peace, happiness, and joy. This results in some confusion and the purpose of this section is to try to disambiguate Aquinas's thought, if possible.

Aquinas's most extensive treatment of the relation between peace, joy, and happiness, as we have seen, *In Sent. IV*, d. 49, q. 1, a. 2. It is still difficult, even in this text, to find a coherent position. Therein, he presents peace as the lack of obstacles to the appetitive order. When relating peace to happiness, Aquinas says that peace is the most proximate disposition to beatitude, something without which beatitude will not be had. He calls peace a *medium* between desire and love, love being the final proportion to the end and desire being the beginning of that motion. When pressed further on the relation between peace and the end, happiness, he says, peace is something closer to the end than the motion itself, but it is not the end. The ultimate end is activity, not the termination of activity. The tensions in this text, or at least lack of explanations, is clear. How is it possible that peace is *aliquid amoris* but yet a lack of obstacles? How is it possible that peace is a *medium* through which desire passes and yet most proximate to the end? Despite these tensions, it seems in his early thought, Aquinas's most direct explanation is that peace is a lack of obstacles to the end, the means through which desire passes to love, and the cessation of motion. He says something similar and confirms this in his early thought on concord. He says, peace is not to be totally reduced to concord because concord is the union of wills itself and peace is the lack of discord.

In Aquinas's mature thought he again treats the relation of peace, joy, and happiness very briefly in a reply, *ST* I-II q. 3, a. 4, ad 1. This is the only other explicit text we have from him. We have seen this text before. In it the objector makes a similar objection as in the *Scriptum*. Man's happiness consists in peace and peace is appetitive, so happiness must be appetitive too. In the body of Aquinas's response, he makes it clear that the attainment of the end is an act of the intellect and "does not consist in an act of the will."[5] Thus, Aquinas

---

5. *ST* I-II q. 3, a. 4, co.: "*impossibile est quod consistat in actu voluntatis.*"

claims that the very essence of beatitude is an act of the intellect from which joy follows in the will when the end is present and desire when the end is absent. In his response to the objection, Aquinas also claims that peace is not essential to happiness, but this time he locates it as both *antecedenter et consequenter.* Antecedent inasmuch as it removes obstacles and consequent inasmuch as attaining the final end, desire is quieted. Gone is the language about peace being a *medium* or most proximate and dispositive to the end.

At first, it seems the same doctrine on peace, happiness, and joy is taught in the *Scriptum* and the *Summa Theologiae,* save the addition (which is implicit in the *Sent.*) that peace is also consequent to happiness in the quieting of desire. This pushes the interpreter to say that there has been development in Aquinas's thought: peace no longer functions solely as a *medium* (if by medium and a lack of obstacles Aquinas means the same thing) but also follows from the good, but essentially the same doctrine is taught, namely, that happiness is an activity of the intellect subjectively and the good objectively, when the good is obtained by the intellect then joy follows in the will. Peace is dispositive in some sense to this inasmuch as it is the lack of obstacles to the good (on the part of the will) and is the cessation of desire once the good is obtained. So why shouldn't one just take these two texts as Aquinas's final word on the topic?

Aquinas's other comments and texts complicate this picture and show that Aquinas does not really have a settled doctrine on this issue. What he said was occasional and is qualified and in tension with other texts. The first complicating factor in taking these two texts as definitive is that Aquinas develops the relation between desire and love from his early to his late thought. In his early thought peace has a place as the *medium* through which desire passes to being love, the lack of obstacles. Desire comes first and love is the termination. Aquinas reverses this order in his mature thought. In Aquinas's mature thought, love is the initial proportion and desire is born from it, not the reverse. Though it does seem possible to continue to see peace as a *medium* (now between love and desire rather than the reverse), the development at least complicates it. Aquinas says peace is something of love in his youthful thought—yet in his mature love is something at the beginning and not solely coming at the end. Second, Aquinas also begins to identify peace more closely with union (and to identify order/union and the good). His encounter with Dionysius' *Commentary on the Divine Names* (as well as his commentary on the Pauline corpus) pushes him strongly in this direction. This also pushes him to associate peace more closely with love, which is a union, bond, or proportion to the good. How can peace be a medium, simple lack of obstacles to the appetite, or merely the termination of motion when it is identified with order/union and so is love? Likewise, in the *Summa* treatment of the relation between happiness and peace, Aquinas does not even seem to have order/union in mind, but only rest/tranquility. Yet order/union are peace too, as Aquinas says in other texts.

Additionally, there are other complicating factors. First, Aquinas's doctrine of peace being order/union implies, as we saw earlier, that the subject of rest is not just the appetites. The intellect also has a proper order/union to its object. It can rest in the truth; it can have a lack of motion because its object is attained. It can be the subject of peace, in other words. This brings up questions about the relation of peace to happiness anew, since Aquinas says the activity of contemplation is the activity of happiness on the part of the subject.[6] Second, Aquinas suggests other relations between peace, joy, and happiness in his mature thought, especially concerning the relation of peace and joy. In one group of texts, Aquinas suggests that peace follows and perfects both joy and charity.[7] Elsewhere he suggests that joy follows from peace.[8] In some texts, he identifies joy and

6. Cf. Rik Van Nieuwenhove, *Thomas Aquinas and Contemplation* (New York: Oxford University Press, 2021), 2.

7. See *ST* I-II q. 70, a. 3 for how peace perfects joy. *In Gal.* c. 5, l. 6, n. 330: "*Sic ergo gaudium dicit caritatis fruitionem, sed pax caritatis perfectionem. Et per haec homo interius perficitur quantum ad bona.*" See also *Super Io.* c. 17, l. 3, n. 2220: "*Ideo autem gaudium ad unitatem sequitur, quia unitas et pax faciunt perfecte gaudere.*"

8. Note though that Aquinas seems to switch this order in his *Commentary on John*, at least with reference to what I've termed the positive. See also *Super Col.* c. 3, l. 3 where Aquinas claims that joy follows peace.

(consequent) peace.[9] In one text, he identifies rest (peace) with delectation.[10]

Given the confusion of Aquinas's texts and no clear developmental pattern, I think it is fair to say that Aquinas did not see the relation between happiness, joy, and peace as a pressing problem. This does not, however, exempt us from trying to seek a coherent relationship between happiness, joy, and peace, especially one which takes multiple texts of Aquinas into consideration. I think the right way to approach this is to proceed from what is clearer to what is less clear. Hence, I will begin with Aquinas's treatments of happiness and joy on their own and then seek to add peace to the picture.

Happiness, according to Aquinas, is the *finis ultimus* of the human person. It can be taken the *finis cuius* and *finis quo*. The *finis cuius* is typically called "objective happiness" in English. It is the "thing itself in which the *ratio boni* is found." It is the *ipsa res*. The *finis quo* is the *usus sive adeptio sive possessio sive usus sive fruitio sive consecutio* of the thing.[11] In considering the differing good things we could possess, Aquinas eliminates them all as possible contenders for the final end. This ultimate end must be God. The *adeptio* of the mind to this thing, according to Aquinas, is an immanent operation, an act by which we are united to the *bono increato*, "an act by which humans are united to God."[12] Happiness taken subjectively "consists essentially in the union itself to the uncreated good."[13] This is, as we have seen, an act of the intellect essentially because it is by the intellect that is the joining of the human to the end itself. This activity of attaining the end, Aquinas calls by diverse terms listed above. The will, on the other hand, is either desirous of the beloved end when it is

9. See *ST* I-II q. 26, a. 2, co.: "*et ultimo quies, quae est gaudium.*"

10. Cf. *ST* I-II q. 3, a. 3.

11. *ST* I-II q. 1, a. 8, co. *ST* I-II q. 3, a. 1, co.

12. *ST* I-II q. 3, a. 2, ad 4: "*ultima perfectio secundum operationem qua homo coniungitur Deo.*"

13. *ST* I-II q. 3, a. 3, co.: "*Nam beatitudo hominis consistit essentialiter in coniunctione ipsius ad bonum increatum, quod est ultimus finis, ut supra ostensum est . . .*" See also *ST* I-II q. 3, a. 5, ad 1, where Aquinas calls the similarity of the intellect of God one of *unionem vel informationem*: "*et sic perfectionem suam habebit per unionem ad Deum sicut ad obiectum . . .*" *ST* I-II q. 3, a. 8, co.

absent or delights in it when it is present. It is not the attainment of the end itself. In the will, the attainment of the beloved good results in the particular type of *delectation* proper to the will, *fruitio or gaudium*. When Aquinas is asked to specifically identify the very act of the intellect that constitutes the *usus sive adeptio sive possessio sive usus sive fruitio sive consecutio* of the intellect; he calls it *contemplatio*. This act is incomplete in this life though for it fails inasmuch as we are incapable of full unity and continuity. The more it can be *una et continua,* the more perfect it is. Likewise, in this life, our union with the good not only includes the speculative intellect, but also the practical intellect "ordaining human actions and passions."[14] Yet even in the practical order, it is the very act of the intellect that constitutes the subjective side of happiness, happiness inasmuch as it is activity.

The next step in this puzzle is to clarify what Aquinas means by *gaudium* or *fruitio.*[15] This part of Aquinas's thought is also, like happiness when treated directly, relatively clear. In his treatise on the passions, Aquinas treats these topics directly (though more generally and not specifically related to the will). Therein he clarifies that *delectation* is the more general of the terms. All delectation results "from a union with a fitting [good] which is perceived or known."[16] Hence Aquinas distinguishes between types of delectation based on the apprehension from which they follow. All types are in the appetitive order and represent the activity of the appetite when the good is achieved. "It [delectation] is an epiphenomenon, an accident, but an accident that normally is inseparable, a property, *accidens proprium.*"[17] Types of pleasure are distinct by the *diversitas apprehensionis* from which they follow. When it follows the apprehension of reason it occurs in the *voluntas* and is called *gaudium* or *fruitio.* In this way, it represents the perfection of the appetite. It "consists in being perfect."[18]

<hr>

14. *ST* I-II q. 3, a. 5, co.

15. Cf. Daniel De Haan, "*Delectatio, gaudium, fruitio.*"

16. *ST* I-II q. 31, a. 5, co.: "*delectatio provenit ex coniunctione convenientis quae sentitur vel cognoscitur.*"

17. Lottin, *Morale Fondamentale,* 160.

18. *ST* I-II q. 31, a. 1, ad 1.

Many times in Aquinas's corpus he speaks of joy as the cessation of motion, the perfection of the appetitive order.[19] It is the termination of motion toward a suitable good.[20] Nevertheless, when the good is achieved, the activity of love does not cease: *"Licet enim delectatio sit quies quaedam appetitus, considerata praesentia boni delectantis, quod appetitui satisfacit."* It is another good added to the good of the operation.[21] It "consists in the state of completion,"[22] and it is a type of motion because there is still an impression on the appetites.[23] The pleasure itself is not an operation but is the completion of the operation.[24] The proper metaphysical category would seem to be a proper accident—a quality and not an action. Presumably, this would apply to joy since it is simply delectation in the will. Nevertheless, when Aquinas treats joy, he says clearly it is an action (or is at least ambiguous on the issue). "[it is] a certain act or effect."[25] *"Gaudemus de bono divino."*[26] Joy, like pleasure, is a proper accident of love's completion but also the fullness of the act itself of the will. Joy represents the fullness of perfection for the individual.[27] In this way, it is not distinct from charity.[28]

As one can see, at least one part of Aquinas's thought on joy is unclear. Is it rest or act? As seen in the last chapter, rest is a negation of motion—of change—caused by the attainment of perfection. It is the perfection of the act that precludes motion. Yet Aquinas (and

19. Cf. *ST* I-II q. 31, a. 3, ad 2; also, I-II q. 33, a. 4, co.

20. Cf. *ST* q. 31, a. 1, co.

21.Cf. *ST* I-II q. 32, a. 1, co. : *"Unde oportet quod omnis delectatio aliquam operationem consequatur."*; cf. *ST* I-II q. 33, a. 4, co.

22. *ST* I-II q. 31, a. 1, ad 1: *"delectatio, quae consistit in perfectum esse, ut dictum est. Sic ergo cum dicitur quod delectatio est operatio, non est praedicatio per essentiam, sed per causam."*

23. Cf. *ST* I-II q. 3, a. 1, ad 2.

24. Cf. *ST* I-II q. 32, a. 1, co.: *"Unde oportet quod omnis delectatio aliquam operationem consequatur."*

25. *ST* II-II q. 28, a. 4, co.: *" Sic ergo gaudium non est aliqua virtus a caritate distincta, sed est quidam caritatis actus sive effectus."*

26. *ST* II-II q. 28, a. 1, ad 3.

27. Cf. *ST* II-II q. 28, a. 3, co.: *"Unde gaudium beatorum est perfecte plenum, et etiam superplenum, quia plus obtinebunt quam desiderare suffecerint."*

28. Cf. *ST* II-II q. 28, a. 4, co.

here is the difficulty) identifies joy with rest throughout his corpus. "Joy is compared to desire as rest to movement."[29] Also, "the ultimate rest [*quies*] consists in joy."[30] Rest is full when there is no more movement.[31] So is joy a proper accident (of the intellect), consisting in the perfect act of the will, or a lack of motion? One can see immediately the import of this question for peace. Peace, as Aquinas describes it, is the rest of union or the tranquility of order. In other words, how we answer this question has import for both Aquinas's thought on joy and peace and certain answers to this question would seem to preclude a real distinction between interior peace and joy. If one answers that joy is rest, a lack of motion, then Aquinas's thought seems contradictory or to simply identify peace and joy. Texts can certainly be found to support this reading.[32]

One might think that Aquinas's texts where he explicitly treats both peace and joy would help us to sort this out. Nevertheless, those texts find Aquinas struggling to find a distinction. For example, when discussing the fruits of the Holy Spirit (of which peace and joy are both identified), he relates them as follows: joy is the result of the union of beloved to lover. Peace comes after this and perfects joy in two ways. First, peace removes exterior disturbances and trains the heart to enjoy one object so that others do not even get a thought. This perfects joy because we cannot rejoice fully if it is disturbed. Second, peace calms our fluctuating desires. It makes us perfectly satisfied with the object of joy. Hence, "after charity and joy, peace is placed third."[33] This is obviously an attempt to make sense of the order Paul gives in Galatians, but is somewhat ad hoc. The first way peace comes after joy only applies to exterior peace, or concord. Yet in substantial ways, concord is essential to peace and not simply anterior, as we have seen. The second way peace follows from joy in

29. *ST* II-II q. 28, a. 3. co.: "*Gaudium autem comparatur ad desiderium sicut quies ad motum.*"

30. *ST* I-II q. 26, a. 2, co.: "*et ultimo quies, quae est gaudium.*"

31. Cf. *ST* I-II q. 25, aa. 1–2.

32. Cf. *ST* I-II q. 3, a. 3.

33. *ST* I-II q. 79, a. 3, c.

this text is also shaky. What does perfect satisfaction add that is not already contained in love and joy? Likewise, calming fluctuating desires is done by love and joy. What could peace add? Furthermore, Aquinas reverses the order between peace and joy in other places. In those texts, he says that peace precedes joy. He says that joy follows from unity (meaning union, and we know from the last chapter that peace is union).[34] He says: "Joy, which follows from peace."[35]

So, what are we to make of all this? On the one hand, Aquinas certainly seems to think joy and peace are distinct (even though he identifies both with rest at other points). He writes about them in different questions in *ST* II-II q. 28–29, for example. But his attempts to relate them are not mutually coherent. Likewise, even though the above solutions on their relation are not coherent with each other, the fact that Aquinas makes an attempt to distinguish peace and joy means, at the very least, he wants to make a distinction between peace and joy. He could have easily said they are only intellectually distinct and left it at that. The confusion only confirms, as I said before, Aquinas does not seem very concerned about this question, and one must use the texts of Aquinas to try to build a coherent Thomistic option.

I want to defend the claim that joy is the *perfectum esse* of the appetitive order and an act to distinguish it from peace, which is *quies*. In other words, one should distinguish between two senses of termination of motion—one which Aquinas calls the perfection and continuing impression of the operation of attainment on the subject's will. This is joy and the fullest fruition of the spiritual life. It is, strictly speaking the perfection of the act of love, a proper accident (of the intellect's act) and an activity of the will.[36] It is the fullness of volitional activity, in fact, and is caused by the presence of God *vera et physica*.[37] In one sense, joy can be named a lack because it precludes

---

34. Cf. *Super Io.* c. 17, l. 3, n. 2220: "*Ideo autem gaudium ad unitatem sequitur, quia unitas et pax faciunt perfecte gaudere.*"

35. *Super Col.* c. 3, l. 3: "*quia caritatis effectus est gaudium, quod sequitur ex pace.*"

36. Cf. Ramirez, *De Caritate*, 565: "*gaudium potest esse nisi consequens operationem aliquam.*"

37. Ramirez, *De Caritate*, 561.

any further motion or lack of any imperfection. Nevertheless, the negation of motion itself is not the full perfection in the end, but is rather implied by it. Joy is the completion of the order/union of the will to the good. Peace, in its negative *ratio,* is the naming of this order/union as lacking further motion and being undisturbed (by having other orders/unions).

Thus, a distinction presents itself to us that allows us to make sense of all of Aquinas's texts (or at least try). Joy is positive, it is a *res,* an *actio* following from charity (through acts of *dilectio*) attaining its good.[38] It is *quies* in the sense of perfection as *actus.*[39] Peace, then, is the negative side of this, a negation of motion, *quies* in the sense of negation. It is not a *res.* It is not consequent from order/union in the sense of a proper accident, but rather as a negation follows from an affirmation.[40] Peace, in its negative ratio, is only logically distinct from order/union since it is a negation of order/union's opposite— disorder/disunion/conflict, etc. In its positive *ratio,* peace is order/ union (as Aquinas says many times). Indeed, it would be odd for Aquinas and for the Christian tradition to claim that joy is simply a negation (i.e. a negative sense of rest). Joy is the intellectual appetite's pleasure. Joy is full in heaven. Can the pleasure/joy of heaven be a negation? Can a lack of motion have degrees in itself? It would seem not. This pushes us to think of joy as positive and peace as negative.[41] This gives both a clear place in Aquinas's thought, but also helps to preserve the arguments of the last chapter—that peace, as both *unio/ordo* and *quies/tranquillitas*—belongs to the transcendental order. A negation is not a *res* and is not categorical, but joy certainly is. Peace is *unio/ordo* and the negation that follows from it.

What about the order between peace and joy? What does the above solution imply for the order of joy and peace? Part of answering

---

38. Cf. Ramirez, *De Caritate,* 564–65: "*hoc est, actio vel passio.*"

39. Cf. De Haan, "*Delectio, Gaudium, Fruitio,*" 544

40. I think this is the way to understand Aquinas's (and the Thomistic tradition's) claim that *quies* is *naturaliter comitatur consecutionem finis.* See Ramirez, *De Ordine,* 20.

41. Alternatively, one could claim that joy is not exclusive to charity as rest, but applies to the operation of any virtue *delectabiliter.* Peace is the rest of charity in God. I think this solution would not work on Thomistic terms because *delectabiliter* is not rest.

this question requires that we use some of the distinctions laid out in Chapter 2. Simply speaking, peace, in its general *ratio*, seems to precede joy both in the mind and will's unions. Joy is the completion of this order/union to the good. So in this way, joy perfects peace and flows from it inasmuch as the order/union obtains in a rational appetite. This would not hold for any inclination/order/union (except with an analogous sense of joy as appetitive completion). When one is outside of an appetitive order one cannot speak of joy (or even of pleasure). For example, take the intellect. Aquinas is willing to speak of order/union and rest (and so of peace), but not of joy, which is appetitive. Joy is the will's act which follows from the operation of the intellect. So there can be peace without joy, but in the appetitive order joy is the perfection of the positive *ratio* of peace.

In our appetites, since joy as the completion and fullness of order/union, it precedes the negative aspect of peace, rest. In its negative *ratio*, peace is the perfection of joy since it is the negation of motion caused by the fulness of obtaining the end. It is the fullness of order/union that joy represents that precludes disunion/discord. Joy is full order/union to the good. Considering this appetitive peace, exterior peace is both dispositive and perfective of joy. It is dispositive because certain obstacles to deeper union must be avoided to achieve joy. Likewise, concord is perfective of joy because it protects from certain exterior types of disturbance in this world. In other words, concord as an order both precedes and follows from the appetitive order, as one order is dispositive or follows from another, depending on the principle in question.

What about the relation of peace to happiness taken as subjective (i.e. the act of the intellect)? Two things must be recalled from Chapter 2 in dealing with this question. The first is that the intellect has an order/union with its object by nature. It is through the will that the primordial order/union is made an effective union (by the will moving the intellect to its respective object under the *ratio* of the good). Second, it is helpful here to recall that we are dealing with categorical peace. Hence, Aquinas's thought on categorical relation will be helpful. In categorical relations Aquinas distinguishes four things: the subject, the term, the foundation, and the relation.[42] The *operatio* of the intellect would certainly be the foundation—uniting the intellect to its intelligible object. The effective union of the intellect, though not the primordial union (which specifies the intellect itself),[43] is something that follows from and is based on the action of contemplation. Happiness is subjectively this act, the foundation of the effective union of the intellect to its object.[44] I do not think it would be right to say that categorical peace is the totality of happiness, even in its positive aspect of order/union (though Capreolus interprets the union as essentially beatitude).[45] Likewise, Aquinas does imply this at least once.[46] Nevertheless, peace here is a categorical relation based on contemplation and inheres in the subject (the intellect) through the act of contemplation, which in turn is efficiently caused by the will moving the intellect toward its object. The will moves the intellect to a *intuitus simplex* of "non-discursive insight into truth."[47] In this contemplation not only extends to the speculative order, but the practical, and sapiential as well.[48] Nevertheless, in none of these orders can a created intellect have essential knowledge of God (on this side of heaven) or have comprehensive knowledge of God.[49] Rest is consequent logically and obtains in the intellect to the degree its object is obtained effectively/really.

42. Cf. Svoboda, "Aquinas on Real Relation," 150.

43. Cf. *ST* I q. 77, a. 3, co.

44. For more on the relation between the intellect and will in contemplation, see Bernard Blankenhorn, "Mystical Theology and Christology in Thomas Aquinas," in *Ephemerides Theologicae Lovanienses: Commentarii de Re Theologica et Canonica*, vol. 95, is. 2 (June 2019): 299–315.

45. Cf. Capreolus, *Defensiones*, vol 1, book 1, d. 1, q. 1, ad 3: "*unio quidem per actum intellectus est essentialiter beatitudo, quia per illam capitur Deus ut praemium.*" Yet he says that the "*perfectissima unio animae ad objectum beatificum ... non est de essentia beatiudinis.*" That's because he includes the union in the will, which is consequent to beatitude.

46. Cf. *Comp. Theo.,* II c. 9: "*Vocatur etiam beatitudo, inquantum excellentiam designat. Potest et pax vocari, inquantum quietat, nam quies appetitus pax interior esse videtur, unde in Psal. CXLVII, 3, dicitur: qui posuit fines tuos pacem.*"

47. Van Nieuwenhove, *Thomas Aquinas and Contemplation*, 46–47.

48. Cf. Van Nieuwenhove, *Thomas Aquinas and Contemplation*, 147ff.

49. Cf. Bernard McGinn, *The Harvest of Mysticism in Medieval Germany*, vol. 4 of *The Presence of God: A History of Western Christian Mysticism* (New York: The Crossroad Publishing Company, 2005).

Considering the contemplative life as a whole though and not just the act of contemplation in the intellect, Aquinas is clear that "the perfection of the contemplative life involves both knowledge and love of God."[50] There is a dual union here and thus a dual *quies.* Something similar could be said for each of the powers of human beings as for the intellect. Peace is the order/union of the power to its object primordially (e.g. the concupiscible appetites), but through the will this union becomes effective and causes a proportionate degree of rest (non-activity) in the corresponding power moved. Hence, inasmuch as these powers belong to the definition of happiness, one can have peace in each or all of them, i.e. the rest of the power in its object. Nevertheless, it is the union of all of them, each in particular and all of them collectively, which counts as a fuller peace. It is this fuller peace that Aquinas links specifically to the virtue of charity.

### GRACE, CHARITY, AND PEACE

According to Aquinas, peace consists in the love by which God loves us. Our peace is only achieved when God is pacified with us.[51] This makes perfect sense, given Aquinas's philosophy and theology of peace seen in the last two chapters. Nothing can be at peace unless it is constituted in the good, living right order within itself, with God, with others, and the harmony constituted by God for the universe. God achieves this by pouring his own peace into human hearts through the special characters of the Son and the Holy Spirit. Here we are nearing the very heart of Aquinas's conception of

---

50. Van Nieuwenhove, *Thomas Aquinas and Contemplation,* 128.

51. Cf. *ST* I-II q. 113, a. 2, co.: "*Offensa autem non remittitur alicui nisi per hoc quod animus offensi pacatur offendenti. Et ideo secundum hoc peccatum nobis remitti dicitur, quod Deus nobis pacatur. Quae quidem pax consistit in dilectione qua Deus nos diligit. Dilectio autem Dei, quantum est ex parte actus divini, est aeterna et immutabilis, sed quantum ad effectum quem nobis imprimit, quandoque interrumpitur, prout scilicet ab ipso quandoque deficimus et quandoque iterum recuperamus. Effectus autem divinae dilectionis in nobis qui per peccatum tollitur, est gratia, qua homo fit dignus vita aeterna, a qua peccatum mortale excludit. Et ideo non posset intelligi remissio culpae, nisi adesset infusio gratiae.*"

peace inasmuch as it concerns humans. It is also here that we see the deep consonance of Aquinas's conception of peace and his conception of friendship. Friendship is the very heart of Aquinas's notion of peace. As Otto Brunner says, "peace is the state that obtains between friends."[52] Likewise, in his theology of friendship, Aquinas draws together lots of the strands of his thought on peace. We find this nowhere more apparent than *SCG* IV c. 21–22. This text is no less than a treatise on peace in the human life and does an excellent job of using the philosophy and theology of peace to show its implications for human life and activity. It, likewise, shows why Aquinas draws such a close connection between the exemplar causality of the Son, the Spirit, grace, charity, and peace.

At first it is not at all clear why *SCG* IV c. 21–22 should be a treatise on peace in the rational creature. Directly it is a treatise on the effects of the Holy Spirit in creation. Nevertheless, Aquinas's theology of peace shows why this is the case. As we have seen, Aquinas ties peace to the exemplar causality and missions of both the Son and the Holy Spirit. The unity and diversity of God himself is reflected in creation and is exemplified by the processions of the Son and the Holy Spirit. In this conception, Aquinas appropriates all motion and bonding to the Holy Spirit. Since peace is usually tied to the appetitive order and the order of motion, peace is particularly tied to the Holy Spirit. It is the Holy Spirit that unifies and bonds creation and drives it to rest in God. These are the very *rationes* of peace. Hence, any treatment of the exemplar causality of the Holy Spirit bonding/uniting is a treatise on peace in the rational creature and *SCG* IV c. 21–22 is just such a treatise. It is through the Holy Spirit that we are made friends of God.[53]

---

52. Otto Brunner, *Land und Herrschaft: Grundfragen der territorialen Verfassungsgeschichte Südostdeutschlands im Mittelalter* (Baden bei Wien: Rohrer, 1939), 23f: *"Friede gehört etymologisch zusammen mit Freund und frei. Friede ist der Zustand eines menschlichen Verbandes, dessen Glieder untereinander „Freunde" und gegenüber der Außenwelt „frei" sind. Friede ist der Zustand, der zwischen Freunden besteht."*

53. Cf. *ScG* IV c. 21, n. 4: [. . .]-1 *"Cum enim amicitia coniungat affectus, et duorum faciat quasi cor unum, non videtur extra cor suum aliquis illud protulisse quod amico revelat: unde et dominus dicit discipulis, Ioan. 15–15: iam non dicam vos servos, sed amicos meos: quia*

Aquinas begins Chapter 21 by explaining how we become like God in general. He explains, "In whatever way we are assimilated to a divine perfection, in that way a perfection is said to be given to us by God."[54] This he follows up with the claim that we become like the Word in receiving wisdom and the Spirit in receiving love. This love, though it is efficiently caused commonly by the divine persons, assimilates us to the Holy Spirit's exemplarity. Thus it is said *"speciali ratione"* to be *per Spiritum Sanctum.* Through this common effect assimilating us to the Holy Spirit, the Holy Spirit is *in nobis sit, quandiu caritas in nobis est.* In other words, through participation in the Holy Spirit, we are made lovers of God. And since love is a union, the whole Trinity dwells in us by this love and us in the Trinity. Aquinas immediately follows this explanation of the indwelling of the Trinity by naming it friendship. He says of friendship, that it *coniungat affectus et duorum faciat quasi cor unum.* We are made friends of God by the Holy Spirit, and the very notion of friendship is the notion of exterior peace (order/union between two persons). It is clear that here the positive *ratio* of peace, order/union, is accomplished in the Holy Spirit and is identified with friendship with God.

Aquinas follows this with some implications of this friendship/ peace. Friends share secrets and so the Holy Spirit shares the hidden things of God with us. Friends share belongings, since the friend is *homo amicum habeat ut se alterum.* Someone will help a friend as he would help himself. With the Trinity, this sharing of goods especially relates to God's own happiness, the *beatitudinem divinae fruitionis, quae Deo propria est secundum suam naturam.* This too is communicated to us in the Holy Spirit, who is the gift of God and also moves us to act in accord with these gifts. Likewise, friendship removes all offenses since offense is opposed to friendship. Since the Holy Spirit makes us friends of God, God forgives our sins *per ipsum*; As Aquinas says elsewhere, God "becomes pacified with us"[55] through the Holy Spirit.

*omnia quae audivi a patre meo, nota feci vobis. Quia igitur per spiritum sanctum amici Dei constituimur."*

54. *ScG* IV c. 21, n. 1.

55. *ST* I-II q. 113, a. 2, co.: *"Offensa autem non remittitur alicui nisi per hoc quod animus*

Since love is an impulsive and unitive force, the Holy Spirit moves us back to God. Aquinas follows with all the ways in which the action of the Holy Spirit unites us with God, orders us to God. As such it is a treatise on peace in act. Aquinas identifies the fundamental aspect of order/union in act as the *simul conversari ad amicum*. Friends turn toward each other by contemplation. Since the Holy Spirit makes us lovers of God, he makes us contemplators of God too. This connects the above section well, since the mind is ordered and rests in its object (happiness subjectively speaking) but is moved by the will's love. Friendship too causes us to delight in our friends, their words and deeds, and to be consoled by them in all anxieties. It is thus through the Holy Spirit that we rejoice in God, *gaudium de Deo*. It is also through him that we have comfort against all the *adversitates et impugnationes mundi*. Likewise, it belongs to friendship that we consent to what the friend wills. God makes his will in the commandments known, and so we love the commandments. The Holy Spirit leads us to fulfill those commandments.

In this Trinitarian indwelling, the concrete extension of friendship on God's part to us, the Holy Spirit leads us not as slaves but free individuals. To be free is to be the source of one's own action. We act *ex voluntate*. The Holy Spirit inclines to act in such a way that *nos voluntarie agere faciat*. He causes us to be lovers of God in such a way that we are internally the source of that love. *Filii Dei libere a spiritu sancto aguntur ex amore, non serviliter ex timore*. In this way, the Spirit frees us from servitude to our passions or false goods. He inclines the will to the true good to which we are *naturaliter ordinatur*. Thus the Spirit mortifies the flesh since the *passionem carnis* turns us from the true good. He leads us there by love.

At least initially, the presence of peace seems to be lacking in the above treatment. Yet if we recall what was written in the previous chapters about peace as order/union as well as Christ's relation to peace, its place becomes clearer. The peace that Christ comes to

---

*offensi pacatur offendenti. Et ideo secundum hoc peccatum nobis remitti dicitur, quod Deus nobis pacatur."*

restore to the world is given through the Holy Spirit who causes us to be in order/union to God, self, and neighbor. The union and nexus of God himself is supremely given in the gift of grace which unites/orders us to God and others. The Holy Spirit is the exemplar of our bonding and given by Christ—who re-orders creation back to God. The Holy Spirit is this very gift of Christ's re-ordering, the one who is given in the reordering.

When the Holy Spirit dwells in us, that is grace. In fact, as noted earlier, Aquinas simply identifies the gift of the Spirit with the gift of grace. Hence, for the full reunification/reordering of creation, grace is required. The precisions and intricacies of Aquinas's thought on grace should not distract us from this broader perspective, but a few points bare out our central point on the relation between friendship, grace, and charity. This grace, which Aquinas calls "habitual" to show it abides, is the immanent cause of charity in the soul. So it is no mistake that Aquinas explicitly connects the Holy Spirit, grace, and the virtue of charity. Charity, which flows from habitual grace inasmuch as it perfects the will, is the subjective means by which humans are rightly ordered/in union with God, their neighbors, and all creation. This likewise gives the most particular connection to peace. Aquinas names peace one of the "acts of charity." "From charity immediately follows peace."[56] Peace is the proper effect of charity.[57] "The union of men in one object and the union of all appetites in one object."[58] Supernatural peace is the proper effect of charity because charity is the direct agent cause of the two-fold union of peace: it is because of this that charity is said to be the bond of the whole spiritual edifice.[59]

It is easy to see why Aquinas connects peace to charity—not only because it is the very means by which the Holy Spirit dwells in us, but also because it is order/union to God. Primarily charity is affective order/union to God. "Charity attains God himself."[60] Aquinas

---

56. *Super Col.*, c. 3, l. 3, n. 164: "*Ex caritate mox oritur pax . . .*"
57. Cf. *ST* II-II q. 29, a. 3, co.
58. *ST* II-II q. 29, a. 3, co.
59. Cf. *ST* II-II q. 4, a. 7, a. 4.
60. *ST* II-II q. 23, a. 6, co.: "*caritas attingit ipsum Deum.*"

specifies habits by their formal object and charity's formal object is God as friend. It is through this fundamental supernatural order/union to God that God dwells in the soul. This, in turn, effects all the results of love: ecstasy, zeal, etc.[61] It is this order that Christ comes to restore. This makes perfect sense given Aquinas's thought on order. If one wants to restore order, one must begin by relating correctly to the principal of that order. This principal, of course, is God who creates and redeems all things. The supernatural order charity brings perfects the deeper likeness to God in creation, a more fundamental order/union.[62] In fact, it is for this very reason that Aquinas claims our loves will not conflict. Loving self, others, and creation is not set over and against love of God, but imply it since the self, others, and creation are a likeness to God.[63] Based on this affective union with God, charity not only seeks effective union with God, but also is the lover's interior peace.

It is by loving God that our diverse desires, projects, thoughts, and powers, are brought into harmony.[64] As Aquinas says, "Similarly, they experience no dissension of will since their whole souls tend *in unum*."[65] This is what Aquinas calls interior peace, or peace inasmuch as it concerns the different power of our souls and their proper objects. As Ramirez says, interior peace is the "tranquil order of all thoughts and wishes of each into God."[66] They (all our powers and thoughts), in an analogous sense, are made friends. It is clear that only union with God can have this kind of integrating function amongst our diverse powers and desires.[67] By ordering/unifying all

---

61. Cf. *ST* I-II q. 28, aa. 3–6.

62. Cf. *ST* II-II q. 20, a. 1, ad 3.

63. Cf. Thomas Osborne, *Love of Self and Love of God in Thirteenth Century Ethics* (Notre Dame, IN: University of Notre Dame Press, 2005), chapter 3.

64. Cf. Ramirez, "La Eucaristía y la Paz Individual," 174. Ramirez says that true individual peace requires three conditions: order, that the order be from the first cause, that it be calm and established.

65. *ST* II-II q. 25, a. 7, co.: "*similiter etiam non patiuntur in seipsis voluntatis dissensionem, quia tota anima eorum tendit in unum.*"

66. Ramirez, "La Eucaristía y la Paz Individual," 174.

67. This is because only love of God above and beyond all things is a true love of self. See Flood, *The Metaphysical Foundations of Love*, 44ff.

our thoughts, powers, and desires to each other based on their relationship through charity to God, Aquinas does not claim that any one of them should be destroyed or repressed. Order/union to God is not contrary to anything good *per se*.

Rather, since God is subsistent goodness, each of our desires can find its proper object preeminently in God. To be directed to God does not destroy our lower appetites, but draws them into themselves. Since all appetites are ordered to God, then they cannot conflict with each other for each seeks the same, *ad unum*. They thus become *unum secundum quid*, an aspect of simplicity of heart.[68] By restoring right relationship/union with God, charity begins the right ordering of our desires. Obviously, this is only possible fully in heaven. On this side of heaven, only the order of our will to God is direct. Directing the other powers (including the intellect in faith) to God is not contrary to their nature, but it is beyond their nature and indirect in this life. This is why Aquinas says that faith is distant from its object.[69] Charity brings it (and our other powers, virtues, etc.) into an ordered unity by serving as the form of the other virtues; it makes goodness himself (God) the object of action.[70] It thereby introduces order to all other things through its respective union/relation to God.

This is what Aquinas means by saying that charity is the form of the other virtues (and gifts) on a supernatural level.[71] It directs all our acts and virtues to God as an end, thereby informing them. Charity does not become the immanent form of each virtue, but commands their acts toward its end, thereby making its end a shared good of all the powers of the soul.[72] It is this end, God, that serves as the final cause of this order and integrates/unites. In this way, God brings peace most concretely. As one can see, Aquinas's thought here is merely an application of his larger thought on order/union. As he

---

68. Wittman, "Not a God of Confusion, but of Peace . . . ," 162 & 166.

69. Cf. *ST* I-II q. 62, aa. 3–4; *ST* II-II q. 1, a. 4, co.

70. Cf. *ST* II-II q. 25, a. 1, co.

71. Cf. *De virt.*, q. 2, a. 3, co.: "*caritas est forma virtutum, motor et radix.*"

72. For an account that claims Aquinas abandons any claim of formal causality for charity see Lottin, *Morale Fondamentale*, 399f.

says, "According to the philosopher, to order is an act of wisdom. Now ordering things is not able to be done unless it is through the understanding of relation and proportion of those things ordered to each other and to the higher, which is their end. For order of things to each other is on account of their order to the end."[73]

Another way of making sense of the order the virtue of charity introduces into our lives is by the distinctions of referential types charity can make to the supernatural end: actual, habitual, and virtual.[74] The habitual order is the widest. Since charity, as a habit, is affective union with God, it orders even acts of a human (not free acts) to God, e.g. sleeping.[75] Virtual reference is caused by the intention of the final end (at some point) by charity and the influence this final end has on our other acts—it virtually (by its power) refers them to God inasmuch as these acts are done as a result of that final intention. In this way, without actual advertence, all actions which flow from and are driven by a previous intention are referred to love of God. Actual order refers to when a human, for the very love of God, does some kind of act. This could be any one of the virtues or acts of virtues inasmuch as charity commands it specifically for its object, God himself. These are differing types of order/union to the ultimate end which charity introduces into our lives. It is in one of these three ways that charity orders/unifies acts which are not directly related to God as friend and extends to the whole of life.

Nevertheless, despite the order/union that charity introduces into human life, Aquinas claims clearly that there will still be disturbances in the life of the believer. Certainly, charity transforms all other good habits and desires by referring them to its end. All the

---

73. *ScG* II c. 24, n. 4: "*Secundum philosophum, in I Metaph. ordinare sapientis est: ordinatio enim aliquorum fieri non potest nisi per cognitionem habitudinis et proportionis ordinatorum ad invicem, et ad aliquid altius eius, quod est finis eorum; ordo enim aliquorum ad invicem est propter ordinem eorum ad finem.*"

74. Cf. Osborne, "The Threefold Referral of Acts to the Ultimate End in Thomas Aquinas and His Commentators," *Angelicum*, vol. 85 (2008): 715–36.

75. Cf. Osborne, "Threefold Referral," 719. Aquinas uses this sense to say that we even refer venial sins to God, but they cannot be actually ordered there because they are sinful.

other virtues and goods thus find relation to each other by their relation to God under the guidance of charity. This precludes some foundational disorder/disunion in our lives by being in union to God, who sufficiently quiets all desire. True rest, the cessation of all desire can only come when there is no good beyond the one possessed. In Aquinas's metaphysics no other object could serve this function of both ordering and quieting. Nevertheless, order/union to the source does not preclude disorder/disunion with others necessarily. This is not only because the believer's charity is not in perfect union with all other humans (though it is the beginning and foundation) and is sometimes not mutual (i.e. there are those who do not inhabit the same order as him and will disrupt his order if given the chance), and likewise because of sin, which is contrary to our ordering to God, as well as the very way charity unifies our powers, but also there is still distance between all other powers and God,[76] that does not constitute distance for the will. Because of this, there will inevitably be *per accidens* conflict between the will's union with God and our union with the goods of this world, as each power seeks union with its proper object and is only then directed by the will toward a greater order/union to God. This conflict is not a sign of sin—for even Christ experienced it in the Garden of Gethsemane. In a substantial sense, Aquinas's explanation for the ongoing lack of peace in creation more generally between species (and within) is replicated with non-sinful conflict amongst our powers under the direction of charity. The virtuous person's life is a harmony, not an identity; some kind of disorder/disunion is inevitable even when all our powers inhabit the same ultimate order.

Likewise, Aquinas claims that charity is going to be the bond not only of our differing powers and thoughts, but also between humans, of exterior peace. Aquinas reminds us that friendship is ultimately based on union, a union of likeness.[77] Friendship is based

76. This is one of the reasons charity is more perfect than faith and hope, so even more the infused cardinal virtues.

77. Cf. *ST* II-II q. 27, a. 3, co. The union about which Aquinas is speaking here is not true union, it is a unity, a oneness that is had by sharing the form of humanity. That is

on this unity, but adds something to it, an additional kind of union, a union to a common end and thus to each other. The order/union of one to another is a relation that subsists in each toward the other. It does not float between them, so to speak. As, Schwartz shows in his study on Aquinas and friendship: "By friendship Aquinas always means one's friendship towards the friend, that is a relational property inhering in oneself, rather than a relationship conceived as something, as it were, 'hovering' between two friends."[78] Based on this common love they are ordered to each other. Based on their love for one another (which is the bond/order/union to the other) the two inform each other and transform each other, for each dwells in the other in the mode of an object of love.[79] This is a conformity of wills based on mutual willing of a good for the other. Nevertheless, charity can only do this because it draws both humans into an integrating good that is the foundation of their relation/order/union. Charity is the union to this integrating good affectively.[80]

Supernaturally, the order to God is the very basis of their relation to each other and God is the primary good that each wills for the other. Charity unites humans in true friendship, provides a true bond based on love of God in which one wills the other's good as one's own. It makes believers love their neighbor as themselves and "makes us want to do his will even as our own."[81] The friend becomes another self by the very indwelling caused by love. The two begin to inhabit the same order, resulting in no substantial conflict between them. This is preeminently lived in the Church as we saw when treating Aquinas's ecclesiology in the previous chapter; the Church is the very communion of the lovers of God in the Holy Spirit. To be at peace with others we must not be opposed to their good, bring sympathy to

---

why he calls it elsewhere union metaphorically speaking. See IV *Sent.*, d. 1, a. 1, a. 1, sc. 2 and d. 5, q. 1, a. 1, co.

78. Daniel Schwartz, *Aquinas on Friendship* (New York: Oxford University Press, 2007), 8.

79. Schwartz, *Aquinas on Friendship*, 27.

80. Cf. *ST* II-II q. 28, a. 1, co.

81. *ST* II-II q. 29, a. 3, co.: "*Aliam vero, prout diligimus proximum sicut nosipsos, ex quo contingit quod homo vult implere voluntatem proximi sicut et sui ipsius.*"

their faults, bring succor to action, and correct their sins.[82] These are, and this is not surprising, all caused by love.

Finally, charity is also the basis of our union/right relationship with the rest of material creation too. We saw this in the chapter concerning the restoration of order in Christ. Aquinas does not speak of this often, but there is an untapped potency in this part of his thought. The right order/union to God, self, and neighbor ultimately includes a restored relationship to the rest of creation. In fact, it is through this relation to humans that the rest of creation finds its redemption, since it was this aspect of creation that was damaged through the fall; creation did not fall in itself but in its relation to humans (or rather humans in relation to it).

In other words, the connection between charity and peace is identity in peace's positive *ratio*, order/union. This deeper connection is something many miss given that Aquinas calls peace an "act of charity."[83] In saying this Aquinas does not mean that peace is one act among others such that sometimes charity enacts peace and other times it is beneficent or fraternally correcting. He does not even seem to want to place peace in the accidental category of *actus* (as he seems to want to do with *gaudium aut fruitio*). We saw in the previous chapter that order/union is reduced to relation, not act. Likewise, it would be an odd thing to say, since all the acts of charity are born of order/union and contribute to rest/tranquility and charity itself is order/union. I think Cajetan's (and Bañez's) commentary on II-II q. 29, a. 4, co. holds the key to understanding Aquinas's thought on the relation of peace to charity most concretely. As Cajetan notes, Aquinas's language concerning peace as an 'act' of charity should not be taken literally. Bañez continues this line of interpretation. "This truly seems more probable, that peace is in us just as health in animals. It is not some quality distinct from the concord of the four humors . . . but health is the very proportion of the qualities. So, peace

82. Cf. *ST* II-II q. 45, a. 6, ad 3.

83. *ST* II-II q. 29, a. 4, co.: "*Cum igitur pax causetur ex caritate secundum ipsam rationem dilectionis Dei et proximi, ut ostensum est, non est alia virtus cuius pax sit proprius actus nisi caritas, sicut et de gaudio dictum est.*"

is the concord itself and proportion of the appetites and virtues among themselves."[84] Aquinas's statement that peace is an interior effect of charity does not exhaust his thought. Peace cannot only be an interior effect of charity based on *dilectio*, at least not if we mean peace in its full analogical and transcendental sense concerning God himself, creation, non-appetitive powers, etc.[85]

Since love is union, I would say that proper order/union, inasmuch as it is lived in humans and concerns the will, is identical to charity itself in some sense, which is an affective union. It will tend to effective order and union since it orders all other thoughts, appetites, virtues, etc. properly. Inasmuch as it does that or negates disunion/disorder between humans, peace can be called an act of charity, but inasmuch as it is order/union itself, then it is identical with charity and simply a formality of it.[86] In some sense, charity even presupposes peace, since Aquinas calls the likeness of similitude on which charity is based, a type of *union*. In this way, one might say, categorical relations/order/union presuppose transcendental order/union. The categorical affective union of charity with God, and the effective union that follows from it, are based on a prior order/union in creation, the fundamental similitude of the creature to God. This likeness is in turn dependent on deeper orders, the transcendental order and ultimately the order which is the Triune God.

Considering charity itself, wherever there is charity there is order/union and so also peace. Peace in its positive ratio is simply identified with charity as order/union to God, self, and others. There is no way, properly speaking, it could be simply one of the acts of charity. When Aquinas locates peace as an act of charity, he

84. Domingo Bañez, *Scholastica Commentaria in Secundam Secundae Angelici Doctoris S. Thomae*, XXIX, a. 4, 432.

85. Cf. *ST* II-II q. 28, prol.: "*Deinde considerandum est de effectibus consequentibus actum caritatis principalem, qui est dilectio. Et primo, de effectibus interioribus; secundo, de exterioribus. Circa primum tria consideranda sunt, primo, de gaudio; secundo, de pace; tertio, de misericordia.*" For more here, cf. Reichberg, "Aquinas's Moral Typology," 473.

86. See Cajetan's commentary on Aquinas's *Summa Theologiae* II-II q. 29, a. 4, in *Opera omnia iussu impensaque Leonis XIII P.M. edita* (Leonine ed.), vol. 4 (Rome: Ex Typgraphia Polyglotta S.C. de Propaganda Fidei, 1888), 239.

is simply using shorthand for something "not . . . absolutely distinct from charity"[87] and the *quies* that follows from order/union to God, self, others, and creation as a negation. He means that inasmuch as charity is active, *esse*, it is peace as the fundamental supernatural appetitive order/union to God.

Interestingly, Aquinas is even willing to say that we merit *per pacem*.[88] What could Aquinas mean by this? In one sense, Aquinas certainly means that exterior peace removes obstacles to the meritorious act of charity. Concord with one's neighbor precludes conflict that might interrupt one's good actions (in addition to that concord being good in itself). In another sense, Aquinas means making order/union where there is none: being a peacemaker (as we shall see in a later section). Nevertheless, I think there is a deeper sense in which peace is related to merit. Briefly, according to Aquinas, merit is the achieving of God by human action.[89] It is the ultimate effect of the Holy Spirit in the lives of believers, effective union with God, the fullness of peace. It is through our right order/union with God that we merit eternal life, i.e. achieve God.[90] It is not only through a lack of obstacles to this order that we merit, but the order itself is what Aquinas means when he says we merit. This is nothing other than the relation of presence/effective union, or of the positive *ratio* of peace taken in its fullest sense. In other words, merit is peace in its fullest. Hence, we merit *per pacem*.

As Beestermoller says, "Peace is the state, which obtains between friends."[91] And "that is why the fundamental sense of the word, [peace] is not essentially negative, as we take it today."[92] Returning to the beginning of this section, we can see concretely why the general *ratio* of peace is explained in this way. Peace is order/union, and

---

87. Cajetan, *Commentary*, 239.

88. *Super II Cor.*, c. 13, l. 3, n. 540.

89. Cf. *ST* I-II q. 114, aa. 2–3.

90. Cf. *Super II Cor.*, c. 13, l. 3, n. 540: "*quia homo non meretur nisi per pacem et dilectionem.*"

91. Beestermoller, *Thomas von Aquin*, 64.

92. Beestermoller, *Thomas von Aquin*, 64.

if we understand these analogously, then each type of friendship is a type of peace and every type of peace is a type of friendship. The order/union of one's faculties is a type of friendship between them. The full supernatural order/union between humans is friendship in the Church. The civil polity enjoys a type of friendship (though it was not treated in this section). In each case, the positive *ratio* of order/union is marked by rest/tranquility.

### WISDOM AND PEACE

Charity is not the only virtue Aquinas ties closely to peace. As seen in the first chapter (and one would expect from Aquinas's theology) wisdom is another virtue important for peace. We have seen in a Thomistic theology of peace that it is ultimately about assimilation to God's peace, of receiving his peace concretely. We have seen that just as Aquinas ties peace very closely to the appetitive order, he ties peace very closely to the Holy Spirit as well. Yet as I have argued throughout, peace is not exclusive (at least as a subject) to the appetitive order. This is confirmed in the importance of the Word and wisdom for peace. As Aquinas says, "[Peace] is fittingly attributed to wisdom."[93] "[The intellect's] business is to know order."[94] It is only through the double assimilation, both to the Word and to the Spirit that the peace of God is received by the individual and collectively by the Church.

As we have seen, just as charity is an assimilation to the Holy Spirit, wisdom is an assimilation to the Word. Here we begin to see all of the parallels in Aquinas's thought: between the *ad intra* processions of the Word and Spirit, between their temporal missions, between the intellect and the will, between the virtues which perfect them. One should note here the parallels between how Aquinas thinks about subsistent relations of the Trinity and the temporal missions based on those. In the same way we are redeemed (formally

---

93. *ST* II-II q. 45, a. 6, co.
94. Van Nieuwenhove, *Thomas Aquinas and Contemplation*, 5.

speaking) by wisdom and in the appetitive order by charity. Christ is not only the exemplar origin of creation in his character of Wisdom, but on that basis the origin and beginning of redemption—a return of proper order to creation. The order of wisdom and love in the causality of peace mirrors the ad intra order of the divine processions. Intellect, Christ, and then will, Holy Spirit, and their temporal missions to reorder creation back to the Father.

Wisdom makes peace by putting things in proper order, i.e. by seeing them as unified in their relation to the first principle, God.[95] It perceives the whole and so understands the part.[96] Wisdom extends not only to our thoughts, but also to the practical order—the order of activity.[97] One is wise by judging things in accord with their highest principles, according to the very principle(s) of order. One is wise when one acts in light of the highest good. According to Aquinas, the gift of wisdom is seated in the intellect and judges connaturally what belongs to proper order, i.e. under the impulse of charity.[98] "Gifted wisdom has its cause in the will, that is charity, but has its essence in the intellect, whose act it is to rightly judge."[99] Aquinas even says that wisdom judges according to the *rationes divinas* or divine ideas.[100] That wisdom attains a deeper order/union to God is Aquinas's very reason why it is a superior virtue.[101] Yet this union is itself through charity and the connaturality (union) with God it brings.[102] This gift of wisdom "makes the bitter to be sweet, and our

95. Cf. *ST* II-II q. 45, a. 6, co.

96. McMahon, "A Thomistic Analysis of Peace," 189.

97. Cf. *ST* II-II q. 45, a. 3, co.

98. Cf. *ST* II-II q. 45, a. 2, co.

99. *ST* II-II q. 45, a. 2, co.: "*Sic igitur sapientia quae est donum causam quidem habet in voluntate, scilicet caritatem, sed essentiam habet in intellectu, cuius actus est recte iudicare, ut supra habitum est.*"

100. *ST* II-II q. 45, A. 2, ad 3.

101. Cf. *ST* II-II q. 45, A. 3, ad 1: "*Unde ex hoc ipso quod sapientia quae est donum est excellentior quam sapientia quae est virtus intellectualis, utpote magis de propinquo Deum attingens, per quandam scilicet unionem animae ad ipsum, habet quod non solum dirigat in contemplatione, sed etiam in actione.*"

102. Cf. *ST* II-II q. 45, q. 4, co.: "*ex quadam connaturalitate sive unione ad divina.*"

labors to be rest (*requiem*)."[103] It makes each person having sanctifying grace sufficient to judge and direct his or her own actions, but not necessarily others, in higher mysteries, or in teaching.[104]

By introducing peace into our actions and our thoughts, we are assimilated to the Son of God. "They are said to be sons of God inasmuch as they participate in the similitude of the natural and only begotten Son, according to Romans 8, 'Those whom he foreknew are conformed to the image of his Son', who is begotten wisdom. For this reason we see that through the gift of wisdom, humans attain to the filiation of God."[105] As we have seen, it is by receiving the gift of the Spirit that we are returned to the Son and so it is by receiving charity that one receives wisdom.[106] The missions of the Trinity are reversed in the order of becoming and the order of being. The Son is prior ad intra and in temporal mission, but the Spirit is the first gift to us and through that reception we are returned to the Son and to the Father. Charity gives rise to wisdom and through it to peace. Peace is thus the ultimate effect of wisdom, and that is why it is listed among the fruits of the Spirit.[107]

At first Aquinas's formulation of the relation between the gift of wisdom and peace, found in II-II q. 45, a. 6, seems to preclude what I have been claiming all along, that peace is not exclusive (at least as a subject) to the appetitive order. In this text, Aquinas says it belongs to charity and the appetites to "*habere pacem*" but to wisdom to "*facere pacem*."[108] It seems to limit wisdom to the efficient or formal causality of peace, a kind of extrinsic causality. Nevertheless, based on what we've seen, this cannot be the case. Certainly, Aquinas says

103. *ST* II-II q. 45, a. 3, ad 3: "*sed potius amaritudo propter sapientiam vertitur in dulcedinem, et labor in requiem.*"

104. Cf. *ST* II-II q. 45, a. 5, co. and ad 1.

105. *ST* II-II q. 45, a. 6, co. and ad 1.

106. Cf. *ST* II-II q. 45, a. 6, ad 2: "*dicendum quod illud est intelligendum de sapientia increata, quae prima se nobis unit per donum caritatis, et ex hoc revelat nobis mysteria, quorum cognitio est sapientia infusa. Et ideo sapientia infusa, quae est donum, non est causa caritatis, sed magis effectus.*"

107. Cf. *ST* I-II q. 70, a. 3, co.

108. *ST* II-II q. 45, a. 6, ad 1.

in the *Summa* section on the gift of wisdom that it makes peace, but the will has peace. But one could easily also say that inasmuch as the will influences the intellect and orders it properly—charity causes peace (as Aquinas says elsewhere and is his typical formulation) and the intellect has peace. It is really a question of the principal of the order in question. In the order of specification, the intellect does not have peace but makes it. But inasmuch as it is commanded by the will and moves toward its connatural end—it enters in into the order of exercise and therefore also of movement and rest. Aquinas says that the true comes under the good, as was argued in the previous chapter. In the same way all the faculties come under the good and therefore under peace. Wisdom is itself proper order/union with God as principle of the order of the world and Church. Likewise, wisdom is the act of contemplation, which unites the mind to God.[109] It is the act of contemplation, which is essential to supernatural peace, understood as the mind's order/union to God and our very final end considered as activity.

In this sense wisdom is not simply extraneous to order/union (just as prudence is not).[110] According to the pure extraneous reading, wisdom would be a cause of peace but is not itself properly said to be at peace. The above reading preserves the insight that all virtues and gifts properly order our potencies with respect to their objects and therefore belong essentially to peace as order/union. The alternative reading would be committed to saying that wisdom does not properly order/unify our intellect to the first principle in judgment or peace is not order/union. Those would certainly be odd claims since Aquinas is committed to the idea that wisdom orders our intellect and peace is order/union. Yet, to admit that wisdom orders our intellect properly is to admit that the intellect (through wisdom and the other intellectual virtues) can enjoy peace (order/

---

109. Cf. *ST* II-II q. 184, a. 5, co. "*Sic igitur ex praemissis patet quod ordine quodam quatuor ad vitam contemplativam pertinent, primo quidem, virtutes morales; secundo autem, alii actus praeter contemplationem; tertio vero, contemplatio divinorum effectuum; quarto vero completivum est ipsa contemplatio divinae veritatis.*"

110. Cf. *ST* II-II q. 49, a. 7.

union and subsequent rest in its object). The real question is how do we make sense of both of these, and the above reasoning strikes me as coherent and plausible on Thomistic grounds.

In addition, the solution I offer is based on another aspect of Aquinas's thought—namely, that union is based on deeper union, order based on deeper order. The appetitive order is, in turn, based on the intellectual order and appetitive union with an object is based on previous intellectual/perceptual union. Orders (and the principles on which they are based) are stacked realities, so to speak. In one sense, the intellect orders/unifies the will to its object and so it can be said to be extraneous to the appetitive order. In this way wisdom makes peace, but does not have peace. But the intellect itself is also ordered/unified to its object in a fundamental inclinational sense. Likewise, the intellect is moved by the will toward its object. Based on these orders, the intellect itself enjoys peace. This is simply another way of saying that considering the order of specification, wisdom puts things in order but does not itself belong to that order. Wisdom puts the intellect itself at peace, for it properly orders/unifies the intellect to the highest causes. The rest of the virtues rightly order our appetites so all can be said to cause peace, but wisdom architectonically by ordering all to the first cause and charity by living that order. Yet in another sense, since the act of the intellect is commanded by charity in this case, wisdom is meritorious and does belong to the order of exercise and so can enjoy peace. As Ramirez shows, wisdom operates in the order of exercise as well. "The gift of wisdom, derived from faith and charity, is an instrument of both to order and concrete of one to the other, because it points out according to the principles of faith and something according to the something of charity."[111]

Nevertheless, one might object that Aquinas's teaching on discord contradicts this picture. As we have seen in *ST* II-II q. 29, a. 3, ad 2, Aquinas says that peace does not belong to the intellect and on this

111. Ramirez, *De Caritate*, 902: "*El don de sabiduria, por derivarse de la fe y de la caridad, es el instrumento de ambas en el ejercicio ordenador y concreto de una y otra, porque senala según los principios de la fe y empuja según el apremio de la caridad.*"

very basis claims that one can have disagreements and still be at peace with someone. Certainly, there cannot be order/union between individuals if there is not agreement about the goods that pertain to their very order/union (*bonis conferentibus*), and especially the greatest there, but not as to the lesser goods. Aquinas says friends agree in the "*principalibus bonis*" but not the "*de minimis et de opinionibus*."[112] To differ in these is not discord, nor are differing opinions here to be likened to a lack of relevant concord. In other words, our intellects can fail to be in order/union to an object the same way and this does not count as the contrary of peace since peace does not belong to the intellect.

Of course, in one sense, as I have claimed all along, peace has a special relation to the appetitive order because it is a *ratio* of the good. To deny this would do violence to Aquinas's thought, certainly. Nevertheless, claiming that peace can (also) belong to the intellect as a subject does not contradict this. In fact, the claim that order/union belongs to the appetitive order requires that it first belong to the intellectual order. Aquinas claims that friends can differ in small things, what he calls opinion, and not have it be contrary to peace. But importantly they still agree in the greater goods that are the very basis of their concord (I think this is the force of using *conferre* with *bonum*). In other words, the intellect of the two (or many more) remain fundamentally in order/union on a deeper level and only differ in contingent details (though the scope of this is arguably much wider than most assume).[113] This is why Aquinas says that we are in union through faith[114] and why concord consists *in unitate sententiae*.[115]

Undoubtedly, when Aquinas is writing about the kind of disagreement that is compatible with the order/union of wills, he is

---

112. *ST* II-II q. 29, a. 3, ad 2.

113. Schwartz, *Aquinas on Friendship*, 34. Billuart reads this as those things "*de necessitate salutis*." So disagreement about supererogatory acts or things unnecessary for salvation is not contrary to charity. See Caroli Renati Billuart, *Theologiae juxta mentem d. thomae, moralis tom. IV* (Paris: Facultatis Theologiae Bibliopolam, 1827), 396.

114. Cf. *Super I Tim.*, c. 6, l. 4; *Super Col.*, c. 1, l. 5; *Super Phil.*, c. 4, l. 1.

115. *Super Rom.*, C. 12, l. 3, n. 1005: "*concordia consistit in unitate sententiae*."

mapping it onto distinctions that he drew when analyzing faith. In other words, there can be no fundamental union according to the will without there being a previous fundamental union on the part of the intellect (in faith and wisdom, etc.). It is certainly possible to trace some disagreements on the part of the intellect back to the will, e.g. heresy,[116] but that does not change the fact that a certain degree of intellectual agreement is necessary for concord. The will cannot love something that is unknown nor can it agree with another without it being on the basis of truth claims. In fact, when Aquinas is analyzing faith, he draws similar distinctions as well as clearly saying that the mind is in union with God by faith.[117] Peace can and must belong to the intellectual order too, for why else would Aquinas claim that we must agree in the more general?

A certain amount of disagreement, or rather disagreement about the very goods that can be the principles of order/union between two parties, will damage concord. This is not only because of the intimate relation between the intellectual and volitional orders, but also because a certain degree of difference in the intellect is discord in the will. The intellectual order/union of peace and the appetitive order stand and fall together, especially inasmuch as it concerns the practical intellect.[118] To differ as to the greatest goods amounts to de-facto discord because the two individuals will not belong to the same order simply speaking. Hence, their wills are not in agreement. They are not mutually informed and so are not made one *secundum quid*.

Likewise, the same kind of solution can be given as to a difference not in belief or love, but a difference in action. In one sense, Aquinas's vision of a unified plurality requires that there be differences in action toward the common good. These are part of the distinctions that make up the perfection of concord. Concord has

116. Cf. Schwartz, *Aquinas on Friendship*, 37ff.

117. Cf. See *ST* II-II q. 11, a. 1; *ST* II-II q. 12, a. 1, co.: "*quae quidem diversimode fit, secundum diversos modos quibus homo Deo coniungitur. Primo namque coniungitur homo Deo per fidem.*"

118. Cf. *Super Rom.*, c. 12, l. 3, n. 1005.

cooperation and mutual dependence built in, so to speak. As Aquinas says, "The distinction of states and responsibilities better preserves the peace of the mind and the earthly city, inasmuch as it enables more to share in the public actions."[119] Likewise, according to Aquinas, you can have more or less fitting ways of pursuing common ends as well as coordinated cooperation (different contributions and aid to one another) to the same end.[120] This is an important part of preserving the distinction and diversity of agents cooperating toward a shared goal, but it is also the very foundation of *per accidens* conflict. It is not, however, sinful even if it is a lack of a certain kind of order/union.[121] In other words, Aquinas is saying that differing in this way (as to actions seeking the same goal or actions seeking differing proximate goals) is a lack of order/union, but it does not arise to the destruction of peace, and can be seen as inevitable and foreseeable given that peace is the order/union of diverse subjects. As a confirmation of this, Aquinas says that these conflicts will not exist in heaven where there will be perfect order/union between the minds and actions of diverse individuals. Of course, this disorder/disunion could be (and very often is) caused by sin, but that is not necessarily the case for Aquinas. Just as disagreement is not always the contrary of order/union neither is practical conflict.

### JUSTICE AND PEACE

The link between justice and peace is deep and biblical, *opus iustitiae pax*. Aquinas cannot help but notice and thus mentions the connection numerous times in his early commentaries.[122] On the other hand, as much as Aquinas notes their connection, he does

---

119. *ST* II-II q. 183, a. 2, ad 3.

120. See, for example, *Super Phil.,* c. 1, l. 4, n. 41: "*Est autem sanctis necessaria unitas triplex . . . Item, cooperationis. Unde dicit collaborantes, etc., ut scilicet unus adiuvet alium.*"

121. Cf. *ST* II-II q. 37, a. 1, co.: "*Et talis discordia non est peccatum, nec repugnat caritati, nisi huiusmodi discordia sit vel cum errore circa ea quae sunt de necessitate salutis, vel pertinacia indebite adhibeatur, cum etiam supra dictum est quod concordia quae est caritatis effectus est unio voluntatum, non unio opinionum.*"

122. See, for example, *Super Is.,* c. 11.

not have an extended discussion of the relation between justice and peace. Part of this is explained by differing definitions of justice. Most of the Old Testament's meaning of justice has migrated to love in the New Testament.[123] As a result, only a few texts can be found in Aquinas on the relation between justice and peace. Love and peace receive the bulk of Aquinas's attention. Nevertheless, that still leaves the question of the relation of justice (as Aquinas means it) to peace.[124]

As we have seen in reviewing Aquinas's works, one of the main places Aquinas treats the relation of justice and peace is question is *ST* II-II q. 29, a. 3, ad 3. This is a response of a mere three or four sentences but gives us Aquinas's most explicit and direct position. In the corpus, which explores the relation of charity to peace, Aquinas identifies peace as charity's *proprius effectus*. Aquinas is clearly talking about supernatural interior and exterior peace as the twofold union of all personal appetites and of one's appetites with another person. Both senses of supernatural peace are caused by charity for it makes us love God and our neighbor. It is in the first objection that he references the relation of justice to peace specifically. An objector claims that peace is not the *proprius effectus* of charity since Isaiah says the work of justice is peace. Aquinas responds that "peace is the work of justice indirectly, since it removes what prohibits peace. It is the work of charity directly, because the proper *ratio* of peace is caused by charity.... For peace is the union of the inclination of appetites."[125]

123. Daniel Philpott, "Reconciliation: An Ethic for Peacebuilding," in *Strategies of Peace: Transforming Conflict in a Violent World,* ed. by Philpott and Powers (New York: Oxford University Press, 2010): 91–118; see pages 97–98

124. In asking this question, I am remaining in theology. So the question is about the infused virtue of justice. Likewise, I follow the revisionist line of relating the infused and acquired virtues—i.e. that they cannot co-exist in the same subject, but that the presence of the infused virtues renders the acquired 'virtual'. See Jean Porter, "Moral Virtues, Charity, and Grace: Why the Infused and Acquired Virtues Cannot Co-Exist," in *Journal of Moral Theology,* Vol. 8, No. 2 (2019): 40–66.

125. *ST* II-II q. 29, a. 3, ad 3: "*dicendum quod pax est opus iustitiae indirecte, inquantum scilicet removet prohibens. Sed est opus caritatis directe, quia secundum propriam rationem caritas pacem causat. Est enim amor vis unitiva, ut Dionysius dicit, IV cap. de Div. Nom. pax autem est unio appetitivarum inclinationum.*"

In this response, Aquinas clearly makes the causality of justice dispositive for the order/union of charity. It removes the obstacles to peace and protects peace from disturbance, but it does not properly and directly cause peace. That is the work of charity as order/union to God, self, and others. Love is a unitive force and so, given that peace is union, it properly belongs to love to cause peace. Put simply, in Aquinas's main treatment justice looks somewhat extraneous to peace. As Aquinas says elsewhere, "Peace is especially disturbed when one man does not give to the other that which is owed to him."[126] Justice guards against this and is therefore important to peace, but only derivatively. This is even true for the peace of the Church.[127] Most Thomistic commentators leave the issue at this. If Aquinas says "justice causes peace"[128] he means that it wards off the impediments to peace. Justice is, and remains, dispositive to peace. As Gilleman says, "superficially one could say that justice divides and love unites."[129]

This all seems relatively straightforward, but other texts of Aquinas complicate the picture somewhat by suggesting justice could have a more integral relationship to peace. For example, in *SCG* III c. 128, n. 6, he says: "Ordered harmony (i.e. external peace/concord) is served among men when each gives to each his due, which is justice."[130] Likewise, Aquinas says that God's justice is the cause of concord (i.e. exterior peace).[131] Elsewhere, he seems to identify

---

126. *Super Rom.*, 14, l. 2, n. 1128: "*Per hoc enim pax maxime perturbatur, quod unus homo non exhibet alteri quod ei debet.*"

127. Cf. *Super II Cor.*, 12, l. 3, n. 750.

128. *ST* II-II q. 180, a. 2, ad 2 : "*dicendum quod sanctimonia, idest munditia, causatur ex virtutibus quae sunt circa passiones impedientes puritatem rationis. Pax autem causatur ex iustitia, quae est circa operationes, secundum illud Isaiae XXXII, opus iustitiae pax, inquantum scilicet ille qui ab iniuriis aliorum abstinet, subtrahit litigiorum et tumultuum occasiones. Et sic virtutes morales disponunt ad vitam contemplativam, inquantum causant pacem et munditiam.*"

129. Gerard Gilleman, *Le Primat de la Charite en Theologie Morale: Essai Methodologique* (Paris: Desclee de Brouwer et Cie, 1952), 299.

130. *ScG* III c. 128, n. 6: "*Tunc autem ordinata concordia inter homines servatur, quando unicuique quod suum est redditur: quod est iustitiae. Et ideo dicitur Isaiae 32:17: opus iustitiae pax. Oportuit igitur per legem divinam iustitiae praecepta dari, ut unusquisque alteri redderet quod suum est, et abstineret a nocumentis alteri inferendis.*"

131. Cf. *Super Iob*, c. 25, l. 1: "*Quasi dicat: ex quo Deus tam magnus est et in iustitia*

peace and justice.[132] Finally, and most tellingly, he says that "peace consists in justice."[133] Each of these could suggest a greater relation than dispositive, but not necessarily. The strongest is the *consistit in* language Aquinas uses. This language is typical of the transcendentals. He also reverses his typical order—here ordering peace toward justice and not justice toward peace. There is a reason Gilleman says "superficially."[134] The relation of justice and peace cannot be explained by only recognizing a dispositive relationship (though that is certainly one relation).

A brief review of Aquinas's thought on justice can show us both why Aquinas writes that justice is dispositive for peace, but also show us why his claim that peace "consists in justice" can also be true. According to Aquinas, justice is lived in and through communities. Justice is the virtue by which right order is lived, between individuals, toward the common good, and from the common good toward individuals.[135] "Human actions are sufficiently rectified toward himself by the moral virtues, which regulate the passions. But actions which are toward another need a special rectification, not only in comparison to the agent, but by comparison to him to whom they are directed."[136] This sense of justice as governing types of relationships between distinct individuals is important for Aquinas. Justice presupposes that two are distinct in some sense. "*Aequalitas*

---

*praecellens ut etiam in sublimibus concordiam faciat, quae est iustitiae effectus secundum illud Is. XXXIII opus iustitiae pax, omnis iustitia hominis divinae iustitiae comparata quasi nihil reputatur.*"

132. Cf. *ST* I q. 96, a. 6, co.

133. *Super I Tim.*, c. 6, l. 4, n. 280: "*Item quod mala vitet, praecipue illa quae sunt nata coinquinare fidem. Cuius ratio est, quia sicut princeps saecularis ponitur ad custodiendam unitatem regni, ita spiritualis ad servandam unitatem spiritualem. Pax autem regni consistit in iustitia, et ideo ille ordinatur ad iustitiam; sed unitas Ecclesiae est in fide, et ideo principaliter monet ad custodiam fidei.*"

134. Gilleman, *Le Primat*, 299.

135. Cf. *ST* II-II q. 61, a. 1, co.

136. *ST* II-II q. 58, a. 2, ad 4: "*dicendum quod actiones quae sunt hominis ad seipsum sufficienter rectificantur rectificatis passionibus per alias virtutes morales. Sed actiones quae sunt ad alterum indigent speciali rectificatione, non solum per comparationem ad agentem, sed etiam per comparationem ad eum ad quem sunt.*"

*autem ad alterum est.*[137] As Aquinas says, "Justice . . . implies equality so from its very meaning justice is *ad alterum,* for nothing is equal to itself, but to another."[138] This Aquinas names the formal object of justice, the *ius* of our neighbor. In other words, the living of relations to those who are *alter* requires justice so that we can desire and act toward the *ius* of our neighbor and attain *aequalitas.*[139]

Aquinas divides the formal object of justice—the *ius,* into the *ius commune et ius privatum.* Based on this distinction he distinguishes types of justice. General, or legal, justice is the habitual rectification of an individual toward the common good (and the other as part of the common good). This inevitably recalls all previously written about the common good. To briefly recall it here, according to Aquinas communities have a two-fold order. There is the intrinsic ordering of the community members to each other, the intrinsic common good, and there is the ordering of all members to an extrinsic common good that gives the intrinsic common good its relations. General justice is the virtue that rectifies relations with the intrinsic common good. Particular justice, on the other hand, regards the *ius* of the individual either from the perspective of the common good (distributive justice) or from another private individual (commutative justice). Each of these types of justice aim at a type of equalizing—general and distributive at a type of proportional equality and commutative at an arithmetic equality. In this way, general justice is a type of connecting (ordering/unifying) virtue for Aquinas. It commands all acts that can be actually ordered to the internal common good.[140] It observes all just laws as a guide toward the common good, and hence it is often called legal justice. Yet its object is the common good, not the law.[141]

At least a provisional connection between justice and peace

---

137. *ST* II-II q. 57, a. 1, co.

138. *ST* II-II q. 58, a. 2, co.: *"cum nomen iustitiae aequalitatem importet, ex sua ratione iustitia habet quod sit ad alterum, nihil enim est sibi aequale, sed alteri."*

139. Dominic Farrell, "Wanting the Common Good: Aquinas on General Justice," in *The Review of Metaphysics,* vol. 71 (March 2018): 517–49; see page 527.

140. Cf. Farrell, "Wanting the Common Good: Aquinas on General Justice," 538–39.

141. Cf. Farrell, "Wanting the Common Good: Aquinas on General Justice," 540ff.

begins to show itself from the short summary above. Succinctly it can be put in three ways, all of which highlight the transcendental aspect of peace. Justice aims at peace; justice is a type of peace; and justice presupposes peace. All these relations can be defended on Aquinas's vision. I shall start with the first, justice aims at peace. To recall, according to Aquinas, peace is order/union and rest/tranquility. Peace, as the unifying of distinct things, presupposes distinction and alterity, but peace is the order/union of these distinct elements/parts, their relation. This makes peace, in some sense, the object of justice. Justice aims to equalize, live right relation, with our neighbors as parts of a whole or as individuals. In other words, justice aims at some kind of order/union (one can see this especially with general justice, which aims at the order/union of the common good). Therefore, Aquinas can write that justice is ordered toward peace.[142]

In another sense, justice simply is a type of peace (a type of order/union with another). One can see this through their *rationes*. Justice presupposes alterity and distinction, but aims to equalize; this very equalizing is a type of order/union (a relation)—that of equalizing.[143] In other words, just as the good is a more general *ratio* of justice and justice is part of the good,[144] so too peace is a *ratio* of the good (order/union) and thus peace extends to and encompasses all the good extends, including to the order of justice.[145] Justice is a type of relation/order/union with the other (even if it is one that governs alterity itself). This shifts the question about the relation of justice and peace to one concerning different orders and diverse

<hr>

142. Cf. *ScG* III c. 34, n. 2.

143. Cf. Gilleman, *Le Primat*, 302.

144. This is where Aquinas contrasts strongly with most modern ethical systems. Therein a distinction is drawn between the good and the right—Aquinas makes no such distinction. For a claim that Aquinas envisions this distinction see James Keenan, *Goodness and Rightness in Thomas Aquinas's Summa Theologiae* (Washington DC: Georgetown University Press, 1992); see also Lawrence Dewan's response. Lawrence Dewan, *Wisdom, Law, and Virtue*, 151ff.

145. Cf. McMahon, "A Thomistic Analysis of Peace," 183. This relation leads McMahon to imply that justice and concord are synonyms.

goods under differing formalities. To have the virtue of justice is to have a type of peace with the other. Not only does justice aim at a type of peace/concord, but it is also a type of peace/concord.[146] It "perfects the relationships between people."[147]

Granted, supernatural peace is the *proprius effectus* of the virtue of charity, but charity is not the sole cause of order/union or rest in general. Charity does not destroy these other orders but transforms them. Charity unites all our powers and the desires of different humans to the ultimate principle of order and goodness himself, God, and therefore causes the deepest and most lasting peace. In relation to this supernatural peace, justice is certainly dispositive in the sense that it is of a lower order/union. Nevertheless, this does not mean that justice is merely dispositive to all peace—within each order, alterity is essential to order/union, just as *aliquid* to *bonum*.

Finally, in another way, justice presupposes peace.[148] Distinction and alterity only exist within a deeper unity on which they are based. This mirrors the transcendentals. *Unum—aliquid—bonum*. Alterity flows from unity which then gives birth to order/union. This is why Aquinas says that unity is the cause of union.[149] Even the fullest sense of alterity Aquinas gives can only be conceived of and operate within the background of a presupposed union. "Those that are altogether distinct [alterity *simpliciter*], just as appears in two humans neither of which is under the other, but both are under the principle [common good] of the city."[150] Their distinction is seen against the background of their union. This could apply to any two humans, even the most unrelated, since they share in creation (and its twofold common good, i.e. union/order) and human nature (properly a unity).[151] So to claim that justice is totally extraneous to peace

---

146. Cf. Roniger, "Do Friends Need Justice or Do the Just Need Friendship? Natural Law as the Foundation for Justice and Friendship," *Lex Naturalis* 3 (2018): 57–84; 67.

147. Roniger, "Do Friends Need Justice or Do the Just Need Friendship?", 71.

148. Cf. Gilleman, *Le Primat*, 306–07.

149. Cf. Flood, *The Metaphysical Foundations of Love*, 18ff.

150. *ST* II-II q. 57, a. 4, co: "*sicut quod est omnino distinctum, sicut apparet in duobus hominibus quorum unus non est sub altero, sed ambo sunt sub uno principe civitatis.*"

151. In this sense, friendship always takes precedence over justice. Schwartz is wrong

misses the fundamental way in which justice is based on (some kind of) preexisting peace.

If this is the case, then what are we to make of Aquinas's consistent claims that justice is dispositive to peace? Peace is the order/union of distinct somethings. Since justice acts toward the other inasmuch as he or she is other—rendering to the other his or her *ius,* justice's order is merely dispositive toward a deeper union, even though it is a type of order/union in itself. As Antonin Sertillanges says, "The fundamental notion of justice is that of establishing equality in the mean of action. Justice is *ad alterum.* Therefore, justice is possible between two beings in the measure they are *autres.*"[152] Aquinas's statements on the issue drive in this direction. Though both peace and justice have alterity in their *rationes* justice acts toward the other merely at the level of alterity. One must be able to predicate equality to have justice.[153] Because of this, it is in some sense dispositive to peace since distinction is presupposed to order/union (metaphysically this would be natural priority, not temporal). In other words, the more you reduce alterity, the less justice's formality has a place (but also the more it is perfected and transcended). That means the closer to strict unity, the less place there is for the otherness on which justice is predicated. This is confirmed by Aquinas's position on justice in relation to self and in the family. Aquinas says that one can only metaphorically have justice toward oneself.[154] There is unity (in the proper sense of identity) there. Likewise, he says the family is too close a union for justice to obtain in its full proper sense.[155] Yet, he is willing to speak about peace in the

---

to claim that inequality of a certain degree renders justice impossible. There is always some kind of unity/union between all creatures. See Schwartz, *Aquinas on Friendship,* 51.

152. Antonin Sertillanges, *La Morale Philosophie de Saint Thomas d'Aquin* (Librairie Felix Alcan, 1922), 236.

153. Cf. Gilleman, *Le Primat,* 301.

154. Cf. *ST* II-II q. 57, a. 1, co.

155. In this Aquinas is following Aristotle, though I do not think he means that there is no justice full stop. There is distinction/alterity in a family and a virtue to govern that, justice. Rather, I think the closer one gets to unity, the more justice requires charity to operate *qua* justice.

family.[156] He does, however, speak of metaphorical justice within the individual (and presumably would amongst families also, since their union is less than an individual's). This explains why Aquinas usually speaks of justice as dispositive to peace and warding off the obstacles to peace. Justice governs distinction *qua* distinction and distinction is conceptually prior to order/union. Diminishing alterity altogether will not only remove justice but also peace, in the proper sense (as we saw in the philosophical predication of peace concerning God).

Confirming this is that Aquinas often speaks of interior peace being the right order between the powers of the soul, an almost identification between the union caused by charity internally and (metaphorical) justice.[157] Likewise, Aquinas follows Aristotle in claiming that justice and friendship (a union of wills) pertain to the same thing.[158] This is also true of the term 'original justice', which Aquinas uses to name the right order/union between all faculties in the paradisial state.[159] Put simply, justice's *ratio* is made possible to the extent things are distinct and then equalized. For this reason, it shares certain conceptions with peace and is a type of peace. This makes sense of Aquinas's occasional identifications of peace and justice (especially in the civil sphere). On the other hand, being only one type of order/union, it does not exhaust the meaning of peace and presupposes more fundamental forms of peace and tends toward them. In this sense, peace can ground justice as well as perfect it (and thus reduce the need for it in the strict sense).

The claim that the virtue of justice is integral to peace can be supplemented by focusing on Aquinas's general thought on virtue. "Habits extend to many things according to their order toward one something."[160] This 'one something' is the formal object of the virtue, that which specifies the virtue itself. Virtues with different

---

156. Cf. *ScG* III c. 125.

157. Cf. *Contra Impugnantes*, c. 1; *Super Jer.*, c. 14, l. 4; *Super II Thess.*, c. 3, l. 2; *Super Matt.*, c. 5, l. 2; *Super Io.*, c. 14, l. 7; *ST* I q. 108, a. 1, ad 1.

158. Cf. *In* VIII *Ethic.*, l. 9, n. 1662–1664.

159. Cf. *ST* I-II q. 82, a. 1, co.

160. *ST* I-II q. 54, a. 4.

formal objects can have the same material objects, but will still be distinct virtues. The point of a virtue is that it rightly orders us toward these material objects under a certain formality. As Ramirez says, "each virtue rightly orders the acts and affects of its respective potency."[161] And "To have order toward their material objects is fitting to every virtue inasmuch as they are virtues."[162] Virtues introduce order into various faculties. Virtue likewise brings order/union between many material objects under a particular formality. Each power rests in the good through its virtues. These are the very *rationes* of peace. Hence, inasmuch as virtue is possible without charity and grace, so too is peace.[163] Concerning justice then, it does, in itself rightly order (in some provisional and imperfect sense) the appetites of individuals toward each other, toward the common good of the *polis,* and toward the individuals who dwell therein. But the point is more general too. Each virtue is a habitual living of right order/union with a good under a certain formality and establishes order/union between its material objects. For example, Aquinas opposes pride and anger to peace, saying peace is thus established by humility and meekness.[164] This could not be said if peace was merely the order/union established by the virtue of charity.

The above explanations can take into account most of Aquinas's texts as well as the language of dispositive: though peace is order/ union, orders/unions can be dispositive to others. Hence, Aquinas often says that justice is dispositive to peace because he has in mind interior supernatural peace (as he does in *ST* II-II q. 29). This order/ union is the *proprius effectus* of charity. For the supernatural order, certain other orders—the civil, for example—are merely dispositive. Nevertheless, the supernatural order/union is not only possible order/union and so justice is not always dispositive to peace. For

161. Ramirez, *De Caritate,* 895: "*cada virtud ordena debidamente los actos o afectos de sus potencias respectivas.*"

162. Ramirez, *De Caritate,* 461.

163. Obviously, there is a long and protracted debate concerning this very point. See Brian Shanley, "Aquinas on Pagan Virtue," in *The Thomist* 63 (1999): 553–77.

164. *Super Eph.,* c. 4, l. 1, n. 191.

example, when Aquinas says that peace consists in justice he is usually talking about concord or external peace.[165] This is a near identification of concord (exterior peace) with justice![166] This shouldn't surprise anyone. Aristotle also nearly identifies the two as well when talking about civil concord.[167] In other words, when Aquinas says the word peace, he usually, but not always, means interior supernatural peace (the prime instance in the anthropological sense). Certainly, acquired justice is purely dispositive to peace taken in this sense. In other words, when Aquinas says that virtues (justice in particular) are dispositive to peace, he often has in mind ultimate and perfect peace, the final and ultimate order/union with God and our neighbor. In this sense one could say that just as nature is dispositive (negatively) for grace, so too is natural justice for true supernatural peace. On the other hand, once charity is introduced, the same order of justice becomes part of the order/union introduced into the life of the individual and the Church. Charity does not destroy the order of justice, but transforms it by directing it to God. One is in union/ordered to one's neighbor not only in the civil sphere through that common good, but also in a deeper way through love of God.

If Aquinas is willing to nearly identify exterior natural peace with the civil order, then the same arguments apply *a fortiori* to infused justice. In Aquinas's thought grace does not leave any of the virtues untransformed by its touch. The way he usually explains this is to say that charity commands the acts of the other virtues. Yet it goes further than this. Grace transforms the acquired virtues by directing them to a new end and thereby transforming them into the infused cardinal virtues. The acquired virtues really only remain virtually (i.e. the infused counterparts cover the same territory and can do the same things).[168] Inasmuch as justice is considered in this vein, as

165. E.g. *ST* I-II q. 69, a. 3, co.: "*Quantum vero ad virtutes et dona quibus homo perficitur in comparatione ad proximum, effectus activae vitae est pax; secundum illud Isaiae XXXII, opus iustitiae pax. Et ideo septima beatitudo ponitur, beati pacifici.*"

166. Cf. Erb, "Interior Peace," 266.

167. Cf. Roniger, "Do Friends Need Justice or Do the Just Need Friendship?," 79.

168. William C. Mattison III "Can Christians Possess the Acquired Virtues?"in *Theological Studies*, vol. 72 (2011): 558–85.

an infused virtue flowing from the theological virtues and gifts of the Holy Spirit, it is integral to peace and not merely dispositive. Infused justice is the perpetual will to render to the common good and every member of it his or her *ius* as commanded by charity and ordered to God. The deeper union of charity enables infused justice to exist and further commands it on behalf of the divine good. Infused justice is essential to the order of charity, because right relations with others are essential to the order of charity (as are the distinctions that justice governs). In this sense, the fullness of justice is found in friendship with God. Charity does not remove considerations of justice and alterity, but grounds their union/order in a greater supernatural union/order. In fact, if the above arguments are right, they suggest that every virtue is integral to establishing supernatural peace (interior or exterior). Every virtue rightly orders us toward a set of goods considered under its formal aspect; justice specifically orders us to the *ius* of our neighbor and this is an integral part of order/union (especially as concord, but also metaphorically as interior peace).

Charity, since it is the union/order to the universal good, establishes the most universal order/union. Because of this it encompasses and transforms all other orders/unions without destroying them. For this reason, every virtue is integral to supernatural peace because each is an instance of peace in itself. Each becomes part of the order/union to God, self, others, and creation under the command of charity. Considering justice, to act toward another *qua* other is not contrary to order/union with that other person, it is an essential part of it since without the alterity one would not have order/union but unity in the proper sense. In other words, the mean of justice (equality) is both preserved and transformed by the command of charity by union with the *other* precisely as friend. This does not destroy alterity (or the virtues that govern it) but draws it into a deeper order/union.

## Satisfaction and Peace

If I am right above about the relation of justice to peace, then another aspect of Aquinas's thought becomes integral: satisfaction. We recognize that peace will be disturbed in this world not only through inevitable differences, but more so through sin. In other words, the larger role that can be played by justice in relation to peace (as well as justice being a type of peace—an *ordo/unio*), also draws Aquinas's thought on satisfaction into peace (as well as confirming the above arguments about justice constituting an integral part of a greater peace). Granted in Aquinas's thought about redemption, satisfaction is but one concept among many, but the way he speaks about it in relation to order/union makes it important for peace in particular. Aquinas speaks about making satisfaction as a restoration/reunion/reordering. Satisfaction is the restoration of peace (as well as being an act of justice). Hence, satisfaction is (part of) Aquinas's answer to the following question: What are we to do when the proper order/union of humans to God, themselves, their neighbors, and creation is disturbed?

For Aquinas making satisfaction most properly means "restoring friendship with God through penance."[169] This is true both for God and for our neighbors, if we sin against them. Satisfaction is not simply the restoration of geometrical or arithmetic equality, which is restoring order/union only inasmuch as the person is other, but is commanded by charity so that it restores order/union with the other inasmuch as they are one with you (analogously one could say that civic friendship commands acquired justice). Interestingly, just as we saw above, not only is justice integral for peace, but peace (a deeper order/union) is the very context in which justice can operate. Put more directly, for justice to operate correctly it must be situated in a larger order/union. Aquinas's thought on satisfaction is a prime example of how charity commands infused justice (or analogously how social friendship in the common good can ground justice for all those who seek that good).

This is why Aquinas says that satisfaction, an act of justice, is only complete when order/union is restored between two individuals.[170]

169. Rik Van Nieuwenhove, "Salvation, Satisfaction, and Friendship with God," in *The Thomist*, vol. 83 (2019): 521–45; see page 527.

170. In this way, even restitution is itself a type of satisfaction and is also intrinsic to the restoration of peace. Aquinas speaks of restitution inasmuch as order/union is

He does not simply mean the order of justice either. Alterity must be taken up into order/union to be good. As Aquinas says, "It should be said that for satisfaction a man must be reconciled to his neighbor, just as to God. Now reconciliation is nothing other than the repairing of friendship."[171] This is true, preeminently, for the satisfaction Christ made on humanity's behalf, willingly accepting suffering on account of his union with us. Nevertheless, the satisfaction of Christ is a model and an inclusive type of satisfaction. It allows participation. Thus, Aquinas says that suffering, *poena,* can become the vehicle by which we restore right relations. Any suffering can be satisfactory if undertaken voluntarily or subsequently rendered voluntary.[172]

Though Aquinas recasts satisfaction as dependent on friendship (order/union in a deeper sense) the justice aspect remains, albeit transformed.[173] We render something back to the person we sin against (the order/union we damage), for the purpose of restoring

---

disturbed in transactions, of a type that typically occur in commutative justice. At first it seems that Aquinas wants to apply this only to material goods, but he extends it to immaterial goods and to any loss –his concept of *damnum.* We are bound to restitution in anything which causes a loss to another. In this regard, justice is the "*redditionem illius rei quae iniuste ablata est.*" One must render the equal back to the person from whom you took a material or spiritual good. Aquinas uses it for spiritual goods such as a good name—or what is owed to God. Restitution is a reinstatement of the *res* to its rightful possessor or lord (*dominus*—one possessing dominion) of the thing. As Aquinas says, it applies when we consider the equality of justice in exchanges with arithmetic equality. This is why he says restitution is an act of commutative justice. Because of this, restitution only applies in a very narrow section of justice—that of mathematical equality of exchange. Commutative justice restores right order/union inasmuch as it concerns the other precisely as other with the person. On the other hand, this implies that even commutative justice is integral for a type of peace (though not order/union in the ultimate sense). Furthermore, according to Aquinas, some kind of peace/order/union is often required as a basis for commutative justice. This means that Aquinas must have a concept of natural friendship, civil friendship, or supernatural friendship to supplement and ground justice. Put differently, the common good is a more fundamental concept than justice and establishes the order/union between individuals in which justice can operate. Justice is intrinsic to the internal common good of any group, but it is the internal common good that enables justice, not the other way around.

171. IV *Sent.,* d. 15, q. 1, a. 5, qla 2.

172. Cf. *ScG* III c. 157; *ST* II-II q. 97, a. 1, ad 3; *ScG* III c. 145, n. 3.

173. Cf. Rik van Neuenhove, "Salvation, Satisfaction, and Friendship with God," 523.

the order/union. Though it is sometimes not possible to render the exact equal (always in God's case), the deeper friendship enables justice to operate. Aquinas's recasting though, amounts to the claim that we can only satisfy the demands of justice, at least inasmuch as it concerns God and the full extent of justice to our neighbor, through some kind of friendship with him/them. There will be no justice unless both parties first are seeking order/union, unless they are seeking some kind of order/union to be restored. This wouldn't have to be full friendship in the proper sense (which can only be had with few people), but could be a type of civil friendship or the restoration of a type of natural friendship that comes with sharing human nature. Aquinas recognizes it will probably be impossible to right the injustice totally, but we should try to restore the good we have taken—and that we will try to do this because it is the action that flows from charity and from justice. This attempt is taken as enough in friendship, even if it is without absolute equality.[174]

What does this imply for the relation between justice and peace? It seems to confirm that justice is integral to peace. Not only will peace be disturbed when justice is not observed, but it will be deficient in itself. The order/union between the parties will not be a true order/union since the wills of each are not turned toward the other and toward the common good. Nevertheless, there is still a distinction between justice and peace. Peace is the union itself/the order itself whereas justice is the will to render the other party in the order/union his or her due. One acts under the formality of alterity and equality whereas the other is a more general formality of order/union. So in the metaphysical order alterity is presupposed to union (but, again, is also posterior to some kind of union or unity), but in the order of finality it is the union that enables the alterity to be good

---

174. Cf. IV *Sent.*, d. 15, q. 1, a. 5, qcla. 2: "It should be known that, as the philosopher says in Ethics VIII, friendship does not always require the equal, but what is possible. And so if anything has been taken that cannot possible be restored, the will of restoring with as much restitution as possible suffices according to the condition of both to the judgment of good men."

and to operate well qua alterity. Put more simply, both are presupposed for the other but in different orders.

This is again confirmed in Aquinas's thought on merit, another place where the deeper peace can enable justice to be an integral part of its order. "In short, we obtain forgiveness [the reestablishment of right relations/union with God] . . . when we make satisfaction on the condition that this occurs within an overall context of friendship."[175] Charity establishes the possibility of meriting, which is a concept of justice. God accepts, *acceptatio*, our willing penance and penitential suffering, even though these are not strictly or even closely equivalent, because of our friendship and union with him through Christ.[176] This is because among friends when there is an offense, the offender willing takes on the suffering the right restoration entails, and the offended willingly accepts less than that on account of the union (also a type of suffering).[177] This is certainly the case with our relation to God, but often also with our relation to our neighbors.[178]

175. Rik van Neuenhove, "Salvation, Satisfaction, and Friendship with God," 539.

176. Cf. *ST* III q. 85, a. 3, ad 1; *SS* IV d. 15, q. 1, a. 2: "*aequalitas autem in satisfactione ad Deum non est secudum aeuivalentiam, sed magis secundum acceptationem ipsius.*"

177. Cf. *ST* III q. 85, a. 3.

178. Satisfaction is predicated on sin. What are we to do when there is the inevitable loss of peace without sin on anyone's part (a possibility not only envisioned by Aquinas but positively required)? I think Aquinas's thought on love also answers this question. As we have seen, Aquinas is committed to the claim that one can make satisfaction based on order/union that is not owed in justice (even if that order/union is presupposed for justice also). This is important not only Christologically, but also for understanding the supernatural order/union of the Church. Based on this supernatural order/union fellow members of the Church can help us restore peace where it is lost without sin. By dwelling in the body of Christ through the reception of his Spirit, all suffering can become redemptive—satisfactory. Certainly, one would not be required in justice to make satisfaction for the foreseeable but unintended bad effects of one's action (or those of one's neighbor). I think one could attempt to make satisfaction for the inevitable loss of peace that was based on a good action, but it would not be required. It would be an offer of good will and of the desire to be in order/union with all people in the fullness of order/union (which we know is impossible on this side of heaven, but is a worthy goal of our striving). These *per accidens* conflicts are potentially infinite and Aquinas is no utilitarian, requiring that all these be taken into account or claiming that failing to take them into account in action is an omission. Yet, it would seem to be a counsel that Aquinas would urge based on his thought on peace, that we take them into account and right them. As we will see below, he claims that each person has the responsibility to make, preserve, and promote peace (order/union). On the other hand, given the contingency

## OUR RESPONSIBILITY TO MAKE PEACE

In the last section, I briefly covered what must be done if one sins and this destroys peace. Aquinas's answer to this is satisfaction, the restoration of order/union and therefore of rest/concord. This includes attempting to render the loss back to the individual, to attempt some kind of equality, but requires that the offender and the individual both belong to a greater order/union (to have some kind of friendship). In this section, I want to treat our responsibility to make right order/union that is not yet present.

Aquinas's conception of the moral life is one of seeking right order/union with God, ourselves, others, and the natural world; that much is clear. We do this by receiving the peace of God himself. Our peace is a participation in God's peace, especially (though not exclusively as we have seen) through the virtues of charity as well as the gift of wisdom. It is through these gifts that we live the peace of God. In other words, it is not out of keeping with Aquinas's thought to say that the entire goal of the practical order is to seek to live and further peace with God, others, and the world. The entire goal of the moral life is peace. In fact, Aquinas says this explicitly. "The last of all goods is peace for peace is the general end of the mind. For in any way peace is taken, it has the *rationem finis*. And in eternal glory, the directing of others, and the living of common life, the end is peace."[179] Hence, it is no mistake that Aquinas's exhortations to make peace—both within ourselves and with others—are forceful. He exhorts the individual to seek peace with God, himself, others, and the world. This is the entire purpose of our practical lives.

---

and limited resources of any one person, one could only undertake this counsel in a very small sector of one's life. It is only in the solidarity of the Church that more becomes possible. Given the supernatural order/union of the Church, others can step in to help restore that order/union that is lost even without sin (whether it be based on your action or another's). In this way, each member of the Church depends on all others for the seeking and restoring of peace.

179. *Super II Cor.*, c. 1, l. 1, n. 8: "*Ultimum autem omnium bonorum est pax, quia pax est generalis finis mentis. Nam qualitercumque pax accipiatur, habet rationem finis; et in gloria aeterna et in regimine et in conversatione, finis est pax.*"

### Our Responsibility to Make Interior Peace—
### Peace with God and Ourselves

As we saw in the first chapter, Aquinas is adamant that everyone desires peace. Undoubtedly he has drawn this from Dionysius (and Augustine), who is equally forceful on the issue. This makes perfect sense if peace (as order/union) is an aspect of the good. Aquinas's notion of ethics is thoroughly teleological—our achievement of the good is about achieving an end. The final end is happiness. In other words, I want to suggest that the connection of peace to the good not only grounds the universality of desire for it, but also grounds our responsibility to make interior peace. Thus, to explicate Aquinas's thought on our responsibility to seek peace, it is thus helpful to see how he grounds it in the universality of desire for the good.

Although it is not possible to fully attain in this life, Aquinas is clear that every agent desires peace. His usual argument for this is that anyone who desires anything desires to achieve it without hinderance. This makes it seem like peace is purely instrumental, as we have seen. On the other hand, I think I have successfully argued that it is otherwise (at least sometimes) for Aquinas. Peace is a *ratio* of the good. Aquinas is willing to talk about the good as pleasurable, honest, and instrumental.[180] That means we should be willing to talk about peace the same way. Aquinas's arguments for the universal desire of peace trade on the instrumentality of lower orders for higher, but that does not imply that peace is intrinsically and universally instrumental. Often in his arguments for the universal desire for peace he is talking about the relation between two orders, that of natural exterior peace to supernatural interior peace. One good can be instrumental to another, and this is rhetorically helpful to prove his point. On the other hand, it does not imply that peace, even natural exterior peace, is purely instrumental in every sense. One order can

---

180. Cf. *ST* I q. 5, a. 6, co.

be instrumental to another (just as one good can be instrumental to another) without it negating its intrinsic goodness.[181]

Likewise, other times Aquinas speaks of the universal desire for peace non-instrumentally. We saw this above in the quotation that introduced this chapter and he says it clearly in the universal and natural desire for union (as *esse et bonum*).[182] This is a non-instrumental desire for wholeness, perfection, and persistence. In other words, one should not take his standard arguments for the universal desire of peace as expressive of his whole thought about peace. Likewise, based on what we have seen of Aquinas's thought, our desire for the good is already an order/union with the good. So moving from desire for the good to desire of peace can be made in multiple ways. Aquinas often chooses one of them—the sense in which natural exterior peace is merely dispositive to supernatural interior peace— but we need not read the totality of desire for peace this way.

Whether the above is correct or not, Aquinas is clear that the desire for peace is universal. All persons desire to return to this deepest order/union interiorily, this deepest union between their powers that is given by grace and lived in virtue. We desire this because it is integral to the life of happiness, to the flourishing of the human person. It is from this universal desire that follows the universal responsibility to seek interior peace. The nature of our faculties and the claim that they are inclined necessarily to their respective objects, generates the responsibility to seek virtue as the proper ordering toward those objects. This is not something that anyone can opt-out of, since the desires of nature are necessary.[183] Likewise, since the

181. Cf. Daniel McInerny, *The Difficult Good* (New York: Fordham University Press, 2006), 43ff.

182. Cf. *In de Div. Nom.*, c. 11, l. 1, n. 886; *ST* I-II q. 36, a. 3, co; McMahon, "A Thomistic Analysis of Peace," 180.

183. In this way, the desire for peace is a hypothetical ought statement which has some kind of necessity. For more on this, see Steven Jensen, *Knowing the Natural Law: From Precepts and Inclinations to Deriving Oughts* (Washington DC: The Catholic University of America Press, 2015), 167ff. It does not depend on the conscious desire of the individual for peace, but is based on the necessity of nature's ordering to its object (happiness).

desire for peace is identical with the desire for the good, it is not a desire out of which people can opt. It is this very desire that grounds freedom and so freedom cannot be without it. The responsibility to seek interior peace holds everywhere and always. Certainly, someone can incorrectly judge what belongs to interior peace just as one can seek a false good, but he or she can only reject what will truly bring peace by seeking interior peace incorrectly, by seeking a false peace (false order/union to the good and false rest). Hence, all persons not only desire peace, but have the responsibility to investigate how to bring it about in their bodies, souls, lives, and actions. The responsibility to seek interior peace is simply the responsibility to restore order to the soul, to unite the powers of the soul within an integral life.

In our current existential state, we are at a severe disadvantage in the seeking of interior peace. Not only are we subject to the privation of grace by original sin, but our faculties no longer seek the good in an ordered way.[184] After sin, the intellect is wounded by ignorance, the will by malice, and the passions by weakness and concupiscence.[185] This means that after sin it is more difficult to know what is good, desire what is good, and overcome difficulties toward the good. Disorder has taken hold in the very interior of human life. Human powers are in conflict with each other. Each seeks what is proper to it with no integration between its possible objects or into the overall life of the person, with no order/union. Alterity has been severed from order and so gives rise to chaos and boundlessness of desire. Alternatively, one could say, each seeks its object also in a disordered way. The result is interior conflict. Not only do we have a positive responsibility to seek peace based on universal desire, but we are at a severe disadvantage for obtaining that desire.

Nevertheless, Aquinas's thought is helpful here too. It is difficult to seek something that one knows little about, and Aquinas's

---

184. Cf. *ST* I-II q. 82, a. 1, co.: "*Est enim quaedam inordinata dispositio proveniens ex dissolutione illius harmoniae in qua consistebat ratio originalis iustitiae.*"

185. Cf. *ST* I-II q. 85, a. 3, co.

metaphysics and theology of peace give a strong (if sometimes debatable) conception of peace. According to Aquinas, the proper order/union between our faculties is as follows: our sense appetites are responsive to the guidance of reason, and reason (encompassing both the intellect and the intellectual appetite—the will) is subject to God.[186] Aquinas calls this peace original justice (but justice in the metaphorical sense). Put differently, one must order/unify one's desires and, as we have seen, orders always relate to a principle. Reflection on principles in general (and with respect to seeking) begin with the order of final causality (since we are talking about seeking something—though of course order obtains in all the other species of causality as well). So the question then becomes what object (as principle of the order/union of our faculties) can provide an integral life where each of our powers can find order to the others and rest? This is where Aquinas's thought on happiness and peace again coincide and Aquinas has concrete advice for seeking interior peace.

According to Aquinas, it is possible to enjoy provisional order/ union between our powers based on lower orders (e.g. in the city), but only God can bring full and lasting peace. He says this for two reasons. First, an individual can only be happy *perfecte beatus* when there is nothing more to desire or seek. Obviously, only God can sate all desire. Second, each power is determined to its object. The intellect, as he writes in *ST* I-II q. 3, a. 8, co., cannot rest until it knows the essence of the first cause. Hence happiness requires knowing the essence of the first cause and then the intellect will be perfected. However, *ST* I-II Q. 3, a. 8, could give the impression that happiness is purely an intellectual endeavor, but Aquinas's thought on peace shows this to be false. If the goal is to restore inner order/union, it must begin (at least inasmuch as natural causality is concerned and not generation, etc.) with the intellect, but all powers of the soul must be perfected in relation to their objects. As we have seen above, this is accomplished by grace and the transformation (virtues, gifts, etc) grace causes in the soul. The virtues caused by habitual grace

186. Cf. *ST* I q. 94, a. 4, co.; *ST* I q. 95, a. 1, co.; *ST* I-II q. 82, a. 3, co.

reorder the powers to their respective objects—faith to the knowledge of God, hope to the happiness of God, love to the friendship of God, the gifts of the Holy Spirit to God's guidance for contemplation and action, and the infused cardinal virtues for seeking the things of this world inasmuch as they are ordered to God. Each of these is integral to the restoration of peace, to reordering the soul's powers properly toward their objects as well as toward each other.

But doesn't this again introduce the possibility of disorder/disunion in life? Can we not desire many things virtuously which we cannot have at the same time or cannot hold securely? Why would virtue preclude disorder/disunion? Virtues seek diverse goods or the same good under diverse formalities and yet we all recognize it would be impossible to obtain them all simultaneously or hold them securely. This is a good question and one Aquinas answers by claiming that only if all the virtues themselves are brought into order/union, can discord between them be precluded. In other words, the virtues themselves must seek their good (to count as virtue at all!) in an orderly/unified way. The virtues must be connected, to use Aquinas's language. Connectivity is simply another name for the introduction of order/union amongst the virtues, the introduction of mutual dependence and common goal seeking.

As we saw earlier, charity (at least considering the supernatural order) is the immanent efficient cause of this order/union. In other words, virtue is not disconnected (disorderly) in Aquinas.[187] If it were then even with virtue there could be internal conflict. Charity orders all our virtues, desires, powers, etc. by providing a principle of their order/union. Charity orders all powers and objects to God. This in turn allows the virtues to find relation to each other (union) by their common relation to God as commanded by charity. Now they inhabit one supernatural order and because they are a part of an order, they are in union with each other (agreement) about what is to be sought and done. This will not preclude, as we shall see, *per accidens* conflict though. The kind of harmony Aquinas thinks charity

---

187. Cf. *ST* I-II q. 65, aa. 1–5; *ST* II-II q. 23, a. 8.

can introduce into our lives is not impenetrable or such a degree of unity that disorder/conflict is precluded.

Yet charity can only provide this integrating function because its object is God. Aquinas's thought about seeking interior peace is less about one virtue commanding all the others than it is about God, who is the object of charity. Since charity's object is God and it suffers no distance from him but is a fundamental affective union with him, it can give a share of that union to the other virtues. This does not destroy the other powers of the soul or their virtues, but transforms them by ordering them to God. Yet this still begs the question of why God can bring order/union to the powers of our souls, our lives, our actions, etc. where other goods could not fully. Aquinas's metaphysics of peace are the reason he claims God (and only God) can provide this integrating function. Since God is infinite goodness, he contains preeminently the good which each power seeks. As Aquinas says, "Peace is a twofold union. One is according to the proper order of each appetite into one. The other is the union of the appetite of one with another's. Each is effected by charity. The first is loving God with one's whole heart so that we refer all things to him and so all our appetites tend to one. The second is that we love our neighbor as ourselves . . ."[188] Charity does not destroy or even negate/sublimate the order of the sensitive appetites, for example, to refer their action to God. The good that they seek is already so referred by creation. The good they seek in creation is preeminently found in God so that the reference of charity to God is not violent. It does not order them to a good unrelated and contrary to the good they seek, but the profoundest and deepest presence of that good. Hence, charity perfects the good of the other virtues/desires, but also brings them into the deepest order of creation and therefore the most lasting and deepest peace.

It is vital to recognize that supernatural peace is only possible when God serves as the principle of interior order (just like happiness). Only God contains preeminently the good that each power

188. *ST* II-II q. 29, a. 3, co.

seeks. Attempting to return inner peace by referring all our powers to another object (honor, wealth, etc.) will only result in more inner conflict since that object cannot sate all our powers and bring them to rest except by (occasionally—when they conflict with what is selected as the integrating good) destroying their legitimate order to their objects. Charity, by its object (God), is the only lasting basis for inner peace. Only God is the infinite good and thus only God has a non-competitive relation to other goods. As Aquinas says, "For apart from God a man does not have harmony with himself, much less with others, because a man's emotions are in harmony with themselves when what is sought to fulfill one desire suffices to fulfill all desires, and nothing but God can do this, for anything else but God will not be enough for all desires, but God is enough."[189]

The Means of Making Interior Peace: Growth
in Virtue and Spirituality

How does one unify/order one's powers and reduce (as much as this is possible) interior disorder? Practically, this is going to look different for each person (depending on their circumstances), but Aquinas has broad advice for growing in peace, and it reduces to his advice about how to grow in virtue. Yet all this growth, if it is going to contribute to the growth of supernatural interior peace, will be under the formality and command of charity. Since charity is the most fundamental and deepest peace we can enjoy (as direct order/union with God himself) and has no distance from him (indeed based on the affective union it is the very indwelling of God in the soul). Charity thus introduces order/union between our powers, desires, and virtues. So, by way of summary, one can look at how Aquinas advises the growth of charity to gain a small understanding of how he would counsel individuals to grow in supernatural interior peace.

Aquinas gives three stages for the growth of charity and these map onto growth in interior peace.[190] Aquinas divides the progress

189. *Super II Thess.,* c. 3, l. 2, n. 89.
190. Cf. *ST* II-II q. 24, a. 9.

in charity into three grades—*incipiens, proficiens, et perfecta*. When Aquinas identifies the three stages of charity (though one should not take these as strictly divided from one another—for growth does not work this way), he compares it to growth in the body. Aquinas divides the growth in charity based on the diverse *studia* that are pursued in each stage. In the first stage, he identifies the avoidance of sin and the resistance of concupiscence. Yet this stage isn't focused primarily on this, but in *nutrienda vel fovenda* charity so that it may not be corrupted. It is only because we are nourishing the growth of charity that we must spend the majority of time fighting against sin at the beginning. The second stage is marked by a principal intention to grow in the good. After having overcome the principal vices and other sins that would snuff out charity, then the principal intention of the first stage can come to the fore—feeding charity. The third stage of charity comes with the dominant intention not to grow in charity but simply to adhere to God and enjoy him. It is marked by fruition/joy. This final stage is marked by a dominance of the contemplative life—not in the sense of being opposed to action[191]—but of chiefly contemplating (and thus enjoying) God who consumes the soul with his fire.

These stages help explain the growth of peace. To grow in interior supernatural peace, an individual will first work on combatting that which disturbs the growth of interior peace—chiefly personal vice and sin. This is not only for those vices and sins contrary to charity, but all vice and sin can disrupt peace (since order/union between our powers requires all virtues). This is not only because they are dispositive to true peace, but because they are integral to interior order as argued in the last section (if one is solely focused on the order/union of the intellect in contemplation of its object, one can say activities/ virtues are dispositive—as Aquinas sometimes does). Hence, in this first stage, growth in any virtue is the principal aim of one desiring to grow in peace. Now the particular vice that besets each individual

---

191. Cf. Louis Bouyer, *Introduction to the Spiritual Life* (Notre Dame, IN: University of Notre Dame Press, 2013), 101–07.

will be diverse, but will fall into patterns. The Thomistic tradition has a long history of reflecting on the primary ways of fighting sin in this first stage.[192] Nevertheless, the principal method for growing in this stage is the Sacrament of Reconciliation—the sacrament by which God forgives our sins, restores friendship with him, and gives us the actual grace to combat those vices/sins in the future.

The second stage is marked by the principal intention to grow in interior supernatural peace given that the predominate obstacles are being overcome. This stage is focused less on the combating of sin and more on the growth of virtue. Again, this will involve every virtue, since every virtue is integral to our interior order/union. The Thomistic tradition, again, has developed highly specific advice for growing in virtue,[193] but one should also take into account the findings of modern psychology on the growth of habits.[194] Apart from advice about each virtue (which virtue is the focus depends on the person and circumstances) this stage also includes a greater focus on what the Thomistic tradition has called the secondary means of spiritual growth, interior and exterior.[195] These are well known in the spiritual literature and the Catholic tradition has a wealth of them. They include fasting, the Jesuit *Examen*, serving the poor, the Carmelite practice of the presence of God, spiritual direction, gardening, spiritual reading, study, the divine office, almsgiving, and so on. Basically it covers any conditions in life that would nourish love of God and growth in virtue. Each of these will help bring order/union to the soul based on an ever-increasing love of God.

The final stage in the growth of peace is marked by some kind of provisional perfection.[196] According to Aquinas, this stage is not

192. For an example of this see, Antonio Marin, *The Theology of Christian Perfection* (Eugene, OR: Wipf and Stock Press, 2012), Part III, Chapters 5–6, who divides them into active and passive purifications.

193. Cf. Marin, *The Theology of Christian*, 364–496.

194. Cf. Ezra Sullivan, *Habits and Holiness: Ethics, Theology, and Biopsychology* (Washington DC: The Catholic University of America Press, 2021).

195. Cf. Marin, *The Theology of Christian*, 565–614.

196. Cf. Servais Pinckaers, *Sources of Christian Ethics*, 3rd ed., trans. by Mary Thomas Noble (Washington DC: The Catholic University of America Press, 1995), 368.

marked so much by growth but by the enjoyment and contemplation of God. This stage thus marks the highest interior supernatural peace which can be achieved in this life and rest/quiet predominates in the soul. A good picture of what Aquinas thinks this life will look like is found in *ST* II-II q. 179ff. Therein, he shows the consonance between his thoughts on happiness and the contemplative life. The contemplative life is a life one where the principal aim is the contemplation of truth, though he understands this expansively "to do justice to a more broad-ranging notion of contemplation, namely one that could include the contemplation of the ordinary, unlearned, Christian. . . ."[197] This is the contemplative life in its essence, but also involves the will because it is love that drives the intellect to contemplate God.[198] The moral virtues, Aquinas says, are dispositive to this life because they remove the impediments to contemplation (another confirmation that orders/unions can be dispositive to other orders/unions, but not be purely instrumental goods!).[199] The cardinal virtues fight the obstacles to the contemplation of divine truth. Nevertheless, inevitably, the peace of the 'perfect' will be disturbed both by continuing imperfection in virtue and venial sin (the stages are not really temporal, but based on an analogy from motion), but also by the actions of others (both sinful or not).

Though Aquinas divides growth in peace into three stages, counseling different activities in each, he also counsels general means for growing and sustaining peace in any stage: prayer and the sacraments. Prayer and the sacraments are the mainstays of all three stages of growth in interior supernatural peace, but also represent the summit of interior peace. The reason for this, especially in the case of the Eucharist, will be outlined in the next chapter, but here it is important to note why both prayer and the sacraments are such vital and lifelong means toward fostering interior peace according to Aquinas. This is because their *rationes* coincide with the *rationes* of

197. Van Nieuwenhove, *Thomas Aquinas and Contemplation*, 204.
198. Cf. *ST* II-II q. 179, a. 1, co.
199. Cf. *ST* II-II q. 179, a. 2, co.

supernatural peace—order/union to God. Prayer is the union of the mind, heart, and affections to God in act (as opposed to habit).[200] This is because the cause of prayer (even if it is an act of religion) is the *desiderium caritatis*.[201] Prayer's primary purpose is given to it from charity: "to be united to God."[202] Once someone has grace, that person is habitually united/ordered to God in all virtue. But growing in this requires that we act on these in relation to God and our neighbor. This is done toward God especially in prayer, since it is the "interpreter of desire" and "the laying out of our will in the presence of God."[203] It is the *simul conversari ad amicum* with God. Habits are strengthened by repeated acts, as a muscle.[204] So too the supernatural habits are all strengthened in prayer, as their exercise in union with God. In fact, Aquinas defines prayer as a movement of the mind to God under the command of charity and therefore seeking union with God.[205]

Something similar can be said about the sacraments. All the sacraments involve the reordering/reunifying of the individual to God, self, neighbor, and creation. For example, the Sacraments of Reconciliation, Baptism, and the Anointing of the Sick are the very reintroduction of order/union to God and the Church. Marriage and Holy Orders are the entry into a new type of order/union within the Church. Confirmation and the Eucharist augment this order/union and cause its growth. The sacraments are not an optional aside for the growth of interior supernatural peace, but its very introduction, sustenance, and end. Hence, even the perfect who have attained some of the last stages of interior growth in peace will still be

200. Cf. *ST* II-II q. 83, a. 1, ad 2.

201. *ST* II-II q. 83, a. 14, co.

202. *ST* II-II q. 83, a. 1, ad 2: "*Unde nihil prohibet, movente voluntate, actum rationis tendere in finem caritatis, qui est Deo uniri. Tendit autem oratio in Deum quasi a voluntate caritatis mota, dupliciter. Uno quidem modo, ex parte eius quod petitur, quia hoc praecipue est in oratione petendum, ut Deo uniamur.*"

203. *ST* II-II q. 83, a. 9, ad 2: "*oratio sit interpres desiderii.*" *ST* III q. 21, a. 1, co. "*explicatio propriae voluntatis apud Deum.*"

204. For the limits of this comparison, see Sullivan, *Habits and Holiness* (Washington DC: The Catholic University of America Press, 2020), 213ff.

205. Cf. *ST* II-II q. 83, a. 1, ad 1.

sustained and enriched by their prayer and the Eucharist as the enjoyment and augmentation of their union with God, self, other, and creation. Put differently, for Aquinas the spiritual life cannot surpass the sacraments but is culminated therein.[206]

Before closing, some qualifiers need to be added. The above picture may seem too optimistic. Simply because loving God can order/unify our faculties does not mean that it will be easy to obtain (or even possible fully on this side of heaven). Obviously Aquinas is going to take into account the conditions under which our responsibility to seek peace is lived and so he qualifies our ability to achieve interior peace in numerous ways.

Firstly, he envisions the possibility that this peace is partially lost without sin on the part of the individual. Since the powers of the soul are separate powers, even if reordered by virtue and to God by charity, they could still desire a good which is *per accidens* in conflict with another good.[207] This will not be the case most of the time, but the experience of Christ in the Garden of Gethsemane requires that Aquinas take this into account.[208] At one point, Aquinas says that this will be the loss of exterior peace without the loss of interior peace.[209] This, however, seems wrong (though it is clear why Aquinas says this—the loss of exterior peace is the cause of the loss of interior peace). Christ's interior peace was lost as well. In other words, Aquinas admits that one could lose interior peace by having

206. Though Aquinas would see no tension between the heights of the spiritual life and the sacraments, this is not the case for all authors. See Voker Leppin, *Ruhen in Gott: Eine Geschichte der christlichen Mystik* (München: C.H. Beck, 2021), 11.

207. Choosing the lower good in these situations would not necessarily be a sin because the choice of the lower good does not always imply one is willing to lose the higher. Aquinas's claim that sin is loving more the lower good (*magis amat minus bonum*) presupposes that one is in a situation where the choice of the lower necessarily implies a volitional rejection of the higher, i.e. when one is willing to suffer the loss of the higher to reach the lower. See *ST* I-II q. 78, a. 1. This would not be the case in lower goods that remain ordered toward the higher. As Aquinas says, the proximate end (lesser good) does not exclude the ultimate end in this case. See *ST* I q. 65, a. 2, arg. 2 & ad 2.

208. Cf. Paul Gondreau, *The Passions of Christ's Soul in the Theology of Thomas Aquinas* (Providence, RI: Cluny Media, 2018), 372–77; Joel Gallagher, "The Gethsemane Event according to Thomas Aquinas," in *The Angelicum*, vol. 94 (2017): 673–707.

209. Cf. *Super Matt.*, c. 5, l. 2, n. 443.

diverse and conflicting desires. In other words, exteriorly others or the world (with or without sin on their part) could prevent our desires from attaining their proper objects, which could inhibit the fullness of interior peace. Aquinas would undoubtedly qualify the loss of peace that is possible here (especially for Christ!). It is the loss of order/union on the part of the sensitive appetite toward it's object and not the loss of the proper order/union of the intellect/will to God.[210] As Erb writes, "Thomas explains that Christ's suffering was the greatest that could possibly be endured, and while it carried the weight of physical as well as the totality of moral evil, it coexisted alongside the most radiant peace, present in his higher faculties but not overflowing to his lower reason or sensitive powers."[211] Aquinas claims that this deeper order/union cannot be lost without sin on the part of the individual.[212] Nevertheless, the possibility of sinless loss of interior peace remains possible. If the proper order/union of our sensitive appetites can be lost in this life (they are ruled politically and not despotically) even in Christ, then one can expect this even in one highly formed in virtue as well. This could be either because an exterior agent prevents desires from reaching the good or because diverse goods cannot all be obtained but are all desired.[213]

Secondly, the possibility of obtaining this order/union of interior peace can be disturbed in this life by ongoing sinful dispositions and actual sin. The virtues do not (especially at the beginning) reorder their respective powers so potently that previous dispositions do not remain.[214] These contrary dispositions are an ongoing disorder/disunion in the soul. Aquinas follows St. Paul in saying that on this basis there is always going to be a lack of interior peace in the life of

210. Cf. *Super Phil.,* c. 4, l. 1.

211. Erb, "Interior Peace," 273.

212. Cf. *Super Io.,* c. 16, l. 8.

213. Obviously, the loss of peace occasioned by the inability to obtain all the goods one desires can still remain within a deeper interior peace because there is a third and deeper desire that determines which of the lesser goods are pursued, i.e. gives them order/union. In other words, it would reduce one's appetitive stance vis-à-vis one of the goods to that of mere velleity.

214. Cf. *ST* II-II q. 14, a. 4, co.

the believer.[215] There will always be ongoing disunion and disquiet. Likewise, apart from remaining contrary dispositions, there is the positive sin on the part of the agent. This will, more than anything else, disturb the interior peace of the believer. In the *Summa Theologiae* Aquinas lists no sins against interior peace because every sin disorders the agent's desires. Not only does sin disorder an individual, but this is the very punishment for sin. Sin renders one unable to be a friend to oneself (to be unified/ordered).[216] In other words, sin is born from and deepens disorder/disunion in the soul. Aquinas recognizes that this is, in some sense, inevitable. We can avoid mortal sin and each venial sin, but he does not think we will ever avoid every venial sin.[217] Why he thinks this is tangential to the issue at hand, but it is important to qualify the possibility of attaining interior peace in this life. Each of these venial sins reintroduce, in a small way, disorder/disunion into the soul with a resulting lack of rest.

## Our Responsibility to Make Exterior Peace—Peace with Others

What about our responsibility to make peace with others? Is our responsibility to make peace with others as strong as our responsibility to make interior peace? Does it suffer the same possibilities and failures? Does it utilize the same means? To a large extent the answer to these questions is yes. Given the predominance of metaphysics and theology in Aquinas's conception of peace, the same kind of vision and principles lie behind both the making of interior and exterior peace. Hence, Aquinas's statements on the responsibility to make exterior peace are forceful and confirm the intuition that our responsibility to seek peace with others is integral to our responsibility to make interior peace (integral to our flourishing as human beings).

The extent to which Aquinas takes the responsibility to be peacemakers with others becomes clear if we review some of his thought

215. Cf. *Super Rom.,* c. 7, l. 4, nn. 587ff.
216. Cf. Roniger, "Is there a Punishment for Violating the Natural Law?," 297ff.
217. Cf. *ST* I-II q. 109, a. 8, co.

on the issue. One of the main places he reflects on this is in his mature *Commentary on Romans.* The occasion verse states, "If it is possible, be one who lives at peace with all people."[218] Aquinas follows this with a long commentary on what it means to bless and not curse as well as to be "one mind." He says Paul recommends all these things "so that we might have peace with all humans."[219] Of course, he qualifies the possibility of having peace with certain people—a topic for below—but also adds that this should be an impediment on the part of the other person, not on the part of the believer. "Even if they themselves act against peace, nevertheless we ought to do what is in us (*in nobis est facere nos*) so that we seek peace with them."[220] This should not surprise us. God himself is a peacemaker and pours peace into the world through Christ. Believers are incorporated into Christ's peace by the Holy Spirit and become sons in the Son. Thus, when Aquinas comments on the beatitude "blessed are the peacemakers" he says "this is written not because they are pacified right now but because they tend toward peace since they are called Sons of God."[221] Peace is the reason "the Son is said to have come into the world, to gather the dispersed."[222] It is not enough to have interior peace, "but they ought to make peace among those at discord."[223]

This is confirmed in his *Commentary on Psalm* 33 (34). Therein, Aquinas says, "Inasmuch as it relates to your neighbor, he says *seek peace, et cetera.* When it happens that you have a neighbor who is fighting with you, it is yours to seek peace; and for this reason he says, seek peace. . . . and when you have someone seek peace from you, then it is yours to follow him . . ."[224] In other words, if someone

218. Rom 12:18: "εἰ δυνατόν τὸ ἐξ ὑμῶν μετὰ πάτων ἀθρώπων εἰρηνεύοντες" and in Aquinas's Latin: "*Si fieri potest, quod ex vobis est, cum omnibus hominibus pacem habentes.*"
219. *Super Rom.,* c. 12, l. 3, n. 1010.
220. *Super Rom.,* c. 12, l. 3, n. 1010.
221. *Super Matt.,* c. 5, l. 2, n. 407.
222. *Super Matt.,* c. 5, l. 2, n. 439.
223. *Super Matt.,* c. 5, l. 2, n. 438.
224. *Super Ps.* 33, n. 13: "*Secundo quantum ad proximum dicit, inquire pacem et cetera. Sed contingit aliquando, quod habes proximum qui impugnat te, et tunc tuum est inquirere pacem; et ideo dicit, inquire pacem: Rom. 12: si fieri potest, quod ex vobis est, cum omnibus hominibus pacem habentes. Quandoque vero contingit, quod habes aliquem qui inquirat a te*

seeks peace with you you should reciprocate. If someone is fighting with you, it is your responsibility to go and seek peace with that person.[225] This is the very heart of the gospel, which is to become people of peace, "converting enemies into friends."[226] This is because our affections are formed by God's and "God hates dissension."[227] This is no surprise given the theology of peace we have seen in the last chapter. God is peace itself. Disorder/disunion (and whatever else Aquinas labels contrary to peace) cannot but be contrary to him. Believers receive a participation in the peace of God and are thus formed to be people of peace.

Another way of showing the responsibility Aquinas holds for individuals to seek peace is to speak about the relation between exterior and interior peace. According to Aquinas, exterior peace is integral to (an essential part of) interior peace, as one order to another.[228] One can easily see, based on Aquinas's philosophy of the good, why he says this. The good around which humans congregate must be truly shared or common (must perfect each agent), otherwise it could not be shared and could not serve as the principle of order/union between them. Aquinas is adamant that the common good is the good of the individual. Since it is a common good, it perfects all who seek it.[229] Because of this, the responsibility to seek the common good with others is really identical with the responsibility to seek (part of) the individual's good since the common good is integral part of the individuals own good.[230]

---

*pacem, et tuum est tunc sequi eam: unde ait, et persequere eam. Vel de pace loquitur quam in se debet habere; et hanc, inquit, inquiras in vita ista. Sed non plene habetur, quia caro concupiscit adversus spiritum, et spiritus adversus carnem, Gal. 5. Dicit autem, et persequere eam, ut scilicet magis habeas, licet non sit perfecta hic, sed in futuro, ubi sedebit populus in pulchritudine pacis, Isa. 32. Vel, inquire pacem, idest Christum, qui est pax nostra: Eph. 2, et sequere eam: Eccl. 2: quis est homo qui possit sequi regem factorem suum?"*

225. Elsewhere Aquinas suggests this is a counsel. See *In Or. Dom.*, a. 5.

226. *Super Ps.* 40, n. 5.

227. *Super Rom.*, c. 16, l. 2, n. 1220: *"qui dissensiones odit."*

228. Cf. *ST* II-II q. 29, a. 1, co.

229. Cf. Mary Keys, *Aquinas, Aristotle, and the Promise of the Common Good* (New York: Cambridge, 2006), 120ff.

230. Cf. *ST* II-II q. 47, a. 10, ad 2: *"dicendum quod ille qui quaerit bonum commune*

Transposed into terms of peace, the responsibility to seek exterior peace is integral to the responsibility to seek interior peace (though not the totality of it) and rests on the same foundation. In other words, the last section on seeking of interior peace was left incomplete (at best), for it left out one of the essential requirements of seeking interior peace—seeking exterior peace with others. Of course, this is implicit, since one cannot have the sacraments or order in the Church without a type of exterior peace (or many other things necessary for sustaining life as a human), but it is important to note that seeking exterior peace is not divergent or divorced from our interior seeking of peace. They are part of the same journey and are both integral parts of proper order not only because others can disturb my interior peace (they can, because of a lack of order/union with them) but also because the goods I can seek only with others are part of my own order/union. This simply further confirms that justice and the other virtues are integral to peace since charity commands the acts of justice which act toward the common good.[231] Justice, as Aquinas often says, concerns exterior acts and establishes right order/union with our neighbors.

Yet Aquinas is not overly optimistic about our ability to make peace with others, even if it is integral to our interior peace. The reasons for this are threefold. The first reason Aquinas has for tempering our hope is sin. If sin is a principal obstacle to our interior peace, and our responsibility to seek interior and exterior peace overlap in substantial ways, then sin will also be an ongoing obstacle to our peace with others.[232] On the other hand, it is not only our own sinfulness that is an obstacle to exterior peace, but the sinfulness of others as well. Just as sin destroys interior order/union, it can destroy exterior peace as well. This is even true for those sins that are not

---

multitudinis ex consequenti etiam quaerit bonum suum, propter duo. Primo quidem, quia bonum proprium non potest esse sine bono communi vel familiae vel civitatis aut regni."

231. Cf. Jeffrey Hause, "Aquinas on Aristotelian Justice: Defender, Destroyer, Subverter, or Surveyor?," in Aquinas and the Nicomachean Ethics, ed. by Hoffmann, et al. (New York: Oxford University Press, 2013), 161.

232. Cf. Schwartz, Aquinas on Friendship, 69ff.

directly contrary to one's neighbor.[233] Any act of ours or another's that is against virtue will not only contravene the individual's peace, but will disturb exterior peace.

Related to our first obstacle (sin), is the second: exterior peace requires virtue and virtue requires freedom. Concerning the virtue of others, Aquinas is very demure about our ability to produce it. With God's grace having personal supernatural virtue becomes possible, but we cannot produce grace or virtue in others. Natural virtue, likewise, since it is born of the voluntary. Even coercive measures can only produce the voluntary *secundum quid*, which is not sufficient for true virtue.[234] Even if the lawmaker legislates for virtue, even just the natural virtues, it is impossible to make somebody virtuous properly speaking.[235] Updating this, one could say the same thing for social structures.[236] One cannot make someone do the right thing for the right reason. There is always the possibility that someone does the right thing in a *secundum quid* voluntary way simply to avoid punishment or for an evil end. Aquinas is very explicit on this point. For this reason, he says, peace cannot be made through fear.[237] If it is to be true order/union between individuals (and not simply a total lack of contact, which can produce a simulacrum of peace: no conflict), then it must be voluntary. Likewise, our ability to play an instrumental part in producing supernatural virtue comes only through the sacraments and exterior actual graces. Yet neither of these can produce virtue without the willingness of the individual. Again, true peace cannot be made through fear. Certainly, Aquinas recognizes that sometimes we must aim at a mere lack of

233. One can easily see this in Aquinas's claims about the effects of sins. Lust, for example, is a sin against the good of the body, yet it is easy to see its social consequences. It is a capital vice. See *ST* II-II q. 153 aa. 4–5 for Aquinas's take on how lust spawns other sins.

234. Cf. *ST* I-II q. 92, a. 1, ad 2; *ST* I-II q. 96, aa. 2–3.

235. Cf. Matthew Rose, "Can Virtue be Taught? Thomistic Answers to a Socratic Question," *The Thomist,* vol. 77 (2013): 229–60.

236. Cf. Daniel Finn, "Social Structures," in *Moral Agency* within *Social Structures and Culture,* ed. by Daniel Finn (Washington DC: Georgetown University Press, 2020), 29–42.

237. Cf. *ST* I-II q. 29, a. 1, ad 1.

conflict (one not born from order/union), but he also claims that this is not true peace either because the order/union between the parties is involuntary on one side or because it is merely *secundum quid* voluntary (and therefore lacking the fullness of order/union between wills and thus suffering precarity).

Third, disunion/disorder with others is endemic in creation, even without the problem of sin! According to Aquinas, two people can be in conflict without either of them having sinned.[238] One can easily imagine friends differing on the proper way to pursue a shared goal without this being due to malice, weakness, or ignorance.[239] Aquinas explicitly recognizes this possibility, as we have seen. One can even extend this to God's will—people can be disordered/disunited with God's will and will something at variance with God's particular will and not fall into sin.[240] If it applies to our relation to God's will, then *a fortiori* to our (other) friends (whether based on creation, civil, ecclesial, or even deeper friendships). So the concord between the wills of people can be partially lost without it being an effect of a voluntary privation.

Put more directly, Aquinas's defense of the peace of creation does not require that disorder/disunion be caused by the sin of either individual (or group). In other words, recognizing disunion/disorder between two individuals can be answered in a similar way to the presence of natural evil among creation. Humans are free creatures. To be free means to pursue the good through deliberation, choice, and command. This will, on occasion, bring you into disunion/disorder with even your closest friends as each deliberates and pursues the good in freely and in different circumstances. As Schwartz puts it, "Equally rational wills representing the legitimate interests of the parties involved clash."[241] Even when humans pursue a shared good, Aquinas does not require that disagreement be caused by sin on one party's side, provided that the disunion/disor-

238. Cf. II *Sent.*, d. 11, q. 2, a. 5; *ST* II-II q. 29, a. 3, ad 2; *ST* II-II q. 37, a. 1, co.
239. These are Aquinas's three standard sources of sin. See *ST* I-II qq. 76–78.
240. Cf. *ST* I-II q. 19, a. 10, co.
241. Schwartz, *Aquinas on Friendship*, 58.

der is not directly willed by either party or either party is excessive in pursing the good as they see it.[242] The formal conformity of wills, that is regarding the end, suffices for order/union with God or our neighbor. As Ramirez argues, "Pure dissension and contrariety of opinions is not contrariety of wills."[243] This is similar to Aquinas's solution for the goodness of creation. It is because each creature is good and pursues the good that there is true and inevitable evil in the particular; this would be true even if there were not sin. So also with peace. It is because each party is at peace and pursues a greater peace that conflict is inevitable and even, sometimes, fruitful for a deeper peace.

Because of these impediments to exterior peace, God remains the primary maker of peace. Indeed, Aquinas claims that God is the "giver of peace" [244] and "peace is God's characteristic effect."[245] On the basis of this, Aquinas adds "from that depth [of God] in which peace exists, it flows first into the beatified . . . then it flows into saintly men: the holier he is, the less his mind is disturbed. Now because God alone can deliver the heart from all disturbance, it is necessary that peace comes from him,"[246] "peace is loving God,"[247] and "peace is obeying God."[248] We cannot fully and rightly order/unify our wills or the wills of others. We cannot make others desire virtue or make them see that virtue is integral to their quest for peace or the common good. We cannot absolve our sins or the sins of others or make primary satisfaction for sin. All depends on grace; our satisfaction is structurally dependent on his.[249] God must step in to interrupt our sinfulness so that we can have peace. This fits perfectly with Aquinas's theology of grace and of peace. Ultimately it is God the Trinity who must pour peace into the world and reunite all things to each

242. These are the very vices against charity. See *ST* II-II qq. 37–42.

243. Ramirez, *De Caritate*, 785.

244. *Super Rom.*, c. 15, l. 3, n. 1191.

245. *Super Heb.*, c. 13, l. 3, n. 766.

246. *Super Phil.*, c. 4, l. 1, n. 159.

247. *ST* I q. 113, a. 2, co.

248. *Super Rom.*, c. 5, l. 1, n. 382.

249. Cf. *ST* III q. 84, a. 1, co.; *ST* III q. 85, a. 1, co.

other and back to himself. Principally, this is through the incarnation. The Son of God is the one who brings order to others and converts enemies into friends.[250] It is the Spirit who dissolves hardness of heart.[251] So we must be peace-seekers but as mere secondary causes of peace. Any ultimate peace making plan with others that does not recognize our metaphysical place in the universe is doomed to failure (ultimately, but not always proximately). Yet God's primary agency in bringing about peace is a teaching of hope on Aquinas's part. The possibility of peace is the possibility of grace.[252]

The Means of Making Exterior Peace: Virtue, Dialogue,
and Evangelization

As Aquinas says, it is union, *multitudo ad unum*, that makes for exterior peace; all things are created within one order of creation and tend to one final cause. They are ordered/united with each other and God. Because of this, all things desire peace. This provides a starting point for seeking peace with others. In other words, Aquinas thinks that the desire for peace can be a strong starting point toward its pursuit. We can see why this is. The desire for peace is already itself a shared order/union as well as a desire for deeper order/union and so represents and inchoate beginning from which peacemaking can proceed. It is a foundational order/union in which all humans participate, making them friends if even in the most attenuated sense. This forms Aquinas's ultimate basis for seeking exterior peace. In other words, the primary way we make peace with others builds on an existing peace in creation and sharing human nature and is furthered by seeking common projects, by uniting our affections with others, by seeking to be friends (in some sense) with everyone.

Aquinas draws from this conception explicitly. For example, he says,

250. Cf. *Super Ps.* 40, n. 5.
251. Cf. *Super Ps.* 45, n. 7.
252. In this way the question of peace takes on the same dimensions as the question of grace, God's universal salvific will, and the possibility of avoiding sin. Everyone knows the contentious nature of these debates!

> [from] persistence in evil, men are returned in two ways. In one way by a desire to be at peace with others. Against this he says, the way of peace they have not known, i.e., have not accepted: "Among those who hate peace I was peaceful" (Ps 120:6). In another way by the fear of God; but they neither fear God nor regard man (cf. Lk 18:2). Hence he adds, there is no fear of God before their eyes, i.e., in their plans: "The fear of the Lord casts out sin; for without fear a person cannot be justified."[253]

In other words, as we have seen, exterior peace is made by seeking common goods with others—mutual recognition and love of what is truly good (and thus each other), and coordinated pursuit of it. Because peace is reduced to the transcendental good, this is just what we'd expect. Aquinas's theology of peace grounds his counsel for seeking supernatural (or natural) exterior peace. It is not a fruitless task, nor one doomed to failure, but one grounded in the universal desire for peace. What advice does Aquinas have for making this happen more concretely? I think advice based on Aquinas will take two forms—depending on what type of peace one is seeking.

As seen above, supernatural peace (and analogously all the other types) has three basic requirements. First, the two parties' intellects must be trained on God and concur in at least the basic truths about God (the creed) which is a type of union/order in itself. Second, and based on the first, the two parties must have mutual love for God and each other, an affective union/order with each other and God. Third, there must be coordination of their pursuit of God such that they can be said to be sharing a life, a type of effective union in action. This is not a practical union firstly, but will include a volitional and practical union coordinated by mutual pursuit of God. It begins with an intellectual union about essentials and volitional union following from that. Yet God cannot have this integrating function, the highest good sought, which wards off all conflict without grace. All of these requirements need grace. This is why Aquinas says that "grace causes peace and this means that without sanctifying grace [which turns us rightly to God and neighbor] there may be

---

253. *Super Rom.,* c. 3, l. 2, n. 289.

an appearance of peace, but there is in reality no true peace."[254] Our right relations with our neighbors and God cannot be fully achieved apart from charity, which is caused (principally) by God's grace in the sacraments. Thus, put simply, for us to seek exterior supernatural peace with others is to seek to have these conditions fulfilled both in ourselves and in others. Put differently, ultimately evangelization, both of ourselves and of others will be necessary, but also some type of agreement or direction of a shared authority on how we are to pursue God as a common good.[255] This requires believers to overcome divisions and draw everyone into the Church, a seemingly insurmountable task. Nevertheless, Aquinas also gives reason to hope—not in our ability to evangelize, but in God who gives grace and the innate human desire for peace. Hence, he says that we should "trust that anyone who wants peace, wants Christ."[256]

Likewise, the intimate relation between interior and exterior peace implies that virtue is not only necessary for interior supernatural peace but also exterior peace (supernatural or natural—the virtues will change depending on the order/union in question). One can easily see why this is the case. If an individual lacks justice, they will not work or want proper order with the other. If the person does not love (in some sense), they will not have the proper context for justice in either ecclesial life or political friendship. For example, Aquinas says that humility, meekness, patience, and charity are necessary for the peace of a community.[257] This is not only because they are dispositive to peace, but integral parts. For example, if individuals are proud, they will not concur in will with others.[258] If a person is wrathful, they will not seek the proper order of justice. Examples could be given for any virtue. Their lack not only disorders the interior life of an individual but also his or her relations with others.

---

254. *ST* II-II q. 29, a. 3, ad 1.

255. Cf. Yves Simon, *Philosophy of Democratic Government* (Chicago: University of Chicago Press, 1977), 19ff.

256. *Super Ps.* 33, n. 13.

257. Cf. *Super Eph.*, c. 4, l. 1, n. 191. See Tapie, "'For He is Our Peace,'" 125ff.

258. Cf. Schwarz, *Aquinas on Friendship,* 74ff.

Distinguishing between types of peace (based on different orders) allows for at least partial (true) peace with many people that may not be based on grace. Nevertheless, Aquinas claims the conditions and means are similar. Concerning natural peace with others—we must have a common good as the principle of relation/order/union between individuals. Following from this we must have some kind of general agreement on both in what that good consists and how we are to coordinately pursue it. If any of these conditions are lacking, peace will fail. As one can see the central and most important point is that there be some kind of agreement about the common good sought (at least in the more general features of it). Likewise, as we saw earlier, the concurrance around this good must be voluntary if it is to conduce to peace.

Of course, natural peace remains subject to the same limitations as above—the inability to be made based on fear, the inability to produce natural virtue in others, sin, and inevitable disturbance. In addition, natural peace is inherently imperfect by object (the common good sought, even if truly common, is not common in the highest sense and so its potency to produce order/union is mitigated). On the other hand, if I am right that Aquinas has a conception of imperfect natural peace, then even as limited and imperfect as the natural peace is, it establishes the possibility of seeking peace with others based on the mutual pursuit of common goods other than God. The believer will seek these under a differing formality, as ordered to God and on occasion this will cause conflict, but otherwise they will seek the same end so that there can be imperfect natural peace in the practical order.[259]

I think one of the main means of arriving at this shared natural good is dialogue. Granted Aquinas does not use this term, but his thought certainly implies it. To engage in dialogue is simply to

---

259. This will be true, even if, one holds that a Christian does not retain the acquired cardinal virtues. The infused and acquired cardinal virtues are different in their formal object (and thus species), but not in their material object. Likewise, one would not want to claim that grace destroys nature, even if the specification of the infused and acquired virtues diverge in certain circumstances. See *ST* I-II q. 63, aa. 3–4.

search out and find shared conceptions of the good, shared goods, and deliberate about how to coordinate pursuit of them. Aquinas's thought grounds dialogue in already existing types of order/union that humans enjoy simply by being human. According to Aquinas, all citizens are concerned with the final purpose of the civil community because it is happiness and the most general good shared by all. Civil society comes about from the action of individuals seeking a common end, their happiness.[260] In other words, we start as humans with a common good and something we all desire (peace as order/union with this good and each other). The question is what this consists of and how to pursue it. This is the very material for dialogue and the very basis for deeper friendships.

Nevertheless, as Aquinas recognizes, the pursuit of this end is somewhat contingent. In other words, a consensus about the material conditions of this formality and how we will pursue it is necessary. This takes dialogue as well. Yet it also requires authority to have coordinated action toward a shared end, facilitate participation, and coordinate the common pursuit of that shared goal. The requirement for some kind of authority (democratic or otherwise) is not simply predicated upon sin or ignorance, but is born of the very nature of the common good and the contingency of the possible means of pursuing it.[261]

Before turning to peace with creation, I should note the additional limits Aquinas thinks we should have in seeking peace with others. According to Aquinas, one who has true interior/exterior peace cannot be at peace with those whose wills are turned against the good (malice), for this requires concurrence with evil. This consent would thereby destroy not only the individual's or society's peace, but the very foundations of a lasting peace with that other person, namely the good. It is important to note the precise type of person identified here by Aquinas: those with malice. This is what Aquinas means when he says it is impossible for good and evil to be

<hr>

260. Cf. Keys, *Aquinas, Aristotle, and the Promise of the Common Good*, 85.
261. Cf. Simon, *Philosophy of Democratic Government*, 59.

at peace. According to Aquinas, malice is an evil will. It is different from mere nescience, ignorance, or weakness. As he says, a sin of malice is "when the will is moved, of itself, to evil."[262] In some sense, this covers every sin (voluntary choice of evil), whether chosen as an act or out of habit.[263] The point Aquinas is trying to make is that one who sins through malice chooses evil knowingly because it is perceived as good in some way (merely apparent good).[264]

This limit on those with whom it is possible to have peace is born of a commitment to peace on Aquinas's part. To seek peace with those who are filled with malice (precisely inasmuch as their wills are actually subject to malice) is to cease to seek peace, but rather to settle for a simulacrum of peace which will ultimately destroy interior and exterior peace. As Aquinas writes, "Sometimes another's malice prevents us from having peace with them. No peace is possible with them unless we consent to their malice."[265] Likewise, as Aquinas's metaphysics imply, there will be no peace even if you consent to their malice. Evil is a privation and so cannot bring the kind of union/order that is a part of the good. In other words, to seek peace with the malicious is to become an enemy of peace for it entails turning the will from the good and concurring with the malicious one in the very evil they seek.

On the other hand, Aquinas is clear that even another's malicious will does not absolve anyone of responsibility to seek peace with this person or from concurring with them in other goods. True love continues to seek peace.[266] Failing to continue to seek peace and to will disorder/disunion in itself is exactly what Aquinas means by sinning against exterior peace. In other words, when another's will is contrary to union/order it is incumbent on the individual to remain committed to peace. Failing in this means that not only would one's neigh-

---

262. *ST* I-II q. 78, a. 3, co.: "*quando ipsa voluntas ex seipsa movetur ad malum.*"

263. Cf. *ST* I-II q. 78, a. 1, ad 3.

264. Cf. *ST* I-II q. 78, a. 1, co.: "*quasi scienter malum eligens.*" *ST* I-II q. 8, a. 1, co.

265. *Super Rom.*, c. 12, l. 3, n. 1010: "*Quandoque enim malitia aliorum impedit ne cum eis pacem habere possimus, quia scilicet cum eis pax haberi non potest, nisi eorum malitiae consentiatur, quam quidem pacem constat esse illicitam.*"

266. Cf. *De Virt.*, q. 3, a. 1, co.

bor be malicious but the individual as well. Disorder must remain involuntary. As Aquinas says, "Concord is destroyed by discord in two ways, *per se* and *per accidens*."[267] *Per se* is intentional—when one aims at discord directly and wants it. This, Aquinas says, is a mortal sin according to its genus. One's commitment to peace itself can entail discord with another if their wills are malicious, but discord can never be directly voluntary without losing the commitment to peace.[268]

In this case, where one's neighbor is contrary to peace (which is wider than those who are malicious), Aquinas offers two recommendations. The first when one does not have authority over the individual and the second when one does. Fraternal correction is an attempt to reintroduce interior and exterior peace into another. "If the [fraternal] correction is administered in suitable circumstances, the result will be not to disturb peace but rather to strengthen it since the sources of discord will be destroyed."[269] One can imagine that fraternal correction is much more likely to be effective in the case of someone subject to weakness or ignorance rather than malice. Nevertheless, it remains one's responsibility if there is a well-founded hope it will return peace and not increase disorder.[270] In other words, fraternal correction should be foregone if it would result in greater evil. It should be tailored to the circumstances of not only the sin,[271] but also the person corrected,[272] and should extend to superiors (with admonition).[273] In other words, in all of these situations, it is the responsibility of an individual to seek peace but in such a way that it actually conduces to peace and does not introduce more disorder/disunion.[274]

267. *ST* II-II q. 37, a. 1, co.

268. This is how Aquinas claims one can go to war or court (against one's neighbor) without necessarily being in discord with one's neighbor. See CID c. 15, ad 7

269. *De Virt.*, q. 3, a. 1, ad 19.

270. Cf. *ST* II-II q. 33, a. 6, co.

271. For example, Aquinas proposes different measures for public and private sins. See *ST* II-II q. 33, a. 7, co.

272. Cf. *De Virt.*, q. 3, a. 1, co.: "*non est pro omni tempore et quolibet modo observandum, sed servatis debitis conditionibus et personarum, et locorum, et causarum, et temporum.*"

273. Cf. *ST* II-II q. 33, a. 4, co.

274. Cf. *De Virt.*, q. 3, a. 1, co.; *ST* II-II q. 33, a. 6.

If one has authority, then Aquinas makes a distinction. "There are two ways to correct sinners. The first is by simple admonition. This is fraternal correction, and it is appropriate only for people who we believe will accept the correction voluntarily. The second is correction that exerts compulsive force through the infliction of punishment … and this kind of punishment is the prerogative of prelates [i.e. those with some kind of authority]."[275] Punishment, for Aquinas, aims at the restoration of peace—to correct by punishment.[276] In order to remain virtuous in the one that punishes, it must aim at returning order/union, i.e. aim at the good.[277] As Aquinas implies this is primarily the correction of the sinner, the good of the sinner (which would include the individual voluntarily rectifying any injustice to the victim as a restoration of right order/union). If the sinner cannot or will not be returned to union/order, Aquinas says that one can aim at another peace—that of society or other individuals, but this is a failure in some sense. It is to be endured as an implication of the love of peace.[278] Punishment's purpose is to restore peace in the fullest sense, that includes the individual offenders.[279]

In other words, according to Aquinas, it remains our responsibility to make peace without consenting to the evil will of the other person. To seek peace with someone inasmuch as their will is trained on evil is to become an enemy of peace. These claims, undoubtedly, ground Aquinas's commitment to just war and to the possibility of coercion/punishment in favor of peace.[280] We can see here why he says these things. Yet even if these means of making peace are admitted (war and punishment), they must be in agreement with

275. *De Virt.,* q. 3, a. 1, ad 2.

276. Cf. *ST* II-II q. 33, a. 3, co. "*non solum habent admonere, sed etiam corrigere puniendo.*"

277. Cf. *ST* II-II q. 108, a. 1, co.

278. Cf. *De Regno* c. 9: "*unde et interdum malum unius sustinetur si in bonum multitudinis cedat, sicut occiditur latro ut pax multitudini detur.*"

279. As Aquinas says, the punishments in this life (including those inflicted by humans) are primarily medicinal—they aim to restore union/order of the individual and society. For a defense of reading Aquinas's thought on punishment as medicinal, see Koritansky, *Thomas Aquinas and the Philosophy of Punishment,* chs. 4–5.

280. Cf. *ST* II-II q. 40, a. 1, ad 3.

Aquinas's wider vision of the theology and philosophy of peace. Punishment and war have their ultimate purpose in the destruction of disorder/disunion or the preservation of order/union.[281] It is only concerning the very thing willed that, when evil, precludes peace and sends us on the search for other means to restore peace.

For Aquinas, to claim that punishment and war are never ways of seeking peace would imply one of two things, both of which end up turning the individual against peace. It would imply that one abandons the commitment to peace by allowing evil to destroy it (when one ought not)[282] or consents to the very evil itself. In either case, peace is voluntarily destroyed. This is important to see, but it is also important to admit the very limited range of Aquinas's commitment—based on someone with malice, concerning the very good against which he or she is turned, and presuming there are means of restoring the good without harming it more. Aquinas's commitment to the possibility of war and punishment as means of restoring peace does not preclude, based on other goods (natural or supernatural), that there could still be peace. Someone who does not even want what is good is to be opposed by these means, if necessary, but anyone with good will in some aspect is someone with whom peace can be achieved to a certain degree.[283] Likewise, undertaking punishment or war in such a way that does not conduce to some kind of greater peace is unintelligible for Aquinas. It would lose its very *raison d'être*. In other words, even if these means are a possibility, one must deliberate about whether utilizing them would introduce even greater evils and one should forego peace in a certain respect.[284]

281. Cf. Reichberg, "Thomas Aquinas Between Just War and Pacifism," 230ff.

282. Obviously, there are situations where these means should be foregone, i.e. when they would result in greater disorder/disunion. See *ST* II-II q. 108, a. 1, ad 5. See also Manfred Svensson, "A Defensible Conception of Tolerance in Aquinas?," *The Thomist* 75 (2011): 291–308.

283. Cf. Reichberg, *Thomas Aquinas on War and Peace*, 20–27.

284. Cf. *De Virt.*, q. 3, a. 1, ad 4: "*et ideo interdum sunt aliqua bona intermittenda, ut aliqua magna mala vitentur.*" Aquinas certainly seems to hold this for war, but not for punishment. He seems clearly committed to the claim that punishment protects exterior peace even if the offender is totally incorrigible.

Furthermore, one must recognize that in Aquinas's thought war and punishment can only remove disorder in a certain sense and protect existing orders/unions; they cannot create order/union between wills.[285] This follows from Aquinas's philosophy and theology of peace. "Peace is not something that can be forced."[286] Peace must be built on mutual volition, not violence or punishment.[287] Since peace and discord are contraries, "peace does not move discord and make something out of it."[288] War only results in a state of non-conflict (or even more conflict!), the kind of *ens rationis* that follows from a non-relation/non-union/non-order between two parties.[289] War and punishment cannot directly produce the order/union of wills or the rest/tranquility that follows from it (of the individual with their individual good, of the individual with the common good, of an individual with another individual, or of the political wills of polities and countries).[290] It cannot produce the order/union that is the real metaphysical cause of peace. So even if they are admitted as tools to restore or protect order/union, Aquinas's thought implies that we should be very careful when using them and be clear about what they can and cannot do.

### Our Responsibility to Make Peace with Creation

As seen in the last chapter, though Aquinas does not dwell on this aspect at length, Christ seeks to restore order/union to all of creation. Peace is not only, or even primarily, anthropological. It is first divine and Christological. It is knit into the very fabric of creation in the order/union of all things with each other and with God. It

285. This makes sense of Aquinas's claim that for the one who is fighting for justice, war is integral to peace, but not for the other side.

286. Reichberg, "Human Nature, Peace, and War," 35.

287. The success of punishment is likewise predicated upon God's grace. See *De Virt.*, q. 4, a. 1, ad 13.

288. *In I Phys.*, l. 11, n. 90: "*Et similiter est de qualibet alia contrarietate: non enim concordia movet discordiam et facit aliquid ex ipsa, neque e converso.*"

289. *Quies* and *tranquillitas* are also negations and so *enti rationes*. They, however, follow from *ens reale*, union/order.

290. Cf. Erb, "Interior Peace," 263.

is this order that Christ comes to restore and elevate. Hence, inasmuch as we seek to restore peace, we should seek to restore order/ union with all of material creation, not just God, self, and other humans. Likewise, given what we have seen about Aquinas's expansive requirements for peace, it is no surprise that his thought implies that peace with creation is also integral to interior and exterior peace.

Though peace is not primarily anthropological for Aquinas, Christ's and the Spirit's restoration of peace to creation happens through humans as secondary causes. In other words, peace with creation happens primarily by ordering creation back to human use and through human use, to God and others.[291] This is the part of creation that has been disfigured by sin, the relation of material creation to humans (or rather the ethical relation of humans to material creation). To recall, all things have a twofold order: to God, and on that basis, to other things. In fact, the order to God is the more fundamental of these orders, which is (in some sense) left untouched by sin. Material creation is ordered to give glory to God, first and foremost. Secondarily, and based on that union/relation/order to God, it is ordered toward human use.[292] Part of the glory material creation gives to God is through its use by humans. In other words, as Aquinas says when discussing the work of Christ, God's means for restoring the peace of creation is to restore humanity.[293] Where the relationship has gone wrong is on the human side, and it is through the fall of humans that the rest of creation has fallen.[294] Hence, the means Aquinas would propose for reuniting/reordering creation are

291. Cf. *De rationibus fidei* c. 5.

292. Cf. *ST* I q. 96, a. 1, co.

293. Cf. *De rationibus fidei*, c. 5: "*Inter creaturas autem a Deo conditas per verbum suum, gradum praecipuum tenet creatura rationalis, intantum quod omnes aliae creaturae ei subserviant, et ad ipsam ordinari videantur; et hoc rationaliter, quia sola rationalis creatura dominium habet sui actus per arbitrii libertatem, ceterae vero creaturae non ex libero iudicio agunt, sed quadam vi naturae moventur ad agendum. Ubique autem quod est liberum, praeeminet ei quod est servum, et servi ad liberorum famulatum ordinantur, et a liberis gubernantur. Lapsus igitur rationalis creaturae secundum veram aestimationem magis aestimandus est quam cuiuscumque irrationalis creaturae defectus.*"

294. Cf. *ST* I q. 96, a. 1, co.

primarily the same he would recommend for reordering the individual or human society: virtue. This is no mistake, if we wish to observe peace in its fullest sense, interior, exterior, and with creation, we must be rightly ordered and that is through virtue.

The virtues central to the use of external goods are Aquinas's primary picture of how to reorder creation back to proper order/union to humans and are thus the means of restoring peace with creation. These, centrally, would be temperance and fortitude (in relation to ourselves) and justice/charity in relation to God and our neighbors. Though it may not be a popular answer, the reason Aquinas thinks environmental degradation is wrong is not because it destroys nature *per se*. Nature is partly constituted by its ordering to human use and human use of creation always involves introducing non sinful privations into other beings (eating them, whether plants or animals, for example). The reason environmental degradation is wrong is that it distorts the character of the actor. Someone who acts that way has disordered desires and is being unjust/unloving toward themselves or others. Others have outlined Thomistic ecology in more depth, so there is no need to dwell on this point.[295] What is important to note, again, is the centrality of virtue for peace (indeed, their identification inasmuch as virtue simply is order/union with the good). If we wish to attain peace with creation, we must begin by reflecting on those ways of relating to creation that are vicious and disordered and the practices that sustain and inculcate those vices structurally and individually.[296]

---

295. For example, see Christopher Thompson, *The Joyful Mystery: Field Notes Toward a Green Thomism* (Steubenville, OH: Emmaus Road Publishing, 2017).

296. Cf. Daniel Daly, *The Structures of Virtue and Vice* (Washington DC: Georgetown University Press, 2021).

5

# Peace and Thomistic Sacramental Theology

Thomistic thought on peace culminates in the sacraments. God is peace and created the world through his Word and in Love. When the fullness of time came (cf. Gal 4:4), God himself became incarnate in order to save the world from disorder, decay, and death through his own dying and rising. In this he sends his own Holy Spirit to unite us back to himself and back to one other. Because of this, we live his peace by bringing order/union to our lives, the lives of others, and with the rest of creation. This is achieved preeminently by love and wisdom (and justice), but also by every virtue. It is in relation to this general picture that Aquinas's thought on the sacraments completes his vision of peace. It is the sacraments that are the most concrete manifestation and communication of God's peace. It is through them that Christ reorders our lives back to God, self, neighbor, and creation. Nevertheless, in order to see the intimate connection between peace and the sacraments, one must step back a bit and visit Aquinas's theology of worship.

## THE SACRAMENTAL ORDER IN AQUINAS

Though all of creation has a fundamental and untouchable peace with God, humans are called to enter freely into these fundamental relations of peace. We are called to voluntarily take up what we are as an ad-extra exposition of God's glory. Aquinas interprets this responsibility as a responsibility to give a special kind of honor to God. This honor that we have for God as first principle, exemplar cause, and final end of creation is expressed through the virtue of *religio.* Through this virtue humans are rightly ordered to God in reverence and worship.[1] Through this potential part of justice, humans live the fundamental order of creation back to God as final cause.

As one can see, this is one of the most concrete senses in which humans naturally live in peace with God, God considered as final cause of the universe, and it is a matter of justice. We owe God honor and reverence simply as creator and final cause of the universe. Again, we see the near identification of peace and justice in a way the supports justice's integral nature to peace. On the other hand, even naturally, Aquinas thinks we also should love God as creator and final cause as well. Again, as seen above, the order of justice does not exhaust order/union to God, ourselves, others, and creation. Nor is it the most fundamental type of order/union we can have with God (even naturally). Justice establishes an inherently imperfect type of order/union because it is enacted, and governs, on the very basis of distinction.

We see this too with the natural virtue of religion. There is an inherent imperfection in the virtue of religion and the acts it elicits. It is only directed to God as end.[2] This is a structural imperfection that is inherent in the peace which is justice. It acts toward the other qua other. In other words, there is need for a deeper virtue (a further specification of this relation) which is union with God, and that virtue is charity. Likewise, religion suffers from another imperfection: humans are sinful. So even the imperfect peace of justice cannot be achieved without grace. Thus their living of this fundamental order and its specification in the type/time/place, etc. of worship is

---

1. Cf. *ST* II-II q. 81, a. 1, ad 4: "*Quia tamen specialis honor debetur Deo, tanquam primo omnium principio, etiam specialis ratio cultus ei debetur.*"

2. Cf. *ST* II-II q. 81, a. 5, co. and ad 1.

marred not only by the imperfection of justice but also by superstition and idolatry.[3]

According to Aquinas the sacraments are provided to perfect us in the worship of God, to perfect us in living toward God as the common good of the universe. "Sacraments of the new law imprint a character inasmuch as through them we are deputed to the cult of God ... and for this reason the character implies a certain spiritual potency ordained to that which is of the cult of God."[4] Aquinas's claim is that the sacraments come to remedy both of these insufficiencies and enable us not only to live the order of creation, but to surpass it in the order of grace. "Sacraments perfect the soul in those things which pertain to the *cultus Dei*."[5] Nor does the order of grace simply mean the remedy of the imperfection of sin, but even of the imperfection of acting purely under the aspect of distinction. Distinction itself is perfected (made good) in order/union. As Aquinas says, the sacraments of the new law are ordered to two things: the remedy of sin and the worship of God.[6] In other words, the sacraments specify our worship in a way that is not superstitious or idolatrous; they provide a concrete remedy for human sin, and unite us to God as friend. In this way Christ's sacraments not only perfect the peace that consists in natural justice but elevate it to a supernatural level by directing it to God as friend, as object.

That Aquinas claims they do these things is not surprising. He views the sacraments as deriving their power from the passion of Christ. "The sacraments especially have their power from the passion of Christ, whose power is in some way united to us through the reception of the sacraments."[7] In other words, the effects of the sacrament are the effects of the passion of Christ applied to us through efficacious signs and in time. It is no mistake that the sacraments

---

3. Cf. *ST* II-II qq. 92–96.

4. *ST* III q. 63, a. 2, co.

5. *ST* III q. 63, a. 2, co.

6. Cf. *ST* III q. 63, a. 6, co.: "*sacramenta novae legis ad duo ordinantur, scilicet in remedium peccati, et ad cultum divinum.*"

7. *ST* III q. 65, a. 2, co.

then have the same potencies and goals as the sacrifice of Christ on the cross. "Christ's passion is the sufficient cause of human salvation. But it does not follow from this that the sacraments would not be necessary to human salvation [also], because they operate by the power of the passion of Christ and the passion of Christ is in a certain way applied to humans through sacraments."[8] Just as Christ's passion aims to reintroduce peace into the world, so too do the sacraments. And it is also no mistake that they are applied in a certain order. This internal order of the sacraments again reveals the absolute centrality of peace to Aquinas's sacramental thought. The very means of reintroducing peace to creation are ordered/unified by their common flowing from their principle in Christ as well as by their subsequent mutual relations to each other.

In *ST* III q. 65, Aquinas asks a question *apropos* to the order of the sacraments, "whether there should be seven sacraments?" He answers that "it is fitting that there should be seven sacraments."[9] They are instituted to perfect humans and as a remedy against sin. In either case, Aquinas says that it is fitting there are seven. In article 2, he asks more explicitly if this is fitting. He writes, "just as *unum* is prior to *multitudo,* so the sacraments which are ordered to the perfection of one person naturally precede those which are ordered to a multitude."[10] Because of this, Aquinas says that marriage and holy orders are last since they concern the perfection of a multitude—its internal order (peace) and against corruption (marriage). Concerning the peace of the individual, he says those which are *per se* ordered to the perfection of the individual are prior to those which are *per accidens*. The latter are penance and extreme unction, which "remove some supervening harmful thing which happens [sin]." Confession/penance restores order/union when lost and broken.[11] In this way, it not only satisfies the demands of justice, but "is above all

---

8. *ST* III q. 61, a. 3, co.
9. *ST* III q. 65, a. 1, co.
10. *ST* III q. 65, a. 2, co.
11. Cf. *ST* III, q. 90. a. 2.

the reconciliation of friendship."[12] Finally, baptism is the first of the final three, which is spiritual birth. Confirmation is ordered to the formal perfection of virtue. Finally, the Eucharist is "ordered to the perfection of the end."[13] As one can see, the whole sacramental order is not only ordered/unified in itself but exteriorly is ordered toward peace, interior and exterior. That is its very purpose, its *raison d'être*.

In some ways, this article obscures how central the Eucharist is for Aquinas's sacramental theology. In the next article, he remedies this and confirms what he says elsewhere. He says in *ST* III q. 65, a. 3 that not only does the Eucharist contain Christ *substantialiter* and the others sacraments are only instruments of Christ, but also "all the other sacraments are ordered to this sacrament as to an end."[14] The sacrament of holy orders has the purpose of offering the Eucharist, baptism to reception of the Eucharist, confirmation against fear abstaining from the Eucharist, penance and extreme unction to receiving the Eucharist worthily, and marriage by its signification of the Eucharist. Likewise, those sacraments that imprint a character enable us to enter into the Eucharist, to receive it, to offer it, and in short, to worship in and through Christ. Put differently, the Eucharist "contains substantially the *bonum commune spirituale totius Ecclesiae.*"[15] Every ministry in the Church is thus ordered toward it.[16] Christ is not only the source of the whole sacramental order by his satisfaction, but this same order returns to him in substantial and effective union in the Eucharist.

Though each of the sacraments retain a relation to the order/union of the Church and all have it as their purpose, the real heart of Aquinas's sacramental theology is the Eucharist. For this reason, in the Eucharist, we shall see the whole sweep of Thomistic thought

12. Romanus Cessario, "Christian Satisfaction and Sacramental Reconciliation," in *Rediscovering Aquinas and the Sacraments: Studies in Sacramental Theology,* ed. by Matthew Levering and Michael Dauphinais (Chicago: Hillenbrand books, 2009), 65–75, see especially page 71. See also *ST* III q. 85, a. 3.

13. *ST* III q. 65, a. 2, co.

14. *ST* III q. 65, a. 3, co.

15. *ST* III q. 65, a. 2, ad 1.

16. Cf. *SS* IV d. 24, q. 2, a. 1, ad 3; d. 24, q. 1, a. 3, qc. 2, ad 1.

on peace. As Aquinas puts it, the Eucharist is "the sacrament of unity and peace."[17] This is no mistake; Aquinas said that the whole purpose of Christ's coming is to return peace to creation and in the Eucharist "the whole of the mystery of salvation is contained."[18] In the Eucharist, the multitude is united with Christ—who is peace incarnate—such that "we carry within ourselves the principle of peace."[19] Unity to Christ not only reorders our interior lives, but also orders us rightly to other humans and creation. It is an "intimate union with the principle of all order, all perfection, and all holiness."[20] In other words, the source and purpose of the whole sacramental order is the Eucharist, and the Eucharist is, in turn, for peace.

### THE EUCHARIST AND PEACE

"The cause or motive of [the Eucharist's] institution ... was the immense love of Christ for men."[21] As seen above concerning satisfaction, it is Christ's love for us that awakens our love for him, his love (the Holy Spirit) who comes to dwell in our hearts (cf. Rom 5:5) and so reorder our lives. It is his peace which causes ours. The same is true in the Eucharist. The means by which Christ, who dwells substantially in it, is to effectively unify himself to us so that the love of Christ reorders our lives.[22] Such a connection is easily established in Aquinas: the Eucharist is nothing other than a re-presentation of the sacrifice of Christ. Now the sacrifice of Christ is the instrumental efficient cause of charity. Hence, the Eucharist is also. The Eucharist effects charity by incorporating believers into

17. *ST* III q. 83, a. 4, co.

18. *ST* III q. 83, a. 4, co.

19. Ramirez, *De Caritate*, 922: "*Llevamos dentro de nosotros al principe de la paz.*"

20. Ramirez, *De Caritate*, 921: "*union intima con el principio de todo orden, de toda perfeccion, de toda santidad.*"

21. Ramirez, "La Eucaristía,"171: "*pro la cause o motivo de su institución, que fue la inmensa caridad de Cristo para con los hombres.*"

22. The citations in this footnote are taken from Emery, "The Ecclesial Fruit of the Eucharist," n29. *ST* III q. 73, a. 3, ad 3; q. 74, a. 4, obj. 3; q. 78, a. 3, obj. 6 and ad 6; q. 79, a. 4, ad 3; q. 80, a. 5, ad 2; cf. q. 78, a. 3, ad 6: "*Hoc autem est sacramentum caritatis quasi figurativum et effectivum*"; *ST* III q. 79, a. 1, ad 1; q. 81, a. 1, ad 3; *ST* III q. 79, a. 1; q. 81, a. 1, ad 3.

Christ and likening them to Christ in its two-fold causality as sacrament and sacrifice.[23] "It has the nature of a sacrifice inasmuch as it is offered up; and it has the nature of a sacrament inasmuch as it is received."[24] As sacrifice, the Eucharist causes charity by reconciling humans with God and by exemplarity. The step from here to peace should be clear from the previous chapter. Aquinas treats the Eucharist as the ultimate cause of peace because it is a representation of the cross. The Eucharist causes peace by uniting the recipient with Christ from whom charity flows.[25]

By re-presenting the passion, the Eucharist effects charity in a two-fold manner. First, it is the very power by which the sacramental aspect (the reception) obtains its effect. The passion is represented and thus the effects of the passion follow; Christ's sacrifice is the efficient cause of our salvation,[26] merits the salvation of all, it is the proper cause of the forgiveness of sins, it delivers believers from Satan's power, it reconciles us with God, and gets rid of the debt of punishment. Hence, the Eucharist, as one can see by the overlay of *ST* III qq. 48–49 & 79, effects the same things. These effects include both charity itself and that which is necessary to preserve it. Second, the Eucharist as sacrifice causes charity in another way as well. It re-presents the efficient cause of our salvation; it is there in the re-presentation of the sacrifice of the cross that we see the exemplar of supernatural charity: Christ's love poured out in sacrifice.[27] This serves the dual function of both exciting the virtue of charity by seeing what great love God has for humans but also informing believers what exactly the proper content of supernatural charity is.[28]

---

23. Cf. *ST* III 49, aa. 2–3. I divide the effects of the Eucharist this way following Ramirez. See Ramirez, "La Eucaristía," 179ff.

24. *ST* III q. 79, a. 5, co.

25. Cf. *In de div. nom.,* 11, l. 3.

26. Cf. *ST* III q. 48, a. 6.

27. Cf. *ST* III q. 48, a. 6, ad 4; q. 46, a. 3, co.

28. Cf. *ST* III q. 46, a. 3, co.; *Super Io.,* 6, l. 6, n. 963; Bruce Marshall, "The Whole Mystery of Our Salvation: Saint Thomas Aquinas on the Eucharist as Sacrifice," in *Rediscovering Aquinas and the Sacraments: Studies in Sacramental Theology,* eds. Matthew Levering and Michael Dauphinais (Chicago: Hillenbrand Books, 2009), 64: "The Eucharist has the very same effects as the Passion itself."

By containing Christ, the sacramental reception of the Eucharist effects charity in a three-fold manner such that "perfected in union with the suffering Christ . . . the Eucharist is called the sacrament of charity, which is the bond of perfection."[29] First, the believer is conformed to Christ's charity. "Just as by coming visibly into the world he brought the life of grace into it . . . so by coming to men sacramentally he causes the life of grace."[30] By the sacramental reception of Christ himself "grace is increased and the spiritual life perfected and made whole by union with God."[31] The increase of grace breaks forth in the soul as charity. Yet this is not only conformity in a generic sense, the reception of grace in the Eucharist is the very reception of Christ's grace, and thus his charity.[32] In receiving the Eucharist believers can begin to love as Christ loves.

Second, under the manner of its giving, food, the Eucharist in its sacramental aspect is also the proper cause of charity. The Eucharist sustains, augments, restores, and delights. It sustains charity by sustaining the supernatural life of the believer, removing the impediments to the activity of charity (venial sin) and protecting the life of charity by protecting against future sins. It augments the life of charity like the assimilation of food augments the body as it is growing. It restores the fervor of charity by removing the impediments to charity's activity and thus renews it. Finally, it moves the believer to acts

29. *ST* III q. 73, a. 3, ad 3: *"Sed Eucharistia est sacramentum passionis Christi prout homo perficitur in unione ad Christum passum. Unde, sicut Baptismus dicitur sacramentum fidei, quae est fundamentum spiritualis vitae; ita Eucharistia dicitur sacramentum caritatis, quae est vinculum perfectionis, ut dicitur Coloss. III."*

30. *ST* III q. 79, a. 1, co.: *"Qui sicut, in mundum visibiliter veniens, contulit mundo vitam gratiae, secundum illud Ioan. I, gratia et veritas per Iesum Christum facta est; ita, in hominem sacramentaliter veniens, vitam gratiae operatur, secundum illud Ioan. VI, qui manducat me, vivit propter me."*

31. *ST* III q. 79, a. 1: *"Per hoc autem sacramentum augetur gratia, et perficitur spiritualis vita, ad hoc quod homo in seipso perfectus existat per coniunctionem ad Deum."*

32. Cf. *ST* III q. 8, a. 1, ad 1: *Super Io.,* 1, l. 10, n. 202: *"Nota, quod haec propositio 'de' aliquando quidem denotat efficientiam, seu originalem causam, sicut cum dicitur, radius est vel procedit de sole; et hoc modo denotat in Christo efficientiam gratiae, seu auctoritatem, quia plenitudo gratiae, quae est in Christo, est causa omnium gratiarum quae sunt in omnibus intellectualibus creaturis. . . . quae scilicet de me procedunt, adimplemini, participatione sufficientis plenitudinis."*

of charity, that is, love of God and neighbor. In short, "This [sacrament] does of the life of the spirit [and thus for charity] all that material food and drink does for the life of the body."[33]

Finally, the species under which Christ is given signifies, but does not contain, the ultimate effect of the sacrament, ecclesial unity. Indeed, ecclesial unity is the direct effect of the sacrament, the *res sacramenti*, yet it is brought about by charity, which Aquinas also calls the *res* of the sacrament.[34] As we saw in the previous chapter, the unity of the Church is lived as a conformity to Christ's love (the Holy Spirit) through whom all are made into lovers of God. Believers are thereby united to each other in their mutual love.

For these reasons, Aquinas claims that "the Eucharist is said to be the sacrament of Christ's charity expressed, and ours made," and "the proper effect of this sacrament is the transformation into Christ through love."[35] The Eucharist both symbolizes our charity and brings it about (in both habit and act) and is thus called the *sacramentum caritatis*.[36]

The connection of the Eucharist to charity gives us an easy connection to peace. The Eucharist is the instrumental efficient and exemplar cause of charity, and charity is efficient cause of supernatural peace., the most concrete way we are reordered/reunified with ourselves, each other, and creation.[37] Hence, the Eucharist is the proper cause of supernatural peace. It causes the twofold notion central to peace, union with God and neighbor.[38] The connection to peace thus becomes very concrete. The Eucharist is the summit of interior peace, the source of a *sobria ebritas*. Mysticism is not disassociated

---

33. *ST* III q. 79, a. 1, co.: "*Et ideo omnem effectum quem cibus et potus materialis facit quantum ad vitam corporalem, quod scilicet sustenat, auget, reparat, et delectat, hoc totum facit hoc sacramentum quantum ad vitam spiritualem.*"

34. For the best treatment of the Eucharist in relation to ecclesial unity see Gilles Emery, "The Ecclesial Fruit of the Eucharist in St. Thomas Aquinas," in *Trinity, Church, and the Human Person: Thomistic Essays* (Naples: Ave Maria Press, 2007), 155–72.

35. *SS* IV d. 8, q. 2, a. 2, qla. 3, ad 5: "*Eucharistia dicitur sacramentum caritatis Christi expressivum, et nostrae factivum.*"

36. *ST* III q. 78, a. 3, ad 6; *ST* III q. 79, a. 4, co.

37. Cf. Hoffman, 164: "*Eucharistia est causa efficiens illius duplicis unionis. . . .*"

38. Cf. Hoffman, 164.

from the liturgy but is the ultimate source of ecstatic peace.[39] The Eucharist is the sign and cause of ecstatic peace.[40] This is why Aquinas speaks of the effects of reception as similar to those of wine. Likewise, in the Eucharist we find the ultimate instantiation of exterior peace. The Eucharist is the "communication of goods and life between friends."[41]

As sacrifice the Eucharist causes peace by re-presenting the very cause of peace, Christ's sacrifice on the cross. This re-presentation causes peace by both efficient causality and exemplarity. The Eucharist as sacrifice causes peace by efficient causality since the very purpose of Christ's incarnation was the restoration of peace. Christ is he who "came to restore all things to a state of peace and calm."[42] He did so by his death. "The passion itself was the maker of peace."[43] It is this very passion which is numerically identical with the sacrifice of the Eucharist, identical *quoad substantium* and different *quoad modum*. Put differently, the very cause of peace is represented in the Eucharist, for Christ is present as priest, victim, and peace offering.[44]

Likewise, in the passion re-presented we see the ultimate example of love, the maker of peace: "If you seek an example of love: 'No one has greater love than this. . . . [to lay down his life for his friends].' This is Christ on the cross."[45] As an exemplar of love, the sacrifice of the cross is also an exemplar of peace, not in its full form without disturbances, but as it exists in this world and in its proper cause. In this way, as re-presenting the very cause of peace, the Eucharist effects unity both interior and exterior. "To cure [the disturbances

---

39. Cf. Ephrem Longpre, *L'Eucharistie est le sacrement de la paix mystique*, 160.

40. Cf. Longpre, 159.

41. Ramirez, *De Caritate*, 864: "*la comunicación de bienes y la convivencia entre amigos...*"

42. *ST* III q. 44, a. 4, ad 3.

43. *Super Matt.*, c. 16, l. 3, n. 1398: "*Voluit igitur ibi pati ad ostendendum, quod mors eorum fuit signum passionis Christi. Item Ierusalem dicitur visio pacis; sed ipsa passio pacifica fuit.*"

44. Cf. *ST* III q. 22, a. 2, co.

45. *In Symb.*, a. 4, co.: "*Si enim exemplum quaeris caritatis, 'maiorem caritatem nemo habet' etc.: hoc Christus in cruce.*"

of peace] Jesus offers them the peace of reconciliation with God . . . which he accomplished by his suffering."[46]

We see concord because of this. The Eucharist causes concord by ordering the diverse appetites of people to desire and seek one good: worship and love of God. The relevance for external peace and the Eucharist can be seen most clearly by separating the three-fold signification of the sacrament: sign, sign and reality, and reality. According to the sign alone, one sees that the Eucharist signifies its ultimate effect of ecclesial unity. "Our Lord has proffered his body and his blood in those things which, from a multitude, are reduced to unity, since the bread is one single reality made of many grains; while the wine is one single drink made of many grapes."[47] From a multitude, the Eucharist brings forth a single reality by ordering us *ad unum*.[48]

Under the second aspect, the *res et sacramentum,* of the Eucharist one also finds the production of concord. The Eucharist makes the Church since "by this sacrament the members of the Church are united to their head."[49] It is by Eucharistic realism that one has ecclesial peace. In the third level of the sacrament, the *res tantum,* one finds the reality of ecclesial peace and unity in full relief. Since one enters into true communion with Christ, believers are "mutually united by [him]."[50] The ultimate effect of the Eucharist is the mutual union of the members of Christ. with one another. In short, the Eucharist is called the sacrament of unity and of peace.[51] The

46. *Super Io.,* 20, l. 4, n. 2532.

47. *ST* III q. 79, a. 1.

48. *ST* III q. 73, a. 3, co.

49. *SS* IV d. 8, q. 1, a.3, q. la 1, sc. 1.

50. *ST* III q. 73, a. 4, co.

51. Garrigou-Lagrange concurs and claims that according to Aquinas, the Eucharist causes peace by uniting all Christians in the profession of one faith. In other words, the Eucharist is like supernatural wisdom and teaches the proper *ordo* of life, an order necessary for true peace. Likewise, it unites the hearts of all the faithful by strengthening charity, which is the very bond of the Church. Furthermore, all the members of the Christian family are united in the Eucharist in common worship. The diverse classes are united as well as the diverse peoples. All this can only be accomplished by causing charity. See Reginald Garrigou-Lagrange, *De Eucharistia et Poenitentia* (Turin, 1943).

Eucharist brings about a union of wills around the highest good, the very notion of concord.[52]

Although it should not be thought of as a different effect from the communal (since both are caused and lived by charity), the Eucharist as sacrament also causes interior peace by communicating to the recipient a participation in the very peace of Christ and ultimately of God himself.[53] "Christ is called the God of peace because he is the giver of peace and one who loves. . . . He is also the author of peace. . . . He also dwells in peace."[54] In short, God pours peace into the world through Jesus Christ[55] and in the Eucharist we receive "the very principle of peace."[56]

Put simply, Eucharistic reception communicates the peace of Christ by uniting the believer to Christ. Union with Christ in the Eucharist not only brings humans together externally but properly orders the subjective desires and faculties toward God the Trinity, the one supreme good. Now, as we saw earlier, union with God is the *sine qua non* of true interior peace. Hence, the Eucharist is the true cause of peace. Put another way, the Eucharist augments and moves toward peace because of what it contains.[57]

Not only does the Eucharist cause peace directly by uniting humans to God and ordering their faculties, desires, *ad unum*. It also wards off the impediments to peace, obstacles both within and without that disturb proper order and rest.[58] The Eucharist forgives venial sin which diminishes the fervor of charity and thus peace. It preserves one from future sins, sins which would disorder the soul and

---

52. The citations in this footnote are taken from Emery, "The Ecclesial Fruit of the Eucharist," 161, n. 27. See also, *ST* III q. 67, a. 2; q. 73, a. 2, s.c.; q. 73, a. 4; q. 80, a. 5, ad 2; q. 82, a. 2, arg. 3 and ad 3; q. 83, a. 4, co. and ad 3.

53. Cf. *Super Ps.* 13, n. 5. For more on the ontological exemplarity of Christ see Thomas Ryan, *Thomas Aquinas as Reader of the Psalms* (Notre Dame: University of Notre Dame Press, 2000), 81ff.

54. *Super II Cor.*, 13, l. 3, n. 540: " . . . *sed ideo Christus dicitur Deus pacis, quia est dator pacis et amator. . . . Ipse etiam est auctor pacis . . . Ipse in pace habitat.*"

55. Cf. *In de div. nom.*, 11, l. 3.

56. Ramirez, *De Caritate*, 922.

57. Cf. *ST* III q. 79, a. 4; Hoffman, 164.

58. Cf. Hoffman, 166.

diminish peace. It even indirectly counters the fomes of sin, the very inclination to sin, which is a cause of conflict. Likewise, it forgives punishment, which is contrary to the will achieving the good and thus contrary to peace. Finally, the Eucharist wards off the outward assaults of demons, who hinder proper love of God and neighbor, the very foundations of peace. By strengthening charity, the love of God and neighbor and source of unity, the Eucharist both causes peace directly and wards off all the agents of conflict.[59] Put differently, the Eucharist sustains and restores peace.[60]

Certainly, the peace attained by the Eucharist, both internal and external, is imperfect in this life; the perfect peace of Christ is only in the life to come. But here also one can see the deep resonances between the Eucharist and peace. Indeed, it is no coincidence that both show the tension of realized eschatology. The peace believers have now is the in-breaking of perfect peace and a participation in the very peace of Christ. As Aquinas says, "Everlasting peace, i.e. spiritual peace, begins here and is completed there."[61]

The Eucharist likewise causes the other virtues integral to peace. This obtains not only efficiently by its augmenting of habitual grace, which breaks forth in the soul as the infused virtues, but also by exemplarity. For example, the liturgy teaches wisdom. Inasmuch as the Gospel is proclaimed at the liturgy, it informs the believer of true order, for "truly, the purpose of the Gospel is peace in Christ."[62] Aquinas claims that "the advantage [his] teaching gives is peace."[63] The Eucharist also concerns justice but goes beyond it by charity. It not only teaches the participant to give the other his due, but to desire the other's due as if it were one's own. As we have seen, this is a necessary condition for justice.

---

59. At least inasmuch as these are contained in the Church and in the mind. See *Super Phil.,* 4, l. 1, n. 159; Emery, "The Ecclesial Fruit of the Eucharist," 162–63; *ST* II-II q. 29, a. 3, ad 2.

60. Cf. Hoffman, 164.

61. *Super II Thess.,* 3, l. 2, n. 89.

62. *Super II Thess.,* 3, l. 2, n. 89.

63. *Super Io.,* 16, l. 8, n. 2174: "*utilitas doctrinae est pax.…*"

Given these resonances between the Eucharist and peace, it does not seem to be a stretch to say that the very purpose of the Eucharist is peace. It was shown above but could also be argued in multiple ways. For example, the purpose of Christ's coming was to bring peace which was accomplished by the sacrifice of the cross. Now that same sacrifice is identical, numerically, with the Eucharist and hence the Eucharist too has the same purpose: to bring peace. Another way of arguing this would be to follow Aquinas's claim that the purpose of this sacrament is its use by the faithful, their sanctification.[64] Now sanctification is simply another word in Aquinas for living proper order, since the saint is "one who has peace amid this life, even in spite of troubles."[65] Hence, the purpose of the Eucharist is to bring peace between all without distinction and to give the heart rest without end. Moreover, since all the other sacraments are ordered to the Eucharist as an end, all the sacraments are ordered toward peace.[66] Hence, I do not think it is a stretch, even though Aquinas never calls the Eucharist the sacrament of peace, to say it is implicit in his thought. The Eucharist sums up the entire sacramental order, an order which is not only unified/ordered in itself but is ultimately ordered toward the introduction and maintenance of supernatural peace, both individual and social.

64. Cf. *ST* III q. 60, a. 5; q. 63, a. 6.

65. *Super Io.*, 16, l. 8, n. 2174.

66. Cf. *ST* III q. 65, a. 3, co.; *SS* IV d. 8, q. 1, a. 2, qla. 2 ad 4, the Eucharist "has all grace and all the effects of the other sacraments singularly."

# Conclusion

When lecturing on Mt 10:12–13 (Christ's instructions for how to greet a household, "peace to this house"), Aquinas makes a claim that this greeting is fitting, or *congruus*. He says: "And this was a fitting way of greeting because the world was at war. In Christ, however, the world is reconciled. For they were the *legati* of the Lord and for what? Certainly, for peace. For this reason, it was a fitting greeting."[1] In some ways, this passage is paradigmatic for Aquinas. A deep insight into the nature of peace, Christ, and discipleship is offered, but only in passing and simply to explain the text in front of him. Aquinas's works are overflowing with passages just like this one. The text in front of Aquinas, or an objector, makes a claim about peace. Aquinas says something about peace in passing but does not dwell or explain the point. In addition, he nowhere relates/systematizes these thoughts. He leaves them scattered across his whole corpus. This partly explains why he is not usually associated with the study of peace. We can see now, however, that this is unwarranted. Aquinas's thought is marked by a deep affinity for peace and the study of peace throws new light over his entire corpus. In addition, Aquinas's thought on peace has much to offer us. In him, we find a framework that combines philosophical rigor with theological precision and encompasses everything from Trinitarian

---

1. *Super Matt.*, c. 1, l. 10, n. 830: "*Et iste erat modus salutandi congruus, quia mundus erat in guerra; in Christo autem mundus est reconciliatus: isti enim legati erant Domini, et ad quid? Certe ad pacem; ideo congrua erat haec salutatio.*"

Theology to environmental ethics. Though Aquinas's thought is not some kind of panacea and requires expansion, especially in a modern context, he does offer us a compelling and synthetic vision of peace.

For Aquinas, peace begins with the triune God. He is the supereminence of unity, beyond all possible division and entirely simple, eternally at rest. Even philosophically, one can predicate peace of God. Theologically, however, Aquinas's thought comes to life. In the Trinitarian order, the Trinitarian Persons are union to each other, subsistent relations to another. God is thus the perfect reconciliation between unity, union, and multitude. This is why Aquinas not only calls God the *auctor pacis* but also peace itself. It is *"ab isto profundo"*[2] that peace is poured into the world. Created peace is a participation in and imitation of the peace found in God. It is no mistake that union/order marks creation necessarily. Creation is an imitation of the Triune God. In particular, the subsistent relations of the Son and the Spirit enter into the causality of peace. The Son as wisdom encompasses all possible created orders, those imitating the supereminent union and multitude of the Trinity. The Spirit, as love and gift, moves these orders into being and exemplifies their bond.

In other words, for Aquinas, God pours his peace into the world with being. Peace is not only predicated of God but also, and because of this, a fundamental law of the universe. Peace is a conforming to the "laws of being itself."[3] We see this in the way that Aquinas describes peace. Granted, his descriptions are diverse and resist easy summary, I found they contain both a positive and a negative *ratio*. The positive is *unio/ordo* and the negative is *quies/tranquillitas*. In unifying Aquinas's descriptions, I found he reduces the positive element of peace to relation and relation to the transcendental good. Put simply, as Aquinas says, peace "adds nothing beyond the *ratio* of the good."[4] This should not come as a surprise. Aquinas predicates

---

2. *Super Phil.,* c. 4, l. 1, n. 159.

3. McMahon, "A Thomistic Analysis of Peace," 176.

4. *ST* II-II q. 30, a. 3, ad 3.

both *ordo et unio* of the Trinity and there reduces both to relation. Wherever the good is found there is union/order and where there is union/order rest and tranquility are as well. This is not only true of humans, but of the whole cosmos, a cosmos born of peace and destined to return to it.

Put differently, for Aquinas, the desire for peace is a *reditus*. All things desire their own perfection, and that desire is a desire for peace. The quest for peace is thus universal, and seeking peace with anyone or anything has an initial grounding in this cosmic friendship, the universal shared orders of creation and redemption. Nor can anyone opt out of this quest for deeper peace, since the quest for peace is simply the quest for the conservation and enlargement of our being itself as well as the deepening of our relationships with God, self, others, and creation. Aquinas not only offers us a rigorous philosophy and theology of peace but also serious grounding for the seeking of peace (both theological as well as psychological).

Aquinas, however, is no utopian thinker. He recognizes the provisional nature of our quest for peace as well as the inevitability of conflict. We often destroy peace in our search for "peace." We settle for a figment, a simulacrum, of peace deluding ourselves that it is the reality (just as we do with the good). Obviously, the primary way peace goes wrong is through sin. In some ways Aquinas's thought on sin is simply a reflection on a lack of peace. Sin is a lack of order for Aquinas, disorder: a destruction of peace. On the flip side, virtue is the primary way that humans order their interior lives and so all virtue is integral to peace. Not all peace is virtue (a good habit), but virtue is the primary way that humans begin to live proper relationships, with God, themselves, others, and creation. This is, of course, preeminently through the virtue of charity. Since charity is union to God, it is the source of the deepest possible peace we can have in this life. As Ramirez says, "love calls to love"[5] and it is no mistake that Aquinas calls peace the *proprius effectus* of both God and the virtue of charity. The very peace of God is poured into our hearts.

5. Ramirez, "La Eucaristía y la pax individual," 173: *"El amor llama al amor."*

Only God can unite all desires without destroying any of them. The same can be said of the whole cosmos. Nevertheless, sin is not the only cause of disorder. Aquinas's theology of creation and of friendship allows us to recognize internal or external discord that is not caused by sin in any sense. For Aquinas conflict is a feature of the universe and a result of the universal quest for peace. In this sense it is unavoidable. In other words, Aquinas offers us resources for understanding sin and peace, yes, but even more so for understanding the causes and goals of conflict—the *sine qua non* of a fruitful/generative discord (if it should even be called that).

In the face of lost peace and inevitable conflict, God reintroduces peace into creation through the very persons in whom creation was initially exemplified and bonded. Christ and the Holy Spirit's external missions are to reintroduce peace. Aquinas could not be more explicit on this point. What God is, is peace. What God is about is peace. The gospel is for peace. Christ is "love's unheard-of peace."[6] In his person, Christ is the new peace God pours into the world; he unites humanity and divinity in his person. Hence, Christ's sacrifice is the cause of peace, and he gives the Spirit, the bond of peace. Peace is the overarching intelligibility of the gospel for Aquinas. The whole point is to restore the cosmic friendship of creation, but also transcend it in the union of the Church, the community of full order/union with God, self, neighbor, and creation. This true order is made most concretely through the sacraments, which transform us into wise and loving people, a community animated by God's own life of peace.

This is Christ's gospel, his great gathering of what was/is divided. The Church is concretely the community of Christ's peace. Through living the order/union of the Church, a multitude is made good. The very heart of this is love, affective order/union to God and others. Put differently, the very bond/union of God's own trinitarian life comes to exemplify and cause our own peace. Our virtues themselves are a conformity to God himself and it is through these

---

6. *Serma Lauda et Laetare,* "*ideo venit sicut pax inaudite caritatis.*"

virtues that we live the very peace of God, making our powers, projects, and desires friends of each other by ordering them *ad unum* as well as making us friends of one another, of creation, and of God. Peacemakers are thus *similis Deo.*[7] Because God himself comes to reintroduce peace into the world, that becomes our very project also. This is our primary aim in praying, frequenting the sacraments, dialoging, evangelizing, learning, and growing. The quest for peace is a quest to live the very life of God in an ever-deeper way. "For where else should peace dwell but in peace?"[8]

Nevertheless, because of the provisional nature of our quest, Aquinas's teaching on peace is a teaching of hope. The seeking of peace is the hope for peace. Any hope that we have of achieving peace here (which Aquinas recognizes is possible but will inevitably be marked by sin and conflict, even among friends) is not ultimately based in our ability to pray, to frequent the sacraments, to grow in virtue, to dialogue, and to evangelize. Aquinas's hope for peace is grounded in the hope that it is through these means that God, the ultimate source and maker of peace, pours his peace into the world. Our peace now is God's work, but God's work is not finished. The desire for peace is ultimately the hope for peace. It is only in attaining God, whose preeminent goodness fulfills all desire, that we will rest individually, with each other, and with creation. Peace is ultimately a gift from God, something we receive now as a foretaste, a foretaste of the fullness found only in heaven.[9]

In conclusion, I have not even mentioned many of the topics I treated in the text. There are many others that could be treated in addition to those in the text. Of course, the first of these is war. Though it is irregular to have an entire text on peace in Aquinas with only brief mentions of war, I think this should be the norm (at least if we approach conflict from a Thomistic perspective). Frequently

---

7. *Expositio in Orationem Dominicam*, a. 7: "*et ideo pacifici dicuntur filii Dei, qui sunt similes Deo, quia sicut Deo nihil nocere potest, ita nec eis, quia nec prospera nec adversa.*"

8. *Serma Osanna Filio David*, "*Primo dico quod appropinquat pacificis sibi. Deus enim est actor pacis; et ubi debet habitare pax nisi in pace?*"

9. Cf. *Super Rom.*, c. 1, l. 3, n. 49.

scholarship on war attempts to understand conflict without serious attention to understanding peace. This makes very little sense. One must study the *res* before one can study the privation. Greater attention to love/relation/order/union would help make sense of many aspects of Aquinas's thought on war, from just causes in going to war to what will make for true peace in post-war reconciliation. If one is looking for a restrictive ethic of war, one born of and tending toward peace, I know of no better than Aquinas's.

Nevertheless, the transformational aspect of focusing on peace goes well beyond Aquinas's thought on war and similar things could be said for almost any topic in Aquinas, from God through the sacraments. Some of these topics I treated extensively (with what quality only the reader can judge); others I treated only in passing and inadequately. Many I bypassed entirely. For example, I treated only briefly the connection between law and peace. This could easily be expanded to include more particular aspects of governance, whether of the universe or the civil sphere. Likewise, I think I only inadequately treated the contraries of peace (e.g. schism) as well as the relation between interior and exterior peace. What I have found certainly holds true, in general, but there are many deep and abiding issues in the particular relations of orders, contraries of peace, and desire in Aquinas. Finally, as an example of a topic I bypassed, I did not treat at all Aquinas's mysticism though the concept of union with God usually evokes mystical claims. One could say something similar for many aspects of Aquinas's anthropology and ethics. Order/union are found throughout his corpus, so I'd be surprised if there were any topics for which peace would be totally irrelevant.

In some sense, and speaking most generally, the entire goal of *sacra doctrina* is peace. Aquinas's entire corpus and thought is at attempt at intellectual peace—order/union between seemingly diverse topics under the formality of coming from and returning to God.[10] Something that has such breadth can only receive inadequate treatments. If peace is really a description of God, then we should

---

10. Cf. *ST* I q. 1, a. 3.

expect it to have all the apophatic mystery that God himself possesses. Hence, my hope is that, if this book is successful at anything, it is successful in beginning a renewed interest in peace amongst Thomists. This is Aquinas's own advice: "serve peace and you will achieve salvation."[11] Aquinas's thought on peace is deep and potent. It spans his thought, from metaphysics to trinitarian theology, from ecclesiology to sacraments, from ethics to Christology, from pneumatology to natural theology. In each of these topics, for those willing to spend some effort, it is possible to see Aquinas's thought anew in the light of peace.

11. *Sermo Osanna Filio Davido*: "*Serva igitur pacem et consequeris salutem.*"

# Bibliography

—— : ——

All in-text translations of primary languages are my own. If I borrowed an English translation, I mention it in the footnotes and include the text in the Bibliography.

### COLLECTIONS

Opera Omnia. Parma: Typis Petri Fiaccadori, 1858–63.
Opera omnia. Rome: Marietti, 1926–65.
Opera omnia, iussu Leonis XIII P. M. edita. Rome: Commissio Leonina, 1882–
Scriptum super libros Sententiarum magistri Petri Lombardi. 4 vols. Edited by R. P. Mandonnet and R. P. Maria Fabianus Moos. Paris: Lethielleux, 1929–47- Summa theologiae. Rome: Editiones Paulinae, 1955.

### WORKS CITED OF AQUINAS (IN LATIN)

*Commentaria in octo libros Physicorum* [Leonine]
*Compendium theologiae ad fratrem Raynaldum* [Leonine]
*De rationibus Fidei* [Leonine]
*De regno ad regem Cypri* [Marietti]
*Expositio in orationem dominicam* [Marietti]
*Expositio in Symbolum Apostolorum* [Marietti]
*Expositio super Isaiam ad litteram.* [Leonine]
*Expositio super Iob ad litteram.* [Leonine]
*In Jeremiam prophetam expositio* [Fiaccadori, Busa]
*In librum B. Dionysii De divinis nominibus expositio* [Marietti]
*In psalmos Davidis expositio* [Fiaccadori, Busa]
*Quaestiones de Quolibet* [Leonine]
*Quaestiones disputatae de malo* [Leonine]
*Quaestiones disputatae de potentia* [Marietti]

*Quaestiones disputatae de veritate* [Leonine]
*Quaestiones disputatae de virtutibus* [Marietti]
*Scriptum super Sententiis* [Mand/Moos]
*Serma Lauda et Laetare* [Leonine]
*Serma Osanna Filio David* [Leonine]
*Sententia libri Ethicorum* [Leonine]
*Sententia libri Metaphysicae* [Marietti]
*Summa contra Gentiles* [Marietti]
*Summa Theologiae* [Leonine]
*Super Boethium De Trinitate* [Leonine]
*Super Epistolam B. Pauli ad Colossenses lectura* [Marietti]
*Super Epistolam B. Pauli ad Ephesios lectura* [Marietti]
*Super Epistolam B. Pauli ad Galatas lectura* [Marietti]
*Super Epistolam B. Pauli ad Hebraeos lectura* [Marietti]
*Super Epistolam B. Pauli ad Philipenses lectura* [Marietti]
*Super Epistolam B. Pauli ad Romanos lectura* [Marietti]
*Super Epistolam B. Pauli ad Titum lectura* [Marietti]
*Super Evangelium S. Ioannis lectura* [Marietti]
*Super Evangelium S. Matthaei lectura* [Marietti]
*Super I Epistolam B. Pauli ad Corinthios lectura* [Marietti]
*Super I Epistolam B. Pauli ad Thessalonicenses lectura* [Marietti]
*Super I Epistolam B. Pauli ad Timotheum lectura* [Marietti]
*Super II Epistolam B. Pauli ad Corinthios lectura* [Marietti]
*Super II Epistolam B. Pauli ad Thessalonicenses lectura* [Marietti]
*Super II Epistolam B. Pauli ad Timotheum lectura* [Marietti]

## OTHER WORKS CITED

Aertsen, J. "Good as Transcendental and the Transcendence of the Good," in *Being and Goodness: The Concept of the Good in Metaphysics and Philosophical Theology*. Edited by Scott Macdonald. Ithaca, NY: Cornell University Press, 1991, 56–73.

Aertsen, Jan. *Medieval Philosophy and the Transcendentals: The Case of Thomas Aquinas*. Leiden: E.J. Brill, 1996.

Aristotle. *Ethica Nicomachea*. Edited by J. Bywater. Oxford: Clarendon Press, 1894.

———. *Politica*. Edited by W. D. Ross. Oxford: Clarendon Press, 1957.

———. *Metaphysica*. Edited by W.D. Ross. Oxford: Clarendon Press. 1924.

Augustine. *De civitate dei contra paganos*. Patrologia Latina. Edited by J.-P. Minge. Vol 41. Paris, 1844–1864.

———. *Sermones*. Patrologia Latina. Edited by J.-P. Minge. Vol 36. Paris, 1844–1864.

———. *Enarrationes in psalmos*. Patrologia Latina. Edited by J.-P. Minge. Vol 36. Paris, 1844–1864.

__________. *In evangelium ioannis tractatus centum viginti quator.* Patrologia Latina. Edited by J.-P. Minge. Vol 35. Paris, 1844–1864.

__________. *Confessiones.* Patrologia Latina. Edited by J.-P. Minge. Vol 32. Paris, 1844–1864.


Austriaco, Nicanor Pier Giorgio, O.P. "Catholic Teaching on Creation and on Human Origins," in *Thomistic Evolution,* 2nd ed. Edited by Nicanor Austriaco. Rhode Island: Cluny Media, 2019, 159–88.

Bañez, Domingo. *Scholastica Commentaria in Secundam Secundae Angelici Doctoris S. Thomae.* Spain, 1615.

Barrios-Andrade, Diego Fernando. "Educación para la paz: una reflexión desde Tomas de Aquino." *Educación y Educadores* vol. 24, no. 2 (2021): 181–96.

Beestermoller, Gerhard. *Thomas von Aquin und der Gerechte Krieg: Friedensethik im theologischen Kontext der Summa Theologiae.* Germany: J.P. Bachem Verlag Koln, 1990.

Billuart, Caroli Renati. *Theologiae juxta mentem d. Thomae,* moralis tom. IV. Paris: Facultatis Theologiae Bibliopolam, 1827.

Blanchette, Olivia. *The Perfection of the Universe According to Aquinas: A Teleological Cosmology.* University Park: The Pennsylvania State University Press, 1992.

Blankenhorn, Bernard. "Mystical Theology and Christology in Thomas Aquinas," in *Ephemerides theologicae Lovanienses: commentarii de re theologica et canonica,* vol. 95, no. 2 (June 2019): 299–315.

Boakye, Lawrence. *Peace Building: the Person, Community, and Authority, A Contemporary Thomistic Approach.* Self-Published, BookSurge, 2009.

Bonino, Serge-Thomas. *Angels and Demons: A Catholic Introduction.* Washington DC: The Catholic University of America Press, 2016.

Bostock, David. *Aristotle's Ethics.* New York: Oxford University Press, 2000.

Bouyer, Louis. *Introduction to the Spiritual Life.* South Bend, IN: University of Notre Dame Press, 2013.

Brachtendorf, Johannes. "Augustine: Peace Ethics and Peace Policy." *From Just War to Modern Peace Ethics,* edited by Heinz-Gerhard Justenhoven and William Barbieri, Berlin: Walter de Gruyter, 2012.

Brock, Stephen. "The Primacy of the Common Good and the Foundations of Natural Law in St. Thomas." *Ressourcement Thomism: Sacred Doctrine, the Sacraments, and the Moral Life: Essays in Honor of Romanus Cessario, O.P.,* edited by Reinhard Hütter and Matthew Levering. Washington DC: The Catholic University of America Press, 2010, 234–55.

Brunner, Otto. *Land und Herrschaft: Grundfragen der territorialen Verfassungsgeschichte Südostdeutschlands im Mittelalter.* Baden bei Wien: Rohrer, 1939.

Burger, Maria. "Thomas Aquinas's Glosses on the Dionysius Commentaries of Albert the Great in Codex 30 of the Cologne Cathedral Library." *Via Alberti Texte—Quellen—Interpretationen,* edited by Möhle, et al. Münster: Aschendorff, 2009, 561–82.

Burt, Donald, O.S.A. "Peace." *Augustine through the Ages*, edited by Allan D. Fitzgerald. Grand Rapids, MI: Eerdmans, 1999.

Cajetan's *Commentary on Aquinas's Summa Theologiae. Opera omnia iussu impensaque Leonis XIII P.M. edita*. Rome: Ex Typgraphia Polyglotta S.C. de Propaganda Fidei, 1888.

Campos, Andrew. "Aquinas's 'lex iniusta non est lex': a Test of Legal Validity." *Archives for Philosophy of Law and Social Philosophy*, Vol. 100, No. 3 (2014): 368–69.

Casella, Pietro. *La pace in San Tommaso* (*Summa theologica: II-II, Q. 29*): *interiorizzazione e attualità di un concetto*. Ph.D. diss., Tipolito Moderna, 1978. Piacenza.

Capreolus, John. *Defensiones theologiae divi thomae aquinatis*. San Esteban: Salmanticae, 1963.

Cessario, Romanus. "Christian Satisfaction and Sacramental Reconciliation." *Rediscovering Aquinas and the Sacraments: Studies in Sacramental Theology*, edited by Matthew Levering and Michael Dauphinais. Chicago: Hillenbrand Books, 2009.

Congar, Yves. "'Ecclesia' et 'populus (fidelis)' dans l'ecclésiologie de S. Thomas." *St. Thomas Aquinas 1274–1974: Commemorative Studies*, vol. 1, ed. Armand A. Maurer et al. Toronto, Ont.: Pontifical Institute of Mediaeval Studies, 1974, 159–73.

Daly, Daniel. *The Structures of Virtue and Vice*. Washington, DC: Georgetown University Press, 2021.

DeHaan, Daniel. "Delectatio, gaudium, fruitio. Three Kinds of Pleasure for Three Kinds of Knowledge in Thomas Aquinas," *Quaestio* 15 (2015): 543–52.

D'Ettore, Domenic. "Una ratio versus Diversae rationes: Three Interpretations of Summa Theologiae I, Q. 13, aa. 1–6." *Nova et Vetera*, vol. 17, no. 1 (Winter 2019): 39–55.

Dewan, Lawrence. *Wisdom, Law, and Virtue*. New York: Fordham University Press, 2008.

Dewey, J. "Peace." In *The HarperCollins Bible Dictionary*, revised and updated. Third Edition. Edited by M. A. Powell. New York: HarperCollins, 2011.

Dionysius. *The Complete Works*. Translated by Paul Rorem. Mahwah, NJ: Paulist Press, 1987.

Doolan, Gregory. *Aquinas on the Divine Ideas as Exemplar Causes*. Washington, DC: The Catholic University of America Press, 2014.

Elders, Leo. *Thomas Aquinas and his Predecessors*. Washington, DC: The Catholic University of America Press, 2018.

Emery, Gilles, OP. "Essentialism or Personalism in the Treatise on God in St. Thomas Aquinas?" *Trinity in Aquinas*, 2nd edition. Translated by Teresa Bede et al. Ann Arbor, MI: Sapientia Press of Ave Maria University, 2006, 165–208.

Emery, Gilles. *Trinity, Church, and Human Person: Thomistic Essays*. Ave Maria, FL: Sapientia Press, 2007.

Emery, Gilles. "Ad aliquid: Relation in the Thought of St. Thomas Aquinas." *Theology Needs Philosophy, Acting Reason is Contrary to the Nature of God*, edited by Matthew Lamb. Washington, DC: The Catholic University of America Press, 2016, 175–201.

Emery, Gilles. *The Trinitarian Theology of St. Thomas Aquinas*. New York: Oxford University Press, 2010.

Erb, Heather McAdam. "Interior Peace: Inchoatio vitae aeternae." *Wisdom's Apprentice: Thomistic Essays in Honor of Lawrence Dewan, O.P.*, edited by Lawrence Dewan and Peter A. Kwasniewski. Washington, DC: Catholic University of America Press, 2007, 260–81.

Farrell, Dominic. "Wanting the Common Good: Aquinas on General Justice," in *The Review of Metaphysics*, vol. 71 (March 2018): 517–49.

Finn, Daniel. "Social Structures." *Moral Agency within Social Structures and Culture*, edited by Daniel Finn, 29–41. Washington, DC: Georgetown University Press, 2020.

Flannery, Kevin. *Cooperation with Evil: Thomistic Tools of Analysis*. Washington, DC: The Catholic University of America Press, 2019.

Flood, Anthony. *The Metaphysical Foundations of Love*. Washington, DC: The Catholic University of America Press, 2018.

Gallagher, Joel. "The Gethsemane Event according to Thomas Aquinas." *The Angelicum*, vol. 94 (2017): 673–707.

Garrigou-Lagrange, Reginald. *De Eucharistia et Poenitentia*. Turin, 1943.

Geenen, Godefridus. "L'adage Eucharistia est sacramentum ecclesiasticae unionis dans les oeuvres et la doctrine de S. Thomas d'Aquin." *La Eucaristía y la Paz, XXXV Congreso eucarístico internacional* 1952: Sesiones de estudio, vol. 1. Barcelona: Planas, 1953, 158–62.

Genovese, Ignazio. "Dalla concordia degli animi alla tranquillità dell'ordine: per una fondazione interiore della pace nella Summa Teologia di Tommaso d'Aquino." *Rassegna di Teologia* 63 (2022): 577–96.

Gilleman, Gerard. *Le Primat de la Charite en Theologie Morale: Essai Methodologique*. Paris: Desclee de Brouwer et Cie, 1952.

Gondreau, Paul. *The Passions of Christ's Soul in the Theology of Thomas Aquinas*. Providence, RI: Cluny Media, 2018.

Grabmann, Martin. *Die Lehre des heiligen Thomas von Aquin von der Kirche als Gotteswerk*. Regensberg: G. J. Manz, 1903.

Gushee, David and Glen Stassen. *Kingdom Ethics: Following Jesus in Contemporary Context*. Grand Rapids, MI: Eerdmans, 2016.

Hahn, Scott, ed. *The Catholic Bible Dictionary*. New York: Double Day, 2009.

Hause, Jeffrey. "Aquinas on Aristotelian Justice: Defender, Destroyer, Subverter, or Surveyor?" *Aquinas and the Nicomachean Ethics*, edited by Hoffmann, et al. New York: Oxford University Press, 2013, 146–64.

Herdt, Jennifer. "Aquinas and the Democratic Virtues: An Introduction." *Journal of Religious Ethics* vol 44, no. 2 (2016): 233–45.

Hoffman, Adolphus. "Eucharistia ut Sacramentum Pacis secundum S. Thomam."

*La Eucaristía y la Paz, XXXV Congreso eucarístico internacional* 1952: Sesiones de estudio, vol. 1. Barcelona: Planas, 1953, 163–67.

Hütter, Reinhard. *Bound for Beatitude: A Study in Eschatology and Ethics.* Washington, DC: The Catholic University of America Press, 2019.

Irizar, Liliana. "Sabiduría y paz. Explorando sus conexiones íntimas desde Tomas de Aquino." *La sabiduría en Tomas de Aquino. Inspiración y reflexión: Perspectivas filosóficas y teológicas,* 107–34. Argentina: Universidad Sergio Arboleda, 2017.

Irwin, Terrance. *The Development of Ethics.* New York: Oxford University Press, 2014.

Jensen, Steven. *Knowing the Natural Law: From Precepts and Inclinations to Deriving Oughts.* Washington, DC: The Catholic University of America Press, 2015.

Jensen, Steven. *Sin: A Thomistic Psychology.* Washington, DC: The Catholic University of America Press, 2018.

Kaczor, Christopher. "Thomas Aquinas's Commentary on the Ethics: Merely an Interpretation of Aristotle?" *American Catholic Philosophical Quarterly* 78, no. 3 (2004): 353–78.

Keenan, James. *Goodness and Rightness in Thomas Aquinas's Summa Theologiae.* Washington, DC: Georgetown University Press, 1992.

Keys, Mary. *Aquinas, Aristotle, and the Promise of the Common Good.* New York: Cambridge, 2006.

Klima, Gyula. "The Changing Role of Entia Rationis in Medieval Semantics and Ontology." *Synthese,* vol. 96, no. 1 (1993): 25–29.

Koritansky, Peter. *Thomas Aquinas and the Philosophy of Punishment.* Washington, DC: The Catholic University of America Press, 2011.

Krempel, *La Doctrine de la Relation chez Saint Thomas: Exposé historique et systématique.* Paris: Libraire Philosophique, 1952.

Labourdette, M. *La Charite.* Paris: Parole et Silence, 2016.

Lawless, George. "Interior Peace in the Confessions of St. Augustine." *Revue des études augustiniennes,* vol. 26 (1980): 45–61.

Legge, Dominic. *The Trinitarian Christology.* New York: Oxford University Press, 2018.

Leppin, Voker. *Ruhen in Gott: Eine Geschichte der christlichen Mystik.* München: C.H. Beck, 2021.

Lombardo, Nicholas, O.P. *The Logic of Desire: Aquinas on Emotion.* Washington, DC: The Catholic University of America Press, 2011.

Longpré, Ephrem. "L'Eucharistie est le sacrement de la paix mystique." *La Eucaristía y la Paz, XXXV Congreso eucarístico internacional* 1952: Sesiones de estudio, vol. 1. Barcelona: Planas, (1953): 158–62.

Lottin, Odon. *Morale Fondamentale.* Tournai: Desclée & Co, 1954.

Ludwig, Paul. *Rediscovering Political Friendship: Aristotle's Theory and Modern Identity, Community, and Equality.* New York: Cambridge University Press, 2020.

MacIntyre, Alisdair. *After Virtue,* 3rd ed. Notre Dame, IN: University of Notre Dame Press, 2010.

Malloy, Christopher. "Thomas on the Order of Love and Desire: A Development of Doctrine." *The Thomist,* vol. 71 (2007): 65–87.

Manser, G.M. "Begriff und Bedeutung der transzendentalen Beziehung." *Divus Thomas,* vol. 19 (1941): 351–60.

Marin, Antonio. *The Theology of Christian Perfection.* Eugene, OR: Wipf and Stock Press, 2012.

Marshall, Bruce. "The Whole Mystery of Our Salvation: Saint Thomas Aquinas on the Eucharist as Sacrifice." *Rediscovering Aquinas and the Sacraments: Studies in Sacramental Theology,* edited by Matthew Levering and Michael Dauphinais, Chicago: Hillenbrand Books, 2009.

Mattison, William C. III "Can Christians Possess the Acquired Virtues?" *Theological Studies,* vol. 72 (2011): 558–85.

McCabe, Herbert. *Faith within Reason.* New York: Continuum, 2007.

McGinn, Bernard. *The Harvest of Mysticism in Medieval Germany.* Vol. 4 of *The Presence of God: A History of Western Christian Mysticism.* New York: The Crossroad Publishing Company, 2005.

McInerny, Daniel. *The Difficult Good.* New York: Fordham University Press, 2006.

McMahon, Francis. "A Thomistic Analysis of Peace." *The Thomist,* vol. 15, no. 4 (1952): 1–52.

Meinert, John. "Alimentum Pacis: The Eucharist and Peace in St. Thomas Aquinas." *Nova et Vetera,* English edition, vol. 14, No. 4 (2016): 1193–212.

__________. "Divine Exemplarity, Virtue, and Theodicy in Aquinas." *The Thomist* vol 82, no. 2 (April 2018): 235–62.

__________. "Peace and the Transcendentals: The Case of Thomas Aquinas." *European Journal for the Study of Thomas Aquinas,* 37 (2019): 18–34.

Moen, Geir U. "Thomas Aquinas Between Just War and Pacifism." *The Journal of Religious Ethics,* vol. 39, no. 2 (2011): 230ff.

Oderberg, David. *The Metaphysics of Good and Evil.* Oxfordshire: Routledge, 2019.

Osborne, Thomas. "The threefold referral of acts to the ultimate end in Thomas Aquinas and his commentators." *Angelicum,* vol. 85 (2008): 715–36.

__________. *Love of Self and Love of God in Thirteenth Century Ethics.* Notre Dame, IN: University of Notre Dame Press, 2005.

Philpott, Daniel. "Reconciliation: An Ethic for Peacebuilding," in *Strategies of Peace: Transforming Conflict in a Violent World,* ed. by Philpott and Powers, 91–118. New York: Oxford University Press, 2010.

Pilsner, Joseph. *The Specification of Human Actions in St. Thomas Aquinas.* New York: Oxford University Press, 2006.

Pinckaers, Servais. *Sources of Christian Ethics.* Translated by Mary Thomas Noble. 3rd ed. Washington, DC: The Catholic University of America Press, 1995.

Plotinus. *Enneads.* Translated by A. H. Armstrong. Cambridge, MA: Harvard University Press, 1966.

Porter, Jean. "Moral Virtues, Charity, and Grace: Why the Infused and Acquired Virtues Cannot Co-Exist." *Journal of Moral Theology*, Vol. 8, No. 2 (2019): 40–66.

_________. *Justice as a Virtue: a Thomistic Perspective*. Grand Rapids, MI: Eerdmans, 2016.

Ramirez, Santiago. "La Eucaristía y la Paz Individual en la Teologia de Santo Tomas de Aquino." *Ciencia Tomista*. vol. 79 (1952): 163–228.

_________. *De Caritate*. Opera Omnia Tomus XII. San Esteban: Salamanca, 1998.

_________. *De Ordine Placita Quaedam Thomistica*. San Esteban: Salmanticae, 1963.

Rathinam, Selva, SJ. "Biblical Understanding of Peace." *Jnanadeepa*, vol. 21, n. 1 (Jan 2017): 11–24.

Reichberg, Gregory. "Aquinas's Moral Typology of Peace and War." *Review of Metaphysics*, vol. 64, no. 1 (2010) 467–487.

_________. "Human Nature, Peace, and War." *A Cultural History of Peace in the Medieval Age*, edited by Walter Simons, 33–50. New York: Bloomsbury Academic, 2020.

_________. "Thomas Aquinas between Just War and Pacifism." *Journal of Religious Ethics* vol. 38, no. 2 (June 2010): 219–41.

_________. *Thomas Aquinas on War and Peace*. Cambridge: Cambridge University Press, 2016.

Rocca, Gregory. *Speaking the Incomprehensible God*. Washington, DC: The Catholic University of America Press, 2004.

Rondet, Henri, S.J. Pax, *Tranquillitas Ordinis*. Real monasterio de San Lorenzo de El Escorial, 1954.

Roniger, Scott. "Do Friends Need Justice or Do the Just Need Friendship? Natural Law as the Foundation for Justice and Friendship." *Lex Naturalis* 3 (2018): 57–84.

_________. "Is there a Punishment for Violating the Natural Law?" *American Catholic Philosophical Quarterly*, vol. 94, no. 2 (2020): 273–304.

Rose, Matthew. "Can Virtue be Taught? Thomistic Answers to a Socratic Question." *The Thomist*, vol. 77 (2013): 229–60.

Rubin, Michael. "The Place of 'Thing' and 'Something' in Aquinas's Order of the Transcendentals." *The Thomist*, vol. 81, no. 3 (July 2017): 395–436.

Ryan, Thomas. *Thomas Aquinas as Reader of the Psalms*. Notre Dame, IN: University of Notre Dame Press, 2000.

Sabra, George. *Thomas Aquinas' Vision of the Church: Fundamentals of an Ecumenical Ecclesiology*. Mainz: Matthias-Grunewald-Verlag, 1987.

Schulze, Markus. *Liebhaft und Unsterblich: Zur Schau der Seele in der Anthropologie und Theologie des Hl. Thomas von Aquin*. Freiburg: Universitätsverlag Freiburg Schweiz, 1992.

Schwartz, Daniel. *Aquinas on Friendship*. New York: Oxford University Press, 2007.

Sertillanges, Antonin. *La Morale Philosophie de Saint Thomas d'Aquin*. Librairie Felix Alcan, 1922.

Shanley, Brian. "Aquinas on Pagan Virtue." *The Thomist*, vol. 63 (1999): 553–77.

__________. *The Thomist Tradition*. Amsterdam: Kluwer Academic Publisher, 2002.

Sherwin, Michael. *By Knowledge and By Love*. Washington, DC: The Catholic University of America Press, 2005.

Simon, Yves. *Philosophy of Democratic Government*. Chicago: University of Chicago Press, 1977.

Spiering, Jamie. "'The Divine Goodness Could Be Manifest through Other Creatures and Another Order': The Source of Aquinas's Convictions about Divine Freedom." *The Thomist*, vol. 83, no. 1 (Jan. 2019): 1–29.

Sullivan, Ezra. *Habits and Holiness: Ethics, Theology, and Biopsychology*. Washington, DC: The Catholic University of America Press, 2021.

Svensson, Manfred. "A Defensible Conception of Tolerance in Aquinas?" *The Thomist*, vol. 75 (2011): 291–308.

Svoboda, David. "Aquinas on Real Relation," *Theologica*, vol. 6.1 (2016): 147–72.

__________. "Thomas Aquinas on Whole and Part." *The Thomist* vol. 76 (2012): 273–304.

__________. *Aquinas on One and Many*. Neuenkirchen-Seelscheid: Editiones Scholasticae, 2015.

Synan, Edward. "St. Thomas Aquinas and the Profession of Arms." *Medieval Studies*, vol. 50 (1988) 404–37.

Tapie, Matthew. "For He is our Peace: Thomas Aquinas on Christ as Cause of Peace in the City of Saints." *The Journal of Moral Theology* vol 5.1 (2016): 111–28.

Thompson, Christopher. *The Joyful Mystery: Field Notes Toward a Green Thomism*. Steubenville, OH: Emmaus Road Publishing, 2017.

Torrell, Jean-Pierre. *Initiation à saint Thomas d'Aquin: Sa personne et son œuvre*. Paris: Les Editions du Cerf, 2015.

__________. *Saint Thomas Aquinas: The Person and his Work*. Translated by Robert Royal. Washington, DC: The Catholic University of America Press, 2005.

Truini, F. *La pace in Tommaso d'Aquino*. Roma: Città Nuova, 2008.

Van Nieuwenhove, Rik. "Bearing the Marks of Christ's Passion." *The Theology of Thomas Aquinas*, eds. Rik Van Nieuwenhove and Joseph Wawrykow. Notre Dame, IN: University of Notre Dame Press, 2005.

__________. "Salvation, Satisfaction, and Friendship with God." *The Thomist*, vol. 83 (2019): 521–45.

__________. *Thomas Aquinas and Contemplation*. New York: Oxford University Press, 2021.

Vauthier, E. "*Le Saint Esprit, principe d'unité de L'Eglise d'après S. Thomas d'Aquin*." *Mélanges de Science Religieuse*, vol. 6 (1949): 57–8.

Weldon, Aaron. "Ad Totius Mundi Pacem atque Salutem Merit for Others and the Divine Plan in Thomistic Thought." *Nova et Vetera, English Edition*, vol. 13, no. 4 (2015): 1125–148.

White, Thomas Joseph, O.P. *The Incarnate Lord*. Washington, DC: The Catholic University of American Press, 2017.

Wittman, Tyler. "Not a God of Confusion but of Peace: Aquinas and the Meaning of Divine Simplicity." *Modern Theology* 32, no. 2 (April 2016): 151–69.

Wippel, John F. *The Metaphysical Thought of Thomas Aquinas.* Washington, DC: The Catholic University of America Press, 2001.

Woznicki, Andrew. *Being and Order: The Metaphysics of Thomas Aquinas in Historical Perspective.* New York: Peter Lang, 1991.

# Index


Analogy, 109n232–233, 123, 244; and
     peace, 71–79
Angels, 8, 20, 29
Annoyances, 91
Apophaticism/Apophatic, 9, 161, 287
Appetible, 70, 82–83, 85, 88, 92, 147, 148
Appetite, ix, 16, 18, 28–30, 33, 38–40, 43,
     47, 63–65, 67–68, 69n89, 72–76, 83,
     85, 87–88, 97–98, 106–12, 141, 154, 157,
     166n228, 167, 170, 174, 176, 180–81, 189,
     191–92, 195–96, 198, 202, 204, 209, 213,
     215, 219, 227, 238, 240, 247, 277
Aristotle, xvi, 10–13, 81, 225n155, 226, 228
Ascetical/Spiritual Theology, xivn3, xvii
Augustine of Hippo, ix, xvi, 4–7, 10, 16, 18,
     28, 32, 37–38, 43, 45, 50, 99, 111n241, 235
Authority, 24, 145, 257, 259, 261–62

Beatitude/Happiness, 16–17, 31–32, 40,
     187–88, 197, 249
Beatitudes, 31–32, 40; 7th beatitude, 32
Being (*Ens*), x, 5, 8–10, 11, 17, 57, 61, 63,
     69–70, 79, 81–88, 92–93, 95–99, 100,
     102, 105, 112, 116, 121–22, 126, 128–133,
     165, 264

Categories, 11, 26, 61, 81, 92, 98–99, 101,
     105, 118, 136
Causality: Divine, 115, 123, 132; efficient
     (agent), 46, 50, 52, 84n143, 86, 103,
     105–9, 126–27, 131, 133–37, 145, 154, 157,
     174–75, 180, 197, 200, 213, 239, 272–73,
     274n32, 275–76, 279; exemplar, 27, 47,
123–31, 134–37, 162–63, 175–77, 179–80,
     199–200, 202, 212, 268, 273, 275–76, 279;
     Final, 46, 79, 83, 87, 89, 103, 107–8, 112,
     126, 131, 133, 135–37, 145, 238; formal,
     46, 50, 52, 57n33, 59, 84n143, 86, 93n185,
     103, 107–8, 124, 126–27, 131, 133–34, 137,
     145, 147, 149–50, 152, 154, 157, 166, 175,
     204n72, 209, 213, 222, 225–27, 229, 232,
     239, 241, 258, 259; material, 46, 50, 52,
     84, 108–10, 112; *per accidens*, 105, 125,
     155–56, 159, 206, 218, 239, 246, 261, 270;
     *per se*, 41, 103, 261, 266, 270
Chance, 105–6, 155
Charity, ix, xvii, 20–24, 32, 40, 44, 48,
     73, 101, 106–7, 142, 174, 180, 189, 192–
     93, 195, 198–99, 202–13, 216n113, 220,
     225n155, 227–29; as a union, 35, 209,
     212, 226, 229–30, 232–34, 239–44, 257,
     266, 268, 272–76, 278–79, 283; as cause
     of supernatural peace, 214–15, 219, 224;
     exterior effects, 35–36; interior effects,
     35–36, 39, 209; stages of growth and
     peace, 242–44
Christ's Passion, 170, 174, 269, 270, 273,
     274n29, 276
Church as community, xvii, 3, 113, 181, 182,
     183, 284
Common good, 66, 68, 72–73, 77n126,
     78, 90, 131, 133n89, 135, 137–40, 143,
     145, 147–49, 183, 217, 221–24, 227–30,
     231n170, 232, 250–51, 254, 256–59, 264,
     269
Community of peace, xvii, 113

Concord/*concordia*, 6, 12, 18, 20, 23, 29, 33, 37–41, 41n137, 45, 65–68, 70, 73–75, 96, 101, 144, 183, 187, 193, 196, 209–10, 216–17, 220, 224, 228–29, 234, 253, 261, 277–78; of the evil, 66–69, 75–79; supernatural, 73, 178–84

Conflict, ix, xviii, 2–3, 5, 7, 9, 13, 34, 44, 64, 65n79, 68–70, 73, 75–78, 88, 94, 95, 97, 103, 113–14, 116n16, 117–18, 133n89, 141, 144n146, 149–50, 154, 157, 159, 167, 176, 185, 195, 203–4, 206–7, 210, 218, 233n178, 237, 239, 240–41, 246–47, 252–54, 256, 258, 264, 279, 283–86; *per accidens* and responsibility, 233n178

*Congregatio Fidelium*, 178

Connectivity of the Virtues, 239

Consequent: naturally, 102; logically, 102

Contemplation/contemplative life, 31, 43, 77n123, 189, 197–98, 201, 212n101, 214, 239, 242, 244

Contraries, 92–93, 264, 286

*Corpus Christi Mysticum*, 178

Covenant, 2–4

Creation: as the giving of *esse*, xvii, 86, 104, 126–32, 133–34; that which is created, xvii, 3, 5, 47, 49, 86, 97, 112, 123–24, 126–33, 136, 139, 146–58, 160, 163–168, 171, 174–86, 199, 202, 208–12, 224, 229–30, 240, 245–46, 253–55, 264–66, 268, 269–70, 272, 275, 282–85

Cross, 3, 20, 37, 48, 151n171, 160, 170–75, 184, 270, 273, 276, 280

Delectation, 190–92

Description of Peace (*ratio*), 46, 50–71, 98–101. See also negative/secondary *ratio* of peace; positive/primary *ratio* of peace; rest; tranquility; *unio/ordo*

Desire, ix, x, 5, 8–9, 17–19, 23, 28, 30, 36–39, 42, 51, 63–64, 65n76–79, 66, 68, 72, 74–76, 83, 88, 90, 92, 96, 98, 100–101, 111–12, 136, 141, 148, 151, 157, 168, 172, 186–88, 193–94, 203–6, 222, 224, 233n178, 235–39, 240–41, 245–48, 254–57, 259, 266, 277–79, 283–86

Dialogue, 2, 255, 258, 259, 285

Dionysius the Areopagite, x-xi, xvi, 7–10, 18–19, 26–27, 30, 37, 45, 50, 189, 219n125, 235

Disagreement, 40, 216–18, 253

Discord, 18, 21, 32, 40–41, 51, 91, 93, 95, 145–46, 155–57, 166, 170, 186–87, 196, 215–17, 218n121, 239, 249, 261, 264, 284

Disorder/disunion, 5, 33, 47, 90, 92–97, 101, 117, 134, 145–47, 152, 154–58, 160–63, 170, 174, 176, 195, 206, 209, 218, 237, 239–40, 241, 247–48, 250, 253, 257, 260–61, 263–64, 266, 278, 283–84; sin as disorder, 20, 40–41, 91–97, 160, 247–50, 283–84

Disposition/inclination, 17, 22, 32, 35, 53, 56, 87, 109–12, 134, 140, 187, 196, 215, 219, 247–48, 279

Disquiet, 93, 95, 133, 145–46, 156, 170, 186, 248

Distinction/distinctness, 28–30, 52, 54, 56, 82, 112, 115–19, 122, 125, 128–30, 132–33, 136, 147–50, 169, 223–26, 229, 232, 262, 268–69; vs division, 118, 122–25, 183

Diversity, xix, 26, 66, 114, 119, 132, 149, 184, 199, 218

Divine Ideas, 47, 128–29, 131, 134, 137, 147, 212

Divine peace, xi, 10, 26–30, 86, 115, 125, 132, 136

Division, 3, 10–11, 28, 44, 50, 70, 71n100, 81, 97, 114n6, 115–16, 118, 121–23, 125, 147–48, 175, 183, 257, 282

Ecclesial unity, 275, 277

End, ix, 16–19, 23, 25, 28–29, 34, 39, 43, 45, 51, 63, 76–77, 79–80, 83–84, 87, 93–94, 98, 110–11, 120, 127–28, 130–31, 137–40, 143–44, 146–49, 168, 187–91, 195–96, 204–205, 207, 214, 218, 228, 234–35, 245, 246n207, 252, 254, 258–59, 268, 271, 280

Eschatology, 279

Essence, 35, 46, 50, 55, 61, 70, 72, 81–82, 85–86, 89–99, 102, 117–19, 122n40, 123, 128, 133–34, 138, 147, 150, 172, 183–84, 188, 212, 238, 244

Ethics, xvii, xviii, 13, 48–49, 185–265, 282, 286–87

Evangelization, 255, 257

Evil, X5, 16, 22–24, 34–35, 39, 41–43, 51, 67, 70, 74, 76, 78–79, 91–93, 95–97, 134, 140–41, 143, 145–57, 169, 175–76, 247, 252–54, 256, 259–63; as the specific difference of human action, 93

Fortitude, 266
Fraternal correction, 261–262
Freedom, 9, 74, 95, 132, 151–52, 237, 252
Friendship, 6, 11–13, 29, 39, 75n115, 115, 136, 182–83, 199–202, 206–207, 211, 224n151, 225–226, 229–34, 237, 243, 253, 257, 259, 271, 283–284; with God, 29, 136, 182–83, 200, 233, 243, 284183, 200, 229, 230–233
Fruits of the Spirit, xiv, 22, 35, 45, 213

God: as cause of creation, 126–37; as *esse ipsum subsistens,* 114, 117, 133; as peacemaker/cause of peace, xvii, 27, 32, 158, 162, 167, 249, 278, 282, 284–285; as peace itself, 117–125; unity and union in, 117–25. See also Trinity; participation; Son; Holy Spirit; Word; Wisdom; Hypostatic Union; Incarnation
Good, 5–6, 11–12, 16–18, 22–25, 28, 35–36, 38–43, 45–46, 48, 51, 57n33, 62–103, 107, 109–12, 117, 121, 130–60, 169, 173, 175–76, 181–83, 186, 188–92, 195–96, 200–201, 204, 206–7, 210, 212, 214, 216–17, 221–24, 227–32, 234–37, 239–42, 246–47, 250–51, 253–54, 256–60, 262–64, 266, 269, 276–79, 282–83. See also unio/ordo, desire, disposition/inclination, joy, love, relation
Governance, 145–48, 286
Grace, xii, 4, 19, 22, 25, 35, 39, 44, 48, 54–55, 73–75, 78, 120, 133, 142, 144, 153–54, 160, 165–67, 169, 174–78, 180–82, 198, 202, 213, 227–28, 236–37, 243, 245, 252, 254–57, 269, 274, 279; grace of union, 55, 164–69, 171
Genus/Genera, 11, 60, 69, 81, 84, 92–93, 98–99, 126, 130, 135, 261

Harmony, 4, 6, 7, 10, 13, 23, 29, 51, 70, 168, 198, 203, 206, 220, 239, 241
Heaven/beatific vision, 7, 16, 23, 34, 40–42, 74, 195, 197, 204, 218, 233n178, 246, 285

Heavenly bodies, 13
Holiness (holy peace), xi, 24, 272
Holy Spirit, 21, 23, 33, 41, 44, 47, 55, 119–20, 130, 135, 139, 178–84, 193, 198, 199–202, 207, 210–12, 229, 239, 249, 272, 275, 284; as accompanying Christ, 179; as bond of the Church, 178–84; as bond of creation or redemption, 180, 199–203; as effect of the action of Christ, 179–81, 284; as gift, 44, 120, 179–84, 200, 202, 204, 213, 239, 282; as union between Father and Son, 41, 120–21, 180
Hope, 3, 6, 43, 48, 182, 206n76, 239, 255, 261, 285
Hypostatic Union, 160, 164, 166–67, 171, 173, 175, 181, 184

Impediments/obstacles, 17–19, 23, 38, 44–46, 48, 51, 63–67, 70–71, 74, 91, 117, 187–89, 196, 210, 220, 226, 243–44, 254, 274, 278
Imperfection, 84n146, 89, 121, 161–62, 166, 176, 195, 244, 268–69
Incarnation, 47, 55n24, 56–57, 158–60, 163–64, 167, 170–72, 177, 179, 180, 254, 276
Individual/individuality, xvii-xviii, 3, 6, 8, 12–13, 16, 21, 23, 36, 38, 41–42, 44, 56, 65–66, 68–69, 73, 79, 90–91, 99, 108n228, 110–11, 130, 138, 141, 143–44, 147–48, 150–52, 155–57, 168, 180–84, 192, 201, 203n64, 211, 216–18, 221–23, 226–28, 230, 231n170, 234, 236n183, 238, 241–42, 245–66, 270, 280
Indivisible/indivisibility, 10–11, 53, 62, 114, 117
Intellect/mind, 24–25, 32–33, 40, 44, 46–47, 51, 54n23, 60, 70, 72, 74n111, 80, 82, 94–95, 100n210, 103, 106–11, 123–24, 127–29, 141, 148n161, 163, 165, 187–89, 190–91, 193–98, 201, 204, 211–12, 214–18, 227–28, 234, 237–38, 242, 244–45, 247, 249, 254, 256, 279n59, 286
Internal/external good of the universe, 134, 143; see also Common Good

Jesus Christ, 3, 20–21, 25, 151, 166, 170–71, 173, 177, 181, 277–78; as head of the human race, 166, 171, 177–78, 277; and peace, 3, 20–21, 25, 158–78, 170–71, 277–78. See also hypostatic union; Wisdom; Word

Joy (*gaudium aut fruitio*), ix, xvii, 4, 17, 21–23, 34–37, 48, 63, 65, 98, 100–101, 179, 186–89, 190, 192–96, 242

Justice, xvii, 11–12, 150–52, 154–55, 171, 230–31, 233, 244, 251, 257, 266–67, 269–70, 279; commutative, 222, 230n170; distributive, 222; general (legal), 73, 75, 222–23; infused, 229; original, 176, 238; particular, 222; and peace, ix, 16, 22, 31, 47–48, 143, 219–26, 228–30, 264n285, 268

Justice in Family, 10, 225–26

Just War, x, xii, xiii, 78, 262

Law, 15, 21, 137–45, 222, 252, 269, 282, 286; divine, 137, 139; eternal, 137, 139, 140; human, 137, 140 natural, 137, 140

Legge, Dominic, 165

Love, xi, 4, 17, 22–24, 30–31, 35–36, 45, 48, 74, 100–101, 112–13, 135, 139–40, 143, 167, 180, 187–89, 192, 194, 198, 200, 205, 212, 217, 219, 239–40, 243–44, 256–57, 260, 262, 268, 272–79, 282–84; as union, 6–8, 11, 20–21, 24, 33–35, 40, 55–56, 63, 67, 106, 120, 121n35, 123, 130, 152, 157, 169–75, 179–80, 182–84, 189, 200–201, 203, 207–9, 220, 228, 233n178, 256, 267, 275, 284, 286

Malice, 75, 237; as a limit on peace, 75, 253, 259–63

McMahon, Francis, xv, 223n145

Mercy, 4, 31, 40

Merit, 40, 152, 171, 175, 210, 233, 273

Metaphysics, xivn3, xviii, 4, 11, 46, 76, 78–79, 80, 82, 96, 162, 168–69, 171, 180, 183, 206, 238, 240, 248, 260, 287

Mission, xvii-xviii, 4, 32, 47, 142, 160, 165, 174, 179, 180, 199, 211–13, 284

Motion, 9, 18, 63, 68, 70, 89, 91, 103, 116n16, 117, 121, 133, 139, 187, 192, 199, 244; ter-

mination of, 18, 64–66, 89, 125, 187, 189, 192–96

Multitude (*multitudo*), 12, 41, 85, 115–16, 121–22, 128, 138, 149, 164, 178, 183–84, 255, 270, 272, 277, 282, 284; multiplicity, xix, 5, 8, 130, 135, 137, 178; as a perfection of being, 121–22

Negation, 51, 60, 63–64, 66, 68–69, 81–82, 88, 90–92, 94–95, 98, 100–101, 103, 111, 114n6, 117, 121–22, 141, 147, 192, 195–96, 210, 264n289

Negative/Secondary *ratio* of Peace, 66, 70, 80, 88–89, 98–101, 103, 106–7, 117, 121, 156, 166, 186, 195–96, 282. See also rest (*quies*); tranquility (*tranquillitas*)

Neo-Platonism, 8–9

Obstacles, removal of, 17–18, 23, 44–46, 48, 63–67, 71, 74, 117, 187–89, 196, 210, 220, 226, 243–44, 278

Oneness: see unity/*unum*

Opinion, 31, 39, 74, 216, 218n121, 254

Order: see unio/ordo

Participation, 27–28, 74, 95, 108, 113, 124–26, 128, 130, 133, 140, 145, 162–63, 171, 173–74, 178, 181, 200, 231, 234, 250, 259, 278–79, 282; participation in God's peace, 10n47, 27–28, 113, 124–25, 128, 136, 145, 162–63, 173–74, 178, 200, 234, 250, 278–79

Peace: christological: 160–178; categorical: 59–62, 77, 93–95, 98, 99, 112, 195–97, 209; contraries of: 20, 25, 28, 30, 40–41, 91–95, 140–141, 148, 156, 204, 206, 216, 218, 229, 242, 247–48, 250, 252, 260–61, 279; development within Aquinas's thought on: 37, 45; exterior: 20, 32, 34, 37, 45–46, 65, 67, 73, 75, 144, 155, 193, 196, 200, 210, 219–20, 228, 235–36, 246–66; false (simulated): 24, 34, 41, 75, 77–79, 95–97, 237; and good: 82–103; imperfect: 39, 78, 161–62, 268; interior: xivn3, 3, 6, 20, 32–33, 65n76, 67–68, 74–75, 177, 193, 203, 226, 229, 235–48, 249–51, 275, 278; and justice:

219–33; natural: 74–78, 144, 228, 258; negative/dispositive: 17–18, 31, 45–46, 186, 188, 196, 220–21, 224–29, 236, 242, 244, 257; perfect: 9, 10, 39–40, 78, 161–62, 175–77, 228, 279; pneumatological: 178–84; and the problem of evil: 146–58; as purpose of the incarnation/gospel: 34, 160, 167–69, 177, 272, 279, 280; supernatural: 74, 76–77, 142, 177, 202, 214, 219, 224, 227–29, 242–45, 256–57, 275, 280; temporal: 23, 34, 43, 76–77, 143; as transcendental: 84–103; trinitarian: 55, 116–25; and unity/unum: 26, 53, 114–18, 121–23, 125; of the world: 24–25, 76–78, 96, 113

Peacemakers, 31, 210, 248–49, 285

Perfection/perfective, 3, 9–10, 17, 20, 23, 27, 34, 36, 48, 63, 77, 83–84, 87, 89, 94, 114–18, 121–22, 126–27, 131–34, 149, 151, 161–62, 164, 166–67, 176–77, 191–92, 194–96, 198, 200, 217, 236, 243, 268, 270–72, 274, 283

Persecution, 15, 32, 65n79, 67

Person (individual), xvii, 12–13, 30, 54–55, 64, 68, 118–25, 129–30, 134–36, 161, 164–69, 173, 180–81, 190, 200, 230–31, 236–37, 241, 245, 250, 257, 259–60, 270, 282, 284

Philosophy, x, xii, xvi, xviii, 1, 47, 50–112, 113, 146, 198–99, 250, 263–64, 283

Plurality, 14, 51, 119–24, 130, 134–37, 217. See also multitude (*multitudo*)

Politics, 12–13, 185

Positive/Primary *ratio* of peace, 51–64, 66, 70, 80, 88, 98–100, 103, 105–7, 109, 115–18, 121–25, 136, 156, 164, 186, 195–96, 200, 208–11. See also *unio/ordo*

Potency/potentiality, xvii, 61–62, 84, 86–87, 89–90, 117, 121, 125, 148, 181, 208, 227, 258, 268–69

Prayer, 35, 244–46

Prime matter, 84–85, 87

Principle, 25, 27–28, 55–56, 61–62, 82, 85–86, 90, 103–6, 115, 119, 126, 130, 134, 147, 165, 182, 186, 196, 212, 214–15, 217, 224, 238–39, 250, 258, 268, 270, 272, 278; of creation, 104; of order, 52–53, 103–7

Privation, x, xviii, 5, 41, 60, 81, 90–96, 100n210, 101, 121, 146–47, 150–51, 154n184, 155, 159–60, 237, 253, 260, 266, 286

Providence, 30, 90n176, 139, 146–47, 152

Punishment, 140–42, 144, 148n161, 150–51, 170–71, 248, 252, 262–64, 273, 279

Quasi-Transcendental, 84–90, 98–101; objections to peace as, 98–103. See also good; *unio/ordo*; unity

Ramirez, Santiago, xv, 52–53, 68, 108, 109n232, 178, 203n64, 215, 227, 254, 283

Recapitulation, 159–60

Reconciliation, 14, 20, 44, 160, 170, 231, 243, 245, 271, 282, 286

Redemption, 171–75, 179–80, 183–84, 208, 212, 230, 283

*Redoublement* of unity and union in God, 117–18

Reichberg, Gregory, xiii, 37, 111

Relation, 51–63, 68–69, 80–88, 90, 92, 94, 98–108, 110–11, 118–24, 126–27, 130–31, 135, 137–40, 144, 146, 156, 161–65, 172–78, 181, 186–90, 196–97, 204–9, 210, 212, 216, 219–24, 230–31, 233, 239, 257–58, 265–66, 268–70, 282–83, 286; *ad aliud*, 51, 59–62, 94, 118–19; as categorical, 59–62, 196–97, 209; as subsistent, 55, 118–19, 122, 124, 130, 164–65, 211, 282; as transcendental, 61, 85–87

Religion, 142, 245, 268

Reorder/reunification, 151–52, 160, 170, 173–74, 179–80, 182, 184, 202, 212, 230, 239, 245–47, 265–67, 272, 275

Rest (*quies*), 26, 28, 30, 32, 36, 38–39, 43, 45–47, 48, 50–51, 62–71, 74–76, 78–79, 80–83, 88–103, 106–11, 117, 121, 123, 125, 137, 146, 154, 156–59, 166, 176–77, 184, 189–90, 192–98, 206, 208, 210–11, 213–15, 223–24, 234, 237–38, 241, 244, 264n289, 265, 278, 282–85. See also negative/secondary *ratio* of peace

Restoration, 141, 159–160, 163–64, 170, 173–74, 177–78, 208, 230, 232–34, 239, 262, 265, 276

Resurrection, 162, 167, 174–78, 180

Sacraments, xviii, 49, 244–46, 251–52, 257,
267–77, 280, 284–87
Sacrifice, 3, 170–74, 270–73, 276, 280, 284
Sacramental Order, 267–72
Sadness, 43, 91, 95, 156–58
Saints, 15, 25, 32, 34, 254, 280
Sanctification, 24, 73–74, 213, 256, 272, 280
Satisfaction, 48, 170–75, 194, 229–33,
233n178, 254, 271
Schism, 40–41, 286
Scripture, xvi, 2–4, 96
Shalom, 2–4
Sin, 15, 20–21, 34, 37, 41–43, 75–77, 113, 140,
144n144, 148, 150–53, 155, 158–60, 166–
67, 170, 174–76, 185, 206, 218, 230–31,
233n178, 237, 242–44, 246–48, 251–54,
258–61, 265, 269–70, 274, 278–79, 283–
84 and choice of lesser good, 246n207;
as contrary of peace (disorder), 20,
40–41, 91–97, 160, 247–50, 283–84; as
privation, 41, 91–96, 147, 160, 253, 286
Specific Difference, 69, 93, 98
Substitutional Theory, 171–72
Suffering, 149–55, 170–71, 176, 231–33, 253,
274, 277

Teleology, 186, 235
Temperance, 266
The Eucharist, xv, xviii, 44, 49, 244–46,
271–80
Theological virtues, 180, 182, 229
Thomism/Thomistic Tradition, xiii-xiv,
151, 243
Totalitarianism, 144
Tranquility (tranquillitas), 9, 22, 24–25,
32–34, 38, 44, 46, 50–52, 56, 62–66, 68–
71, 75, 77, 79–81, 83, 88–91, 96–97, 99–
101, 106–7, 109–11, 117, 121, 146, 156–59,
189, 193, 208, 211, 223, 264, 283. See also
secondary/negative ratio of peace; rest
(quies)
Tranquility of Order (Tranquillitas Ordinis), 4, 16, 25, 32–33, 38, 50–52, 56,
99n204, 193
Transcendental Relation, 61, 85–87
Transcendentals, xviii, 61–62, 80–88, 98–
99, 114, 129, 134–35, 183, 221, 224
Trinitarian Person/Relations, 47, 55, 118–

22, 129–30, 134–35, 165, 282
Trinity, 47, 55, 113, 116–25, 130, 135, 158,
163–66, 180, 200, 211, 254, 278, 282–83;
as cause of peace, xvii, 27, 32, 158, 162,
167, 249, 278, 282, 284–85; relations, 55,
118–25, 130, 164–65, 211, 282
Truth, xi, 32, 41, 43, 70, 82, 108–9, 189, 217,
244, 256

Unio/Ordo and Ordo/Unio, 41, 45–46,
51–64; 66–72, 75–107, 109–24, 130, 135,
138, 141–43, 146, 156–57, 163–64, 170,
173–74, 177, 182, 185, 189, 195–96, 205–11,
214, 216–18, 223–24, 227–30, 255, 260,
262, 264, 268, 282–83; see also peace;
positive/primary ratio
Union/communion/connection, 9–11, 18,
24, 28, 30, 36–41, 45–47 53–79, 87, 91,
94, 104–6, 108–9, 111, 115–20, 130, 132–
36, 154, 160, 164–78, 183–84, 189–90,
193–98, 200, 202, 206–7, 206n77, 209–
11, 212, 215–17, 220, 224, 226, 229, 231–33,
236, 239–40, 255–56, 271, 277–78; affective, 36, 55–56, 108, 157, 203, 205, 209,
240–41, 245–46, 256; effective, 56, 63,
89, 109, 197, 203, 209–10; modes of
union, 54–56; substantial, 55–56; in the
Trinity, 55, 117–25. See also unio/ordo
Unity (unum/unitas), 28–30, 35, 46, 58,
62, 69–70, 79, 82, 85, 88, 97, 102, 114–22,
182, 200, 203–4, 224, 255, 270, 277–78,
285; vs union, 53, 115–18, 121–23, 125
Unity of the Church/faithful, 22, 178–84,
275

Vice, 22, 40, 150, 242–43, 266
Virtue, 11, 13, 37, 40, 47, 72, 75, 126, 142–45,
152, 173, 180–82, 195n41, 204–5, 209,
211–12, 219n124, 221–22, 224, 226–29,
236, 238–40, 240–48, 252, 254, 266, 268,
271, 279, 283–85

War, ix-x, xii-xiii, xviii, 7, 37, 39–41, 43, 45,
78, 185, 262–64, 281, 285–86
White, Thomas Joseph, 176
Whole/wholeness, 2, 6, 9, 11–12, 29, 42,
56n32, 58, 79, 97, 106, 131–37, 139–40,
147, 149–50, 154, 181–82, 212, 236

Will, 33, 39–40, 46, 51, 63, 66–68, 79, 82, 103, 106–9, 141, 144n146, 187–88, 190–98, 210–12, 206, 209, 211, 213–17, 237–38, 244, 260, 279

Wisdom (the Son), 123–24, 130–39, 163–64, 212–15, 282

Wisdom as virtue/gift, 32–33, 106–7, 123–28, 211–18

Word (the Son), 123–25, 135, 139, 163–66, 200, 211

Worship, xviii, 25, 49, 268–72